AF598901

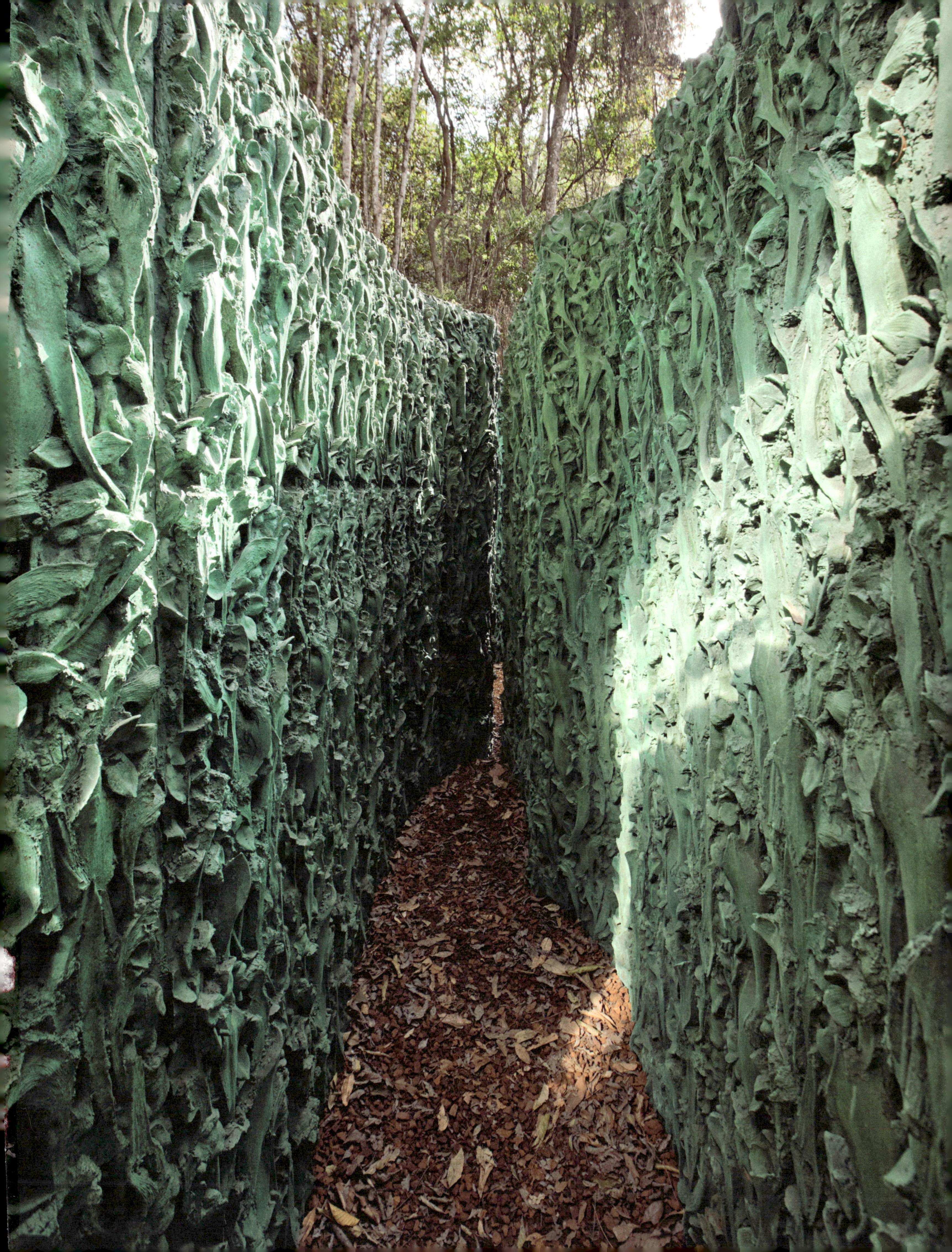

THE ULTIMATE MUSEUM BOOK

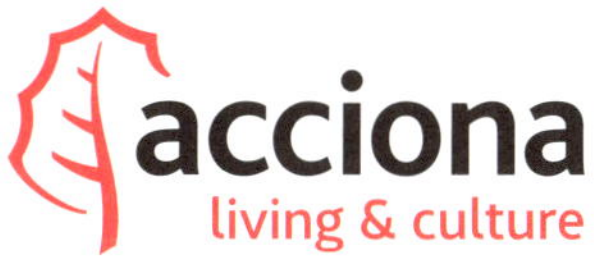

INDEX

This practical guide was developed by ACCIONA Living & Culture, in collaboration with El Otro Muro, as part of a research project examining sustainability practices in over 150 museums worldwide.

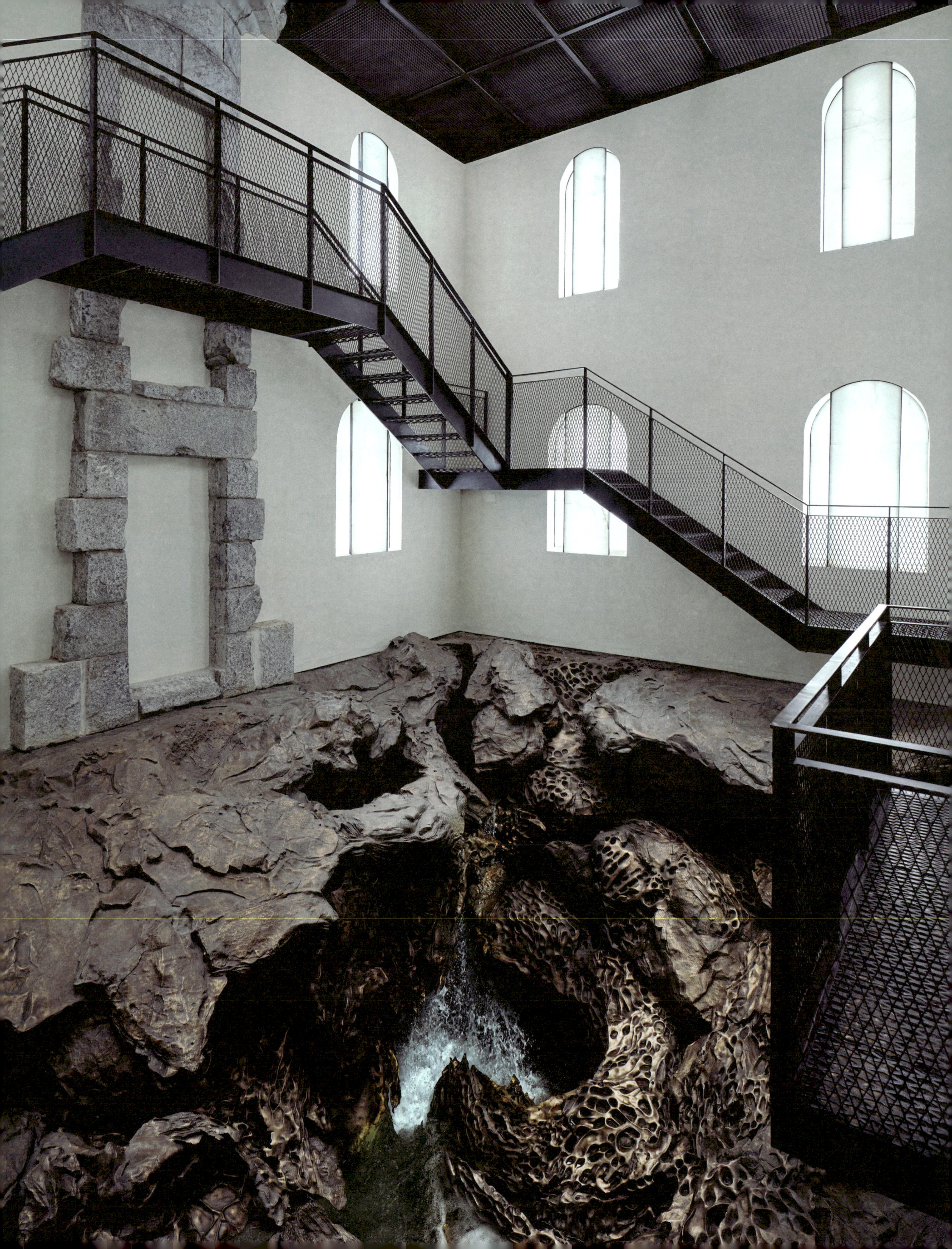

NOTES TO THE EDITION

This guide is the result of research conducted at over 150 museums across the globe in order to assess the degree of sustainability of these institutions.

This eminently practical guide presents a total of thirty-three measures, grouped in fact sheets, that cover practically every environmental and social dimension of sustainability, with the aim of offering museums an inspiring road map to follow. Discovering and becoming familiar with these measures will provide a better grasp of the enormous range of possibilities available to each institution, as well as the challenges involved in implementing them.

The fact sheets, which comprise the bulk of the guide (pp. 18–259), are divided into eighteen colour-coded categories and illustrated by the experiences of institutions that have been most successful in adopting these practices. There is also a section detailing the Sustainable Development Goals (SDGs) of the 2030 Agenda related to each measure.

These are followed by various appendices containing highly relevant information, such as the main international certification systems, which will help museums to legally verify their practices and certify them to a recognised standard (pp. 265–278). The final section presents ten simple yet effective measures (pp. 281–291) for institutions which—due to their size, mission, structural challenges posed by their buildings or simple budgetary constraints—have yet to take the first steps towards devising a sustainability strategy.

Through this book and initiatives such as NEXT IN, a global benchmark event that brings together the most visionary leaders in the museum sector, ACCIONA Living & Culture reaffirms its commitment to sustainability and innovation. NEXT IN reflects our mission to highlight the transformative role of museums as agents of change, driving innovative practices that create a positive impact on both people and the planet.

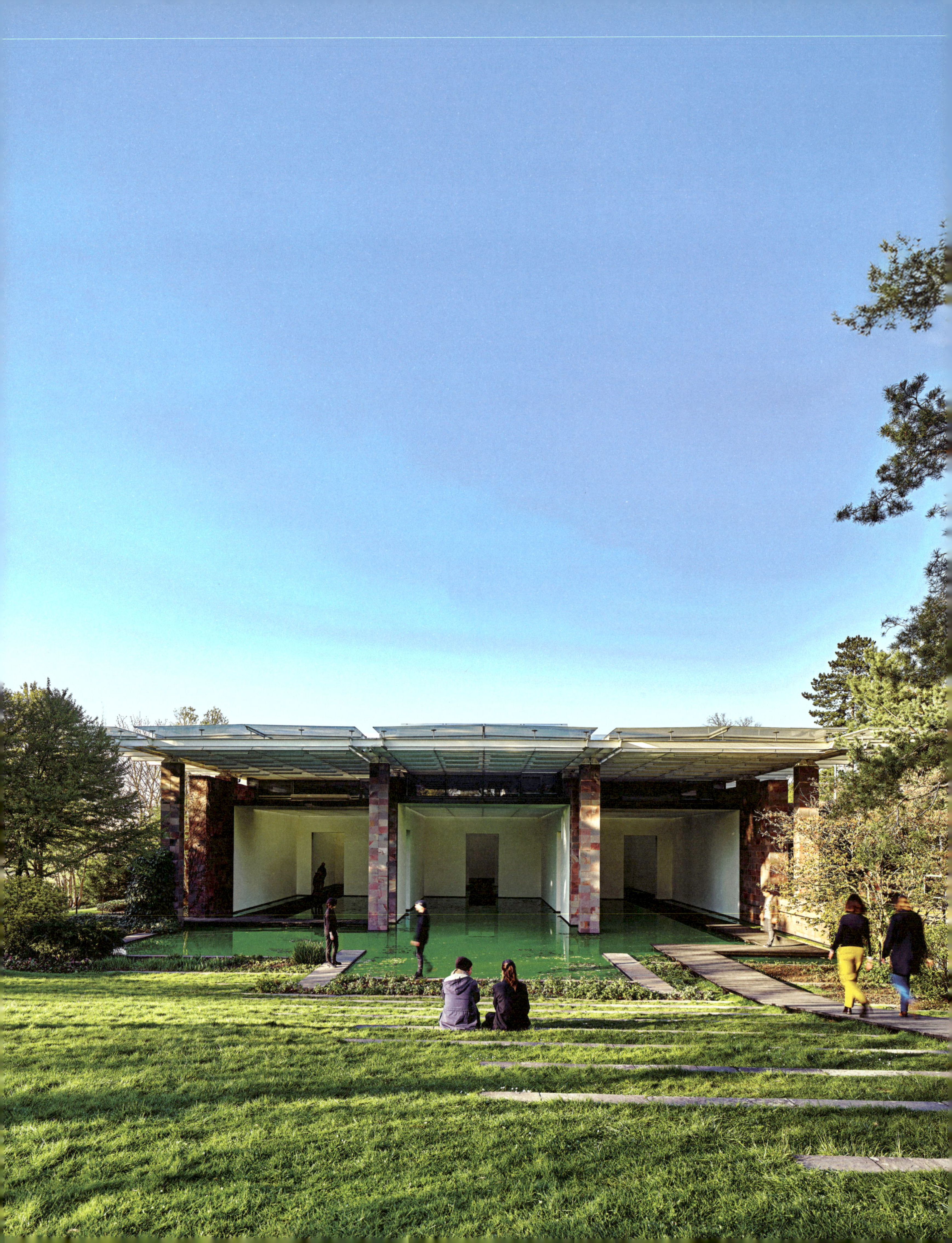

DIALOGUE ACROSS GENERATIONS

Clotilde Entrecanales
ACCIONA Living & Culture

The word "culture" comes from the Latin abstract noun *colere*, which refers to the act of cultivating the land to make it fertile, just as a human being must be cultivated to transition from a wild state to a more refined and elevated one. That is why museums embody one of humanity's deepest aspirations: the quest to transcend our own existence. By preserving cultural, artistic, and natural heritage, they serve as vessels of collective memory and perpetuate human knowledge. Artistic expression connects generations across time, offering perspectives to understand our cultural identity and its evolution.

Through Gauguin's eyes, we see the jungles of Tahiti; through Catlin, the plains filled with American bison; through Tutankhamun, the Nile of his dreams; and with Turner, we are tied to the mast of a ship to capture the fury of the sea. These perspectives provide a fascinating view of how people of different eras comprehended their world. From cave paintings to video installations, art reflects our past counterparts, celebrating beauty and misery alike.

This dialogue with past generations facilitated by museums mirrors the conversation with future generations envisioned in the concept of sustainable development, a core focus of our activities at ACCIONA for over twenty years. Like art, sustainability moves and challenges us to build a legacy—a future where progress, social equity, and environmental conservation coexist harmoniously.

This book, which I invite you to peruse and read, proposes conversations between past and future generations through real projects. On its pages, you will find examples of museums that have had the vision to adapt their exhibition practices and promote initiatives that ensure not only excellence in execution times or the use of the latest innovations but also a new cultural awareness. By embracing sustainable concepts and practices, museums reinforce their institutional mission of permanence, education, and universality, strengthening the link between memory and the ambition for a better future.

Art has never remained indifferent to the great questions and challenges of each era and has often driven the most significant changes in our history. We are particularly proud of ACCIONA's work as ambassadors of our purpose.

The development of an exhibition project demands as much responsibility and rigor in the selection of the pieces chosen to endure as it does in the ethics underlying its execution. Therefore, ACCIONA's philosophy has always been, through its commitment to excellence and making a positive impact on society, to find new technological and creative avenues to integrate artistic and cultural expression into the contemporary world, with sustainability as an essential requirement.

With this book, we want to share our vision when it comes to designing cultural experiences and recognize the efforts many museums are making to take on an active role in the great environmental and social challenges of our time.

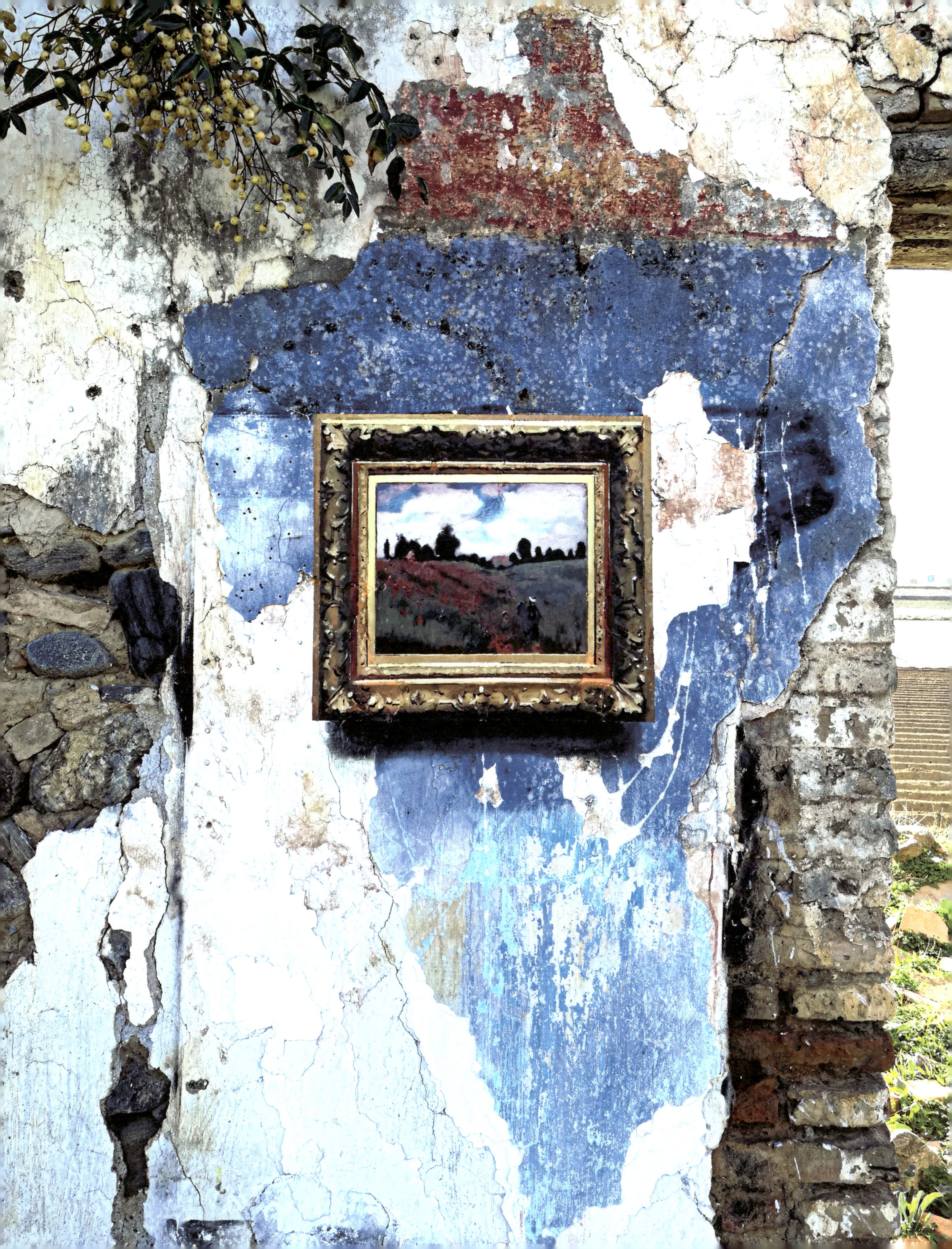

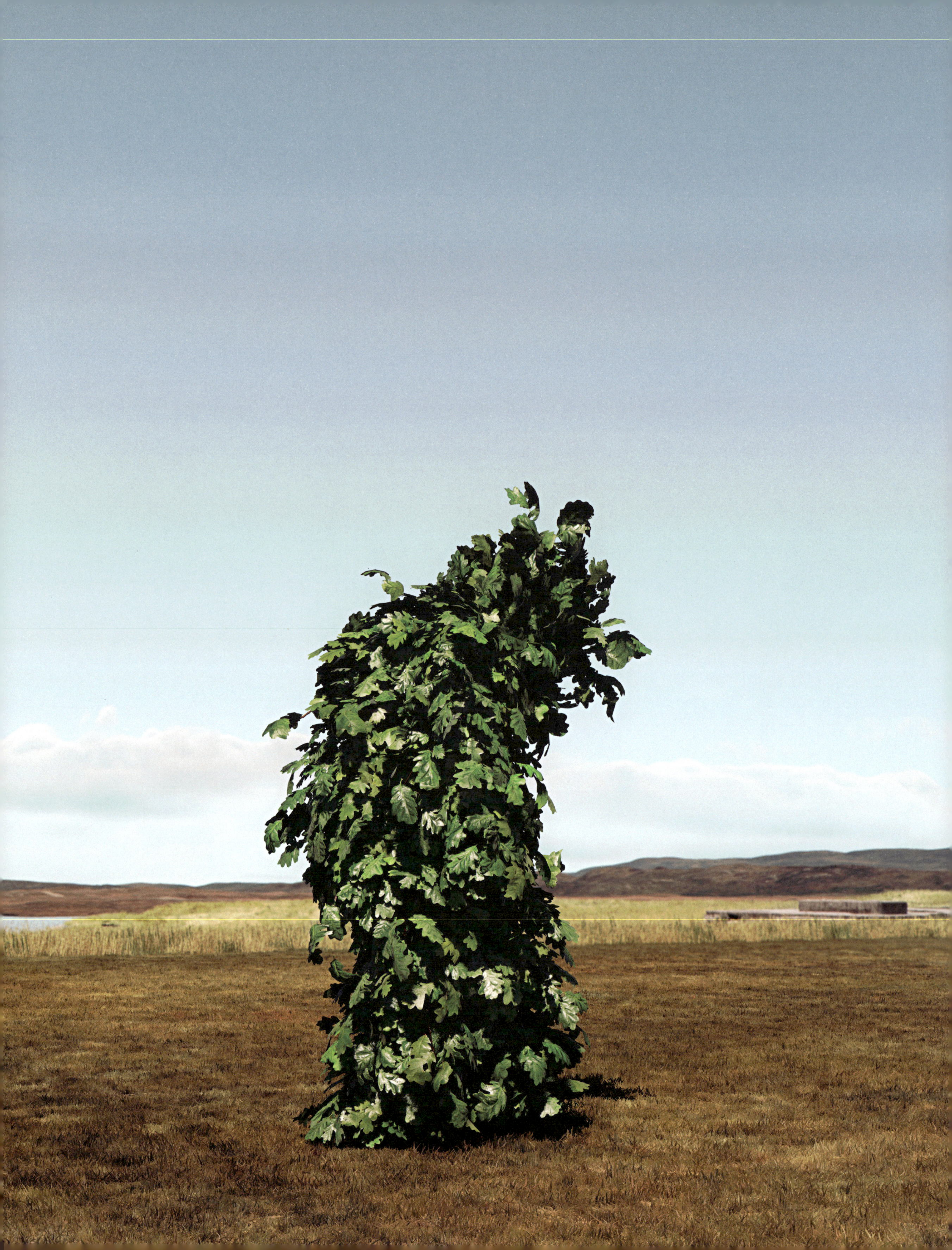

SUSTAINABILITY AND MUSEUMS

Alfons Martinell
Director of the Working Group on Culture and Sustainable Development
Red Española para el Desarrollo Sostenible (Reds)

The 2030 Agenda, despite not explicitly including culture in its seventeen Sustainable Development Goals (SDGs), has spurred the cultural sector to integrate itself into this crucial roadmap to address global societal challenges.

Beyond the 2030 Agenda, museums and heritage sites are facing a complex global landscape: with the climate emergency, the pandemic, inequalities, and conflicts, they have detected a heightened sensibility and concern among the population about the effects of human activity on the planet. Dynamics aimed at adapting to these new problems raise questions about the social role of museums today. This reality triggers different internal reflections on and revisions of their goals and operations, in which they explore the possibilities of the museum's alignment with ecological or environmental principles.

At a basic level, this includes adapting their physical spaces to meet current needs, whether by modifying existing structures or by undertaking new architectural projects that meet the requirements for creating a fully sustainable public space. More directly, many museums are analyzing their internal operations to overhaul practices related to energy consumption, waste management, and carbon footprint impacts. This has led to the adoption of various methodological approaches to align museum practices with sustainability frameworks. There's a notable eagerness among professionals to acquire and brush up on the skills needed to deal with these unexpected scenarios which they were not trained to face. All these efforts reflect a renewed commitment by museums and heritage services to foster a culture of sustainability within their capabilities.

Similarly, this commitment influences the project's core, incorporating new principles into its vision, mission, and objectives, thus adding a contemporary sustainable dimension to museum operations. In some instances, where elements of these orientations already existed, these processes have made it possible to bolster the intentionality of such commitments in cases where it was not as clear as it should be.

Cultural sustainability requires multiple balancing acts in current cultural systems. The first must be between knowing and respecting inherited legacies (history, tradition, heritage, etc.) that are part of our values, ways of life, and identities, and engaging with contemporary cultural life. Each generation processes, adapts, and transforms its cultural context as a fundamental part of influencing and participating in its community. Moreover, sustainability compels us to consider the cultural needs of future societies, fostering foresight and a prospective outlook to avoid passing on "debts" in what might be termed intergenerational justice or ethics. This broader perspective challenges museums to proactively engage in building cultural futures rather than focusing solely on the past.

This dynamic has also supported inclusive creative projects that use art to address and reflect on nature and the climate crisis. Some of these initiatives, previously confined to the fringes or alternative spaces, can find a new home in these museums or heritage sites, creating a nexus for dissemination, creativity, and commitment.

This set of circumstances that museums have encountered on their journey towards sustainability has brought about sweeping changed in the industry, in which adapting to new scenarios has become an opportunity for deeper dialog between the museum, the community, and global issues. These changes also represent a chance to redefine the social role of museums in today's society and, as mentioned, invest in building futures, for commitment to the next generations (a key pillar of sustainability) has become a moral imperative for any organization and its professionals.

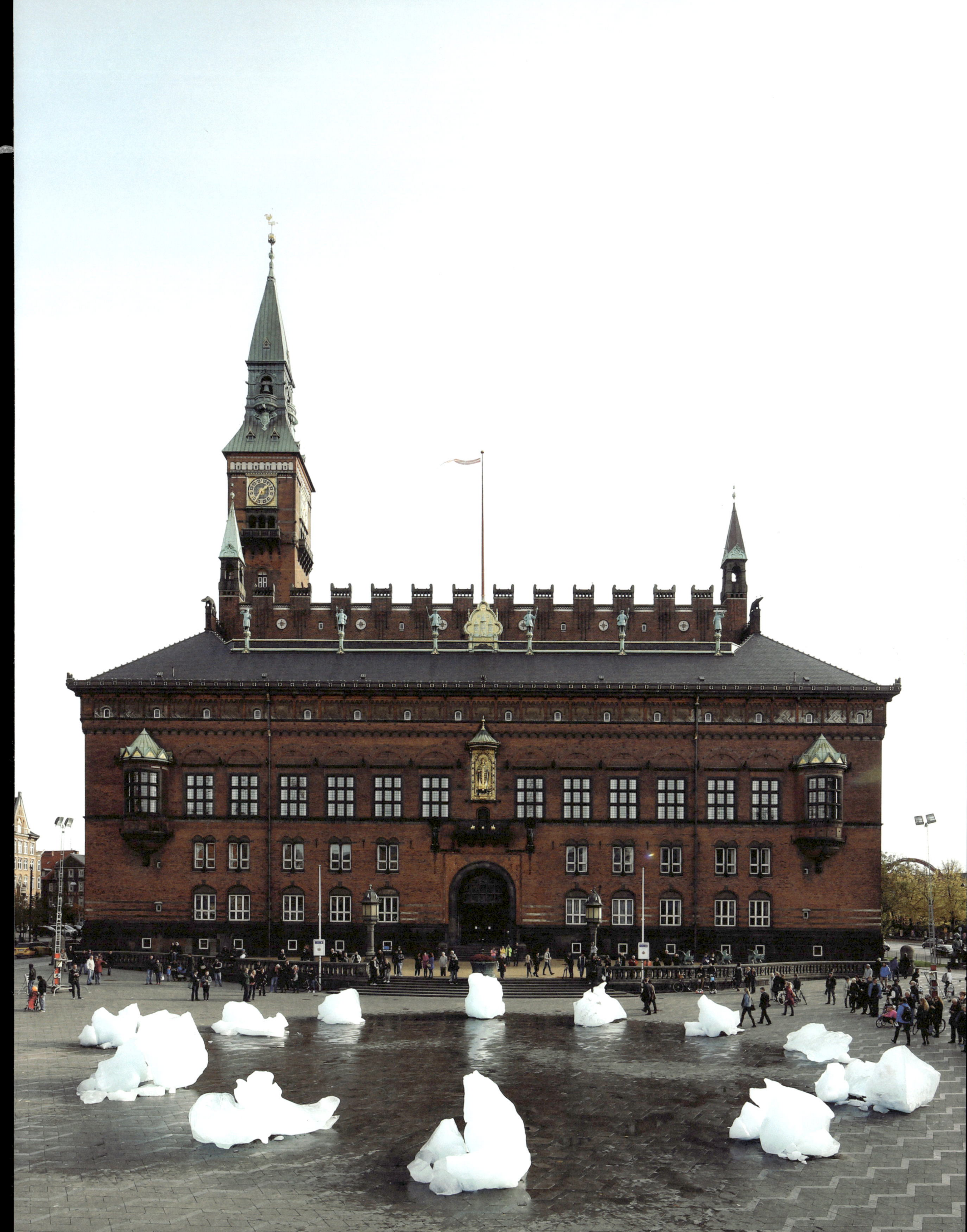

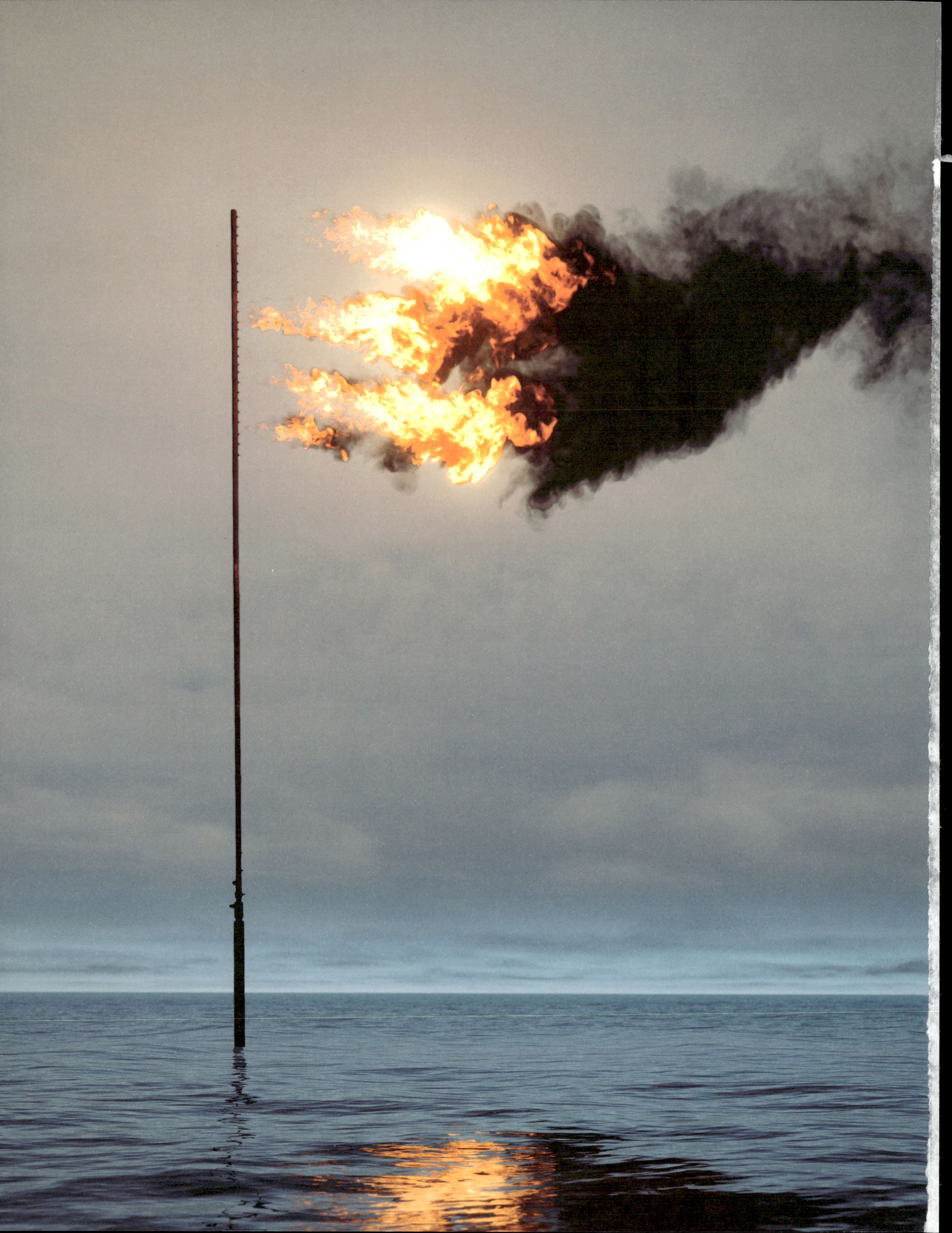

SUSTAINABILITY MEASURES

The following are thirty-three sustainability measures implemented in museums from various parts of the world. Each measure is illustrated with real-life examples of institutions that have successfully carried out these initiatives or projects that plan to do so, demonstrating that change is both possible and achievable. From reducing carbon footprints to implementing inclusive and socially responsible practices, the actions described here offer a practical guide for museums wishing to integrate sustainability into their daily operations.

More than just a simple manual of best practices, this book is an invitation to reflection and action. Museums, as spaces for learning and connection, have the power to inspire their visitors and communities toward a more balanced and respectful model for both people and the planet. Through these fact sheets, we hope that each reader finds applicable ideas and that, together, we can move toward a future where culture and sustainability go hand in hand.

OUTLINE OF CONTENTS

The guide highlights best practices and compelling case studies from museums around the world that have adapted their structures, museographic approaches, and management practices towards sustainability.

Each selected measure and case study is presented in detailed fact sheets that outline the sustainability measures implemented, offer data on the involved museums, and discuss their contributions to the Sustainable Development Goals (SDGs) of the 2030 Agenda.

Categories

- INTEGRATION OF NATURE
- CONSTRUCTION MATERIALS
- WATER USE
- BUILDING ENERGY EFFICIENCY
- PROTECTION AND PROMOTION OF BIODIVERSITY
- CIRCULAR EXHIBITION DESIGN
- ENVIRONMENTAL IMPACT ASSESSMENT OF EXHIBITIONS
- EXHIBITION MATERIALS
- POSITIVE IMPACT OF EXHIBITION PROJECTS
- ACCESSIBILITY, INCLUSION, AND DIVERSITY
- TRAINING OF EMPLOYEES AND WORK TEAMS
- ENVIRONMENTAL EMERGENCIES
- SUSTAINABLE MOBILITY
- CARBON FOOTPRINT
- VISITOR EDUCATION AND AWARENESS
- INTEGRATION OF MUSEUMS IN THE COMMUNITY
- PRESERVATION OF MEMORY AND HERITAGE
- ALLIANCES

Sustainable Development Goals (SDGs)

The seventeen global goals defined by the United Nations address humanity's greatest challenges from a global, cross-cutting perspective. At ACCIONA, as commitment to sustainability is our raison d'être, we contribute to the achievement of the Sustainable Development Goals (SDGs) because we understand that social progress, environmental balance, and economic growth must go hand in hand.

SDG 1	NO POVERTY
SDG 2	ZERO HUNGER
SDG 3	GOOD HEALTH AND WELL-BEING
SDG 4	QUALITY EDUCATION
SDG 5	GENDER EQUALITY
SDG 6	CLEAN WATER AND SANITATION
SDG 7	AFFORDABLE AND CLEAN ENERGY
SDG 8	DECENT WORK AND ECONOMIC GROWTH
SDG 9	INDUSTRY, INNOVATION AND INFRASTRUCTURE
SDG 10	REDUCED INEQUALITIES
SDG 11	SUSTAINABLE CITIES AND COMMUNITIES
SDG 12	RESPONSIBLE CONSUMPTION AND PRODUCTION
SDG 13	CLIMATE ACTION
SDG 14	LIFE BELOW WATER
SDG 15	LIFE ON LAND
SDG 16	PEACE, JUSTICE AND STRONG INSTITUTIONS
SDG 17	PARTNERSHIPS FOR THE GOALS

33 keys to sustainability

01 BIOPHILIC DESIGN

02 LIVE COVERS

03 USE OF RECYCLED CONSTRUCTION MATERIALS

04 INTEGRATION OF INNOVATIVE MATERIALS

05 LOW-EMISSION MATERIALS

06 USE OF NATURAL BUILDING MATERIALS

07 REDUCTION OF WATER CONSUMPTION

08 SOFT WASTEWATER TREATMENT SYSTEMS

09 RAINWATER RECOVERY SYSTEM

10 SEAWATER-FED COOLING SYSTEM

11 LEVERAGING NATURAL LIGHT

12 PHOTOVOLTAIC PANEL INSTALLATION

13 GEOTHERMAL INSTALLATION FOR AIR CONDITIONING

14 LIVING MUSEUMS

15 ISLANDS OF URBAN BIODIVERSITY

16 CIRCULARITY OF TEMPORARY EXHIBITIONS

17 DESIGN OF REUSABLE DISPLAY PANELS

18 ENVIRONMENTAL IMPACT ASSESSMENT MODELS

19 LOW-IMPACT MATERIALS

20 EXHIBITIONS WITH POSITIVE IMPACT

21 ACCESSIBILITY IN MUSEUMS AND EXHIBITIONS

22 TACTILE PERCEPTION OF ARTWORKS

23 EMPLOYEE TRAINING

24 SUSTAINABILITY GOVERNANCE BODIES

25 PREPARATION FOR ENVIRONMENTAL EMERGENCIES

26 PROMOTION OF SUSTAINABLE MOBILITY

27 CALCULATION OF THE CARBON FOOTPRINT

28 EXHIBITION SPACES DEDICATED TO SUSTAINABILITY

29 GAMIFICATION

30 COMMUNITY DEVELOPMENT PROGRAM

31 COMMUNITY REVITALIZATION

32 PRESERVATION OF CULTURAL HERITAGE

33 COLLABORATION NETWORKS AND ALLIANCES

01 BIOPHILIC DESIGN

INTEGRATION OF NATURE   SDG 9 / 11

Biophilic design is a trend in architecture and interior design that aims to reestablish the links between nature and human beings, integrating natural elements and analogies in spaces. This trend maintains that spaces designed under the principles of nature have a positive impact on the physical, emotional, and cognitive health of the people who occupy or visit them.

The *Museo de Ciencias Ambientales* (Museum of Environmental Sciences), inspired by the colonial architecture of the historic center of Guadalajara, Mexico, evokes the process of water erosion that sculpted the ravine that represents the northern boundary of the city. Conceptually, water erosion gives the building an organic form, linking its interior courtyards into a central "canyon" open to the passing public that encourages natural light and ventilation of the space. Its twelve themed gardens familiarize visitors with the natural phenomena presented in the interior galleries.

Museo de Ciencias Ambientales

FOCUS
Environmental Sciences

PROJECT
Snøhetta

LOCATION
Guadalajara, Jalisco. Mexico
University of Guadalajara

CERTIFICATION
LEED Platinum New Construction (requested)

CONSTRUCTION
Began in 2010. Due to open in 2025

SIZE
22,000 m² (7,000 m² for exhibitions)

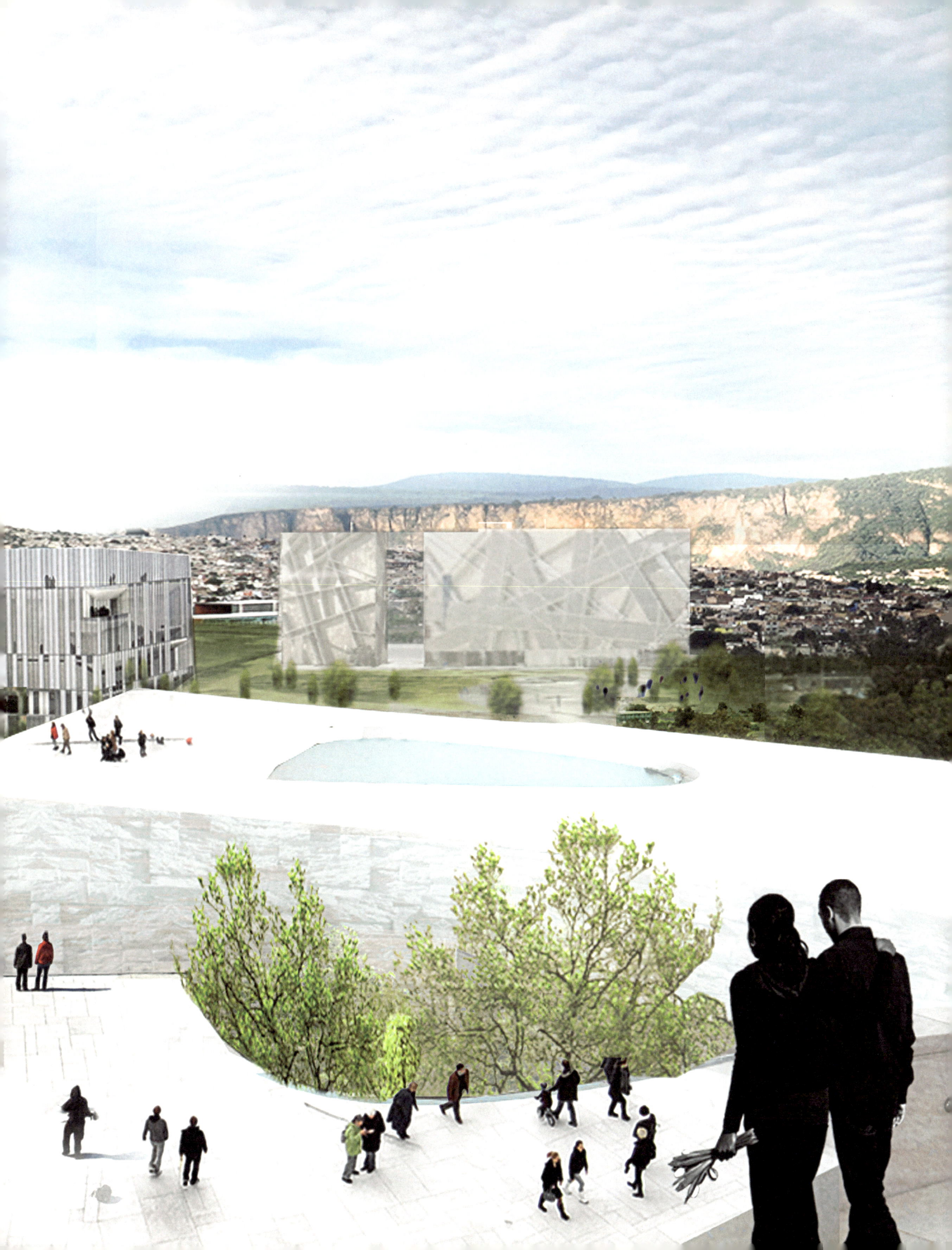

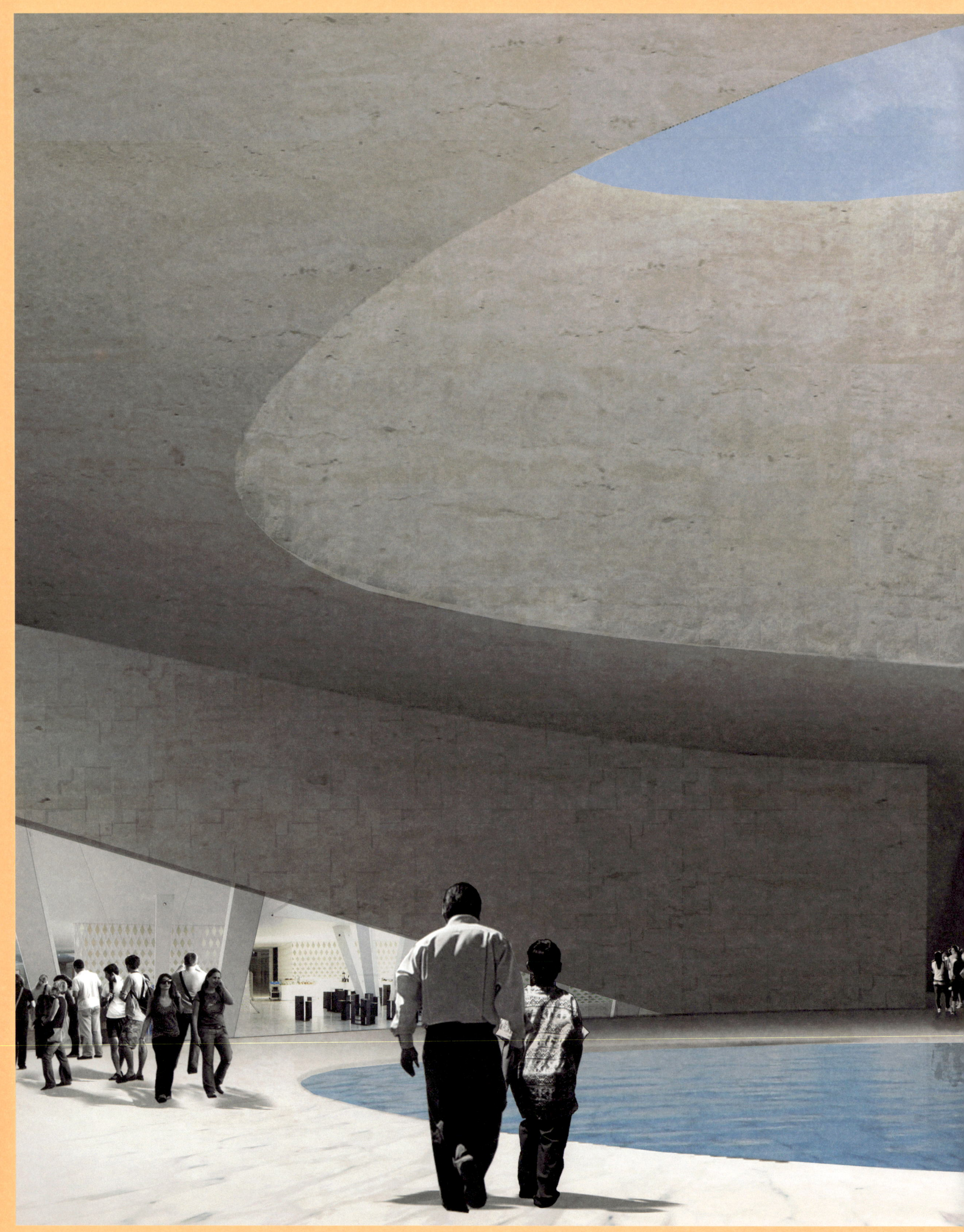

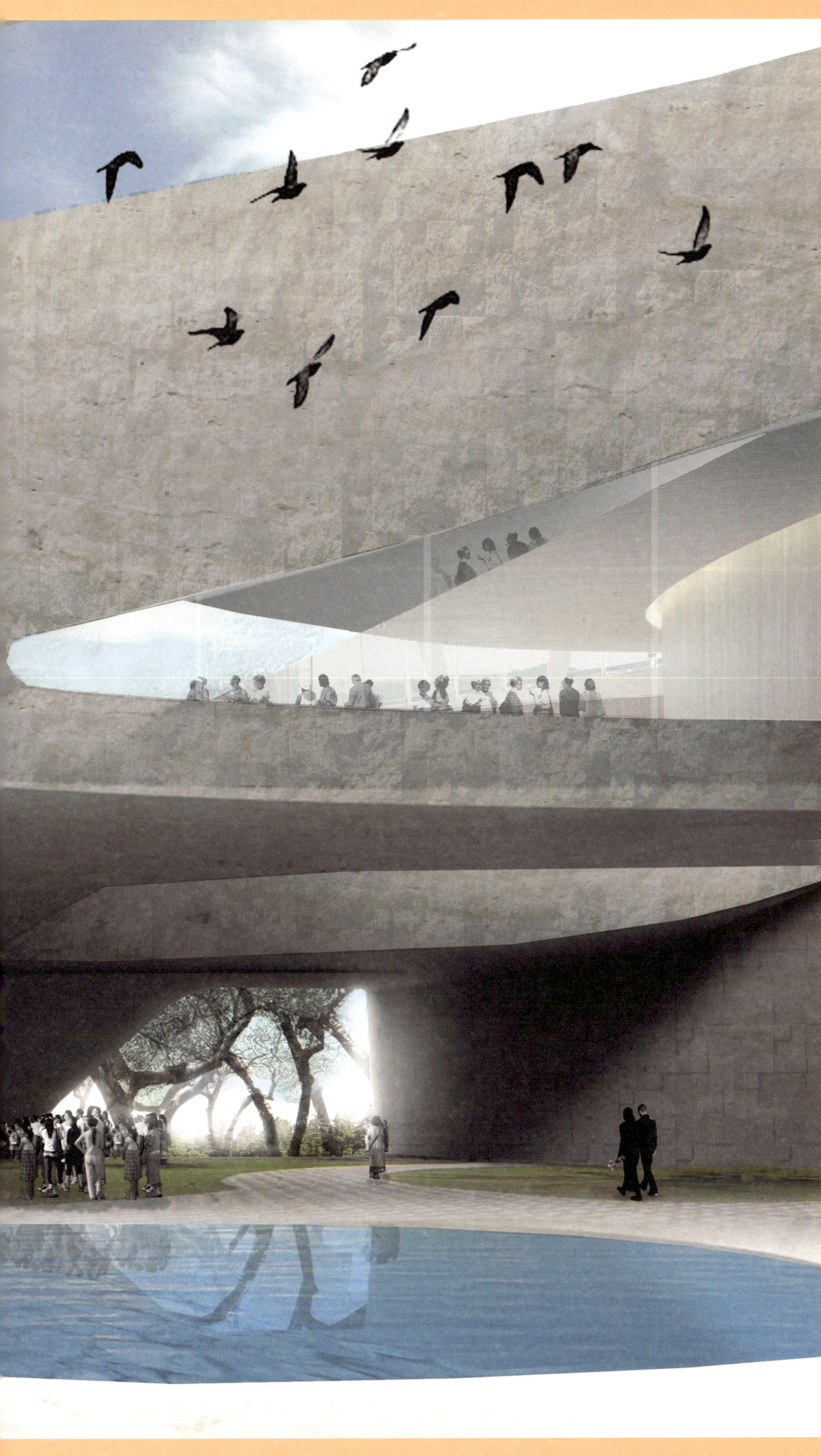

MUSEUMS WITH SIMILAR MEASURES

Fondation Louis Vuitton

PARIS, FRANCE

Efficient building that combines technology, design, and integration with natural surroundings.

Biesbosch MuseumEiland

BIESBOSCH NATURE PARK, THE NETHERLANDS

Designed to camouflage with its surroundings featuring a green roof fully integrated into the natural environment.

Biodôme

MONTREAL, CANADA

A building that combines modernism with biophilic architecture to house each of the museum's ecosystems.

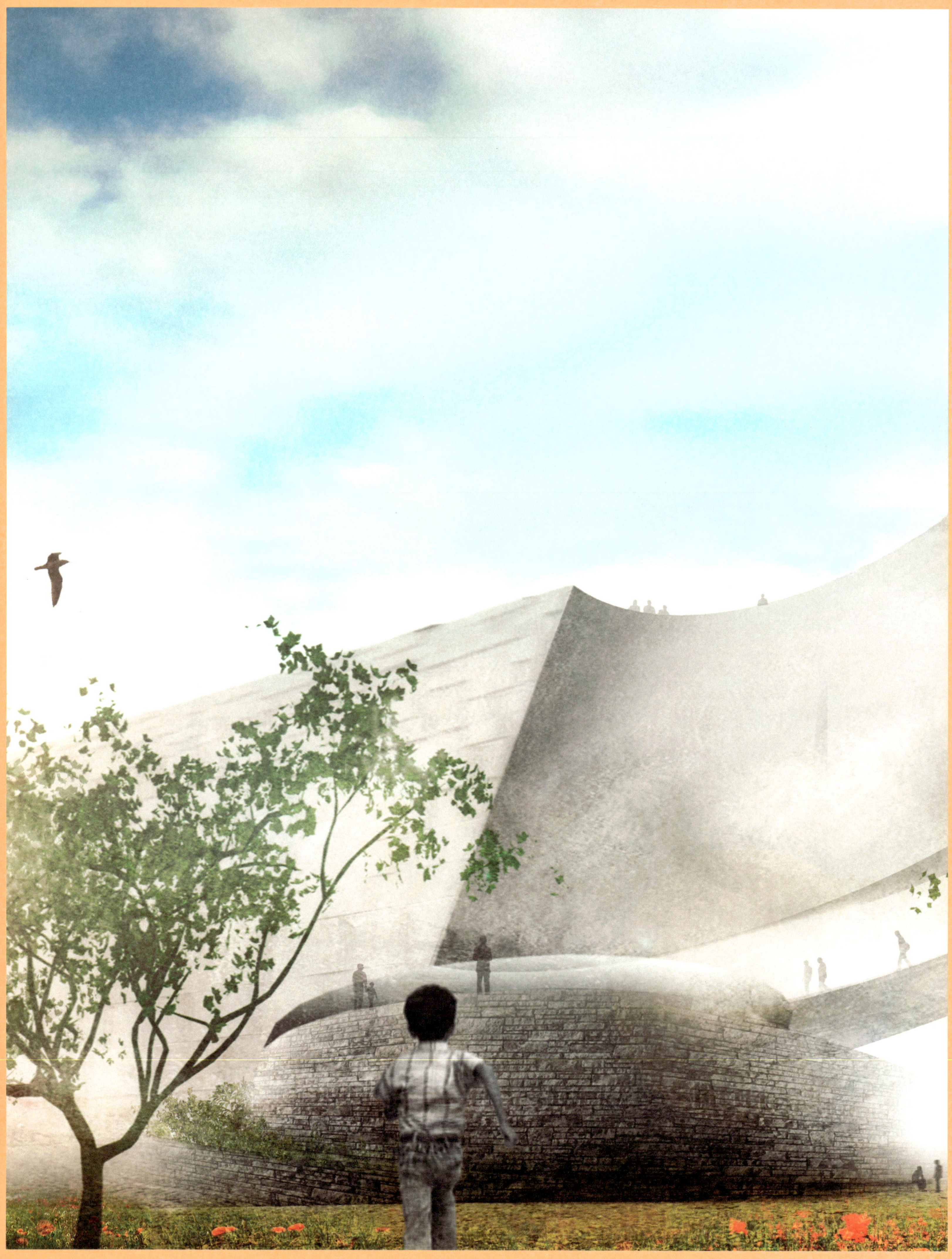

"We will never be truly healthy, satisfied, or fulfilled if we live apart and alienated from the environment from which we evolved."

Stephen R. Kellert

Birthright: People and Nature in the Modern World

02 LIVE COVERS

INTEGRATION OF NATURE SDG 6 / 9 / 15

A green roof is a vegetation layer grown on top of buildings, such as roofs, terraces, or walls, over a waterproof membrane and a substrate blanket. These roofs also incorporate a drainage system to manage excess rainwater.

Landscaped roofs are an important tool of sustainable urban design: they promote the development of biodiversity in urban areas, reduce pressure on drainage systems by preventing flooding, provide thermal and acoustic insulation, mitigate the heat island effect in cities, and help improve air quality.

The California Academy of Sciences boasts a roof that covers more than 10,000 m² and includes 1.7 million plant species.

California Academy of Sciences

FOCUS
Natural History

LOCATION
Periurban, in San Francisco's Golden Gate Urban Park, California, USA

ANNUAL VISITORS
1,000,000

CONSTRUCTION
Created in 1853, it was rebuilt in 2008 by Renzo Piano with Stantec Architecture

CERTIFICATION
LEED Platinum

SIZE
38,000 m²

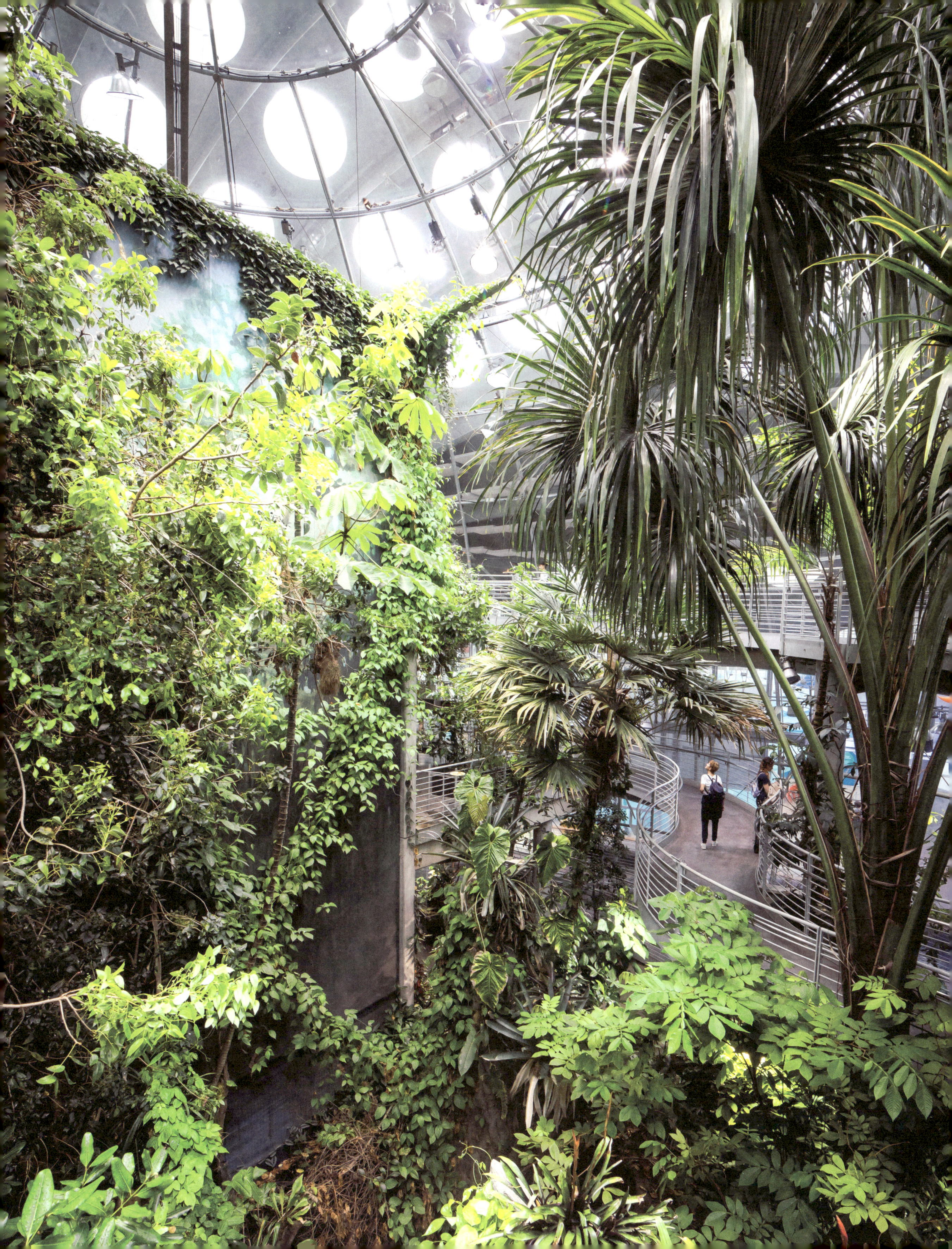

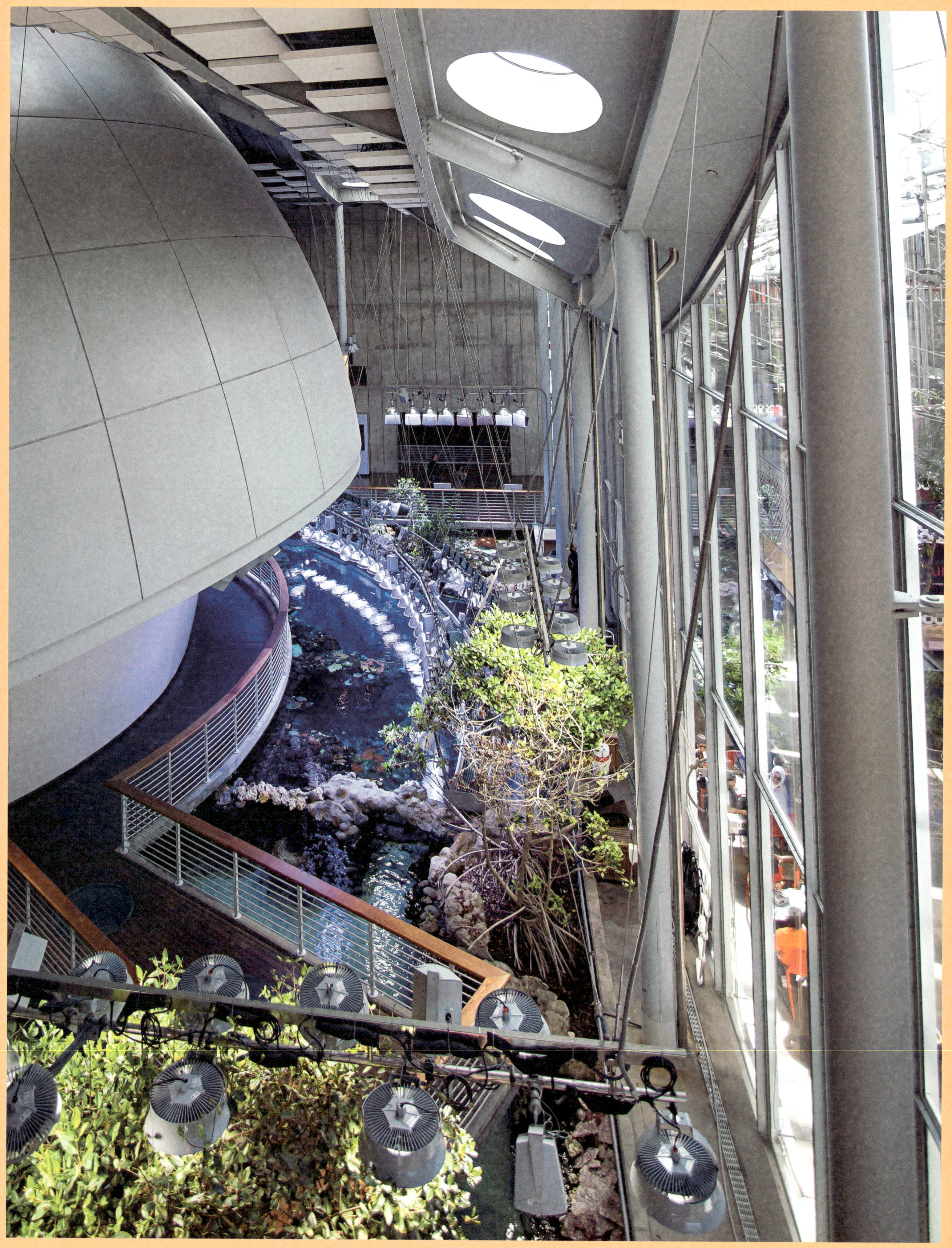

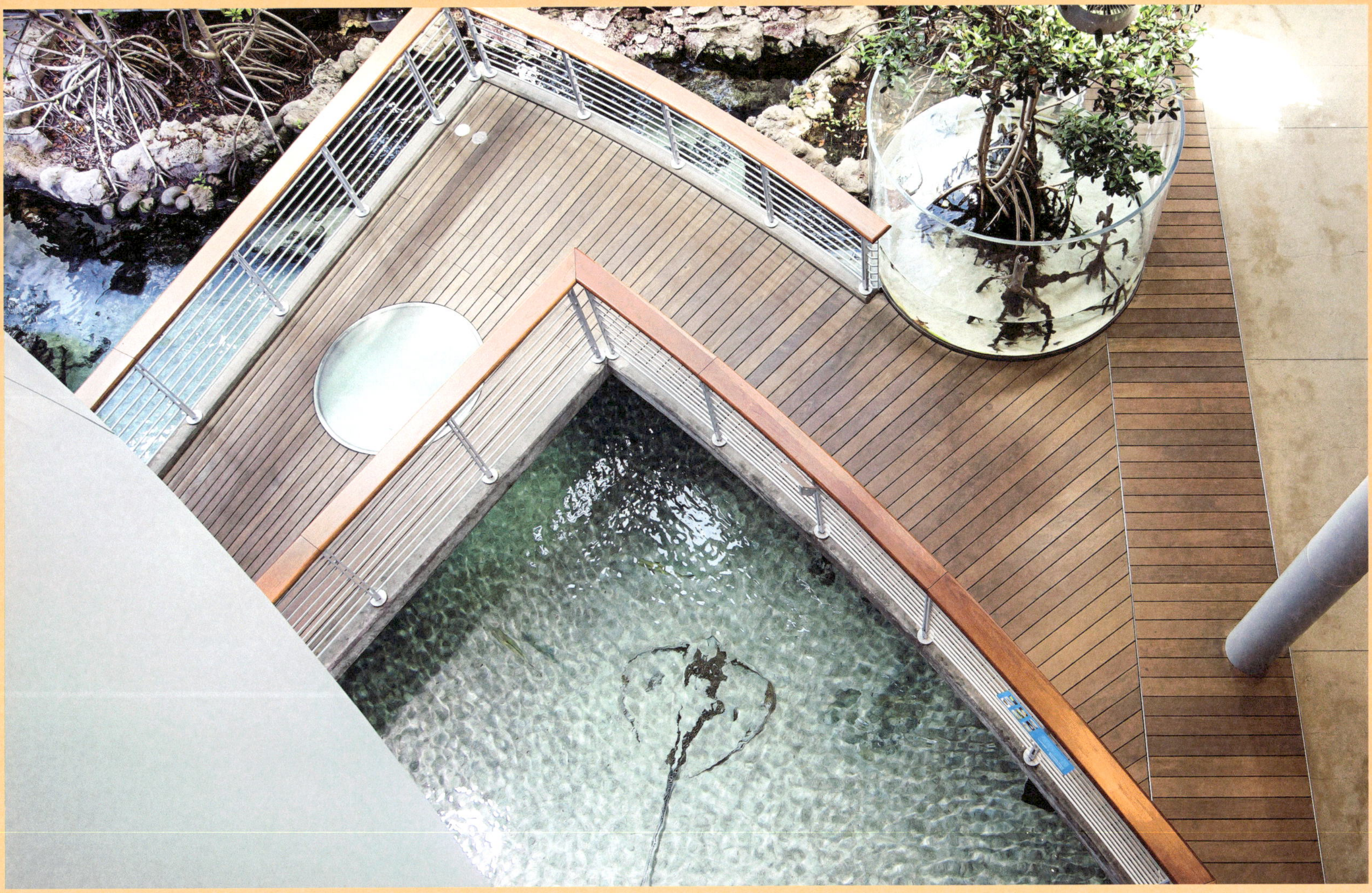

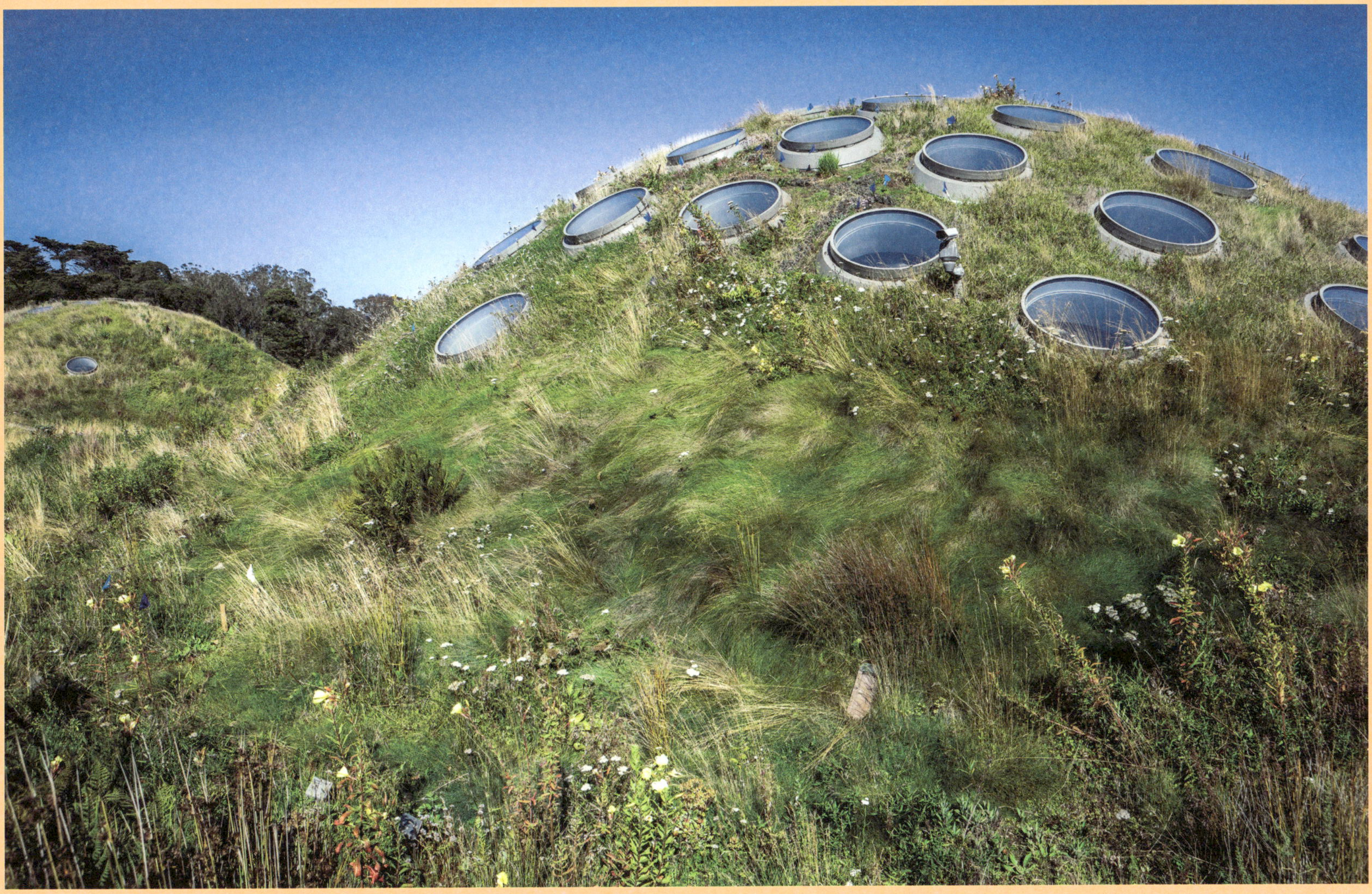

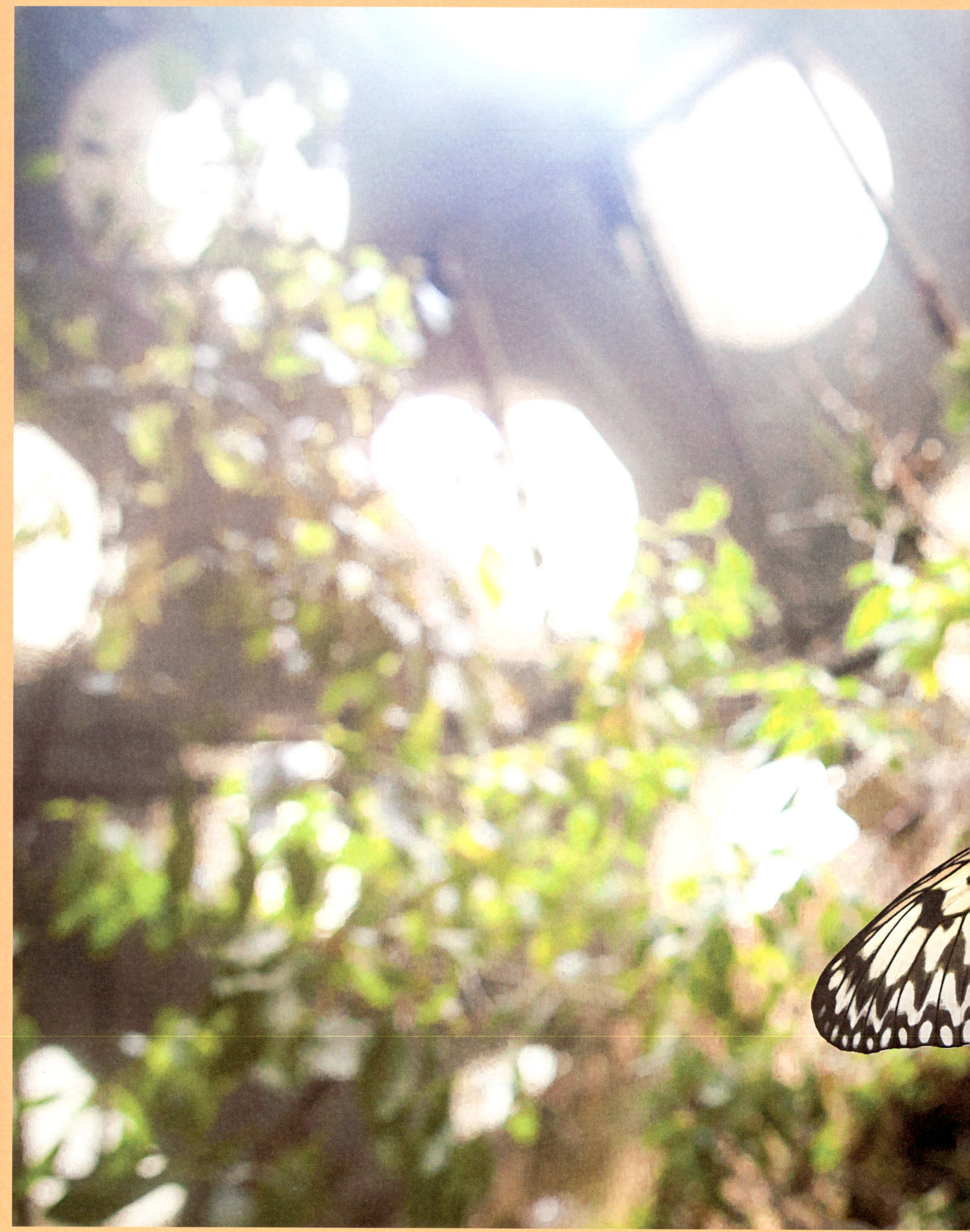

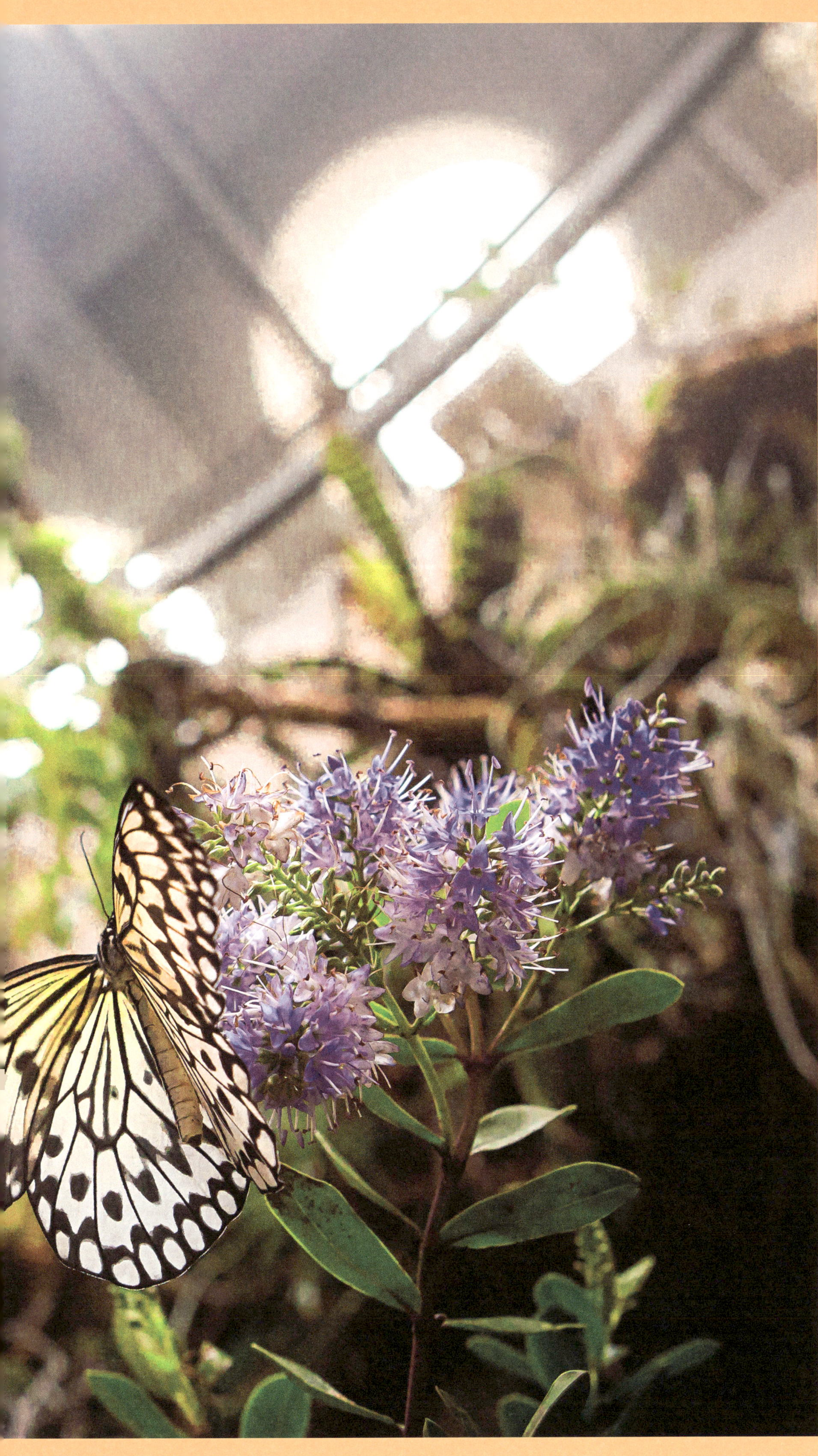

MUSEUMS WITH SIMILAR MEASURES

Musée du Quai Branly - Jacques Chirac

PARIS, FRANCE

Vertical garden, urban biodiversity reserve.

Kunst Haus Wien. Museum Hundertwasser

VIENNA, AUSTRIA

Efficient green roof.

San Francisco Museum of Modern Art (SFMOMA)

SAN FRANCISCO, CALIFORNIA, USA

Vertical garden.

Néprajzi Múzeum
Budapest, Hungary

Landscaped roof integrated
in a community park.

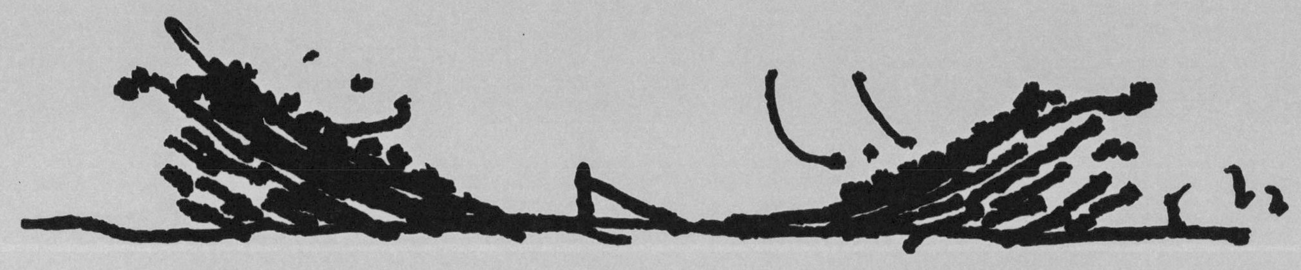

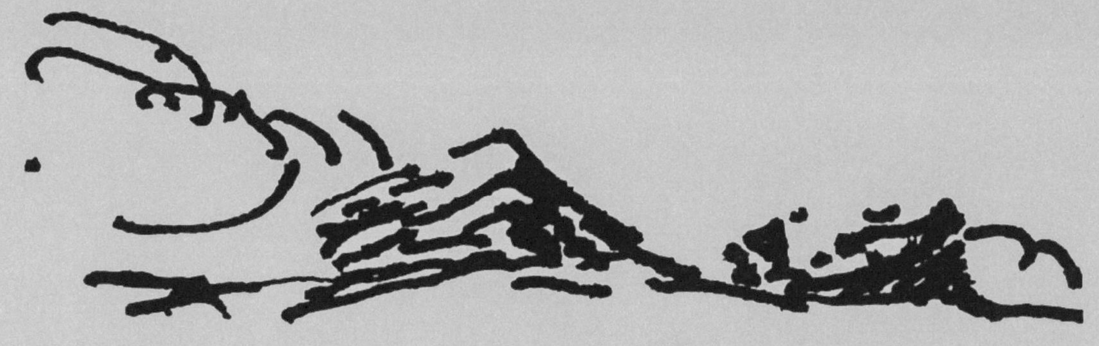

Architect Marcel Ferencz's First Sketch for the Museum of Ethnography Building.

03 USE OF RECYCLED CONSTRUCTION MATERIALS

CONSTRUCTION MATERIALS SDG 9 / 11 / 12

Use of reused or recycled construction elements serves as a sustainable alternative to the production of new materials.

The Ningbo Museum has incorporated rubble waste using the traditional *wapan* technique, which utilizes demolition debris to construct new, heterogeneous walls. The facade is covered with traditional bricks, tiles and recycled tiles, in response to the phenomenon of deconstruction and mass construction in the process of urbanization in China.

In addition, natural materials like stone and bamboo are used in its construction, contributing to the deliberate irregularity of the complex.

Ningbo Museum

FOCUS
Local History

LOCATION
Ningbo, Zhejiang, China

CONSTRUCTION
2007–2008

PROJECT
Wang Shu and Lu Wenyu

SIZE
30,000 m²

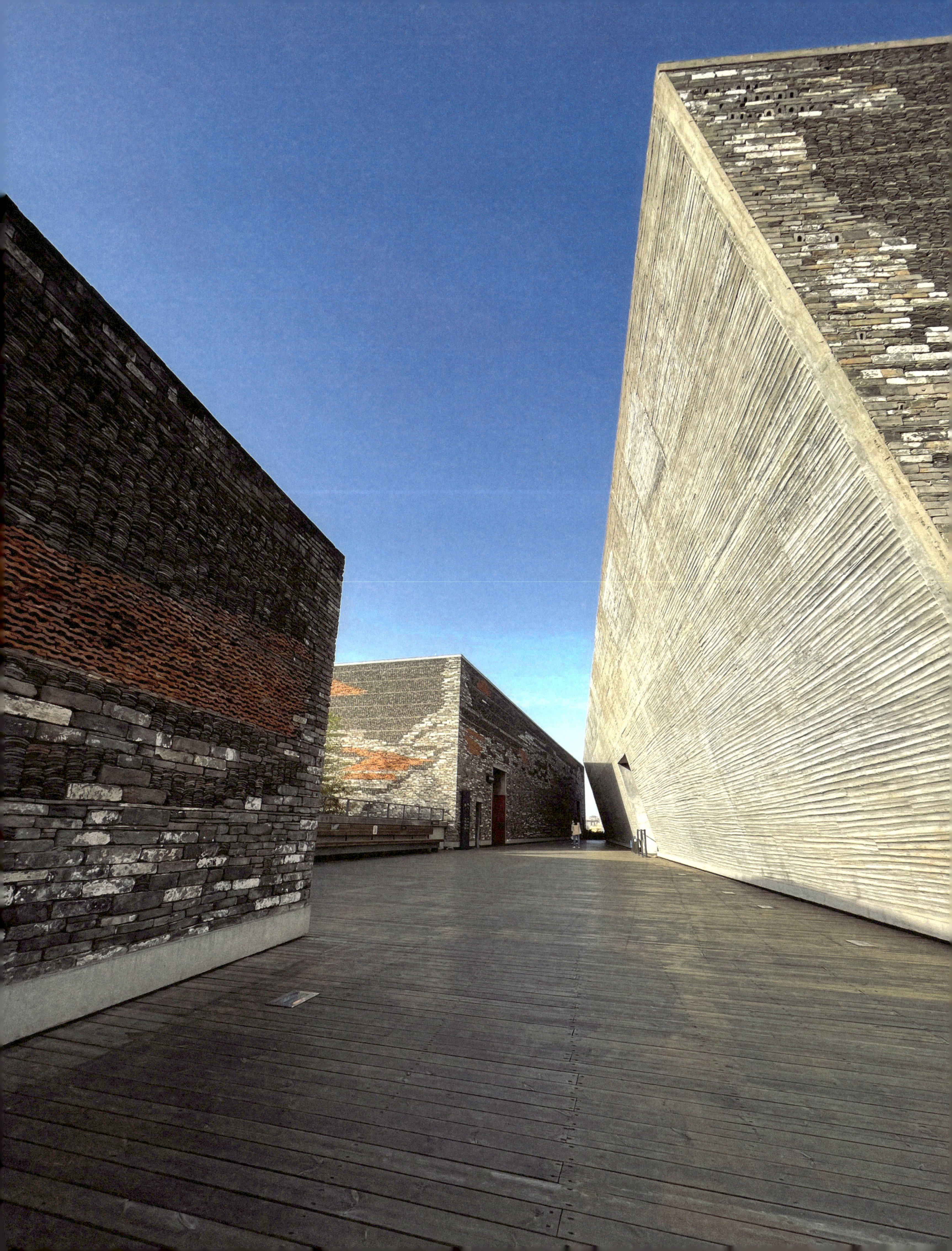

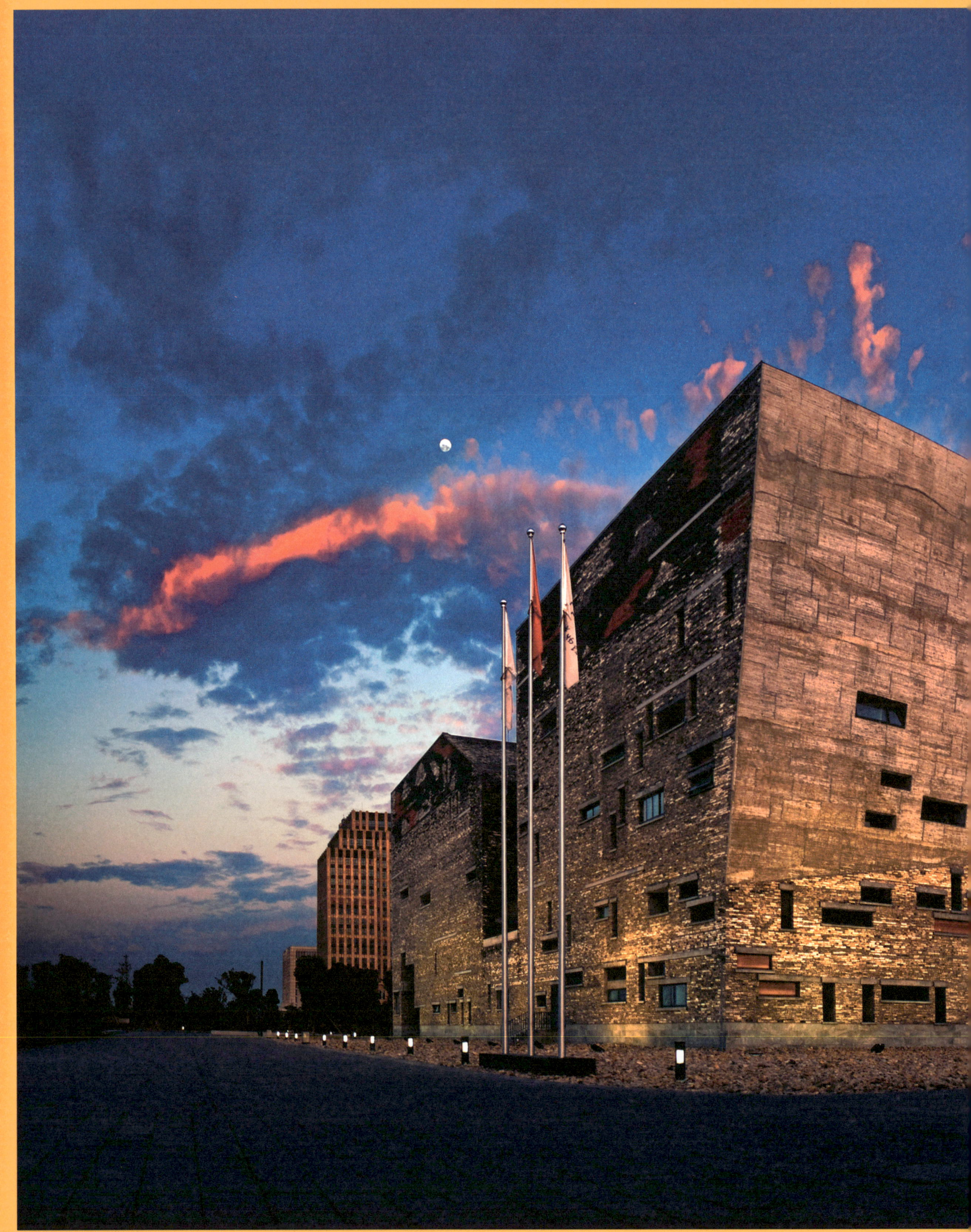

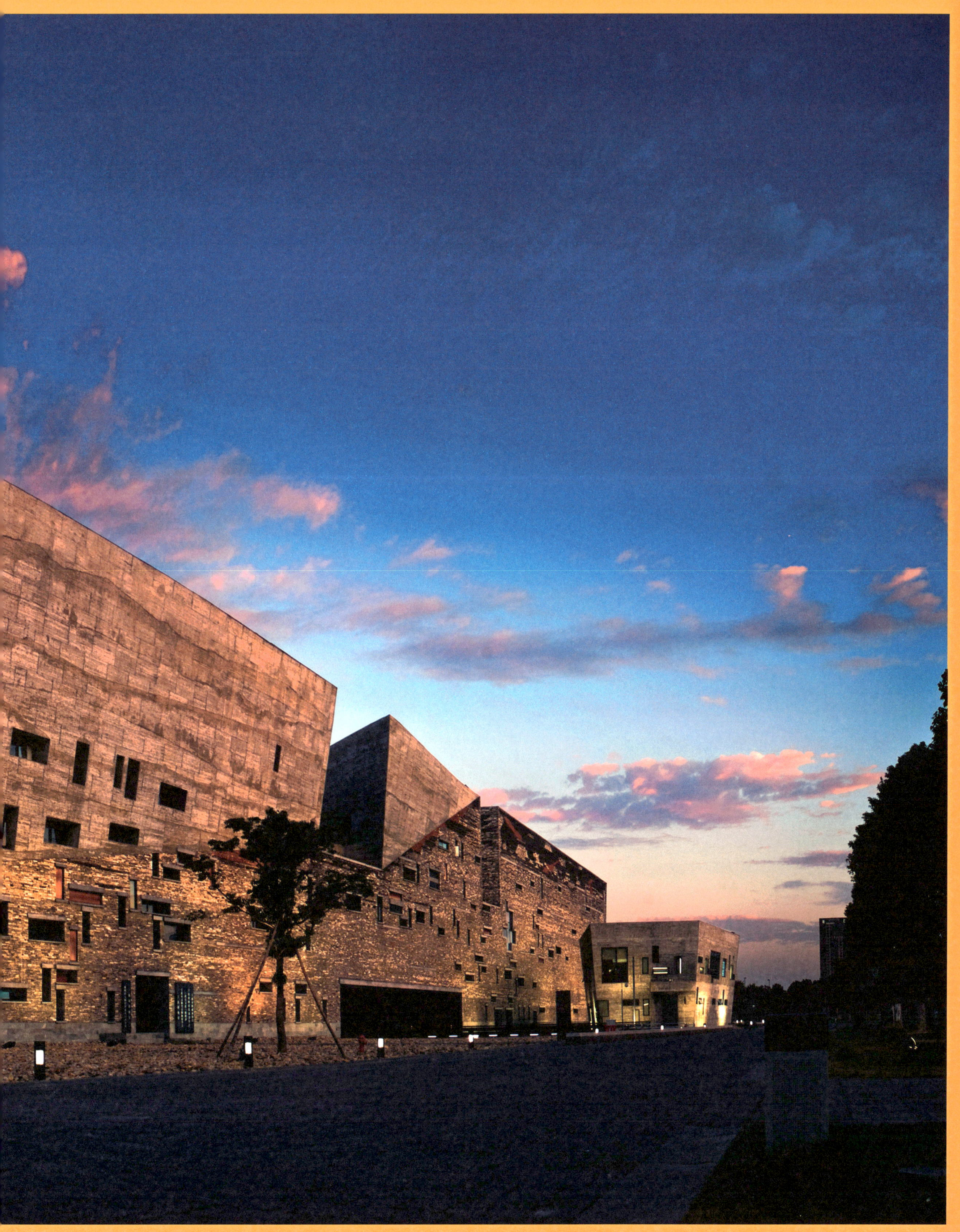

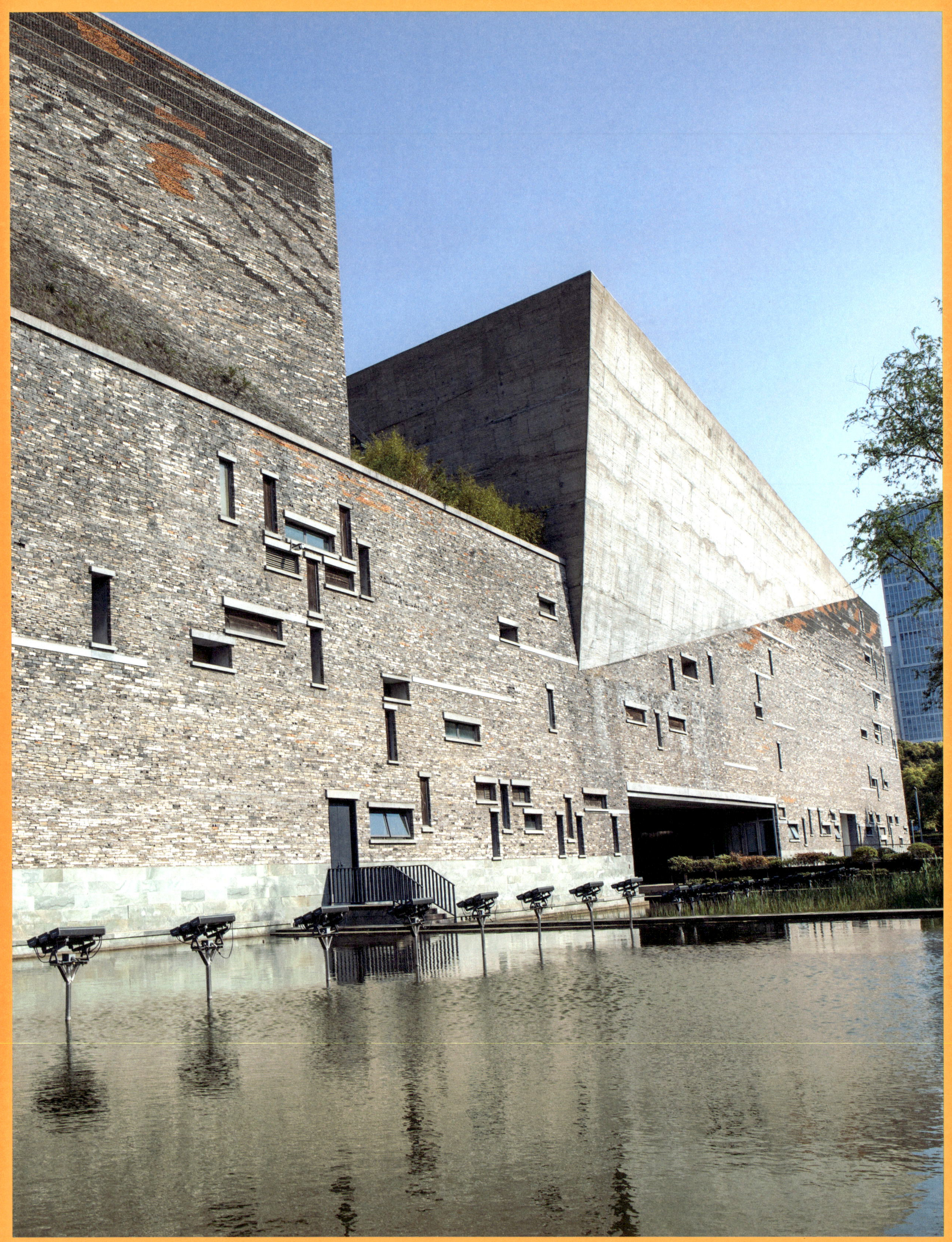

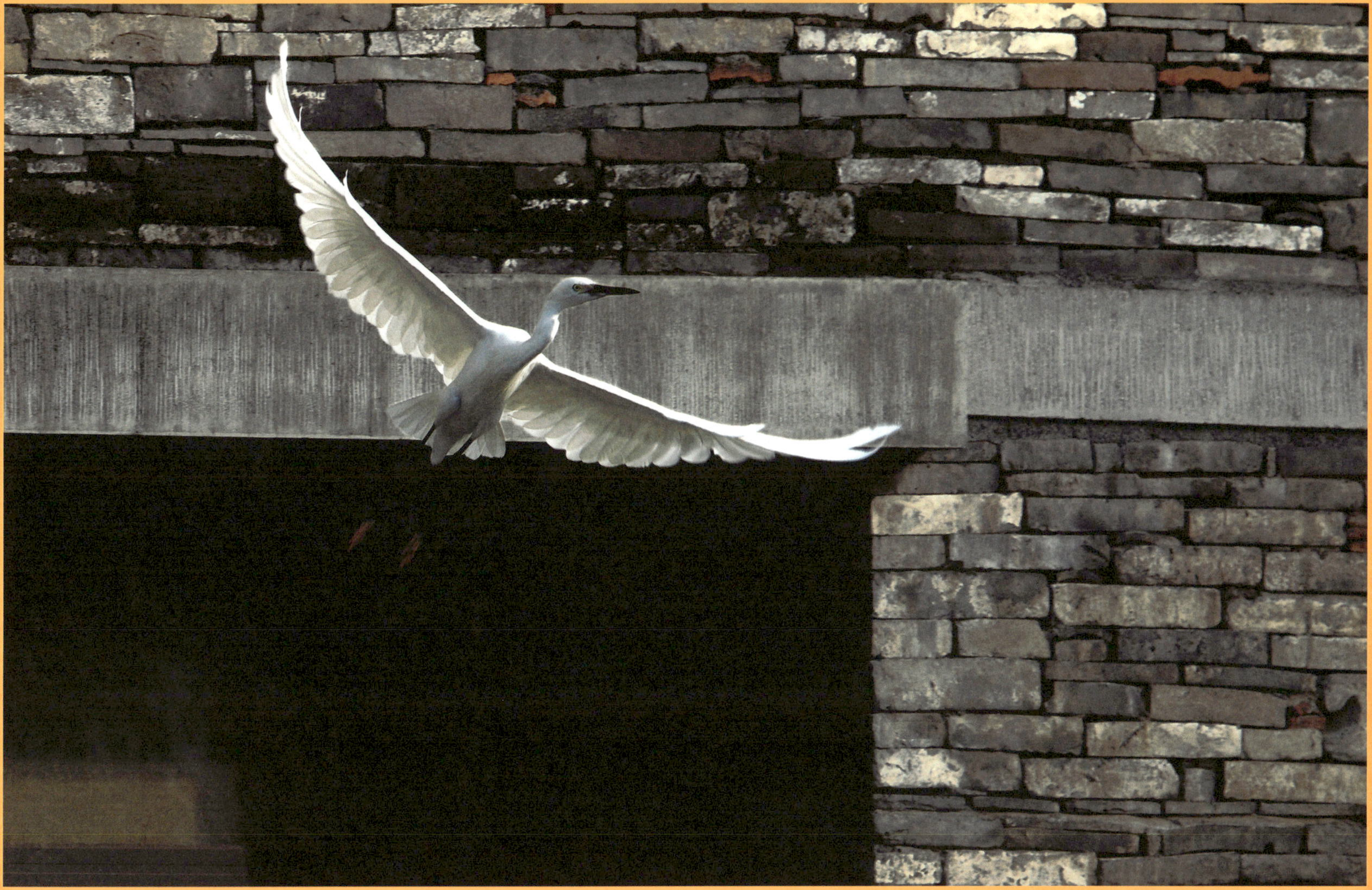

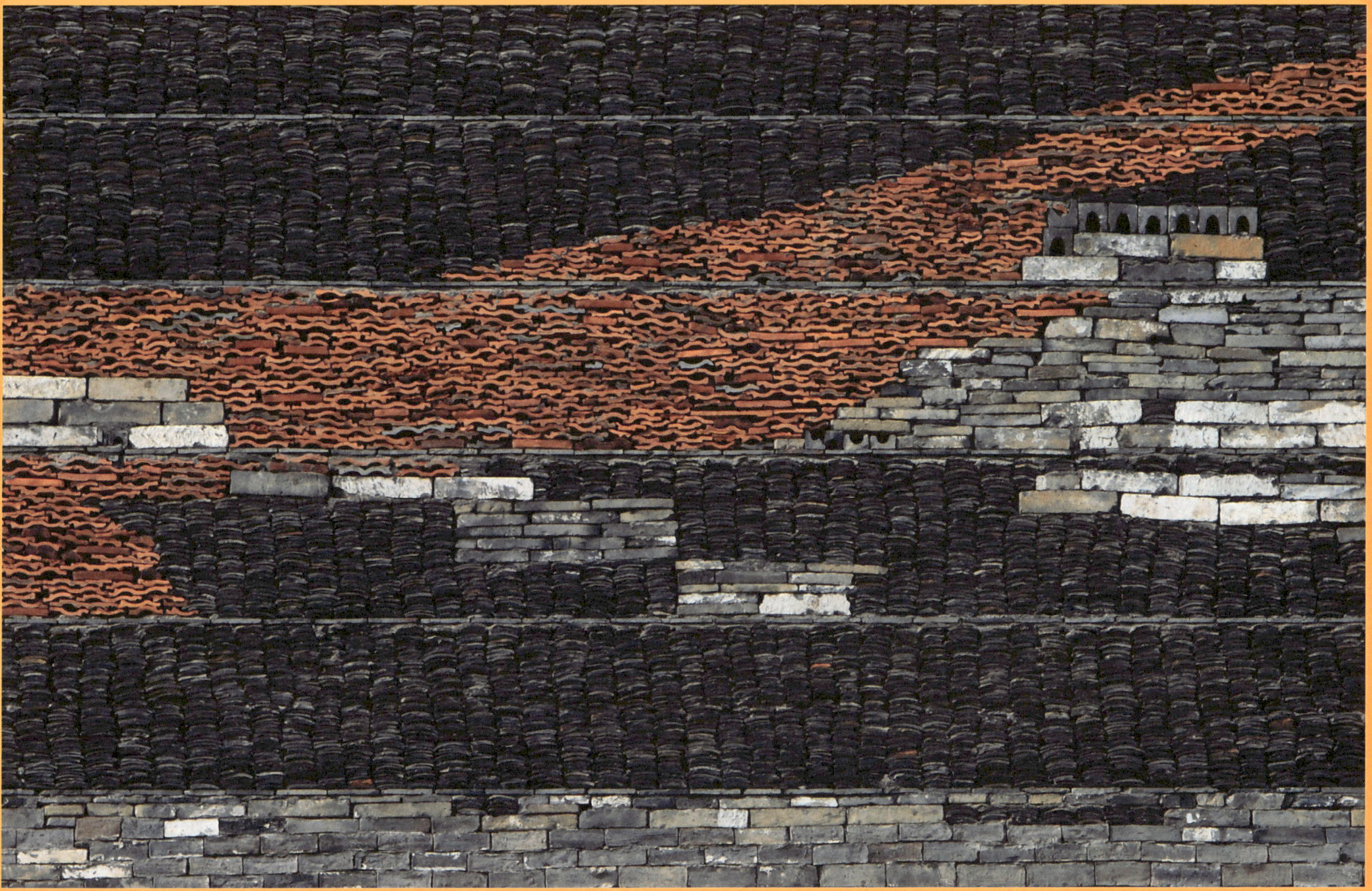

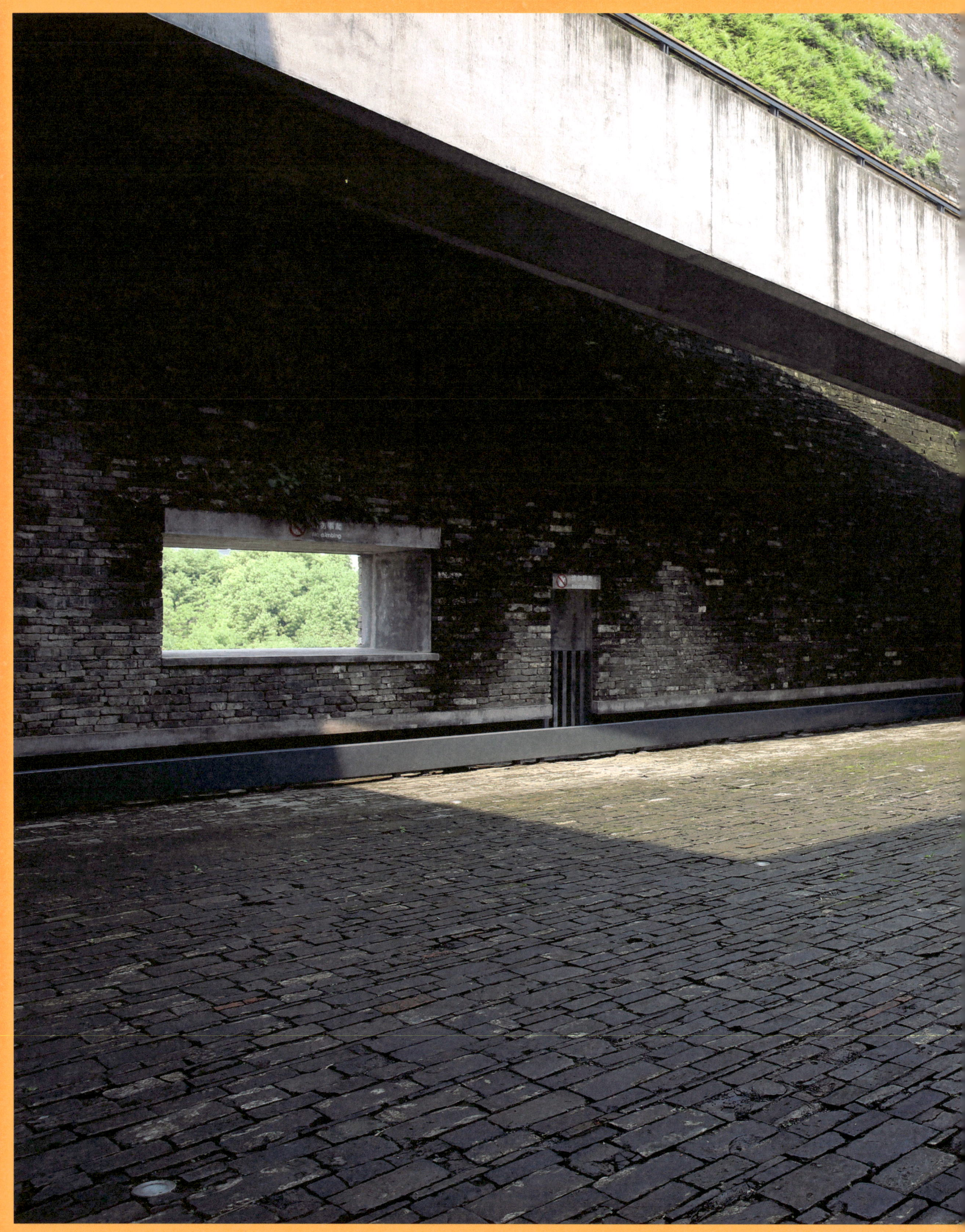

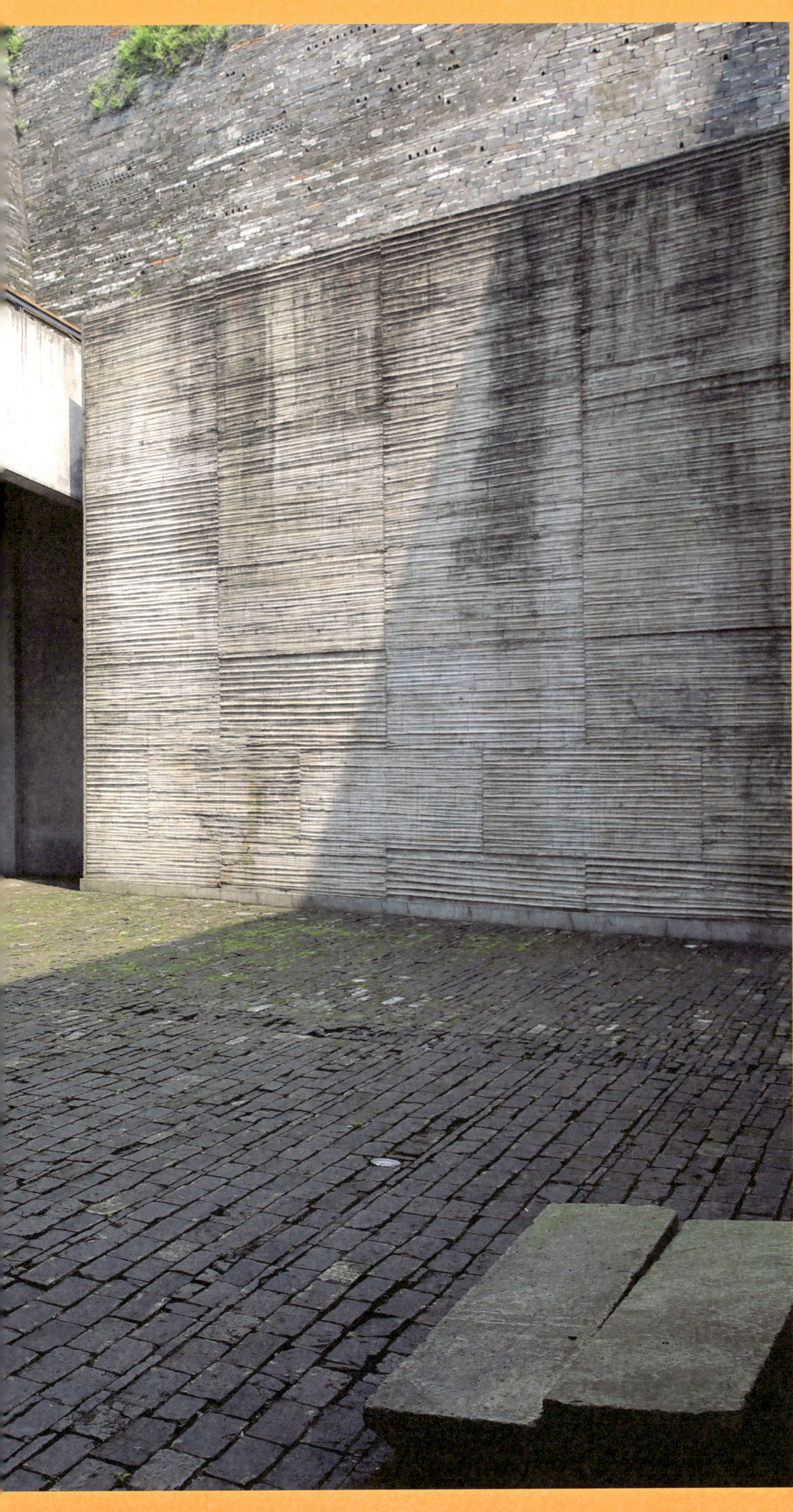

MUSEUMS WITH SIMILAR MEASURES

California Academy of Sciences

CALIFORNIA, USA

Recycling and reuse of debris generated in the demolition of existing structures for the construction of the new building.

Design Museum Gent
Ghent, Belgium

Use of bricks made from municipal construction and demolition wastes.

"Research is one of the fundamental activities of a designer and a design museum. As a design museum, we need to raise awareness about major social challenges, such as climate change. Together with designers, we have the ability to imagine and model possible solutions for this ecological transition. We are proud to be pioneers, along with BC Materials and architects, in this research project. The brick made from the waste of the Design Museum in Ghent has the potential to make this world a better place. We are even more excited to create a space where research has resulted in a real and innovative brick."

Katrien Laporte
Director, Design Museum Gent

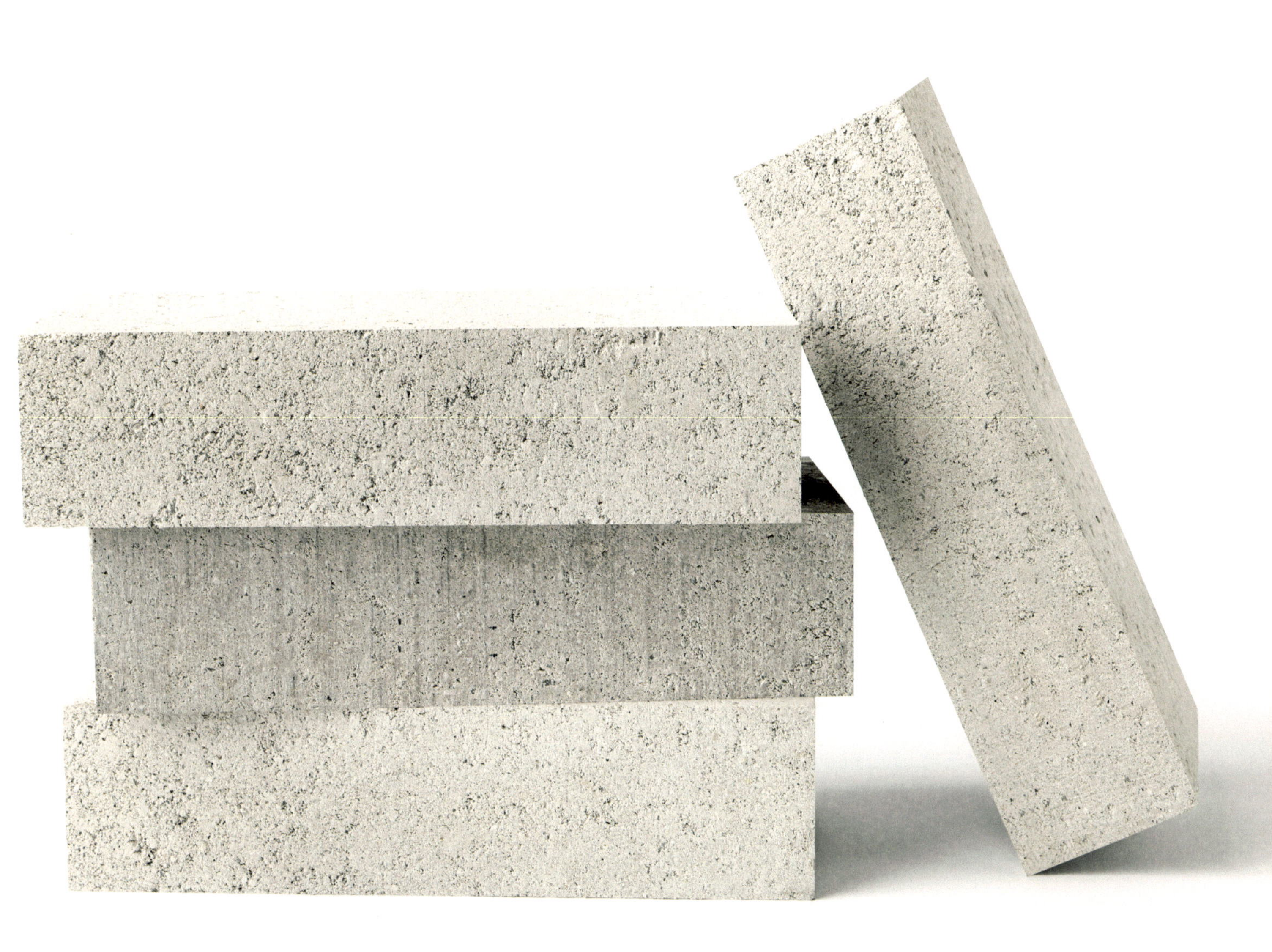

04 INTEGRATION OF INNOVATIVE MATERIALS

CONSTRUCTION MATERIALS SDG 9 / 11 / 12

The integration of technology and creativity for the use of materials with innovative properties enhances the sustainability of buildings that house museums.

In the case of Nanhai Art Center, the museum's roof features a translucent white ETFE membrane. ETFE, a lightweight, transparent copolymer refined from seawater, allows 95% of the light that glass does at just 1% of the weight. Additionally, its low-pressure air filling provides thermal insulation and structural stability against wind or snow loads. The ETFE membrane allows for natural room lighting, insulation, and recyclability with energy-efficient and environmentally friendly technology.

Nanhai Art Center

FOCUS
Art

LOCATION
Foshan, Guangdong, China

CONSTRUCTION
Due to open in 2029

PROJECT
MAD Architects

SIZE
59,445 m²

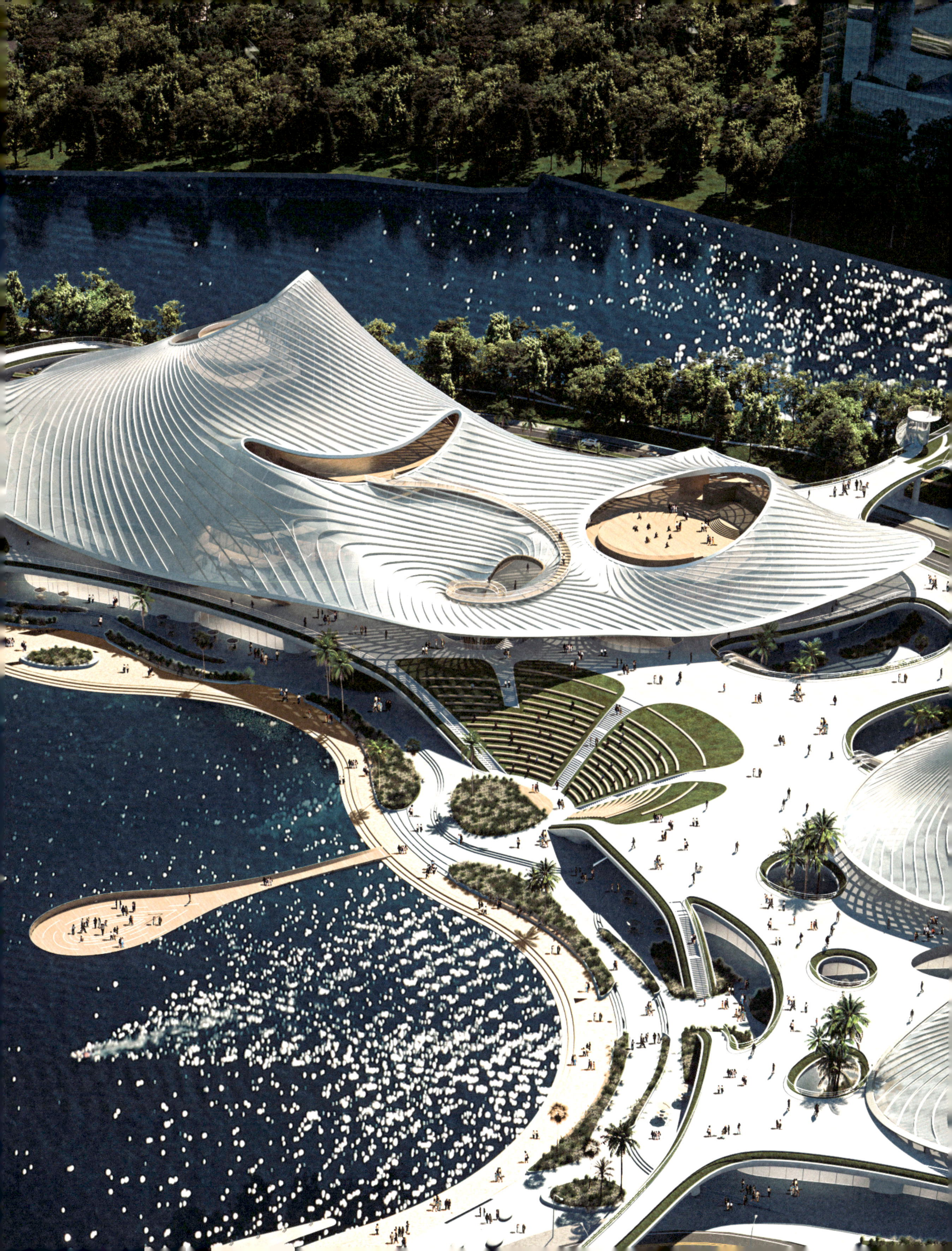

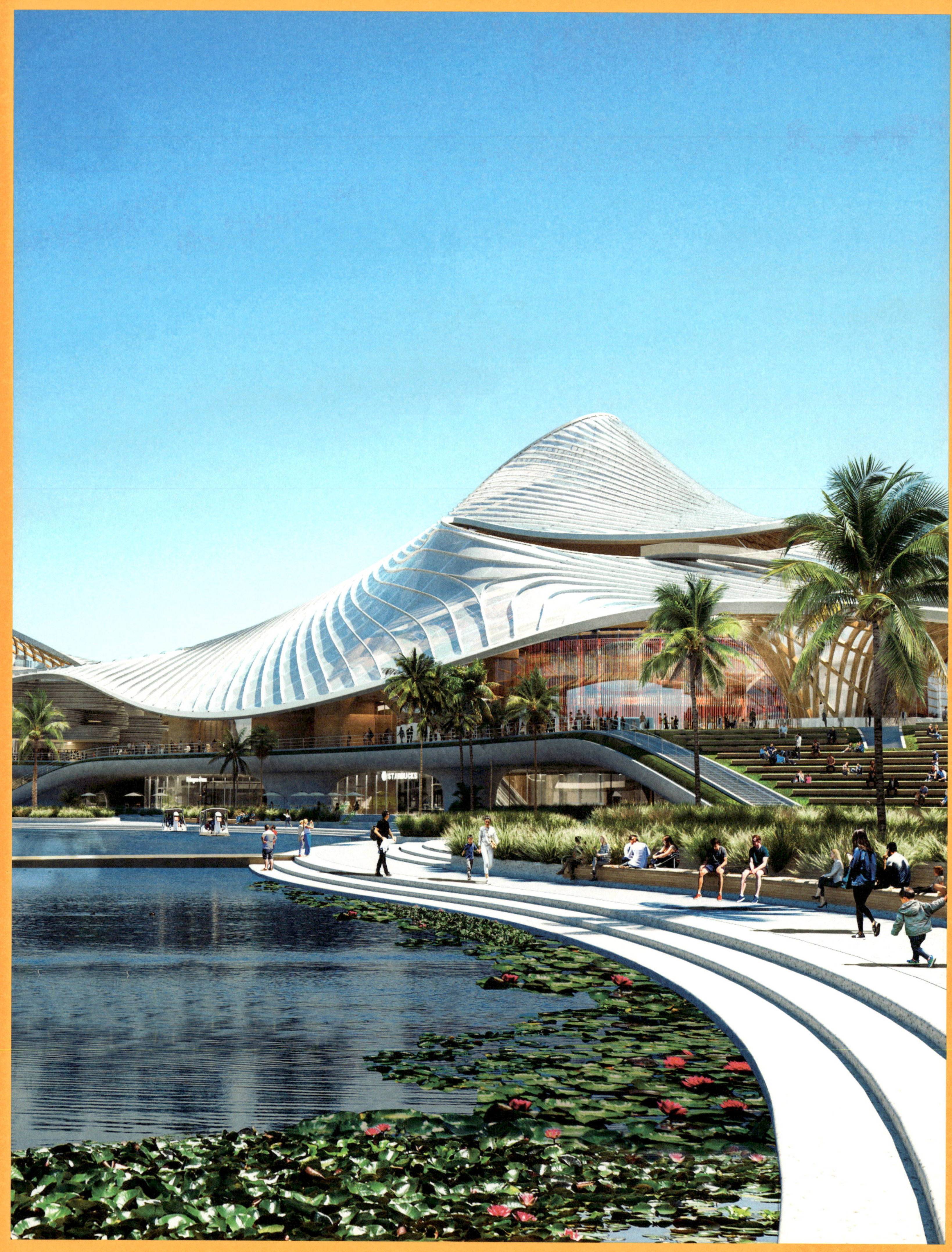
STARBUCKS

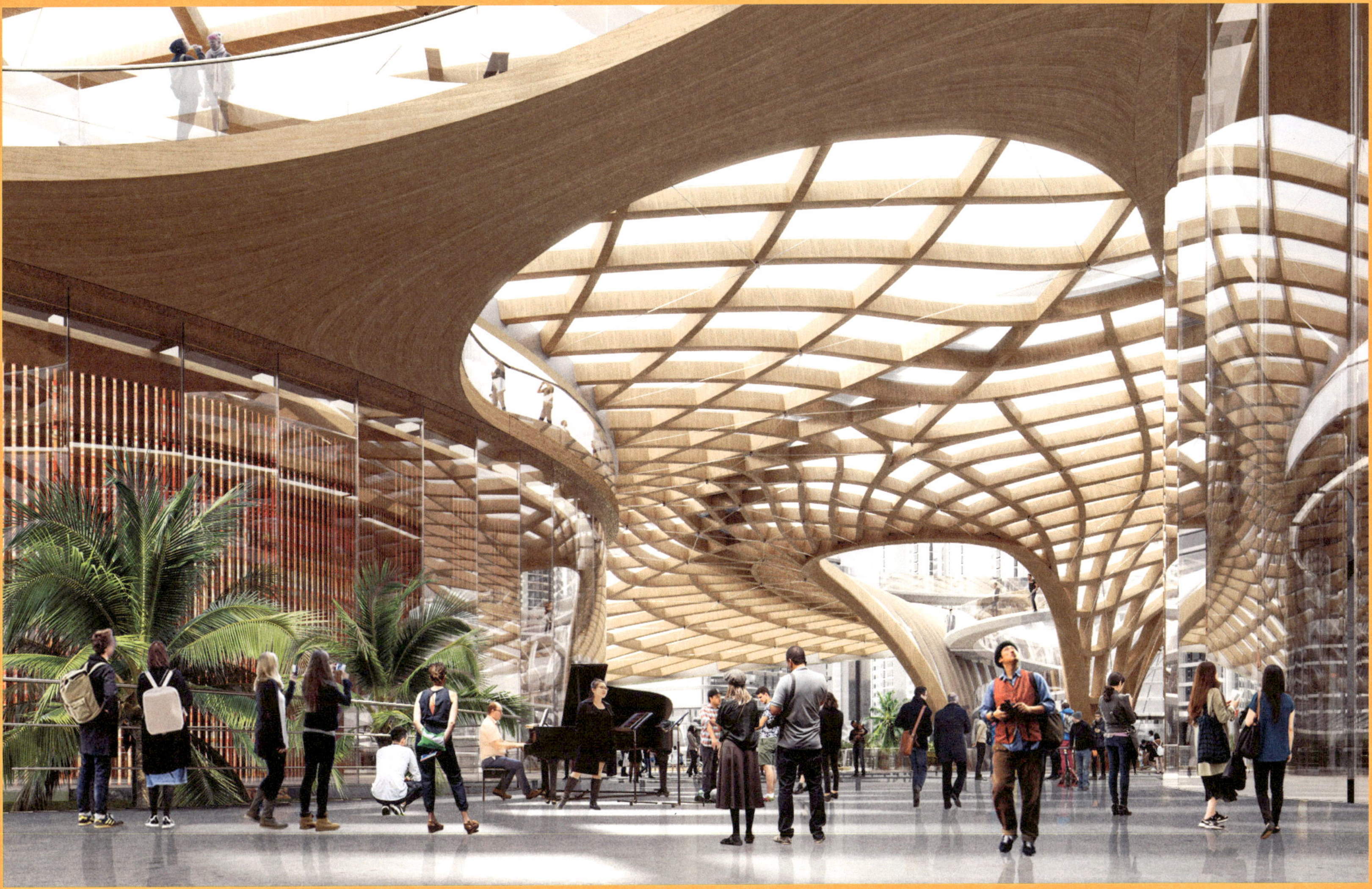

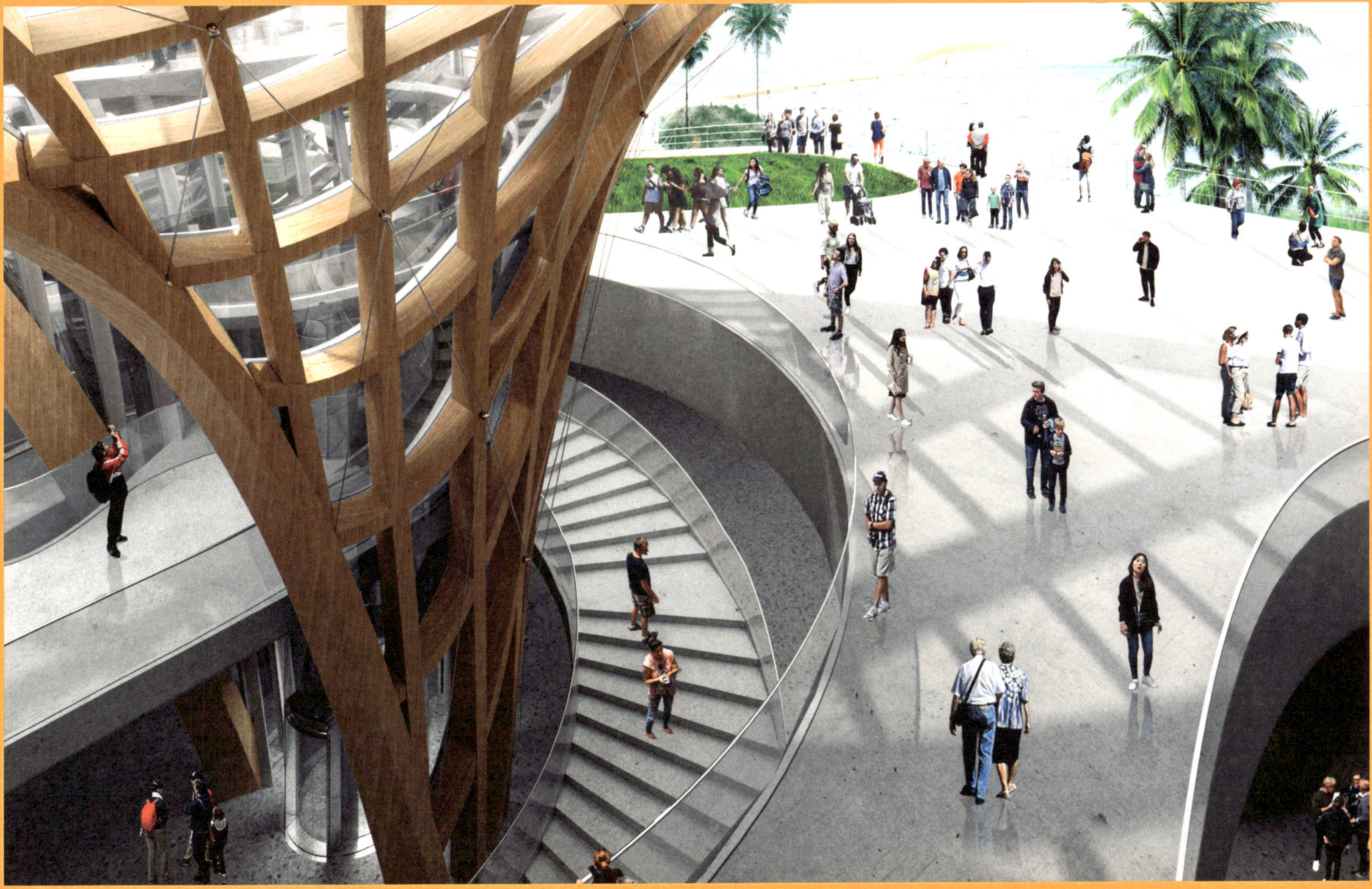

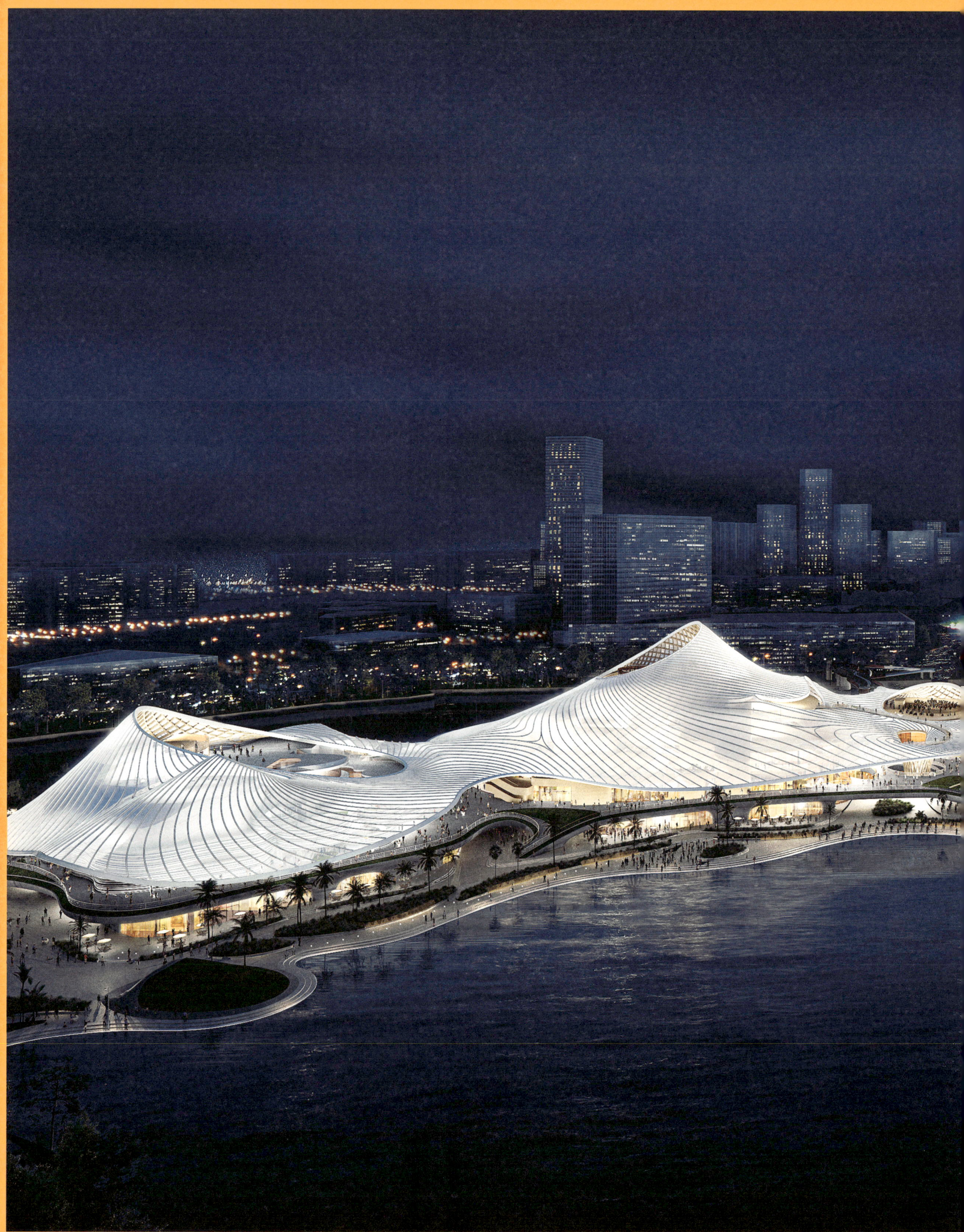

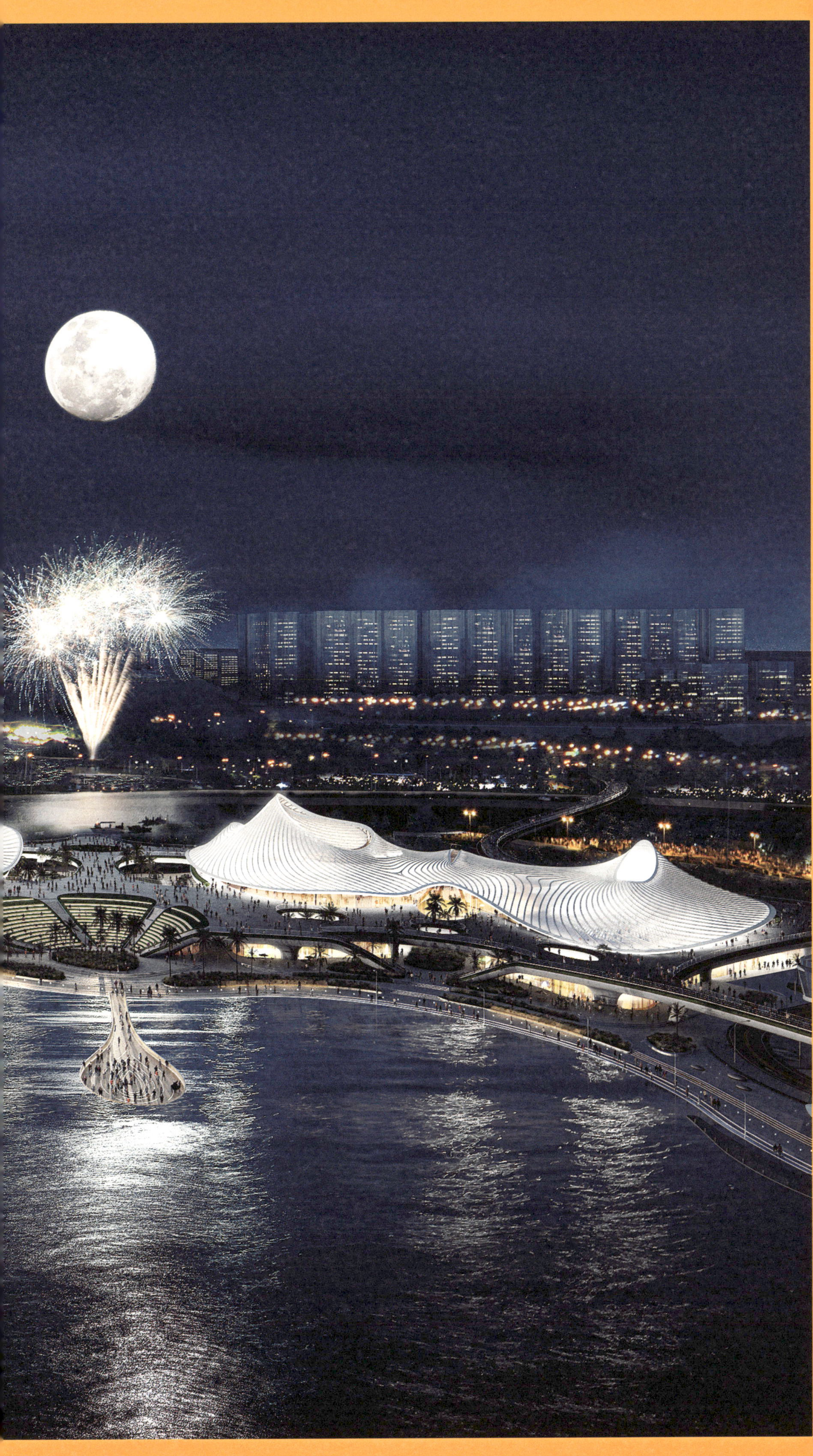

MUSEUMS WITH SIMILAR MEASURES

Fondation Louis Vuitton

PARIS, FRANCE

This museum features innovative construction with a curved glass cover that creates light and mirror effects.

Aspen Art Museum

ASPEN, COLORADO, USA

It uses natural wood siding complemented by supertextured façade panels.

Museum of the Future

DUBAI, UNITED ARAB EMIRATES

Parametric design, passive solar architecture, low-energy and low-water engineering solutions.

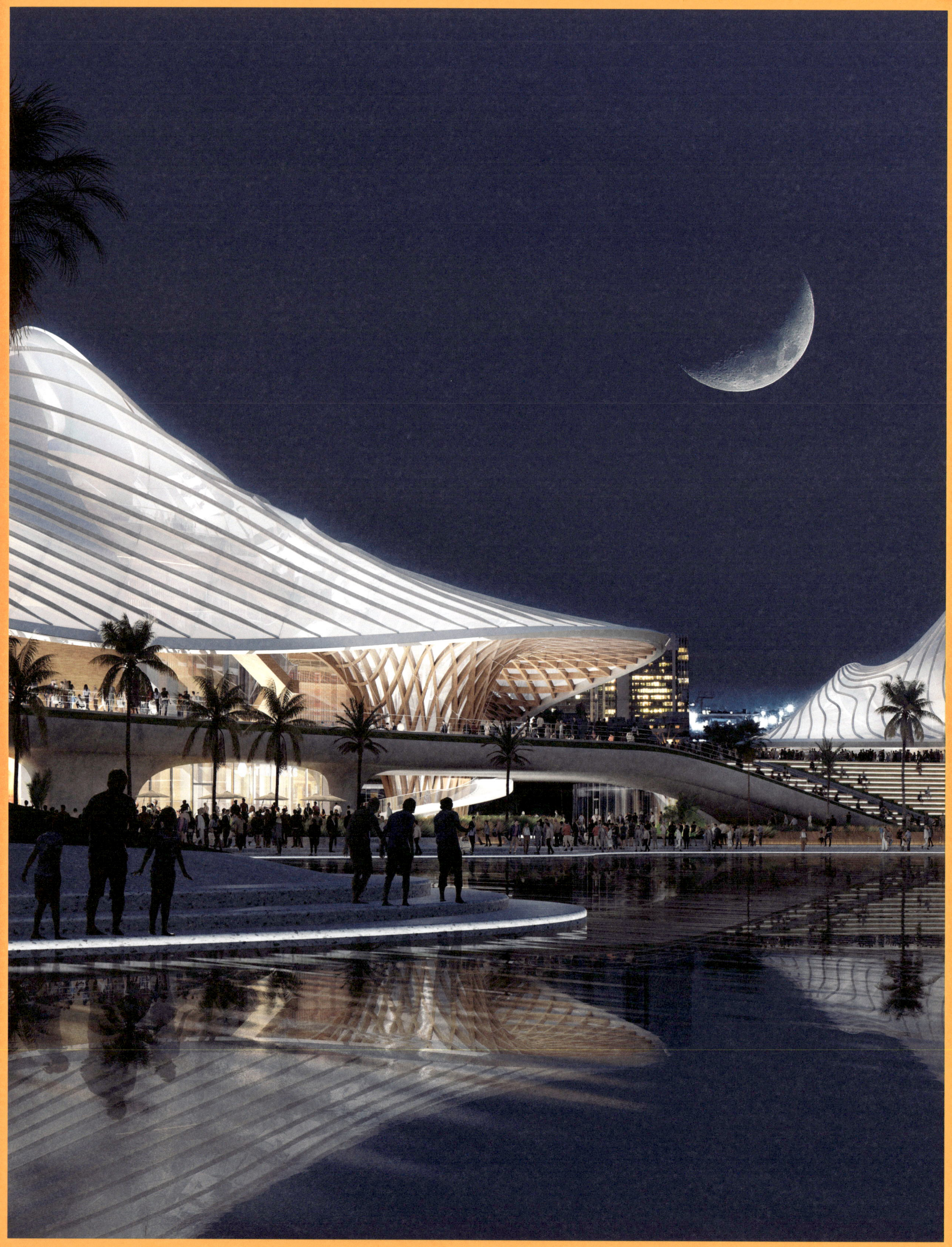

“I think of nature as a material. I understand the function of the whole and the necessary elements to make it functional. But I also want to transfer this functionality, this reality, into something surreal. We seek the spiritual quality of nature.”

Ma Yansong

Founder and Principal Partner of MAD Architects
Archinect

05 LOW-EMISSION MATERIALS

CONSTRUCTION MATERIALS SDG 3 / 9

Volatile organic compounds (VOCs) are substances that easily evaporate at normal temperatures and pressures. Their volatility allows them to spread into the environment and potentially alter their chemical composition, directly and indirectly affecting both the natural world and human health. These compounds are often found in various construction materials, contributing to poor indoor air quality.

To maintain a healthy indoor environment, the National Museum of Qatar has used materials with low concentrations of volatile organic compounds (VOCs). The adhesives, insulators, paints, coatings, carpets, rugs, and wood used throughout the museum have been selected with consideration of their VOC content.

National Museum of Qatar (NMoQ)

FOCUS
History

LOCATION
Doha, Qatar

CONSTRUCTION
2010–2019

PROJECT
Jean Nouvel

CERTIFICATION
4 Star Global Sustainability Assessment System (GSAS)

SIZE
340,000 m²

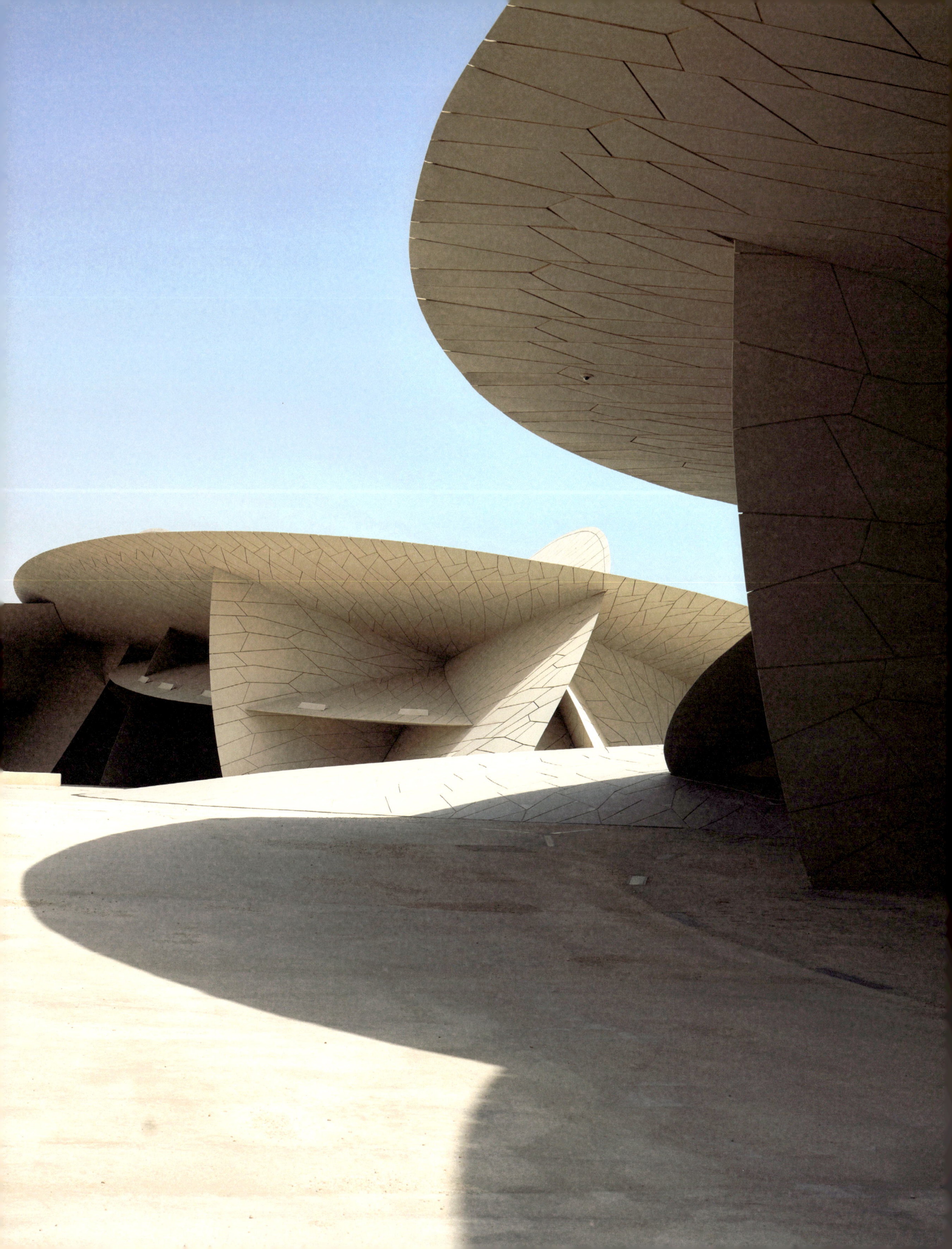

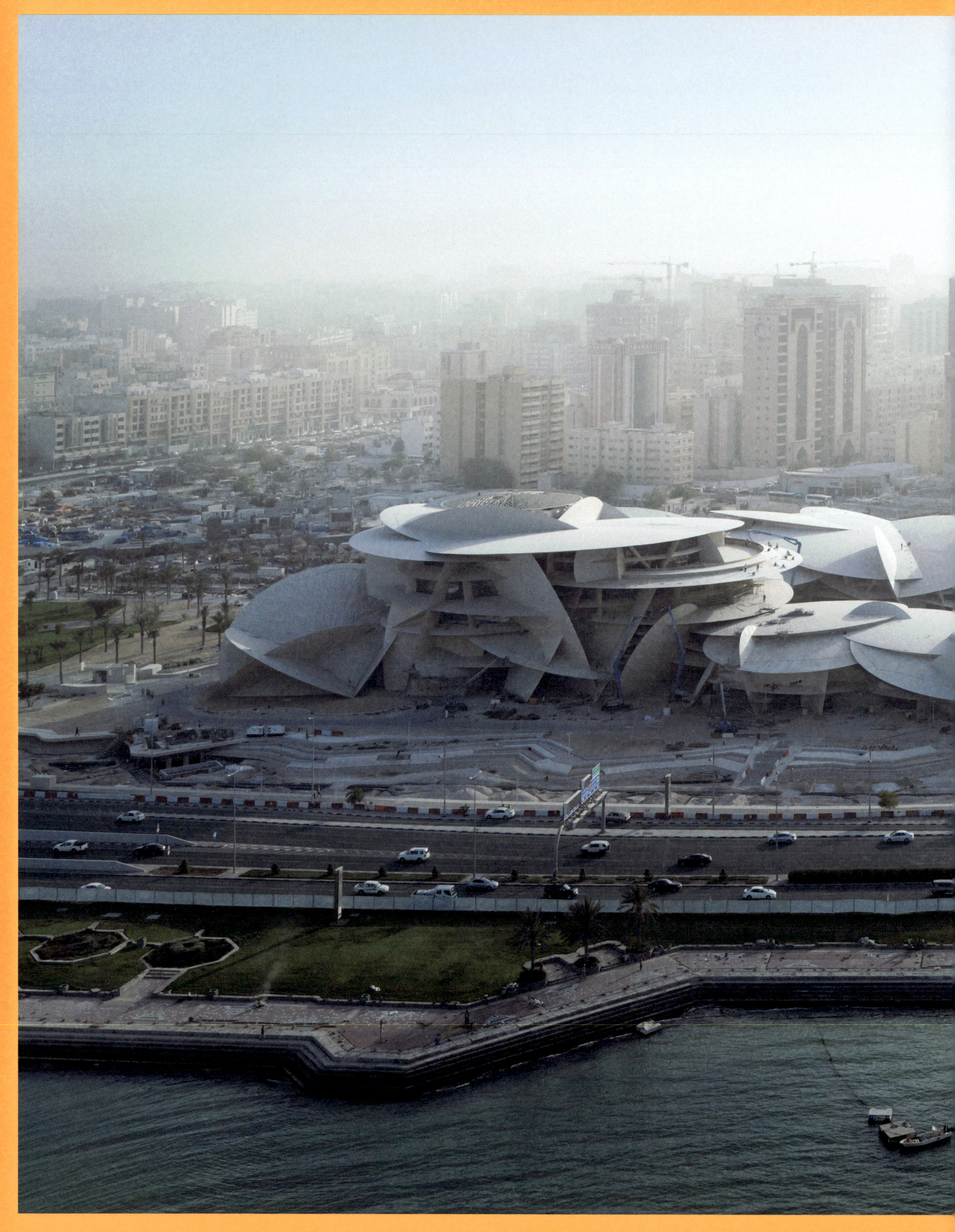

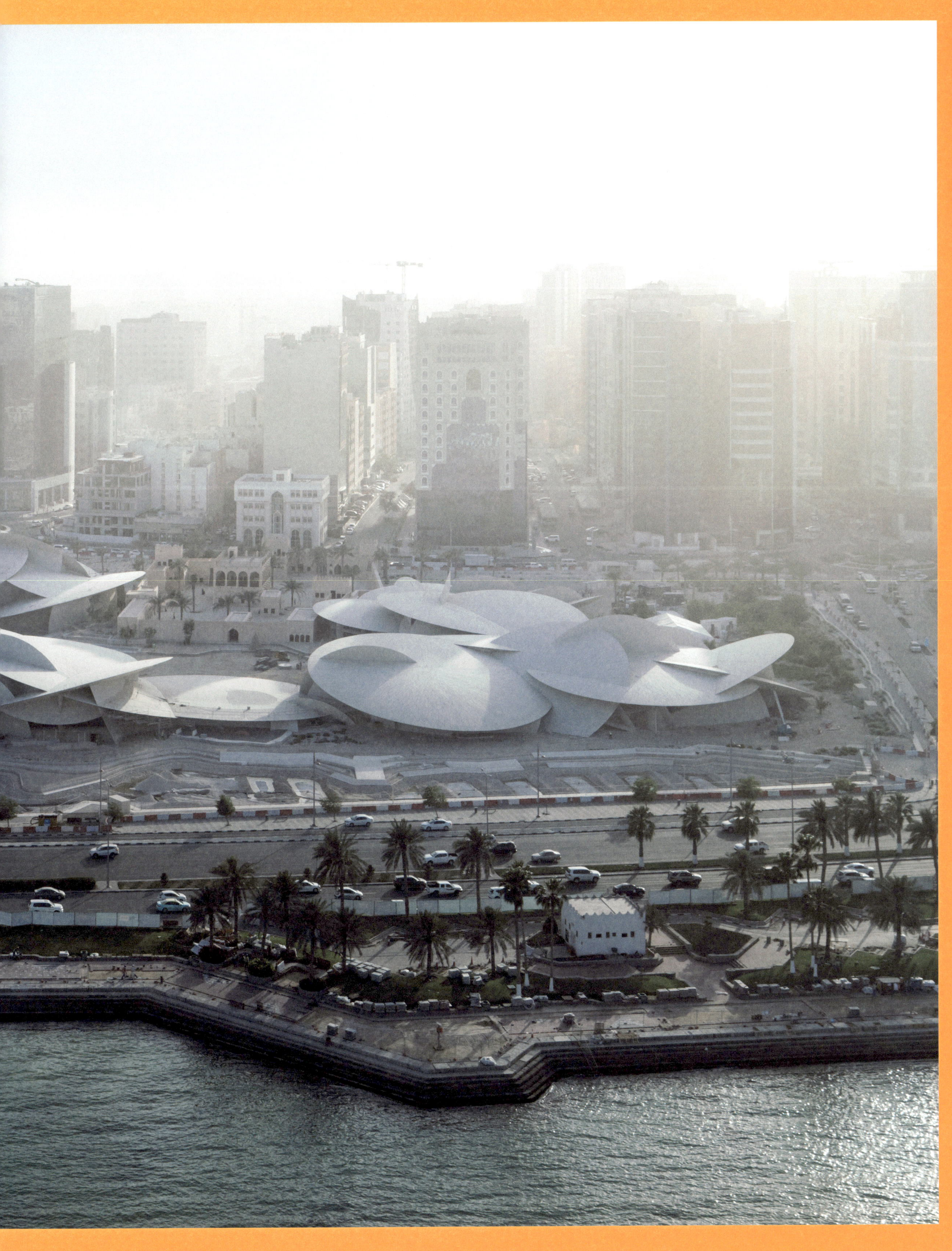

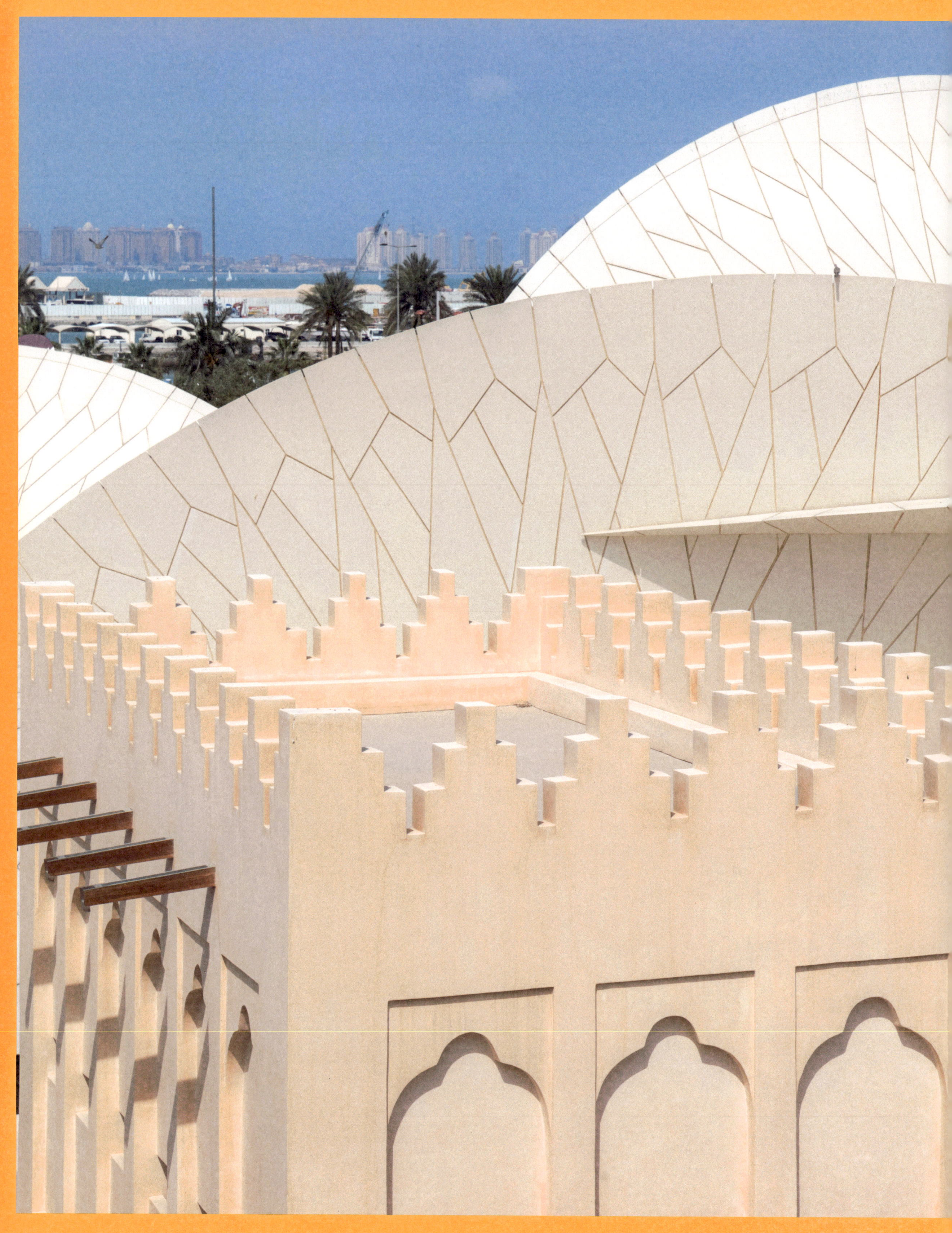

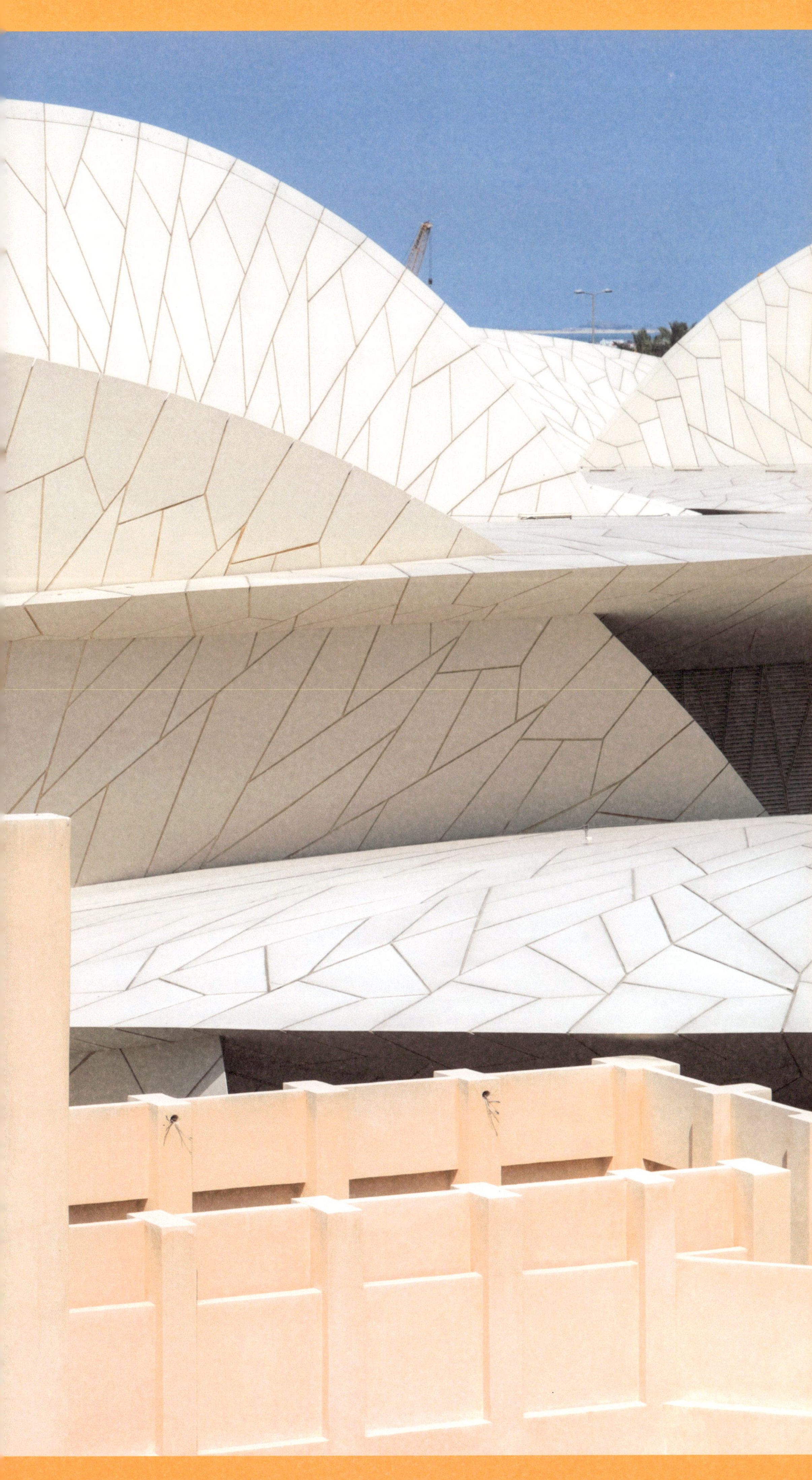

MUSEUMS WITH SIMILAR MEASURES

Children's Museum of Pittsburgh

PITTSBURGH, PENNSYLVANIA, USA

In its renovation, all adhesives, coatings, insulators, paints, varnishes, carpets, woods, and floorboards were certified as low-emission under the building's operating conditions.

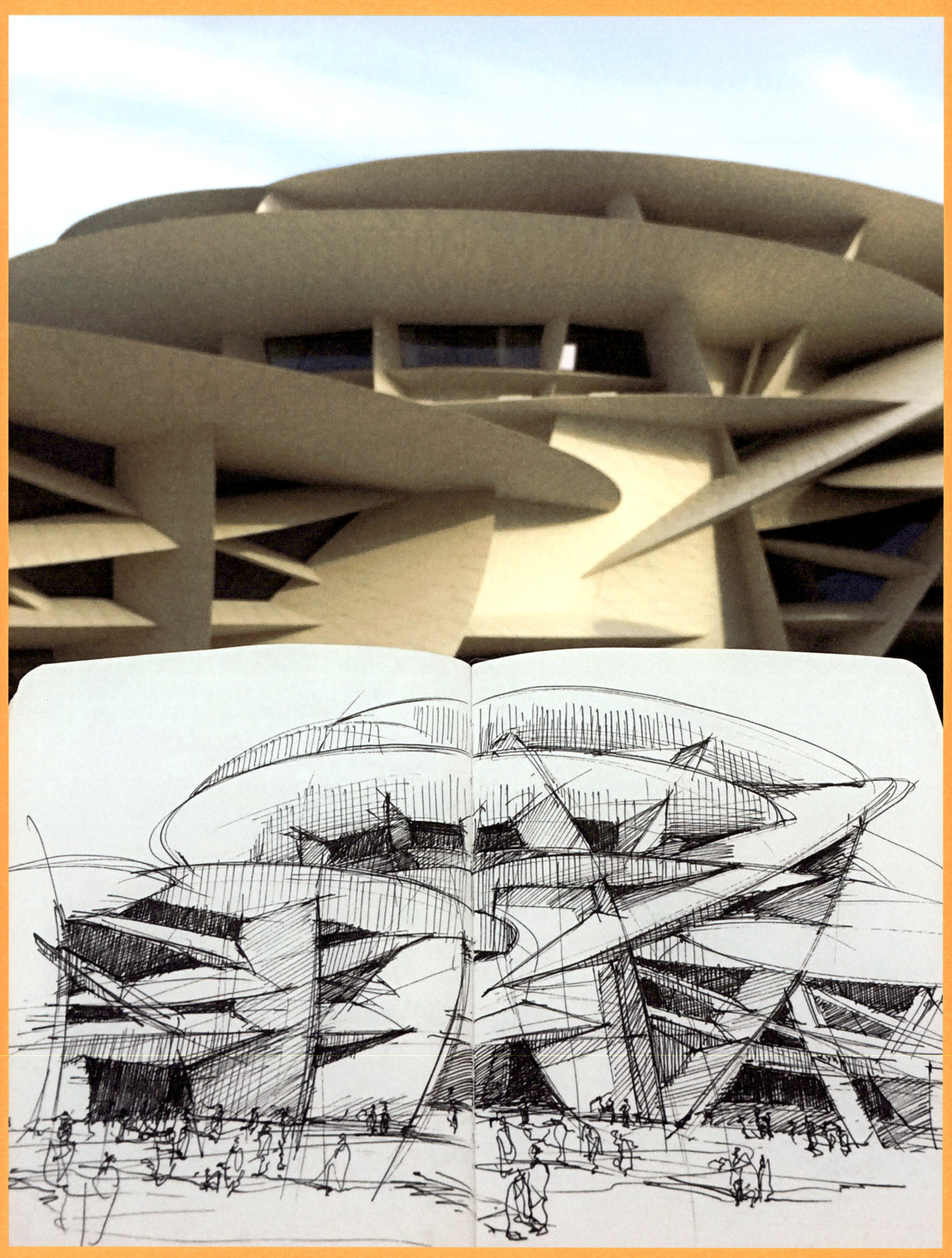

"The Heartbeat of Our Heritage"

قلب تراثنا
النابض

National Museum of Qatar

06 USE OF NATURAL BUILDING MATERIALS

CONSTRUCTION MATERIALS SDG 9 / 12 / 13

Utilizing natural materials in construction not only reduces the carbon footprint but also enhances thermal and acoustic comfort indoors, creating a warm and serene atmosphere.

At the Odunpazari Modern Art Museum, the façade is entirely constructed from wood. This design features interconnected strips of wood forming a unique stacked-box structure. Sustainably sourced wood acts as a carbon sink, thereby reducing atmospheric CO_2 levels. Moreover, the wooden design pays homage to Turkish art, contributing culturally to the city of Eskisehir and the history of Odunpazari.

Odunpazari Modern Museum

FOCUS
Contemporary Art

CONSTRUCTION
2019

LOCATION
Urban. Eskişehir, Turkey

PROJECT
Kengo Kuma & Associates

SIZE
3,582 m²

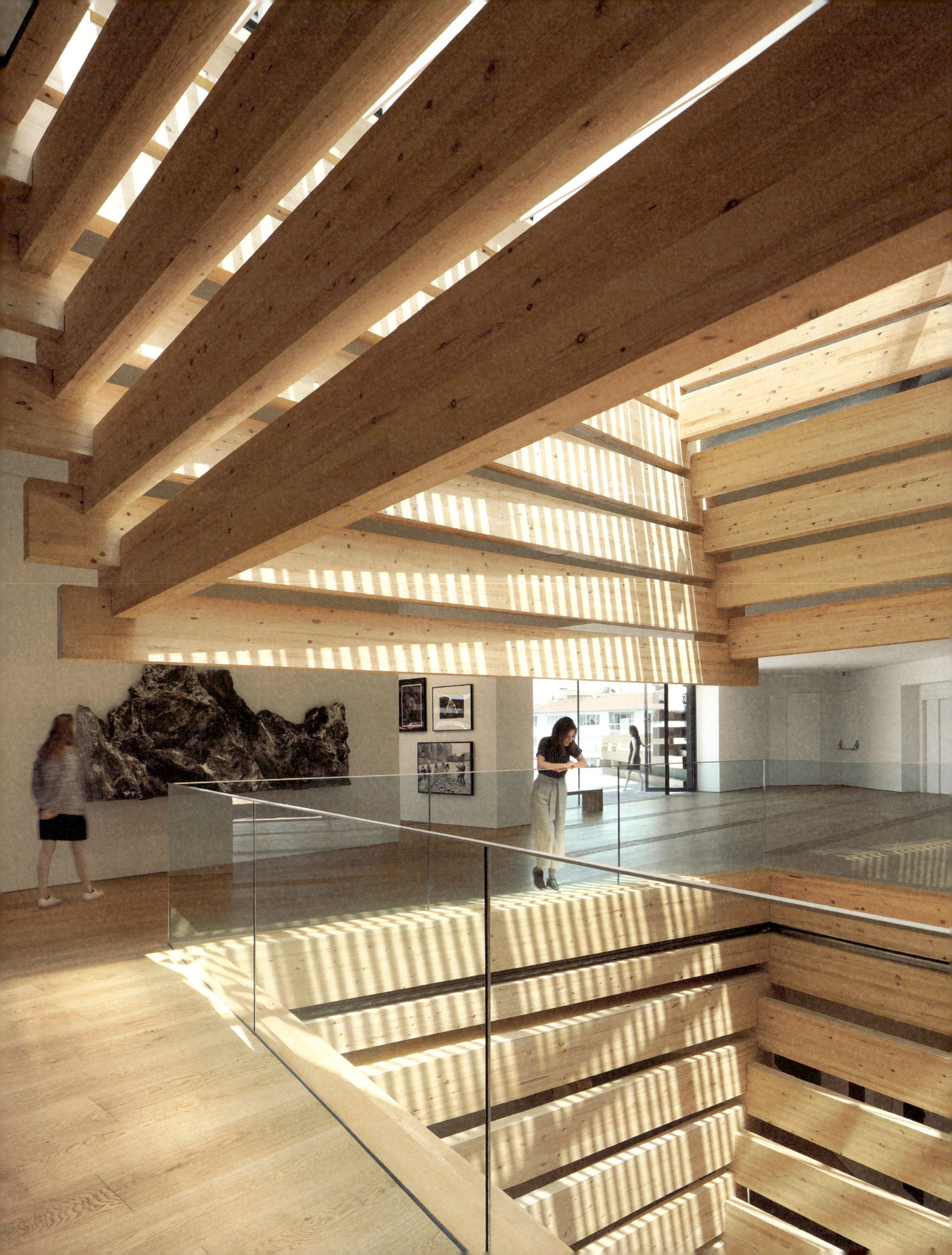

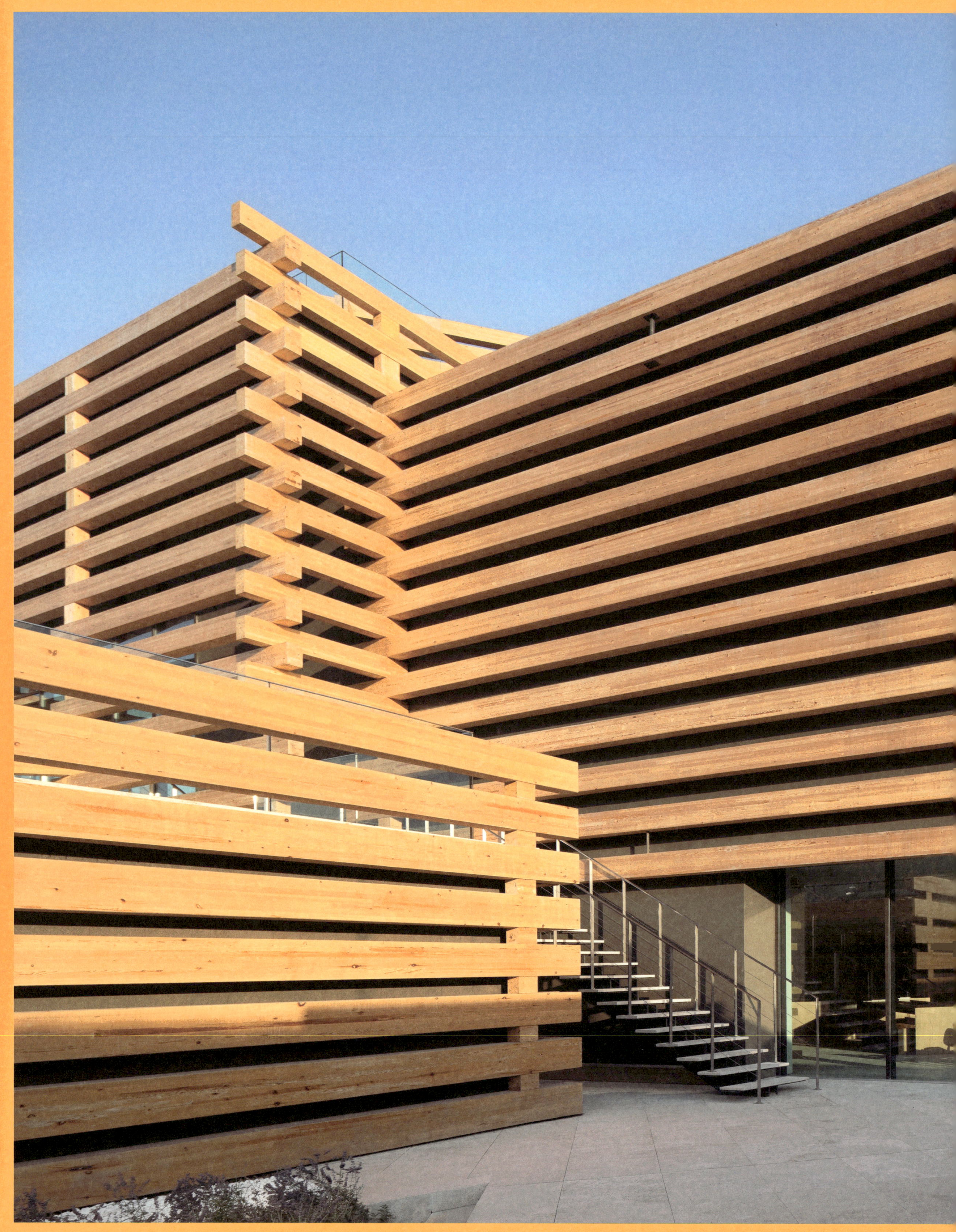

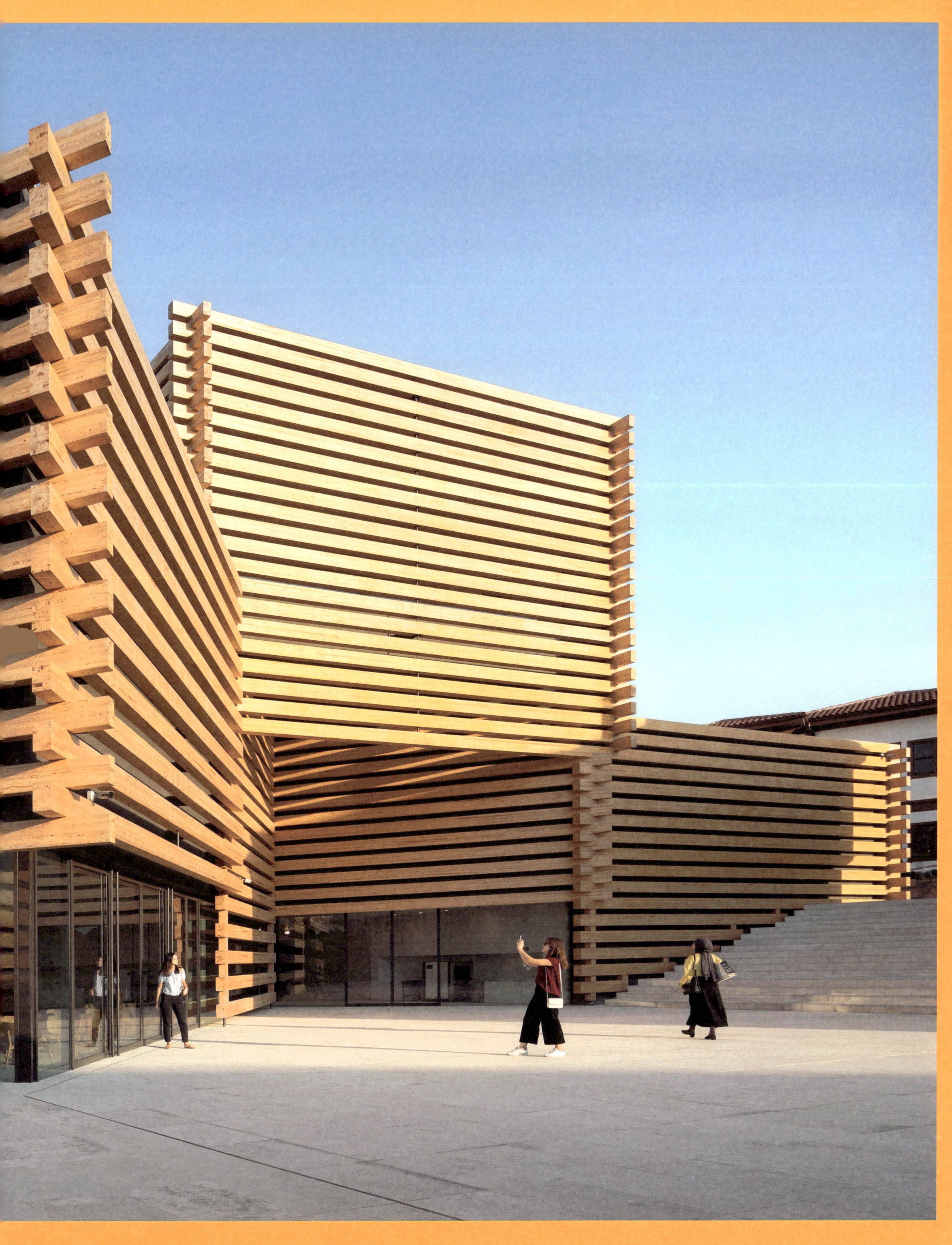

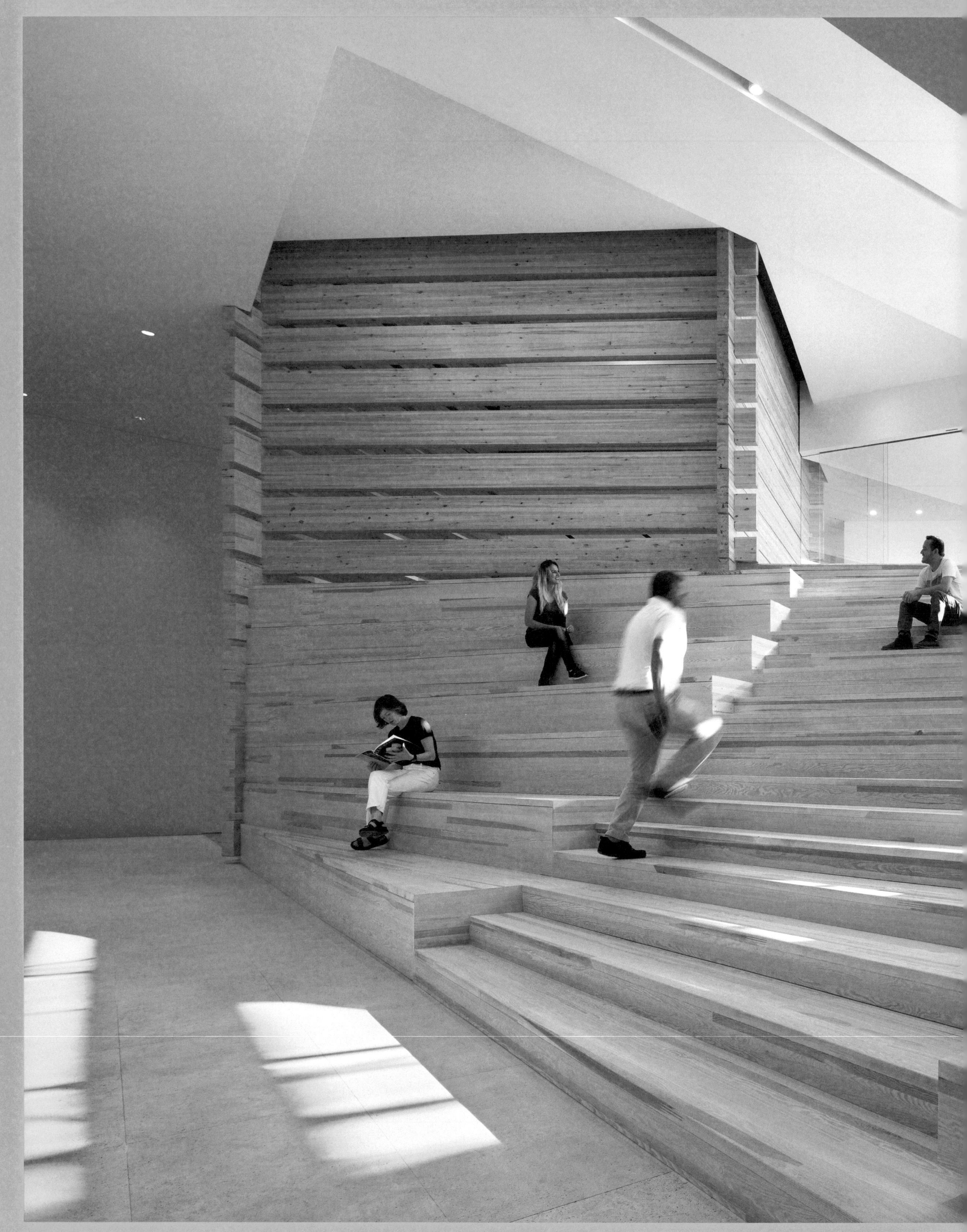

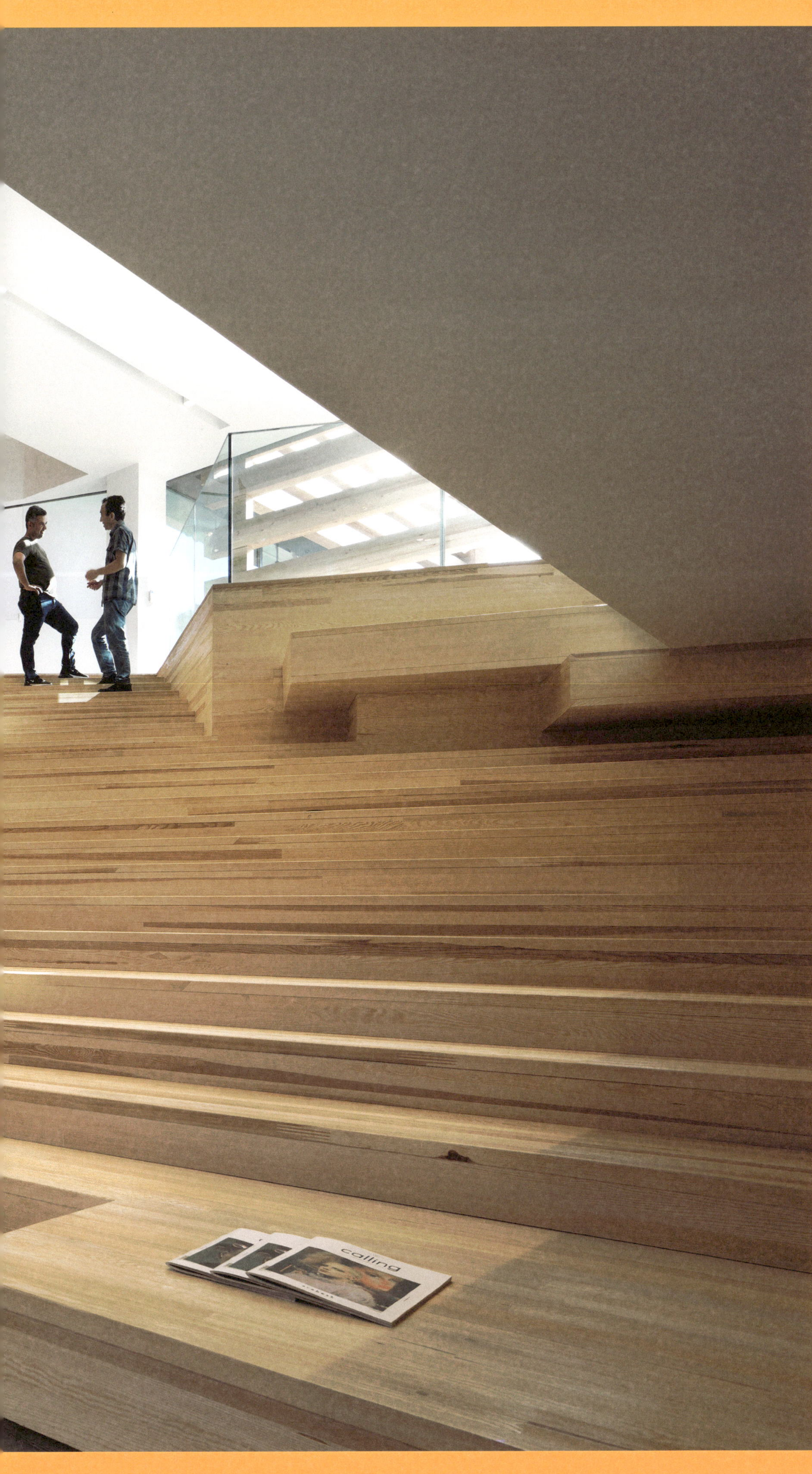

MUSEUMS WITH SIMILAR MEASURES

Yusuhara Wooden Bridge Museum

YUSUHARA, KOCHI, JAPAN

Use of natural materials for traditional construction.

Arte Sella. The Contemporary Mountain

TRENTO, ITALY

Use of natural materials for the construction of the new visitor reception area.

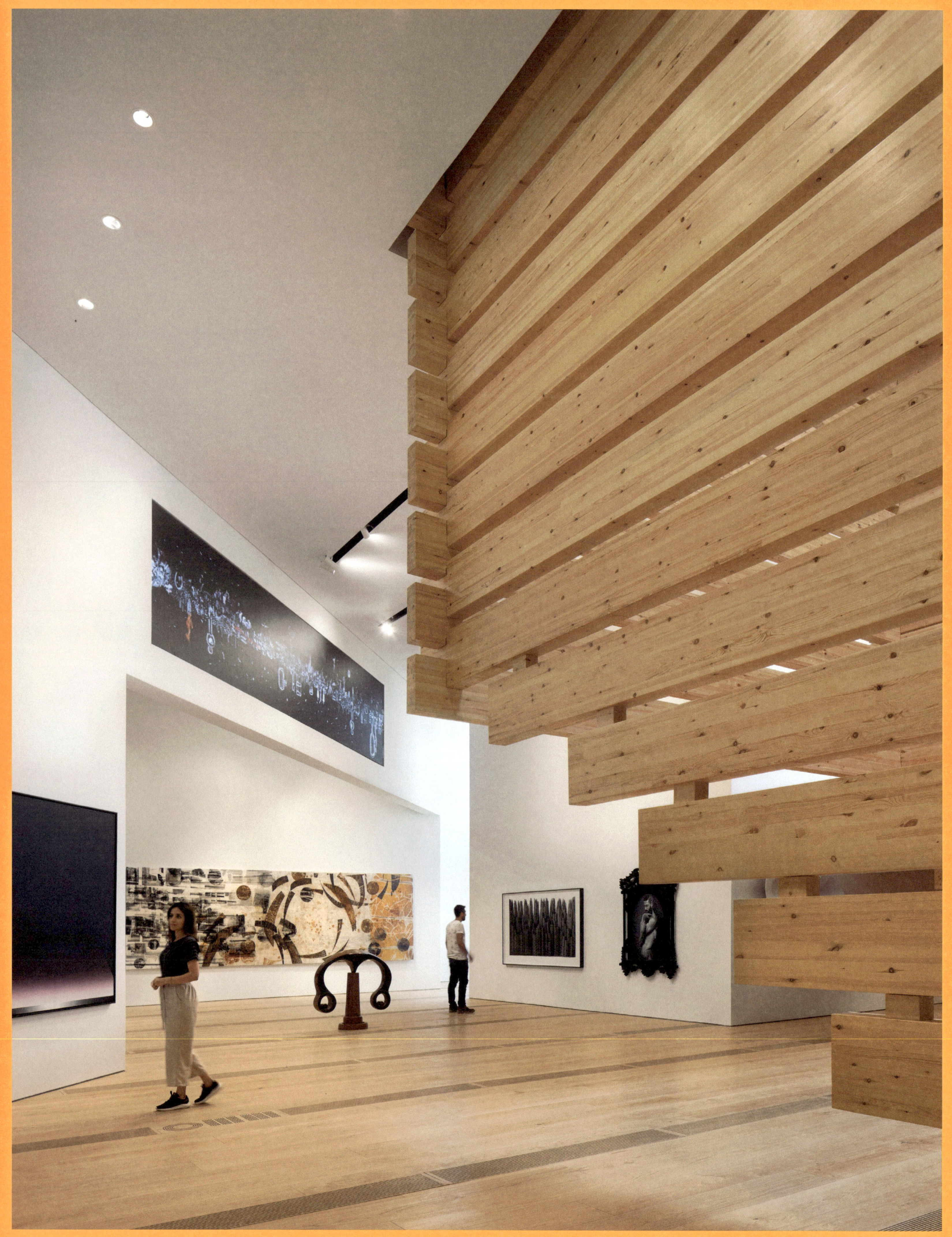

“As architects, when it comes to deciding on the materials we build with, we have a very big responsibility. I think the key is to stop building with fossil resources and start betting on bio-based materials.”

Daniel Ibáñez

Architect, Doctor of Design & CEO at the Institute
for Advanced Architecture of Catalonia
Interihotel 2023

07 REDUCTION OF WATER CONSUMPTION

WATER USE SDG 6 / 12

In a climate change scenario where prolonged drought periods and freshwater scarcity are becoming more frequent, the implementation of innovative measures leading to a more responsible and efficient use of this precious resource is indispensable.

The Huntington Botanical Gardens has upgraded its traditional irrigation technique by implementing an efficient system based on high-efficiency sprinklers, a climate-based irrigation control mechanism, and a drip irrigation system. Additionally, the development of advanced gardening techniques such as mulching around plant beds, deep watering, and replacing turf with drought-tolerant species has significantly reduced water usage in the gardens.

The Huntington

FOCUS
Art Gallery, Library and Botanical Garden

LOCATION
Urban. San Marino, Los Angeles, California, USA

ANNUAL VISITORS
1,000,000

CONSTRUCTION
1928

SIZE
526,000 m²

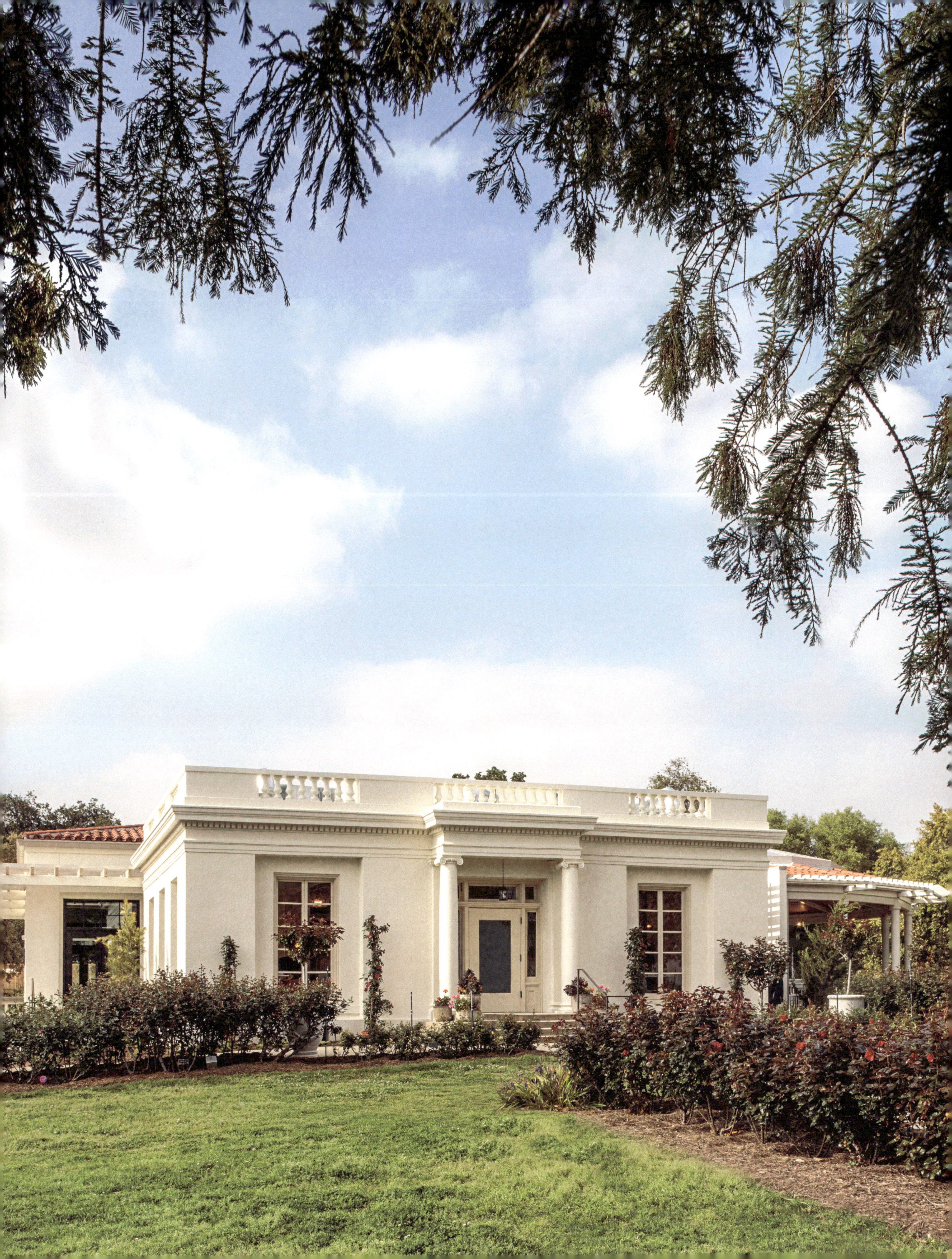

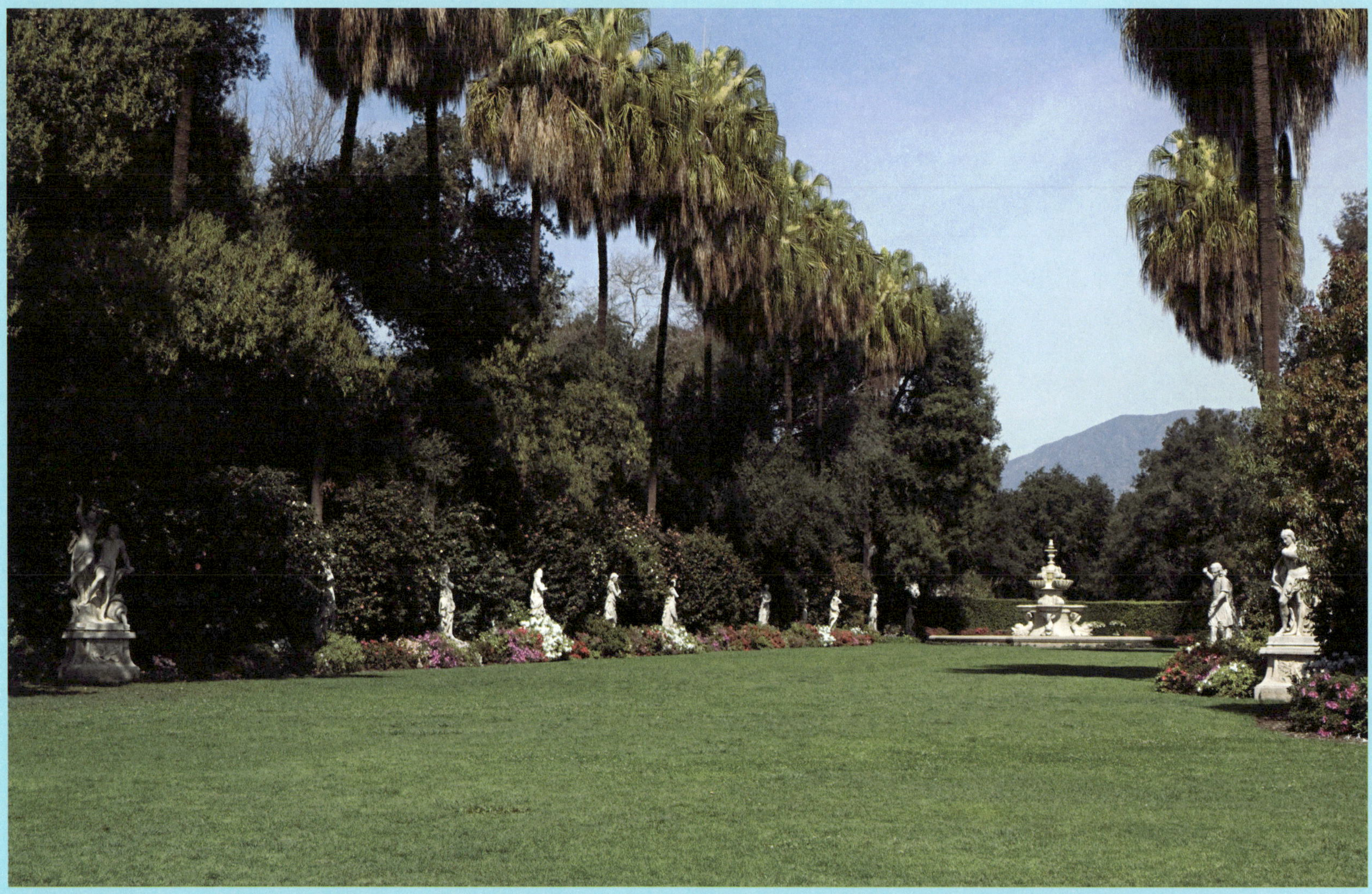

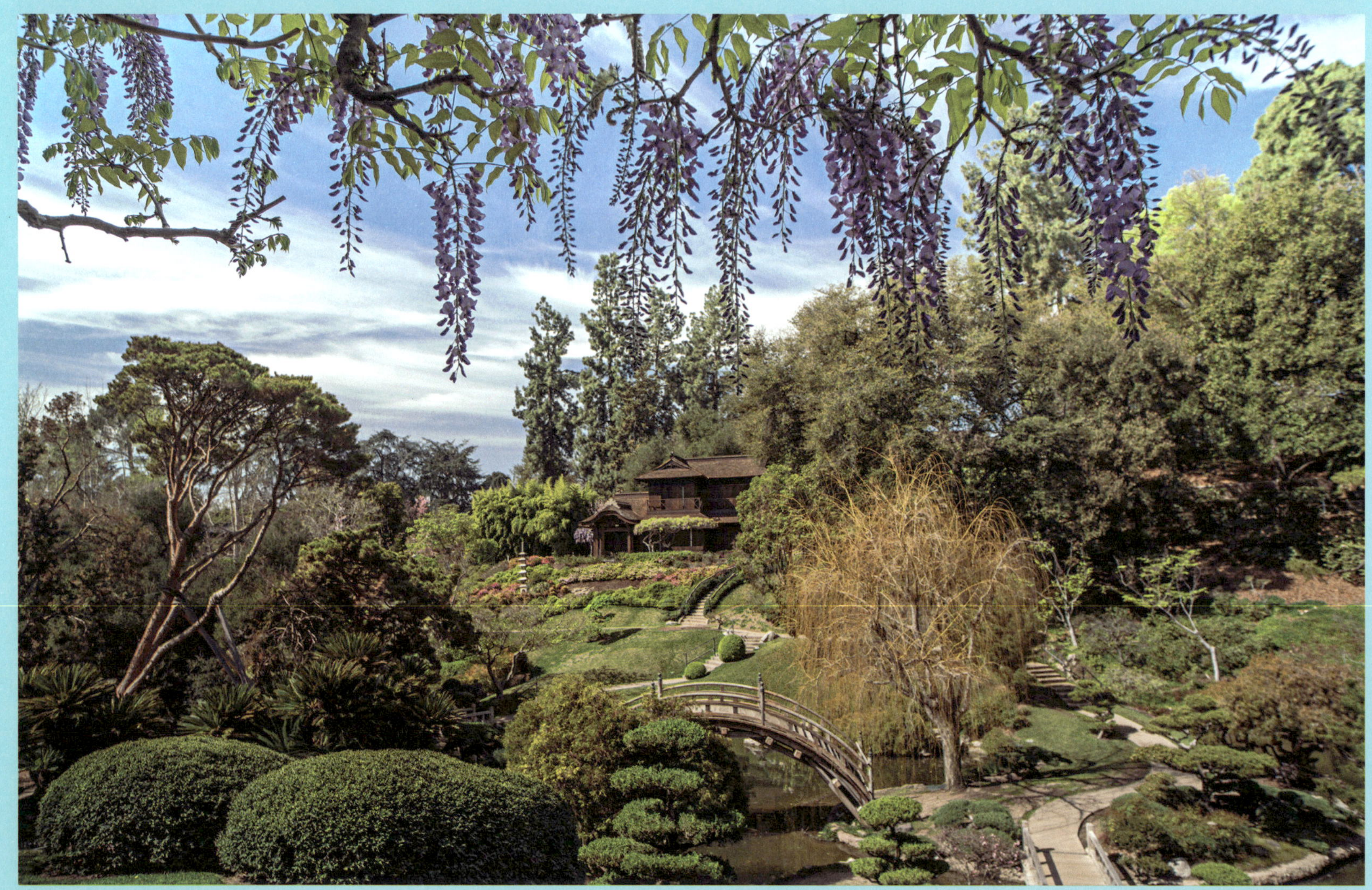

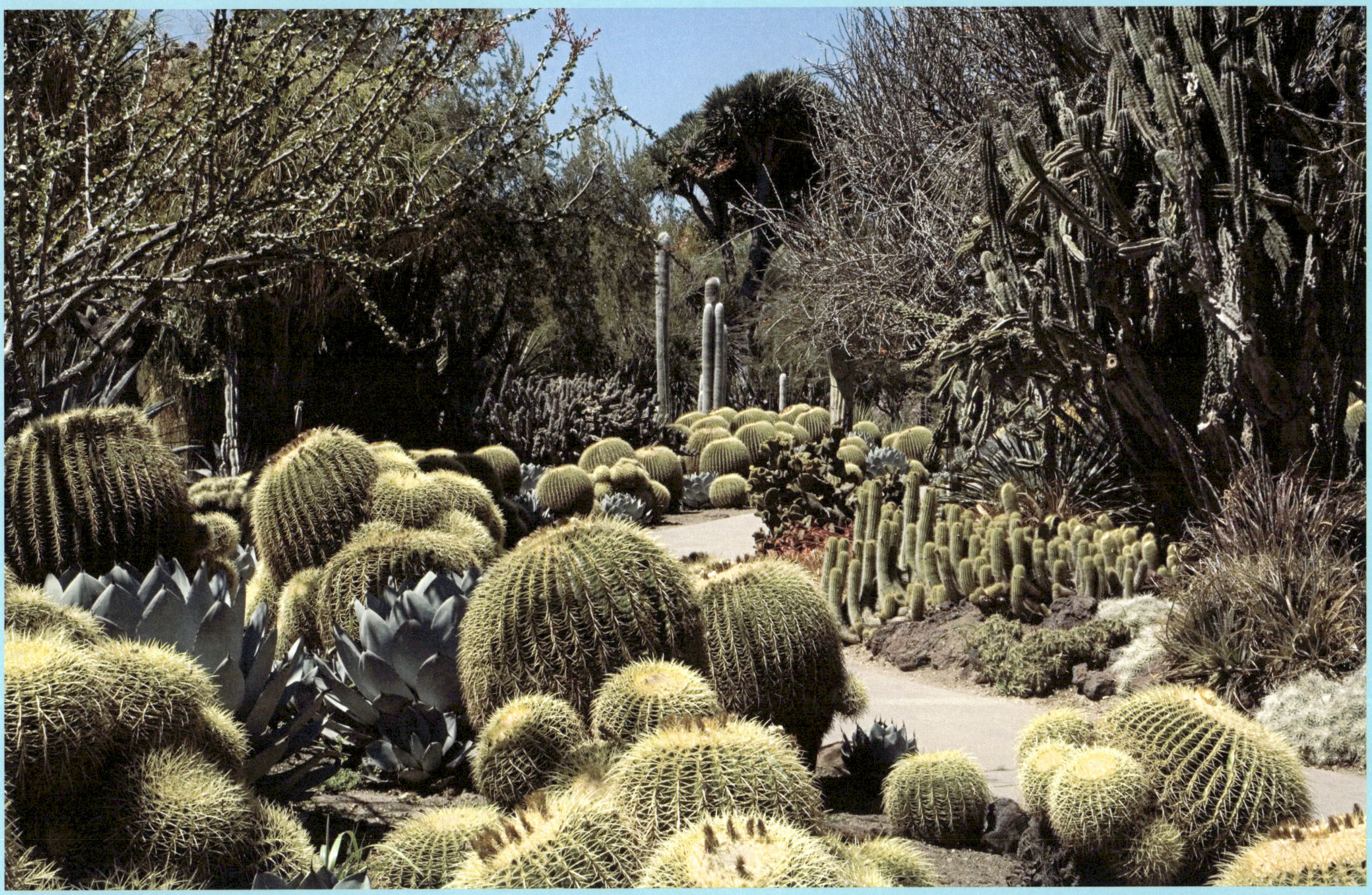

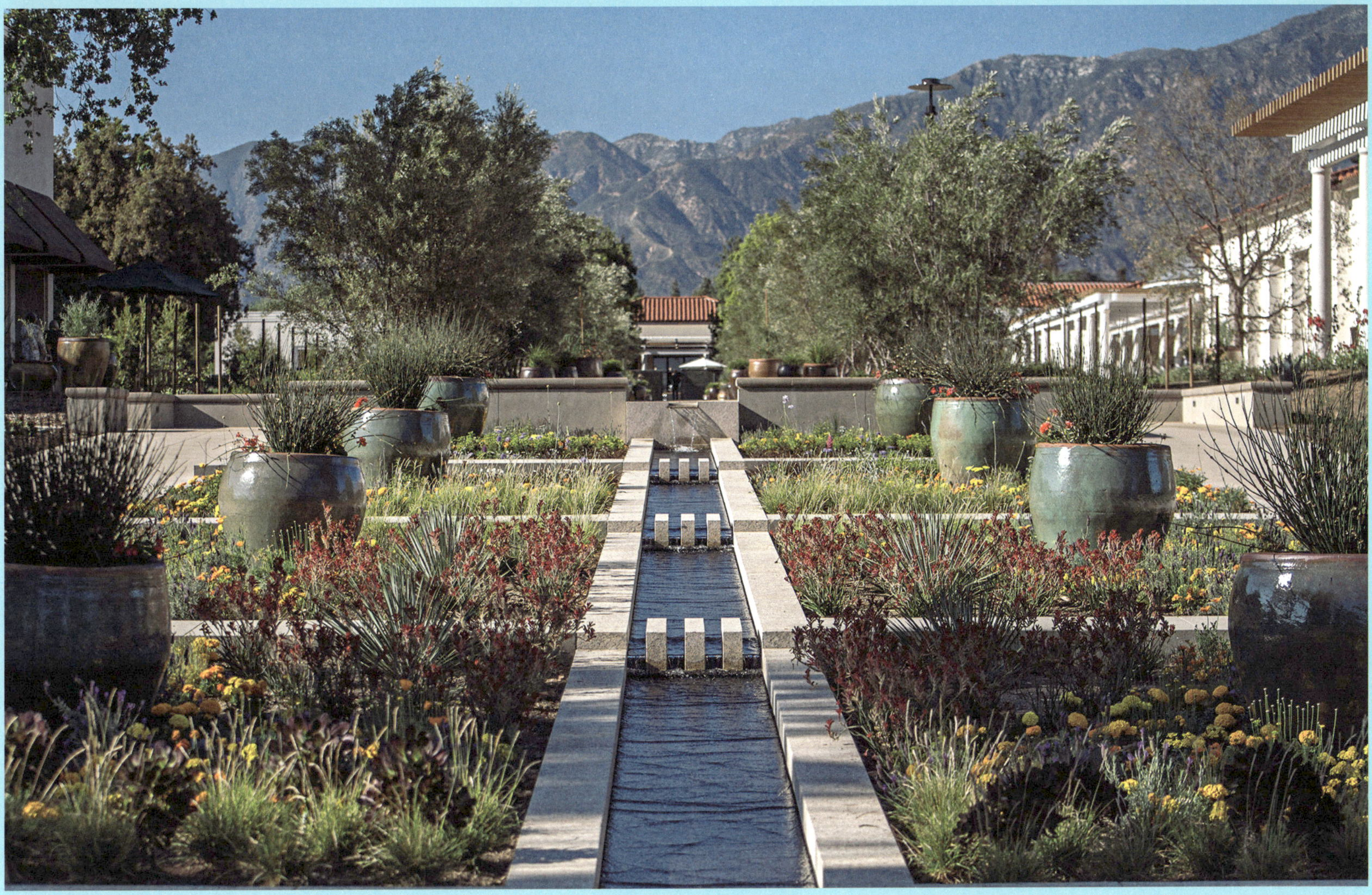

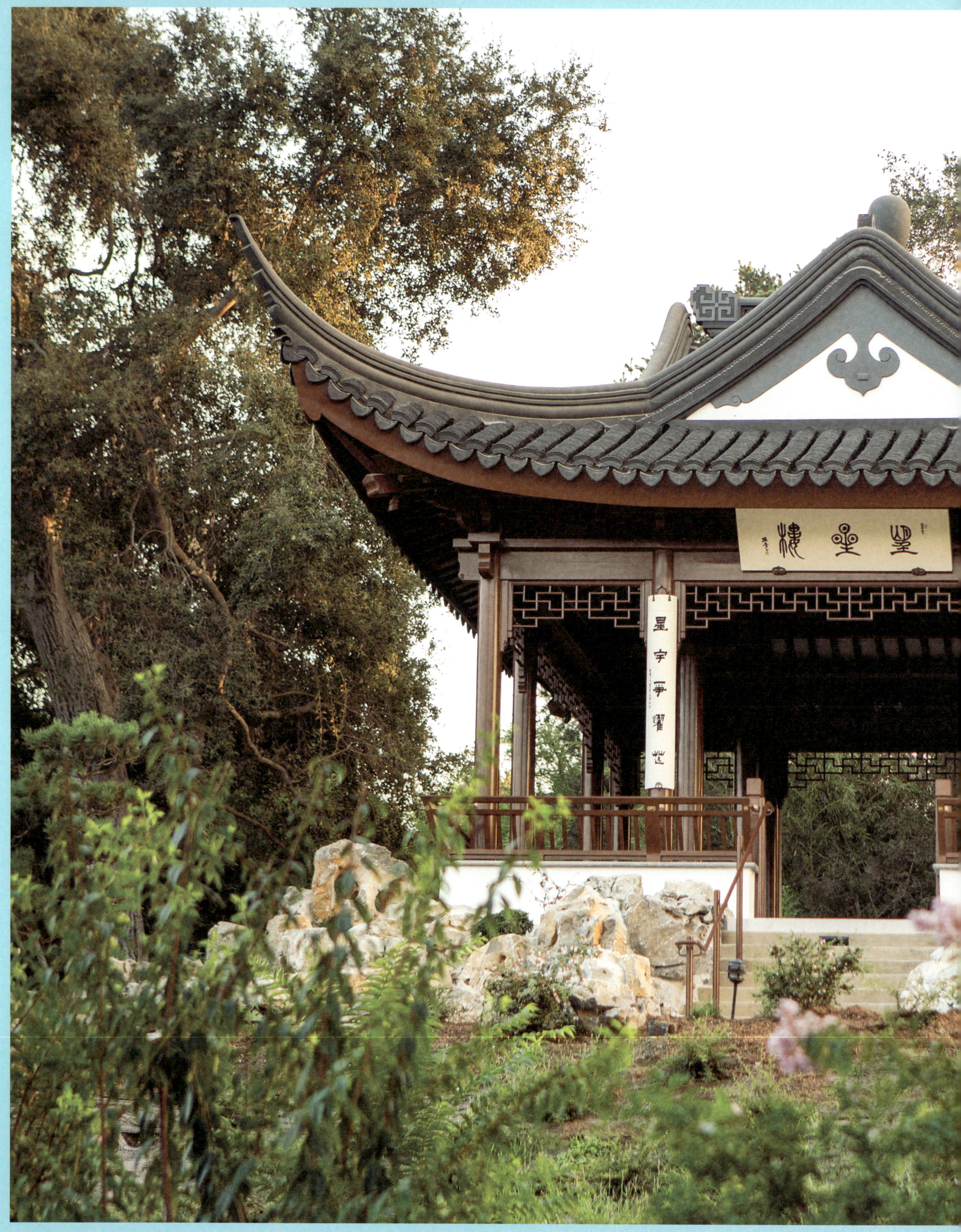

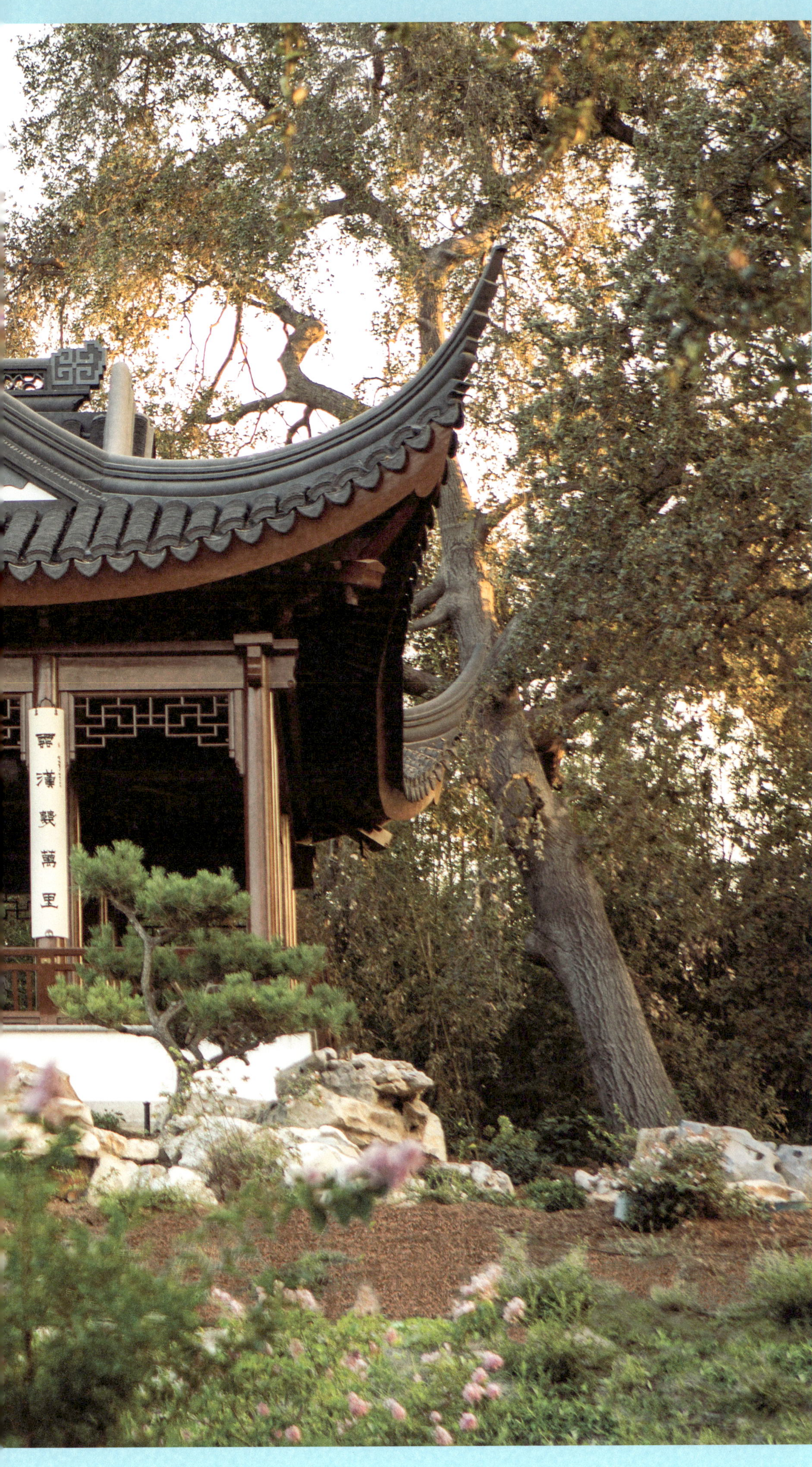

MUSEUMS WITH SIMILAR MEASURES

Museu Nacional d'Art de Catalunya

BARCELONA, SPAIN

Reduction of water consumption through comprehensive plumbing optimization and irrigation systems.

Exploratorium

SAN FRANCISCO, CALIFORNIA, USA

Optimization and reduction or limination of water use in restrooms.

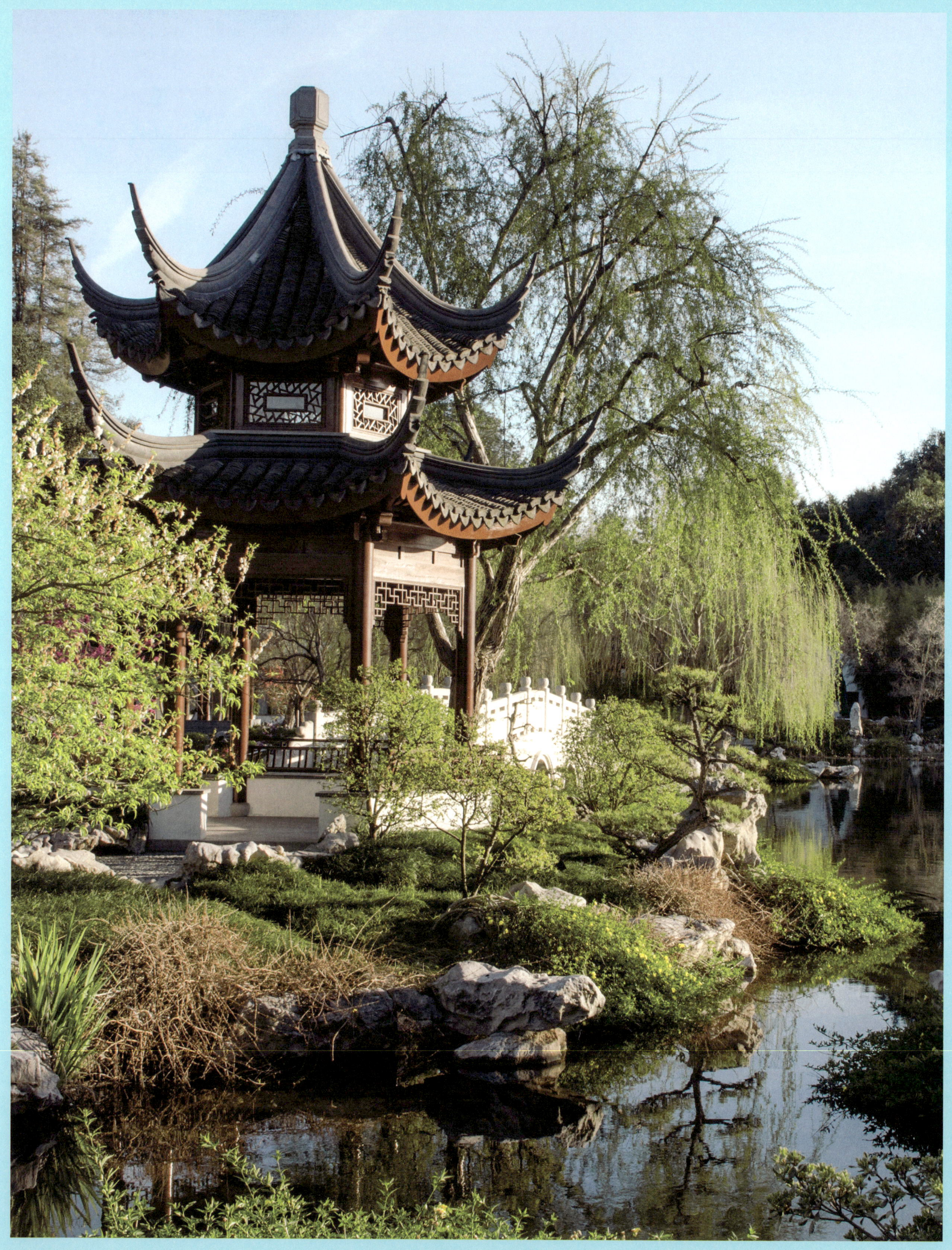

“A drought-resistant landscape doesn’t have to be just gravel and a few succulents. It can be lush, leafy, and inviting.”

Seth Baker

Garden Designer at The Huntington

Dot Magazine

08 SOFT WASTEWATER TREATMENT SYSTEMS

WATER USE SDG 6 / 15

Soft wastewater treatment systems are generally less costly and simpler to operate and maintain than conventional systems. While they do require more land, they are often just as effective at removing organic matter and even more efficient at eliminating pathogens and nutrients. Additionally, these systems use minimal energy, incur low maintenance costs, and require less specialized personnel for their operation.

At the Biesbosch MuseumEiland, wastewater is biologically treated by a forest of willow trees, a species native to the island on which the museum is located, which utilizes the wastewater's nutrients such as nitrogen and phosphorus for growth. The purified water is then discharged into a nearby wetland and eventually flows into a river, generating an entire ecosystem that helps attract and preserve local biodiversity.

Biesbosch MuseumEiland

FOCUS
Science and Technology

CONSTRUCTION
2015

LOCATION
Natural. Biesbosch Nature Park, The Netherlands

PROJECT
Studio Marco Vermeulen

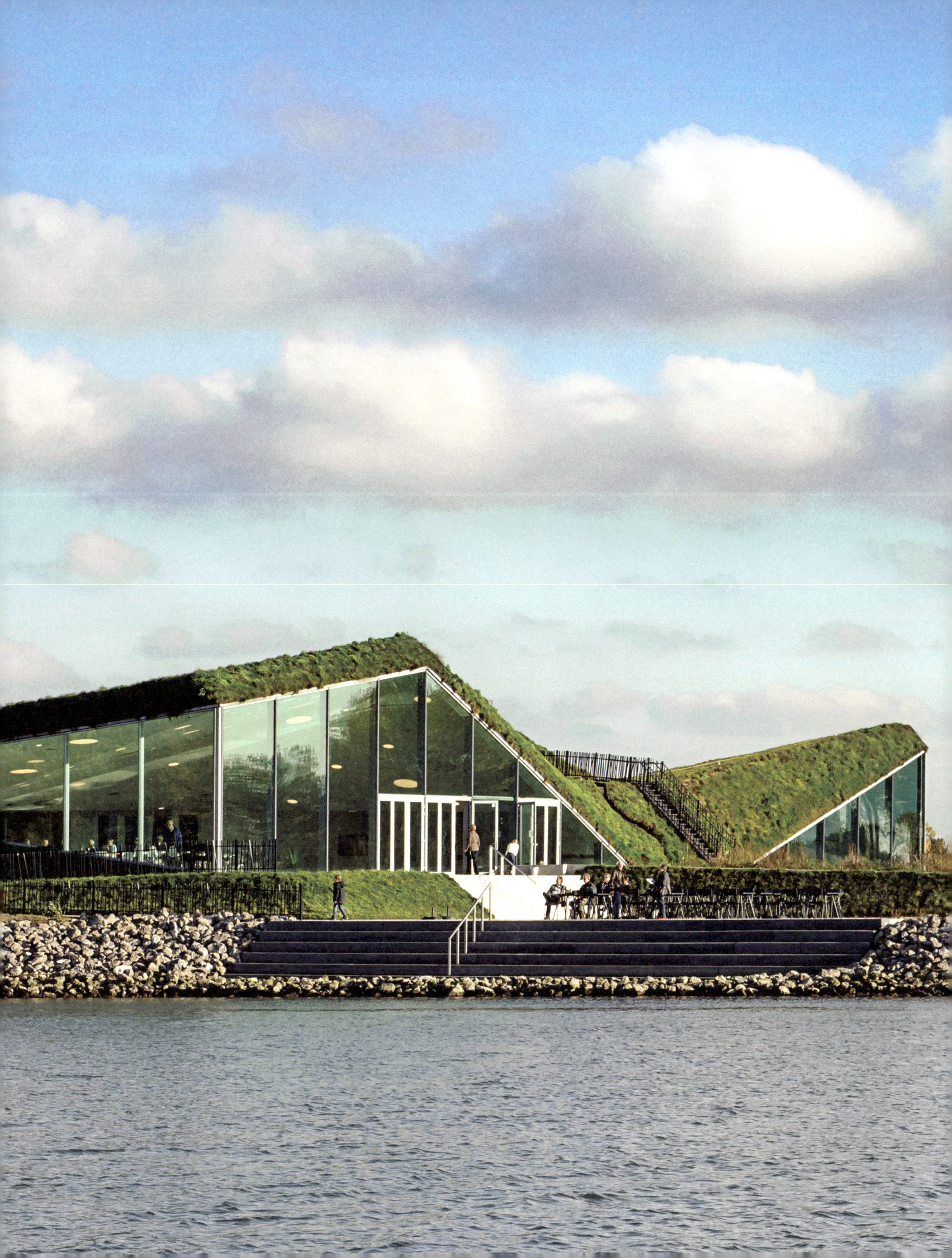

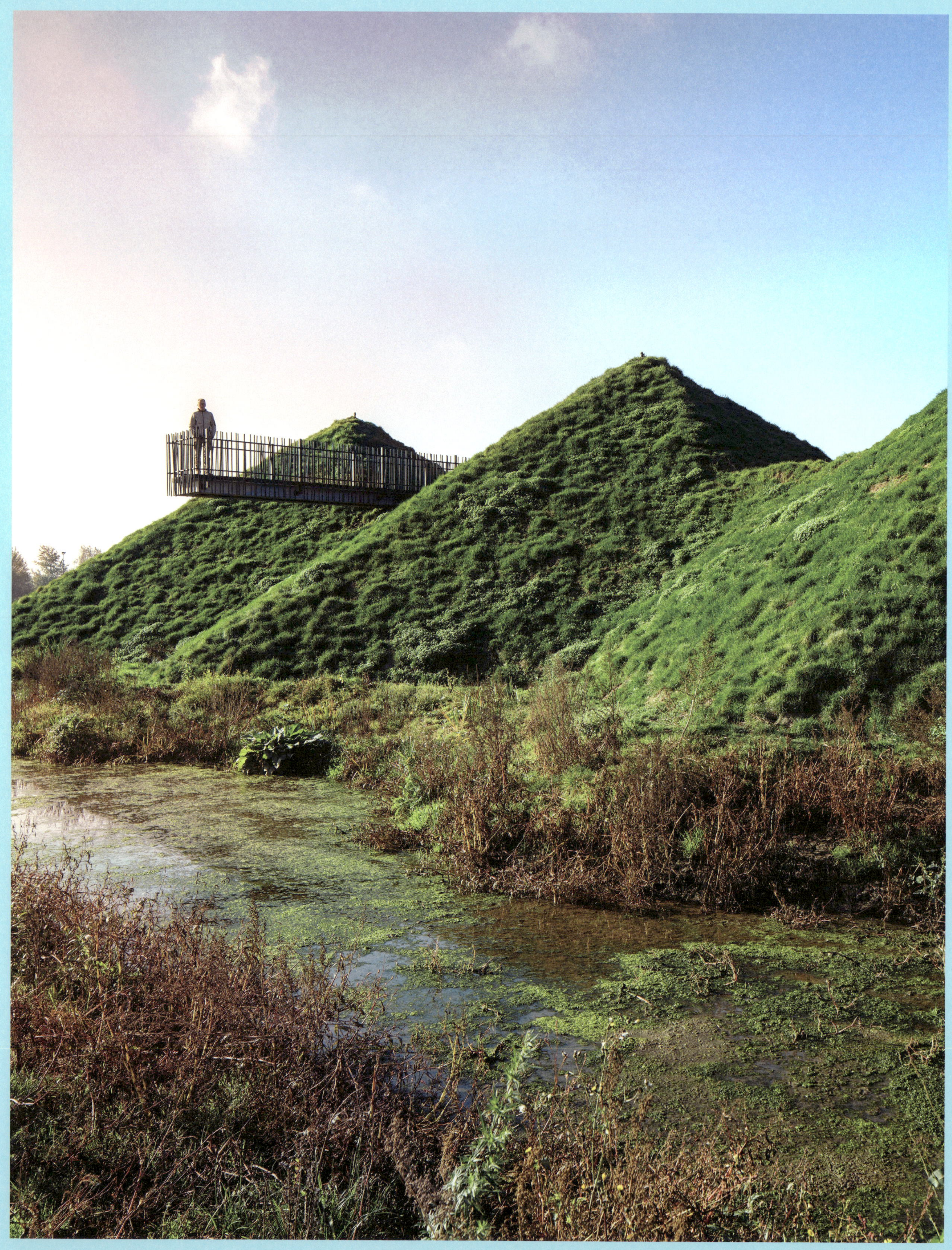

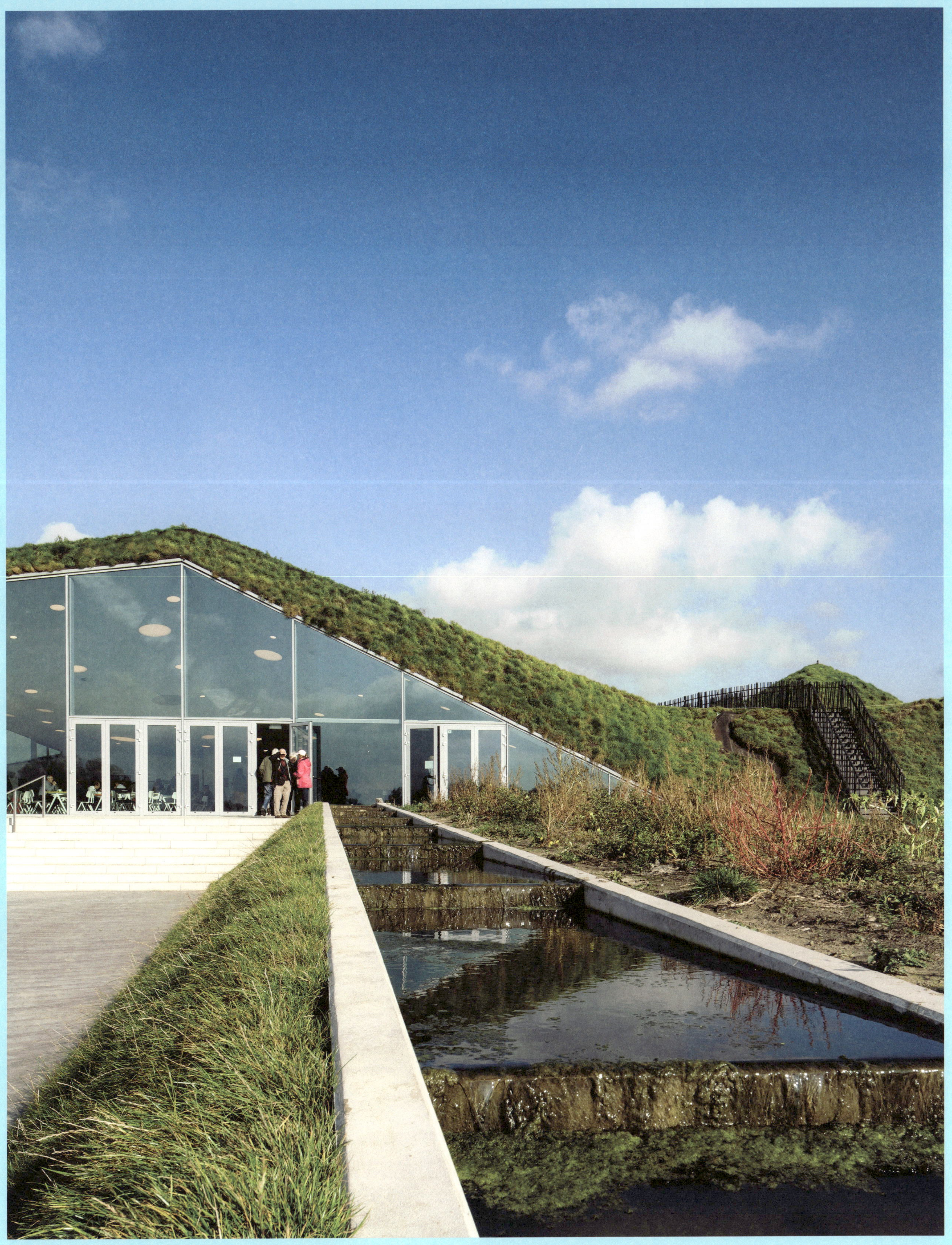

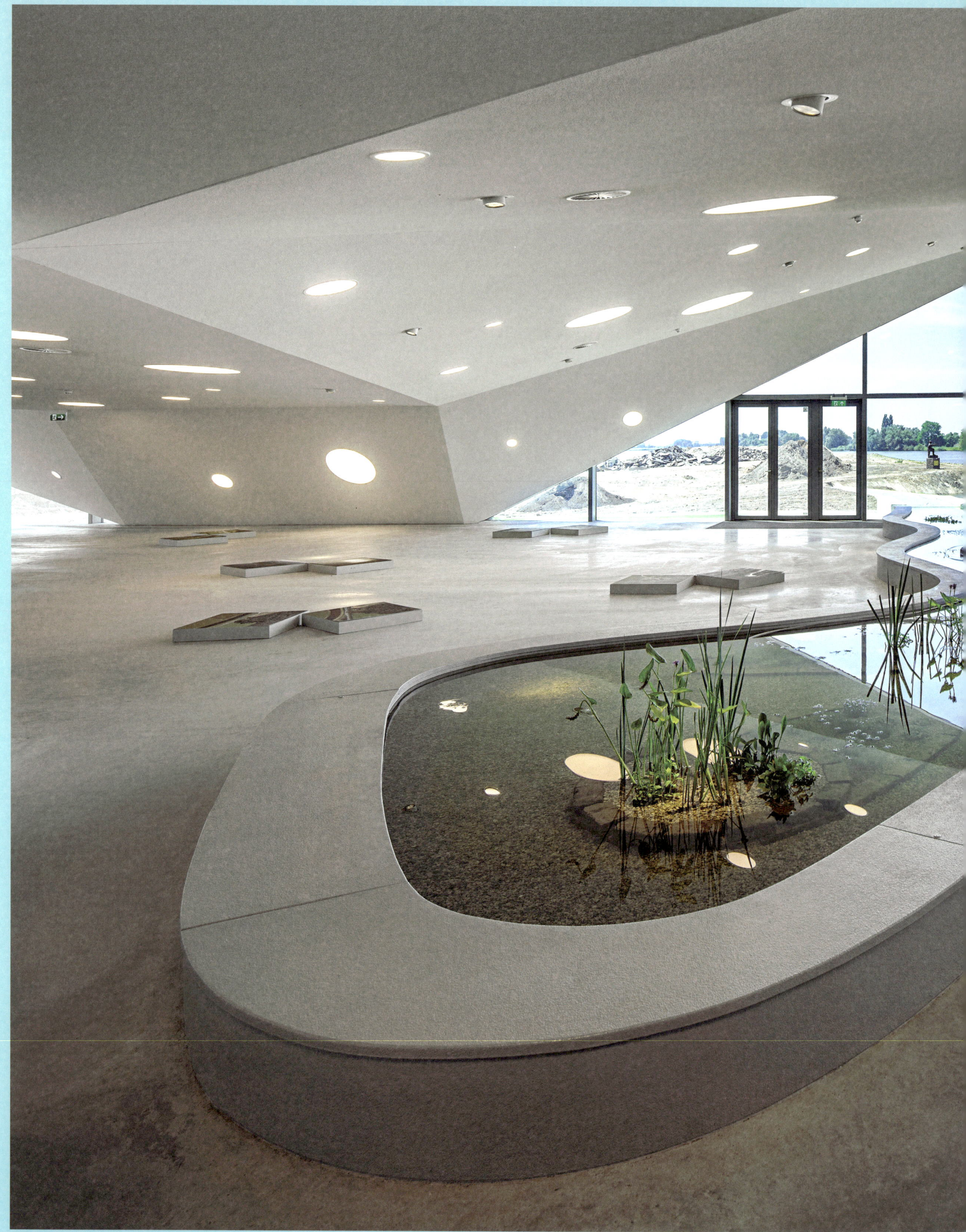

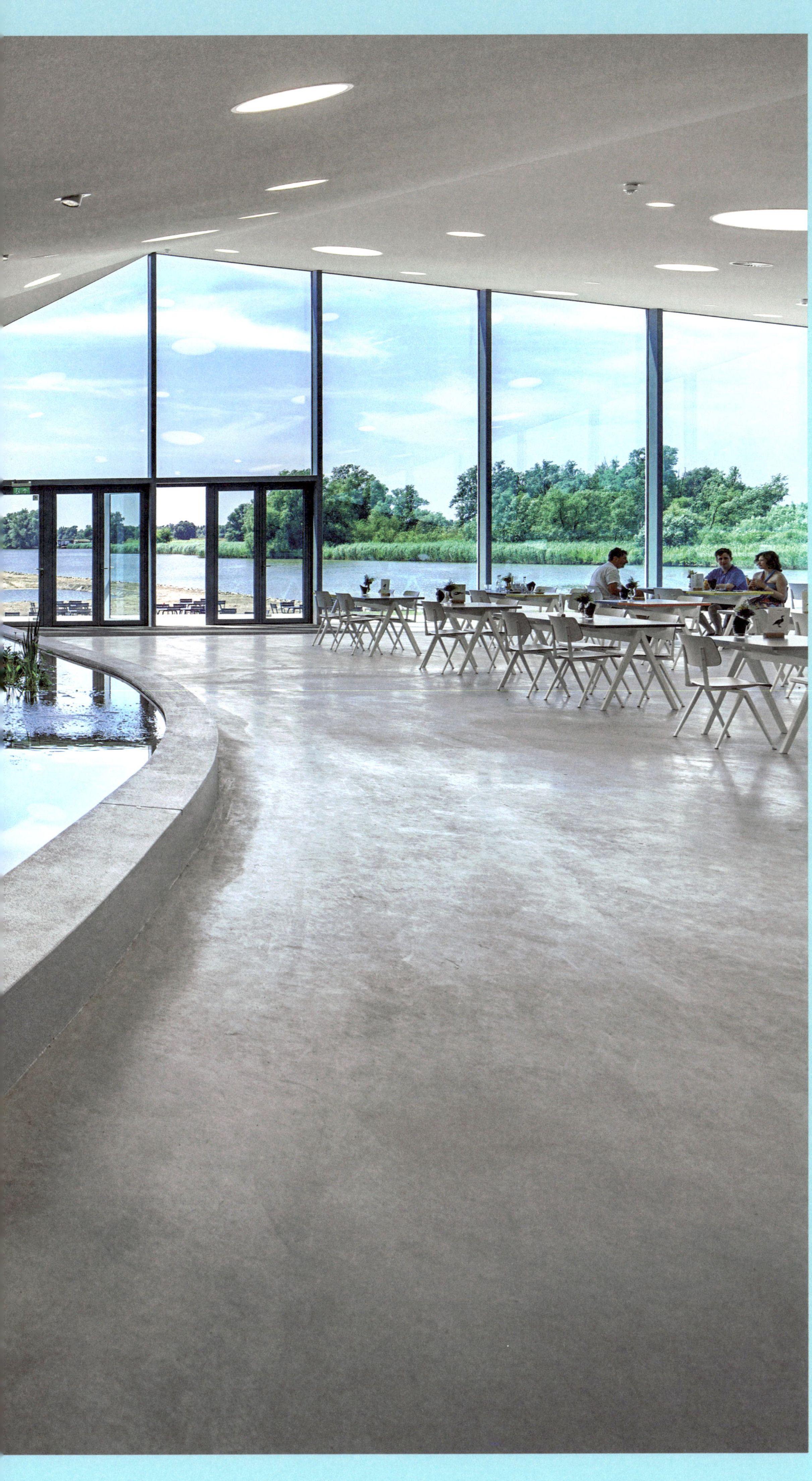

MUSEUMS WITH SIMILAR MEASURES

Arizona-Sonora Desert Museum

TUCSON, ARIZONA, USA

Use of reclaimed wastewater for irrigation of green areas.

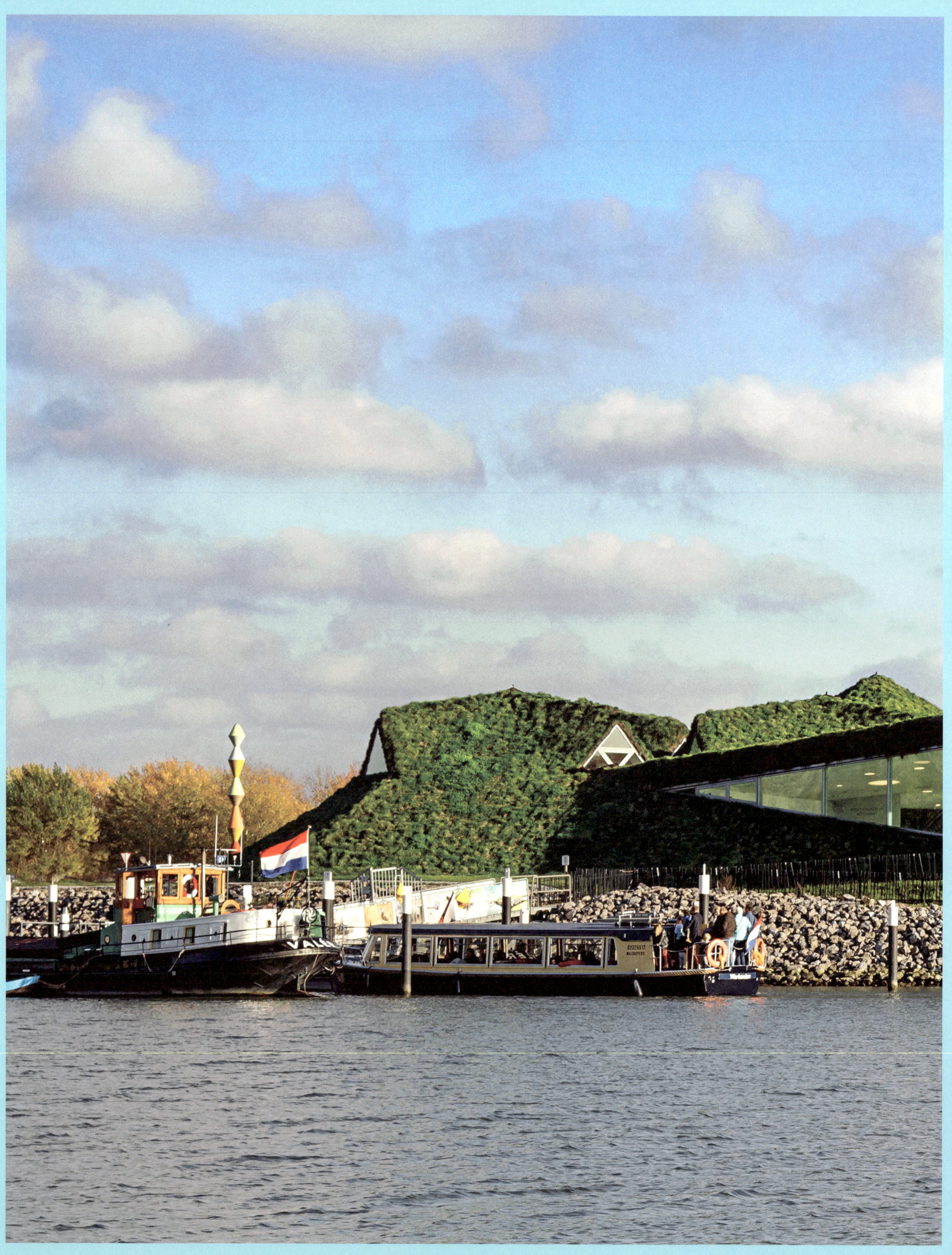

“Water security was the main reason for the development of the Biesbosch museum island. As part of a national program, the 4,450 hectares of the Noordwaard Polder area have been transformed into a water retention area.”

Studio Marco Vermeulen

Dezeen

09 RAINWATER RECOVERY SYSTEM

WATER USE SDG 6 / 12

Rainwater harvesting captures rain from a specific surface, usually a building's roof, and stores it in tanks for subsequent distribution and use via a separate hydraulic system from the drinking water supply.

The ArtScience Museum's lotus-shaped roof funnels rainwater into the central atrium, creating a stunning 35-meter waterfall that ends in a small reflecting fountain. After undergoing filtration and disinfection, this collected rainwater is reused for the building's toilets.

ArtScience Museum

FOCUS
Art and Science

LOCATION
Urban. Singapore

CONSTRUCTION
2011

PROJECT
Safdie Architects

SIZE
5,000 m²

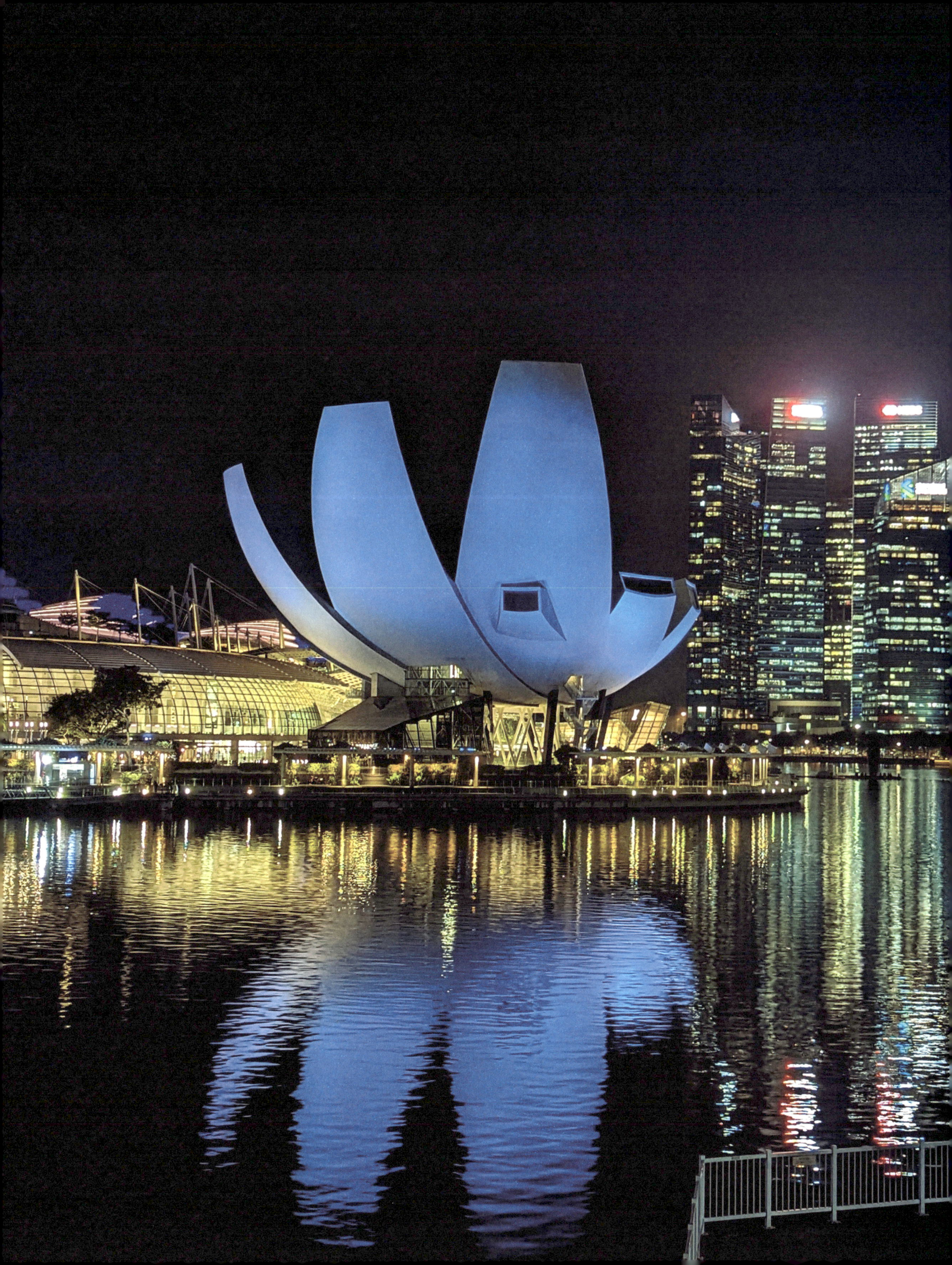

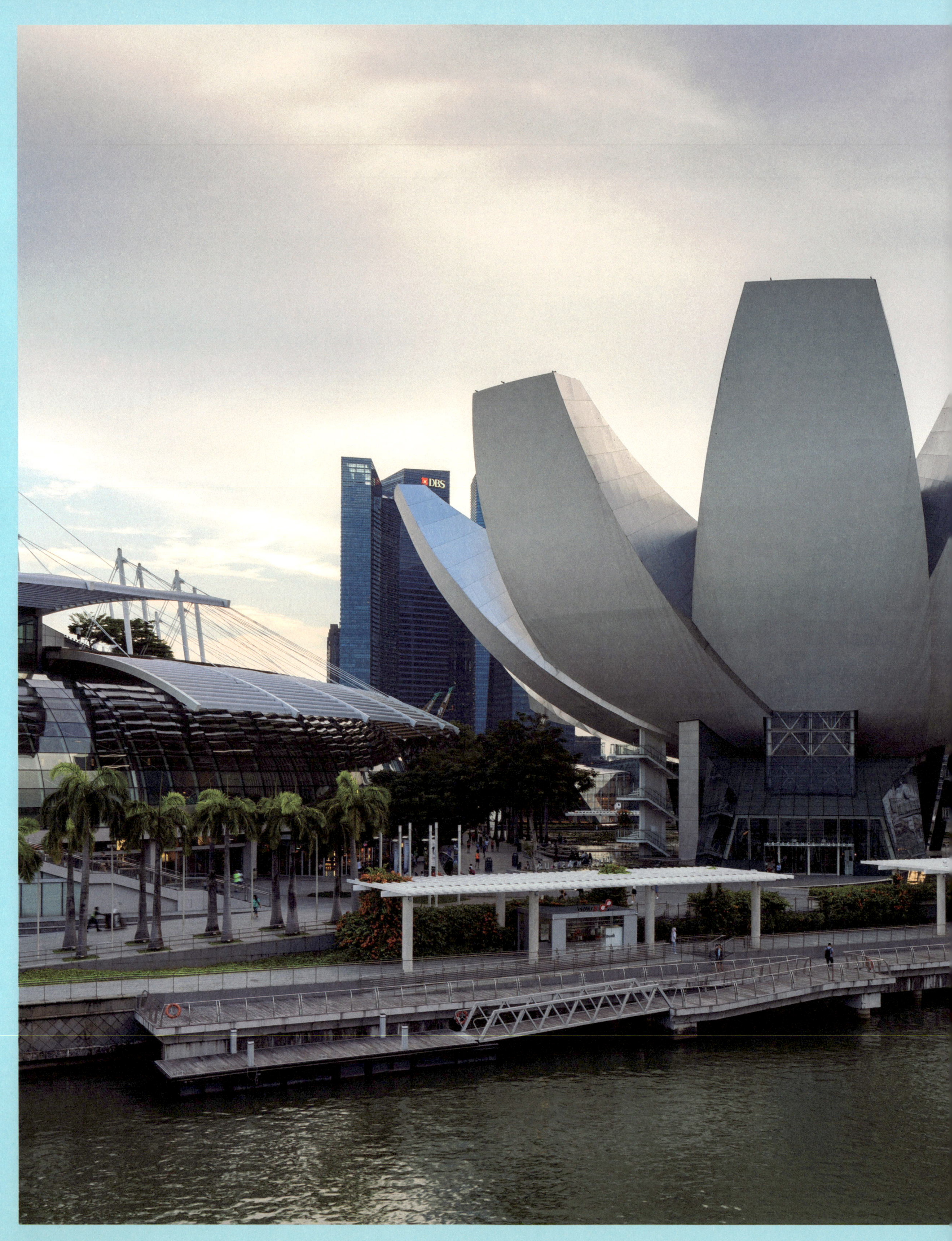
DBS

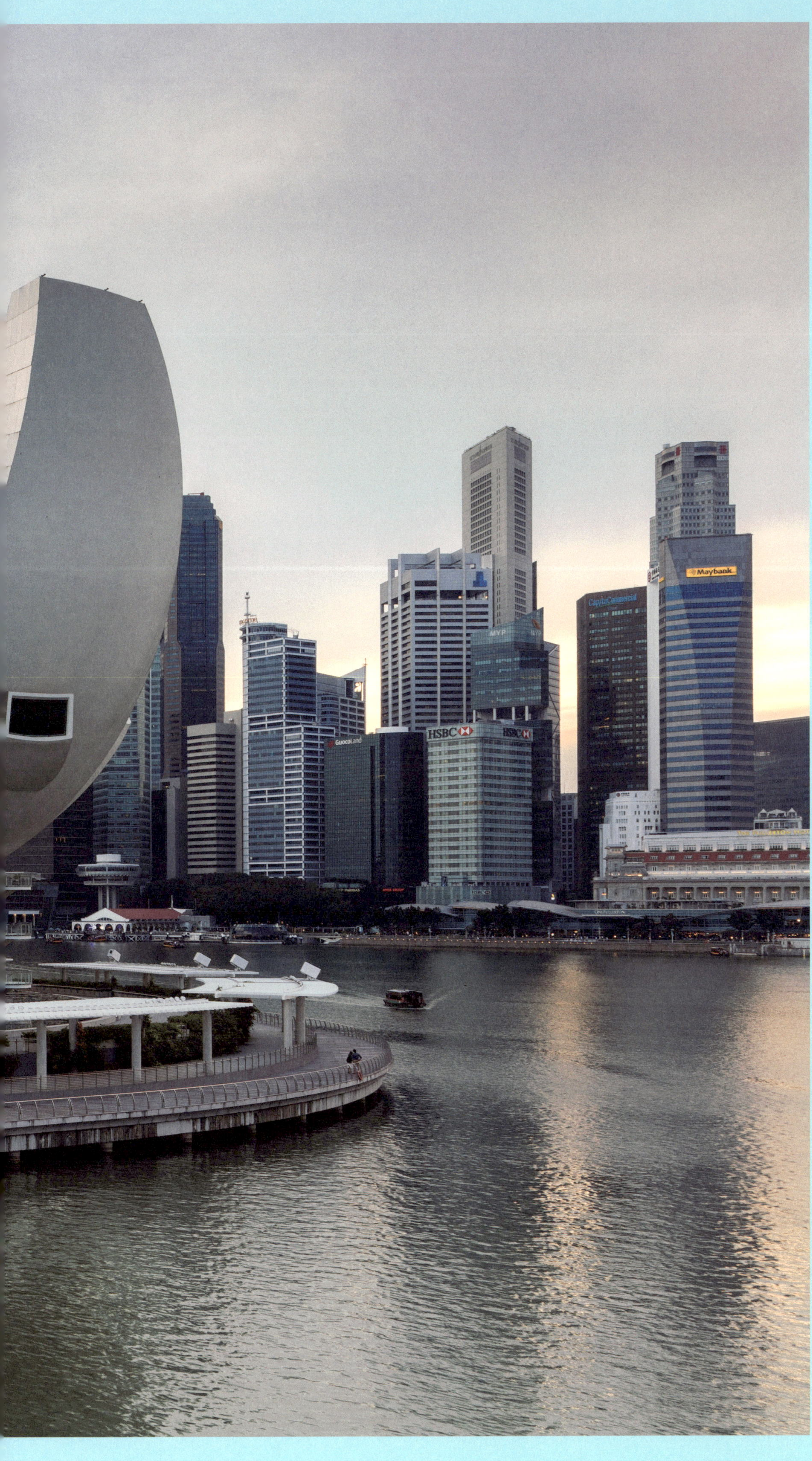

MUSEUMS WITH SIMILAR MEASURES

Perot Museum of Nature and Science

DALLAS, TEXAS, USA

This museum efficiently collects and regenerates condensation from air conditioning units and rainwater for reuse.

Tate Modern

LONDON, UNITED KINGDOM

Harvesting and recycling rainwater paired with an automatic monitoring system to detect issues.

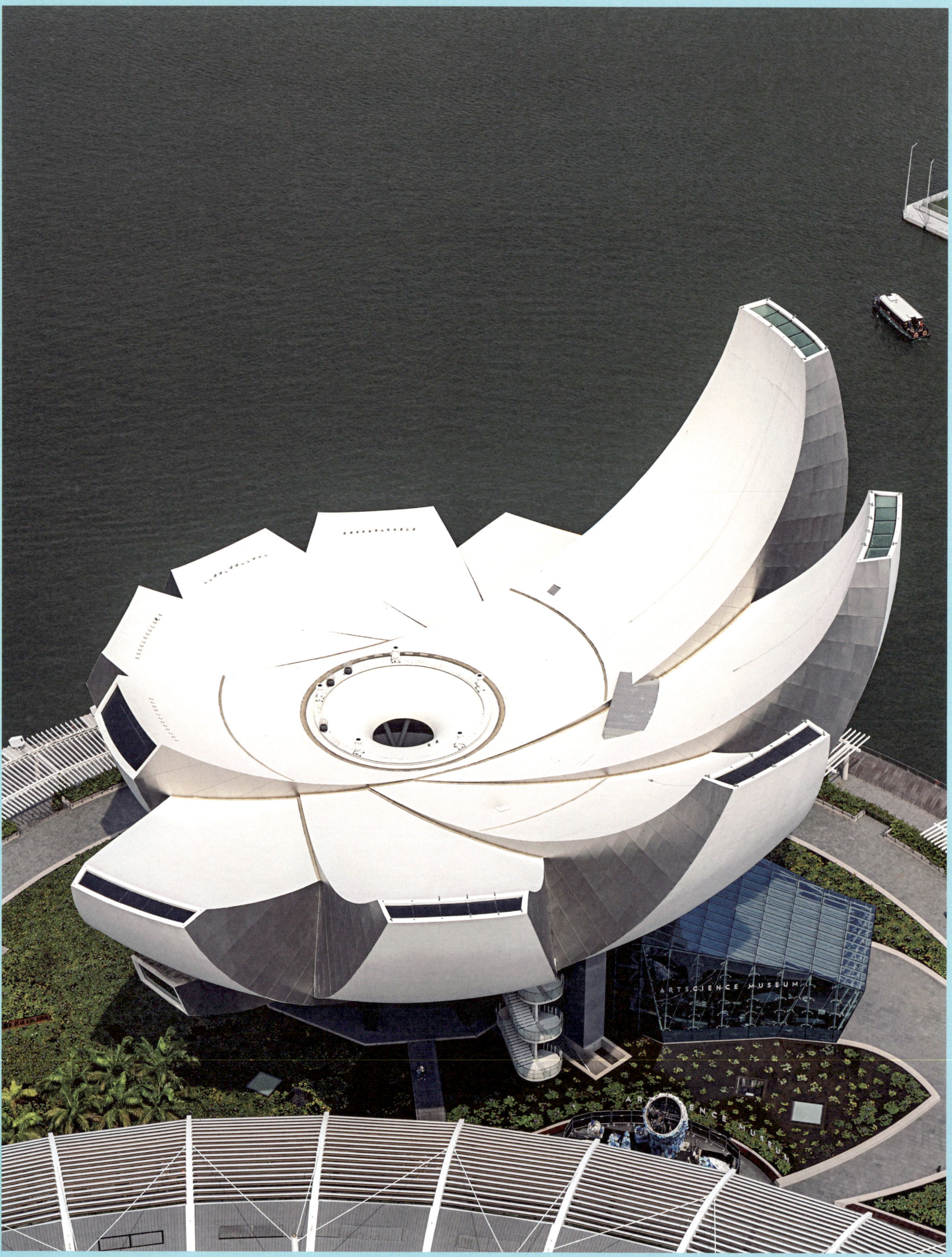
ARTSCIENCE MUSEUM

"If there is a particular aspect of my work that I believe is profound, and that perhaps should be valued, it is that I have not simply imported concepts from one place to another, but have instead subordinated my work to an attempt to understand the essence of each place."

Moshe Safdie

Inexhibit

10 SEAWATER-FED COOLING SYSTEM

BUILDING ENERGY EFFICIENCY SDG 7 / 11

The climate control of museums is a key aspect in ensuring the preservation conditions of the displayed pieces. Climate control systems must meet the most demanding standards in terms of energy efficiency while ensuring the continuity of supply and the proper functioning of the installation.

The Centro Botín in Santander features a cooling system powered by a seawater heat exchanger. This system uses the thermal difference between the environment and the water for heat exchange with the condensation circuit, avoiding conventional solutions based on cooling towers that have excessive energy consumption, higher operational and maintenance costs, and the use of chemical refrigerants.

Centro Botín

FOCUS
Art

LOCATION
Urban. Santander, Spain

ANNUAL VISITORS
166,000

CONSTRUCTION
2017

PROJECT
Renzo Piano, Luis Vidal

SIZE
8,739 m²

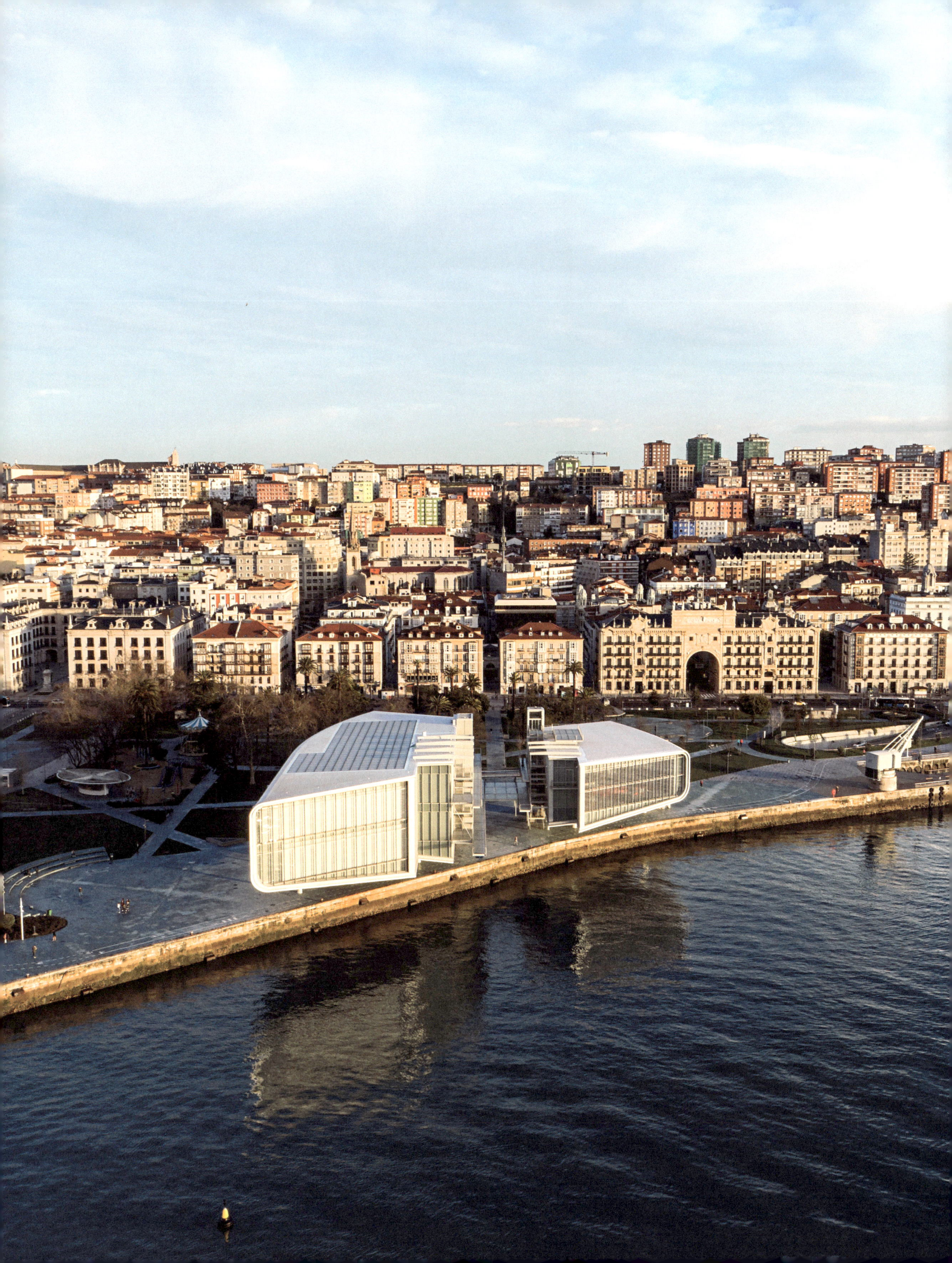

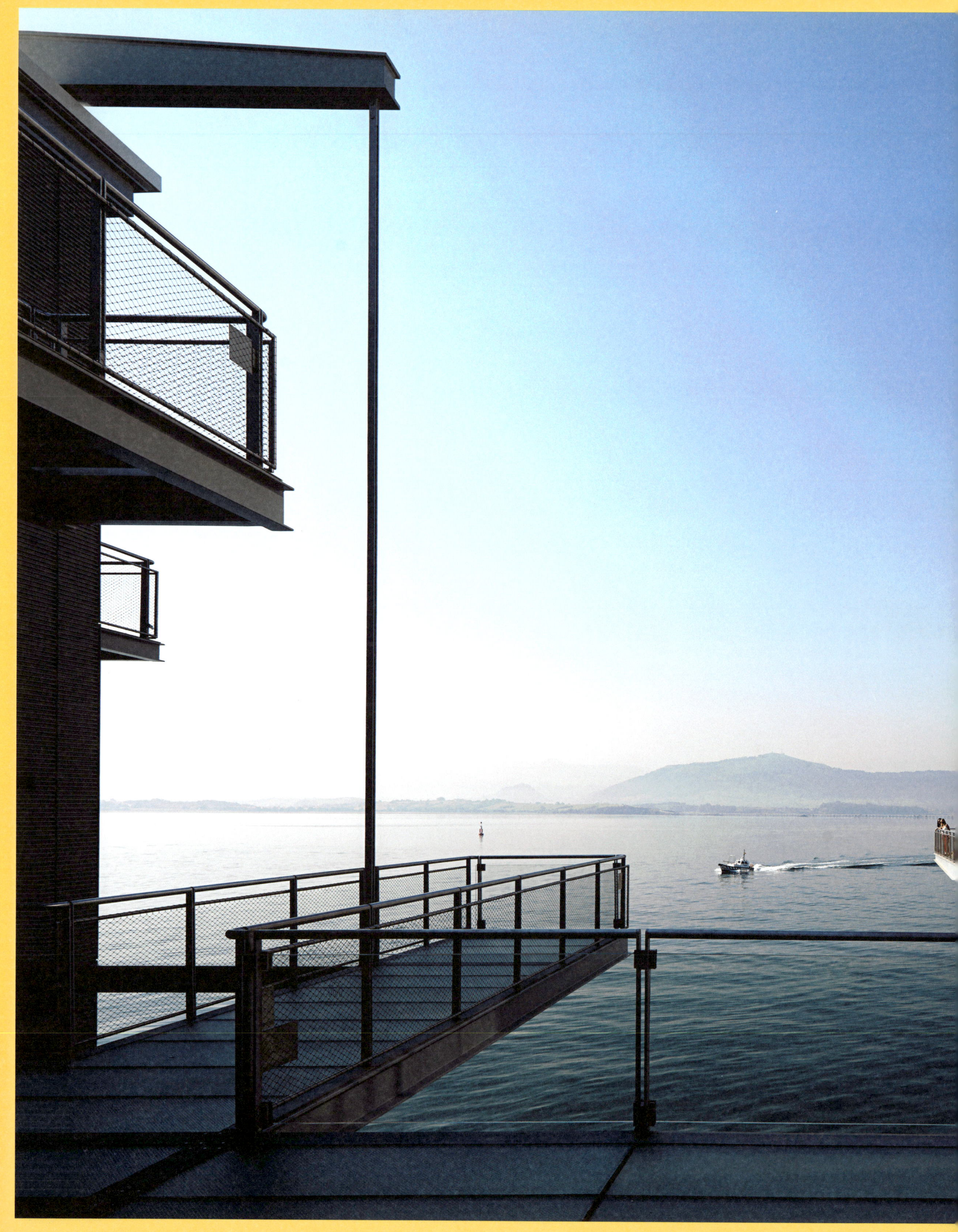

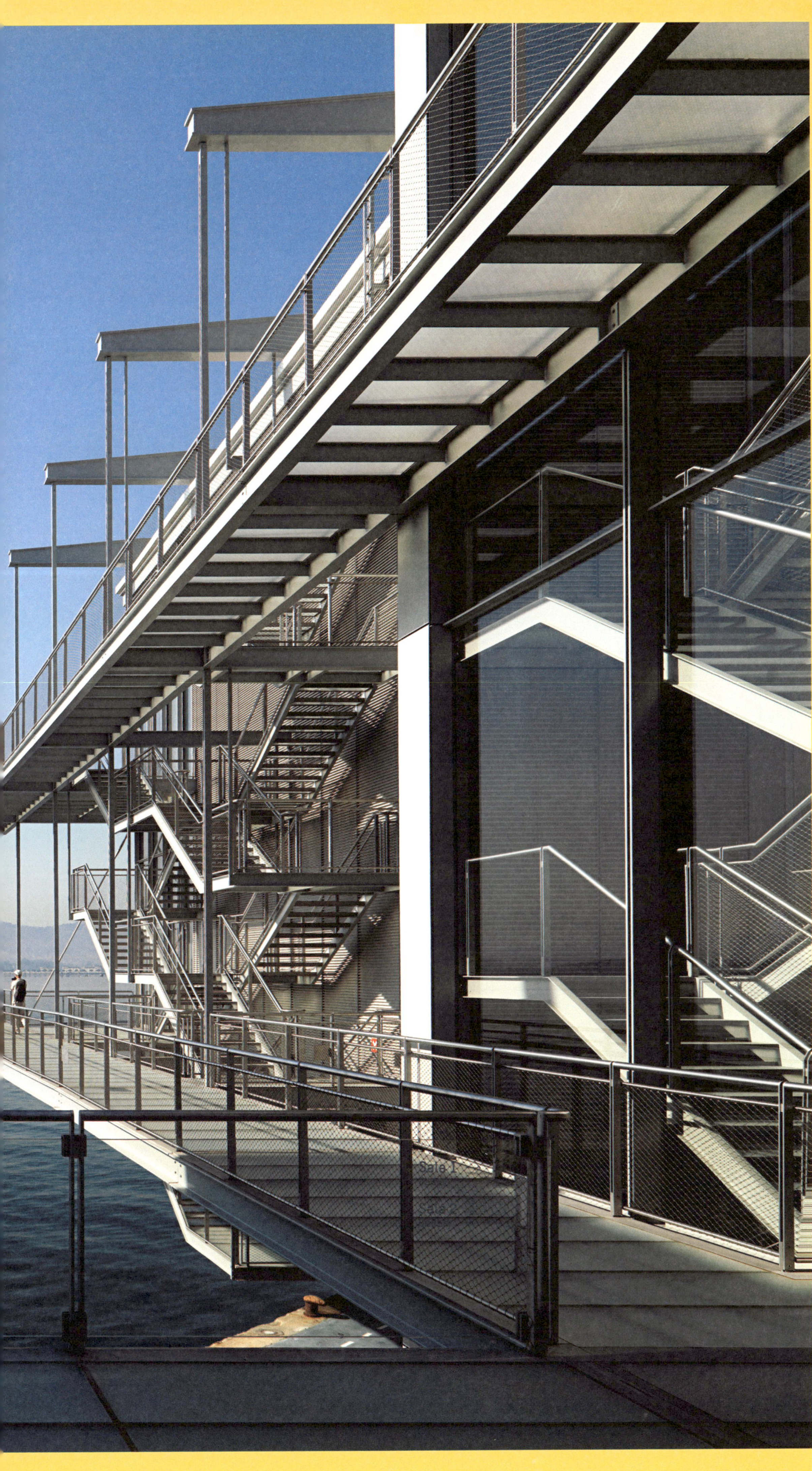

MUSEUMS WITH SIMILAR MEASURES

Museu do Amanhã

RIO DE JANEIRO, BRAZIL

Seawater-fed heat exchanger cooling system.

Exploratorium

SAN FRANCISCO, USA

Underfloor cooling and heating system powered by seawater.

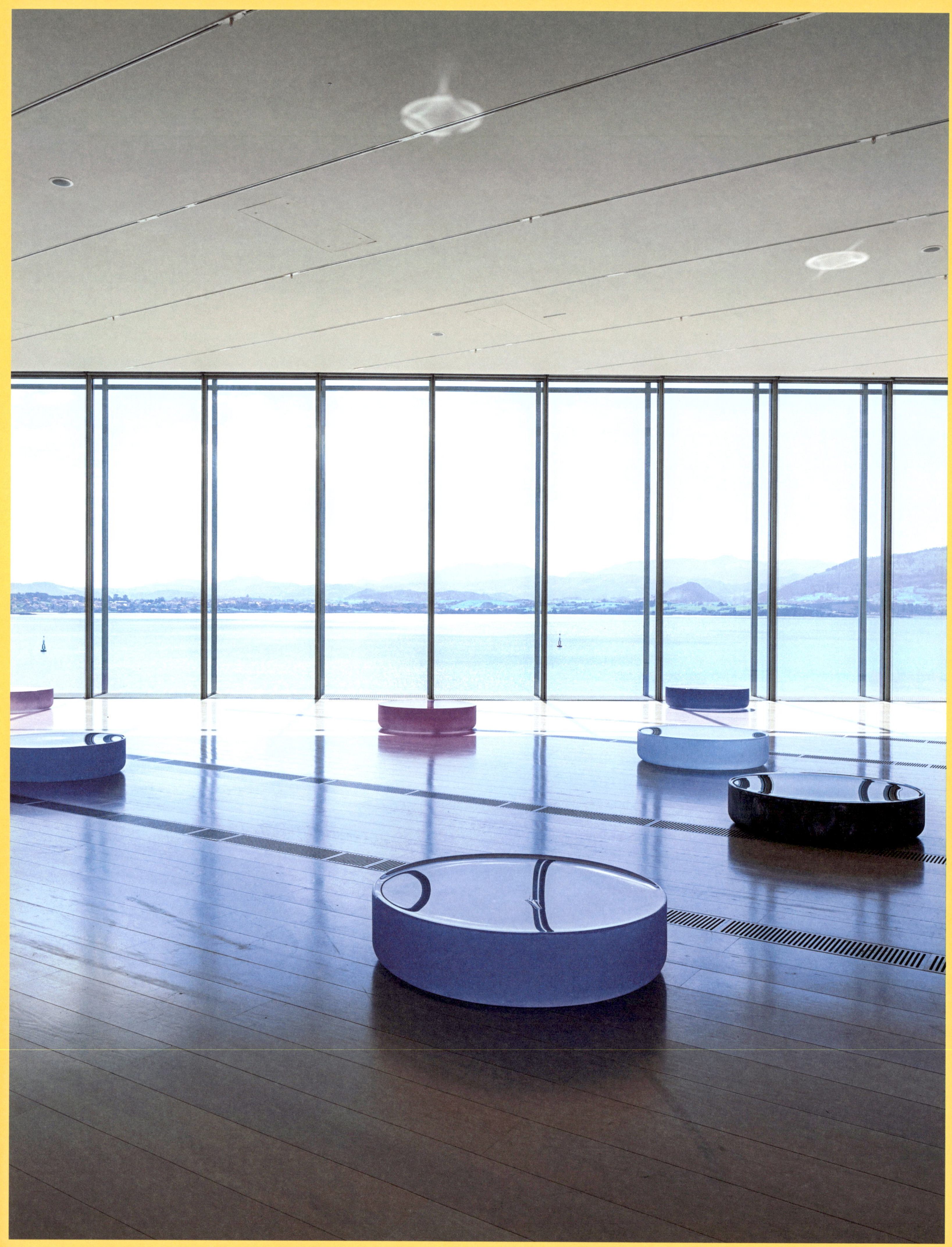

“What keeps you alive is not what you’ve done, but what you have not done.”

Renzo Piano

Alain Elkann Interviews

11 LEVERAGING NATURAL LIGHT

BUILDING ENERGY EFFICIENCY SDG 7 / 9 / 11

The use of natural light not only significantly reduces a building's energy consumption but also adds liveliness and warmth to museum spaces.

The Jeongok Prehistory Museum is enveloped by a stainless steel roof with a pattern of exterior perforations which, in addition to providing a distinctive visual identity inspired by Korean dragon and snake skins, also lets sunlight in during the day. These perforations can be adjusted to suit the lighting needs of each exhibition or weather conditions. Additionally, a double-glazed wall behind the perforations helps maintain a constant interior temperature, reducing air conditioning requirements and minimizing glare.

Jeongok Prehistory Museum

FOCUS
Natural History. Prehistory

LOCATION
Periurban. Yeoncheon, South Korea

CONSTRUCTION
2005.
Opened in 2011

PROJECT
XTU Architects

SIZE
6,700 m².
Land suface: 72,600 m²

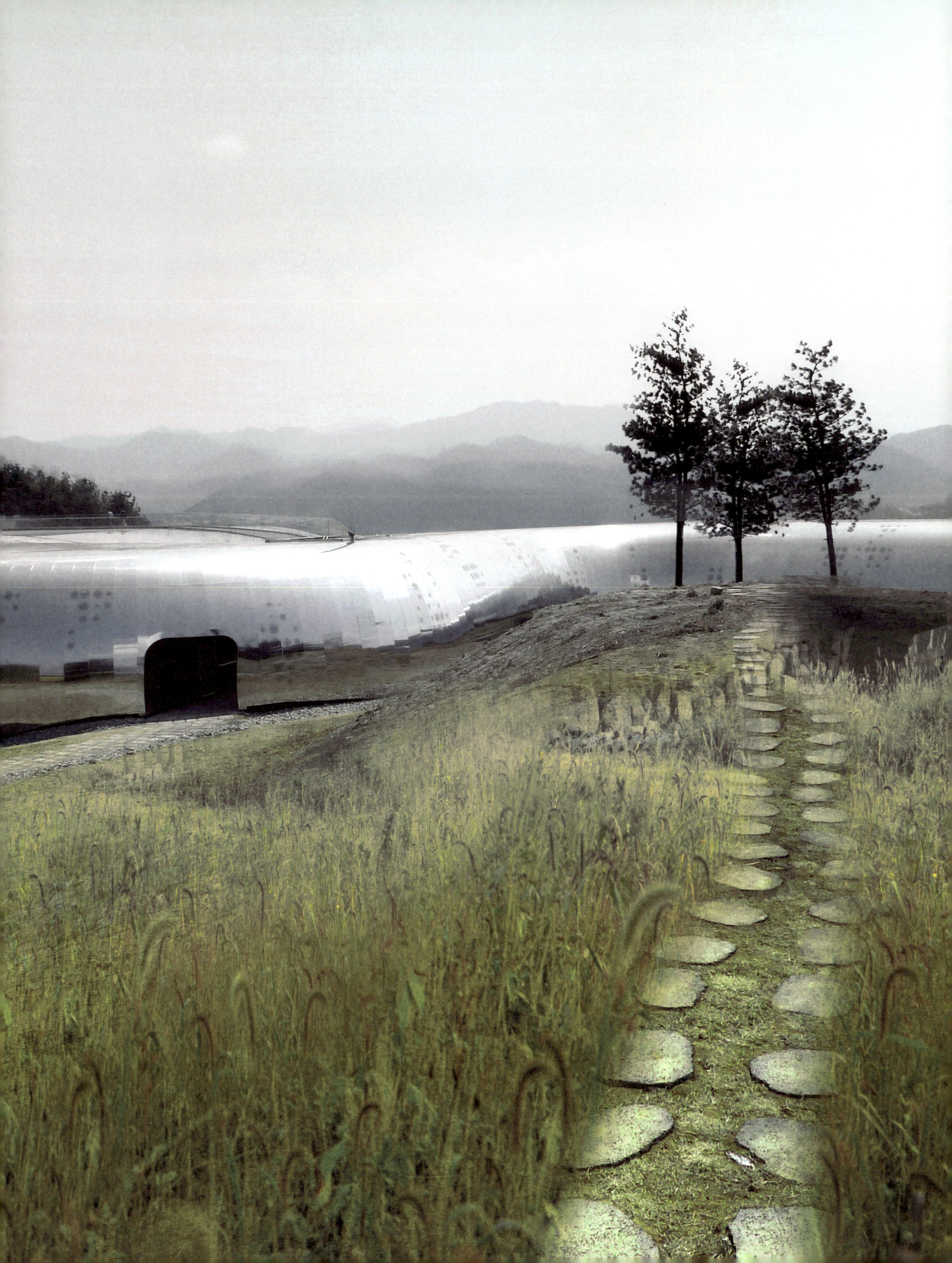

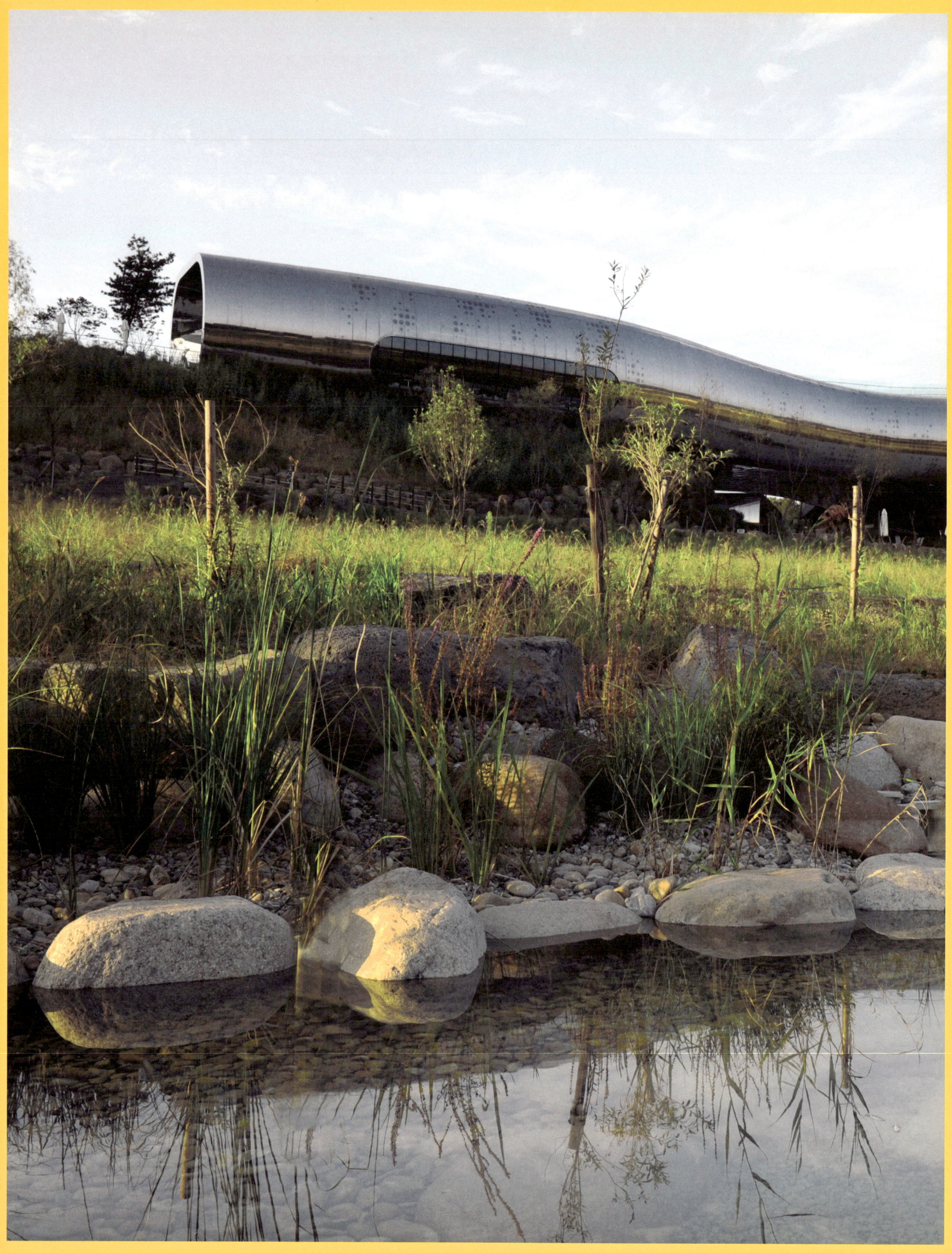

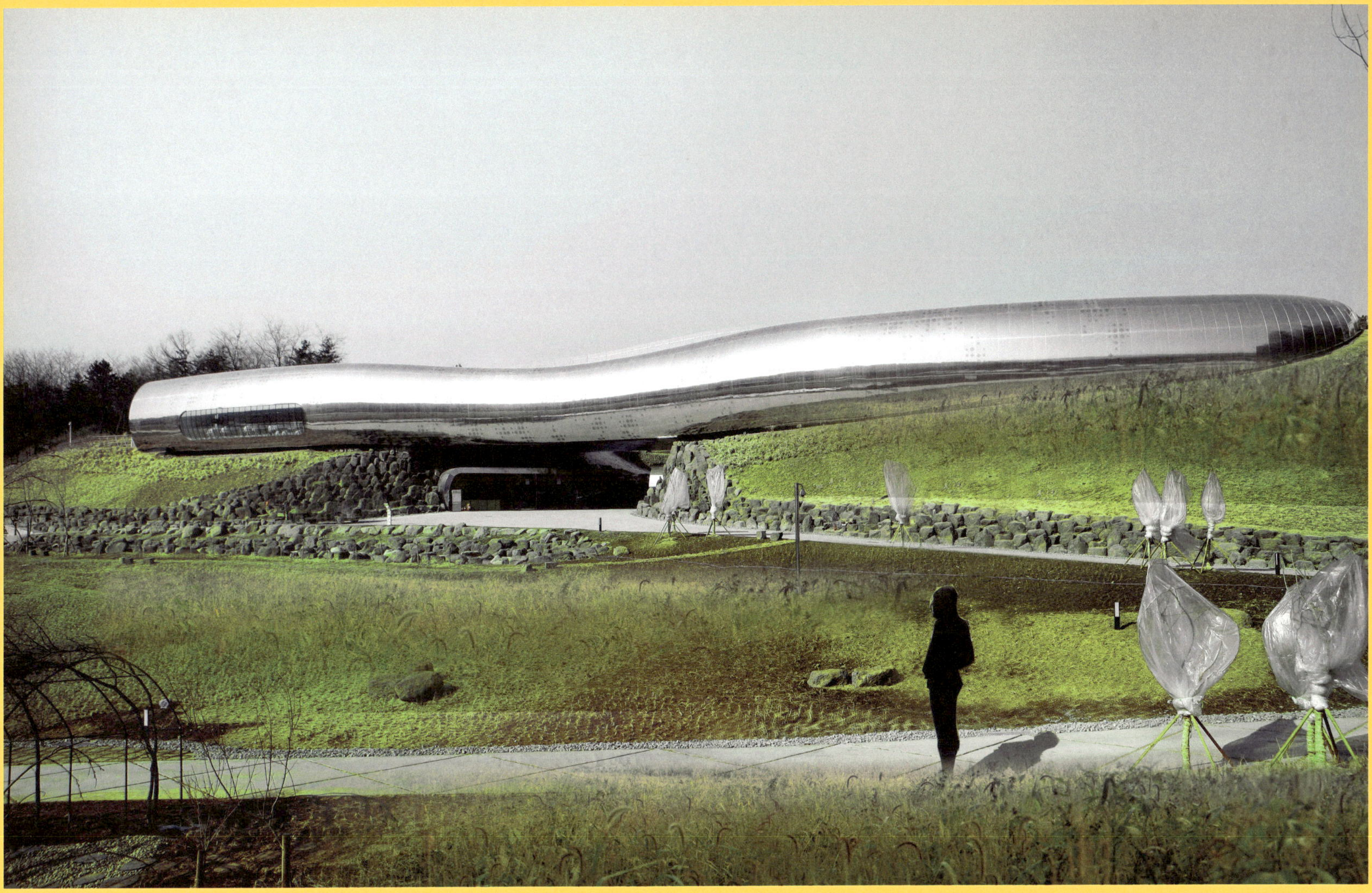

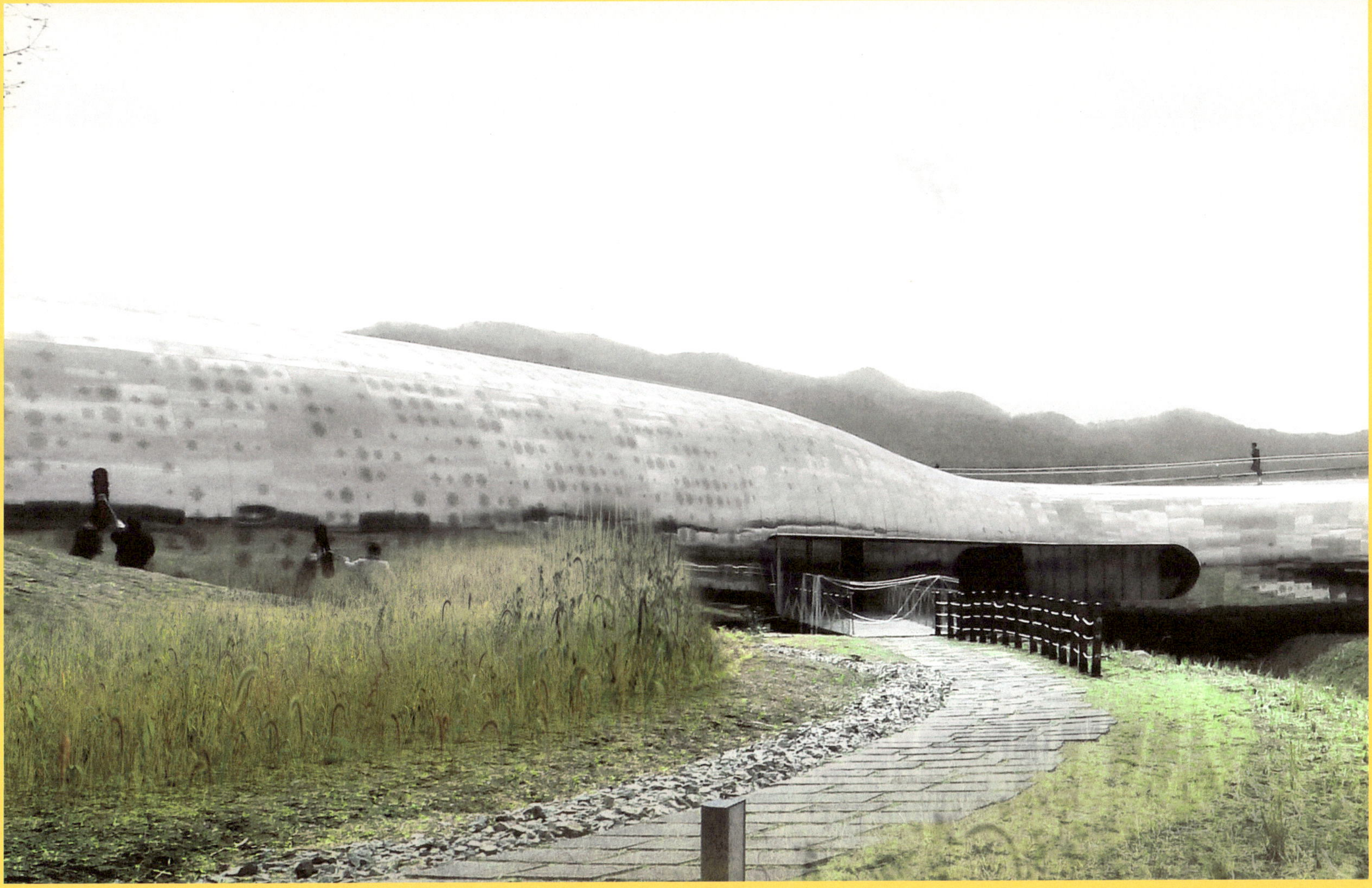

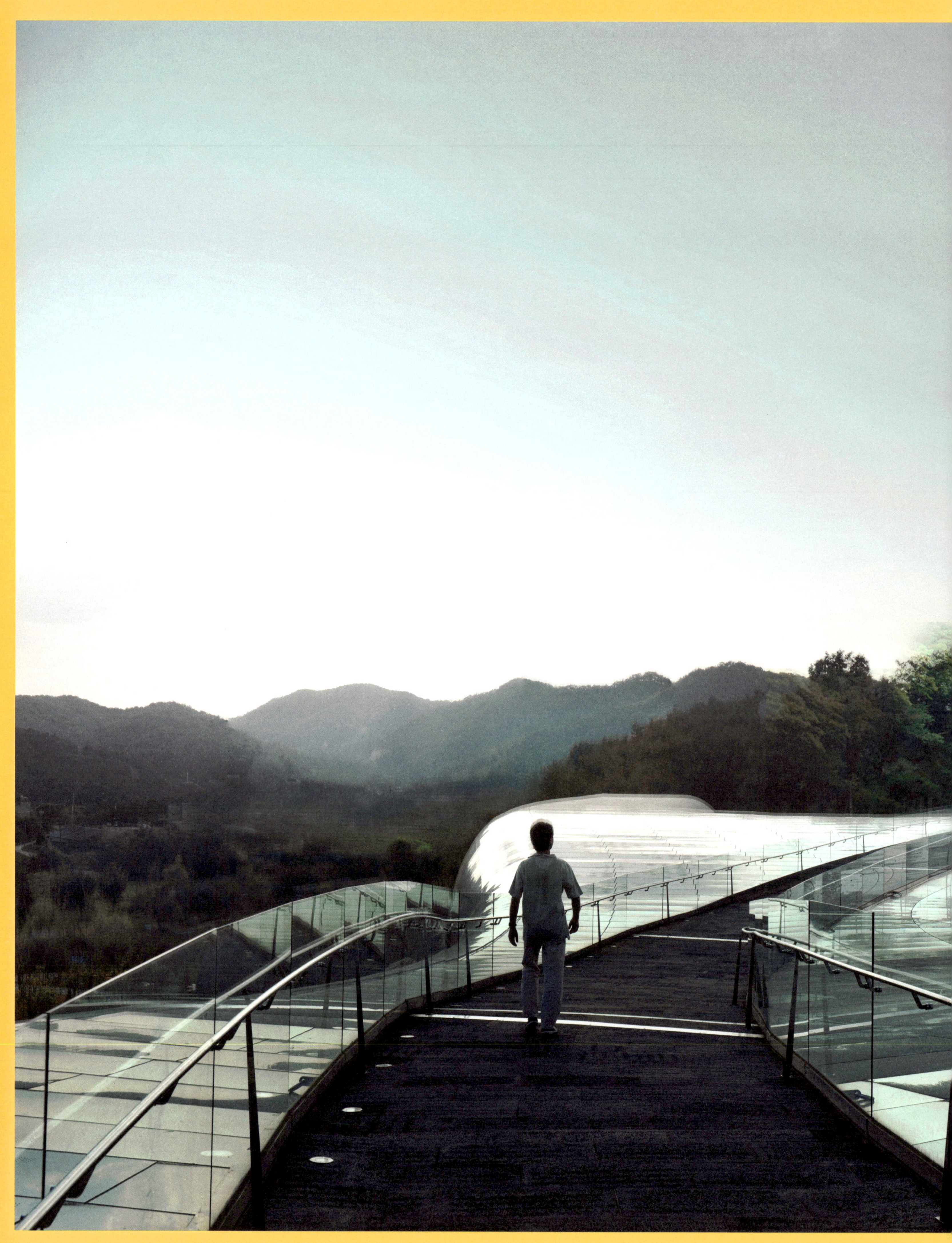

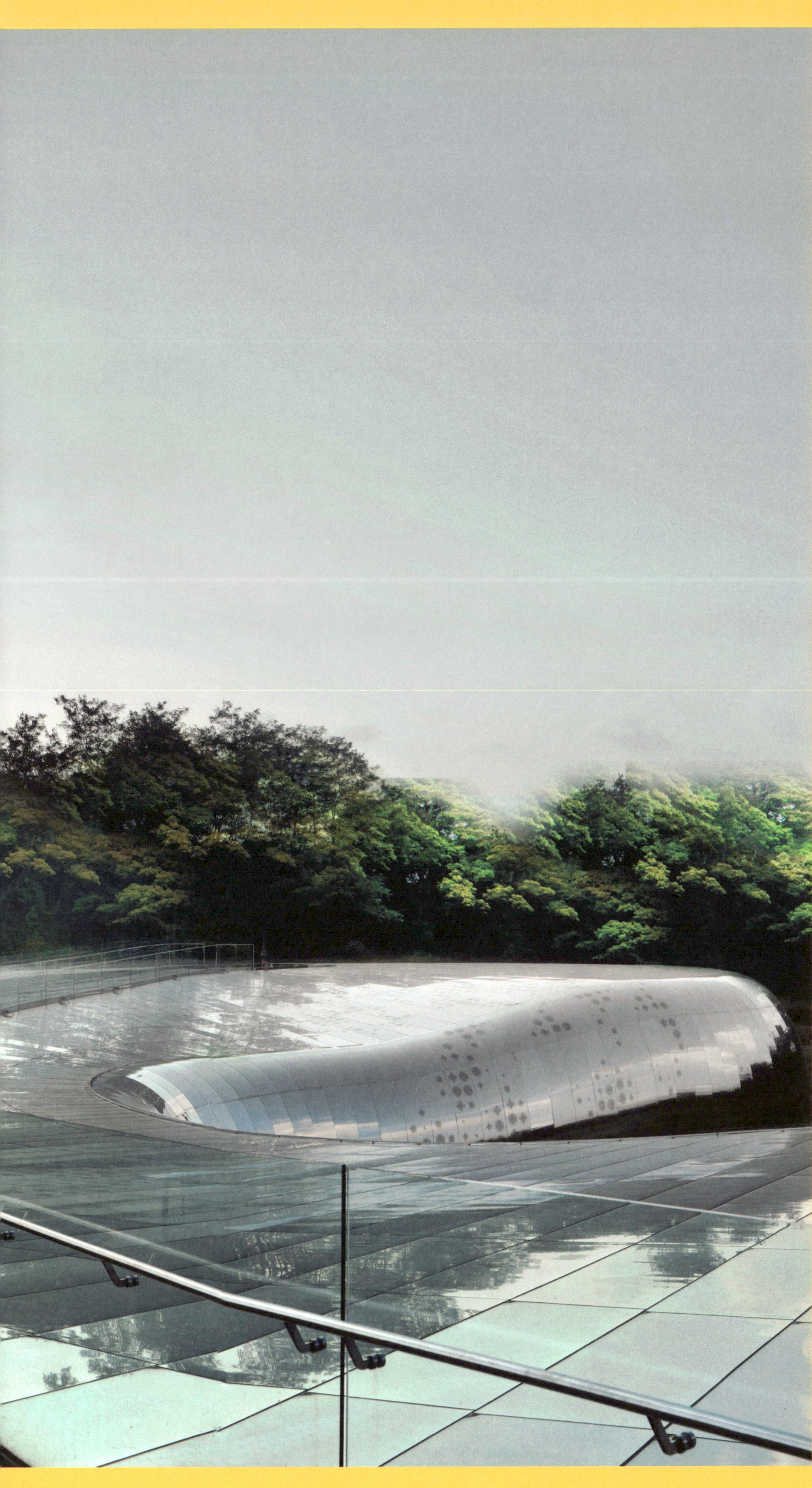

MUSEUMS WITH SIMILAR MEASURES

Art Institute of Chicago

CHICAGO, ILLINOIS, USA

Uses an overhead filter screen to reduce electricity use while maximizing daylight.

Cité de l'Océan

BIARRITZ, FRANCE

The building has undergone sustainable renovations with a focus on enhancing natural light utilization.

Louvre Abu Dhabi

ABU DHABI, UNITED ARAB EMIRATES

Features a dome with optimized perforations that allow natural light to enter without causing excessive solar gain or wind flow.

Papalote Museo del Niño

CHAPULTEPEC, MEXICO

Utilization of natural light with the aim of reducing energy consumption.

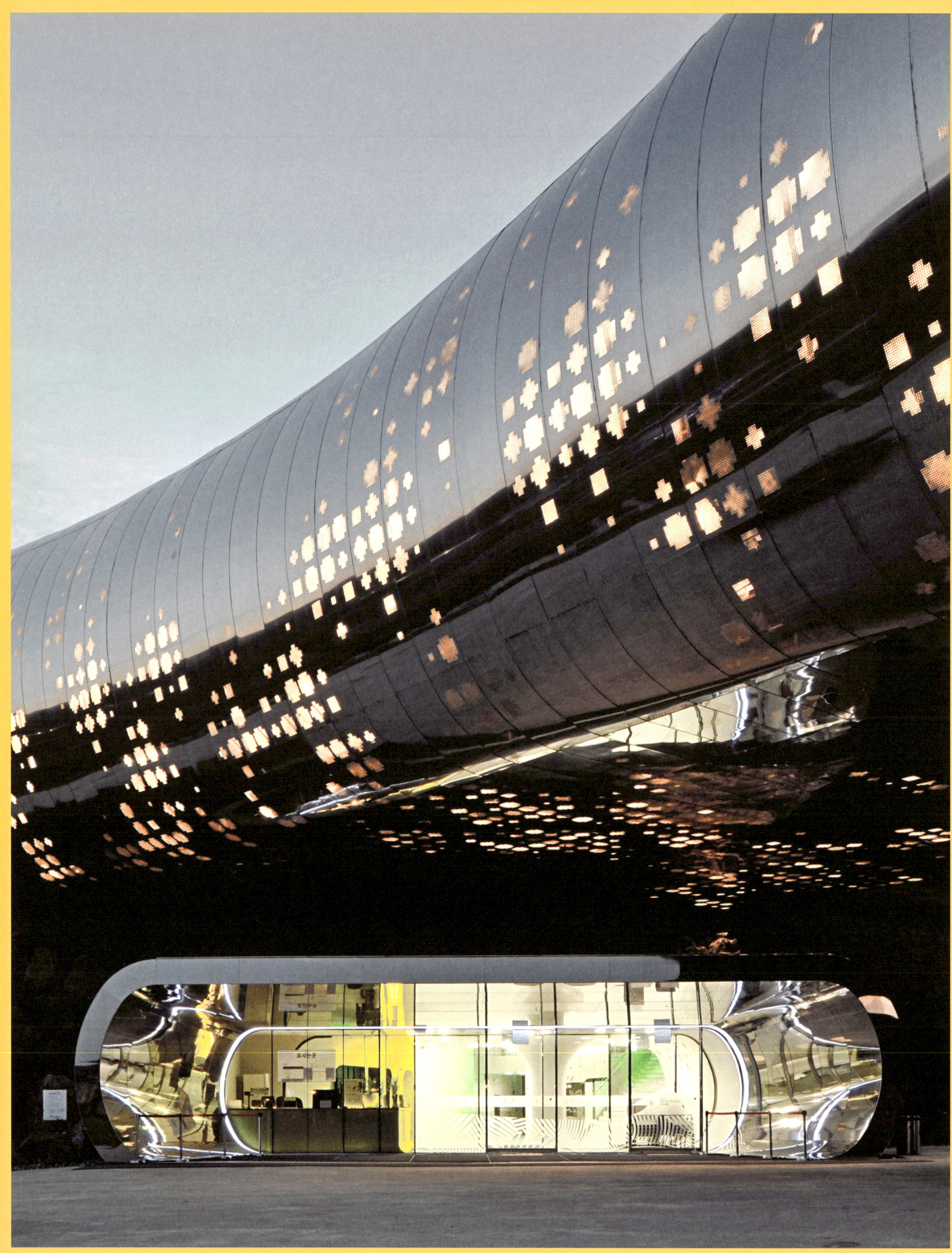

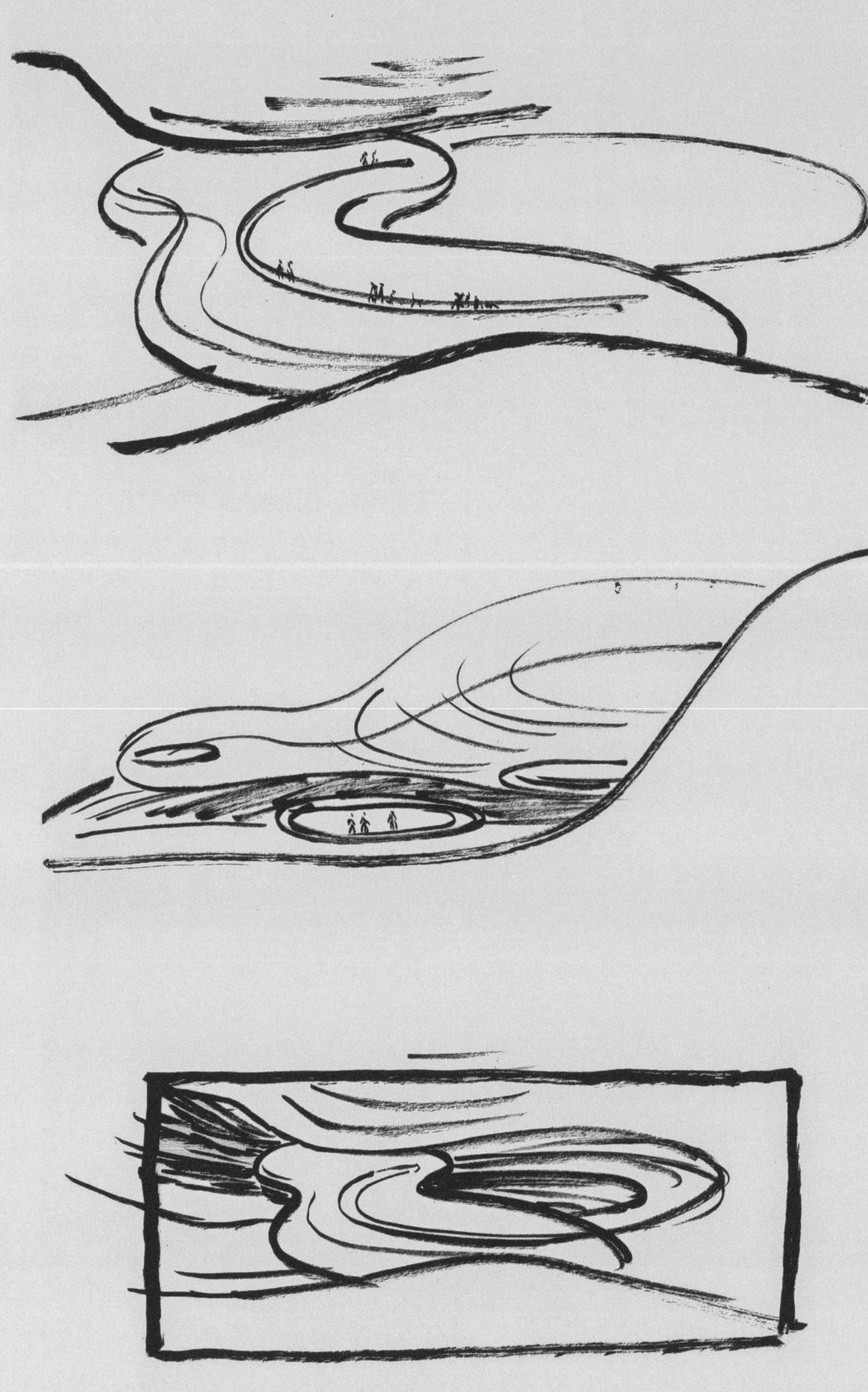

Sketches of Jeongok Prehistory Museum.
Anouk Legendre, co-founder of XTU Architects studio.

12 PHOTOVOLTAIC PANEL INSTALLATION

BUILDING ENERGY EFFICIENCY SDG 7 / 9

The photovoltaic panel is a device designed for energy production, whose modules consist of a set of cells that capture the sunlight which falls upon them and transform it into electricity for conventional use, making it a renewable energy source.

The Guggenheim Museum Bilbao has three hundred photovoltaic panels located on its rooftops, allowing for a savings of around 5% in the Museum's electrical consumption and covering the lighting needs of all its exhibition rooms. The panels were installed on the two largest roofs of the building, fully integrated into its architecture.

The museum's solar panel project, which began in January 2024, is complemented by the installation of photovoltaic panels in its external warehouse, contributing an average of 30% of the building's electricity demand.

Guggenheim Museum Bilbao

FOCUS
Modern and Contemporary Art

CONSTRUCTION
1997

LOCATION
Bilbao, Spain

PROJECT
Frank Gehry

ANNUAL VISITORS
1.3 million

SIZE
24,000 m²

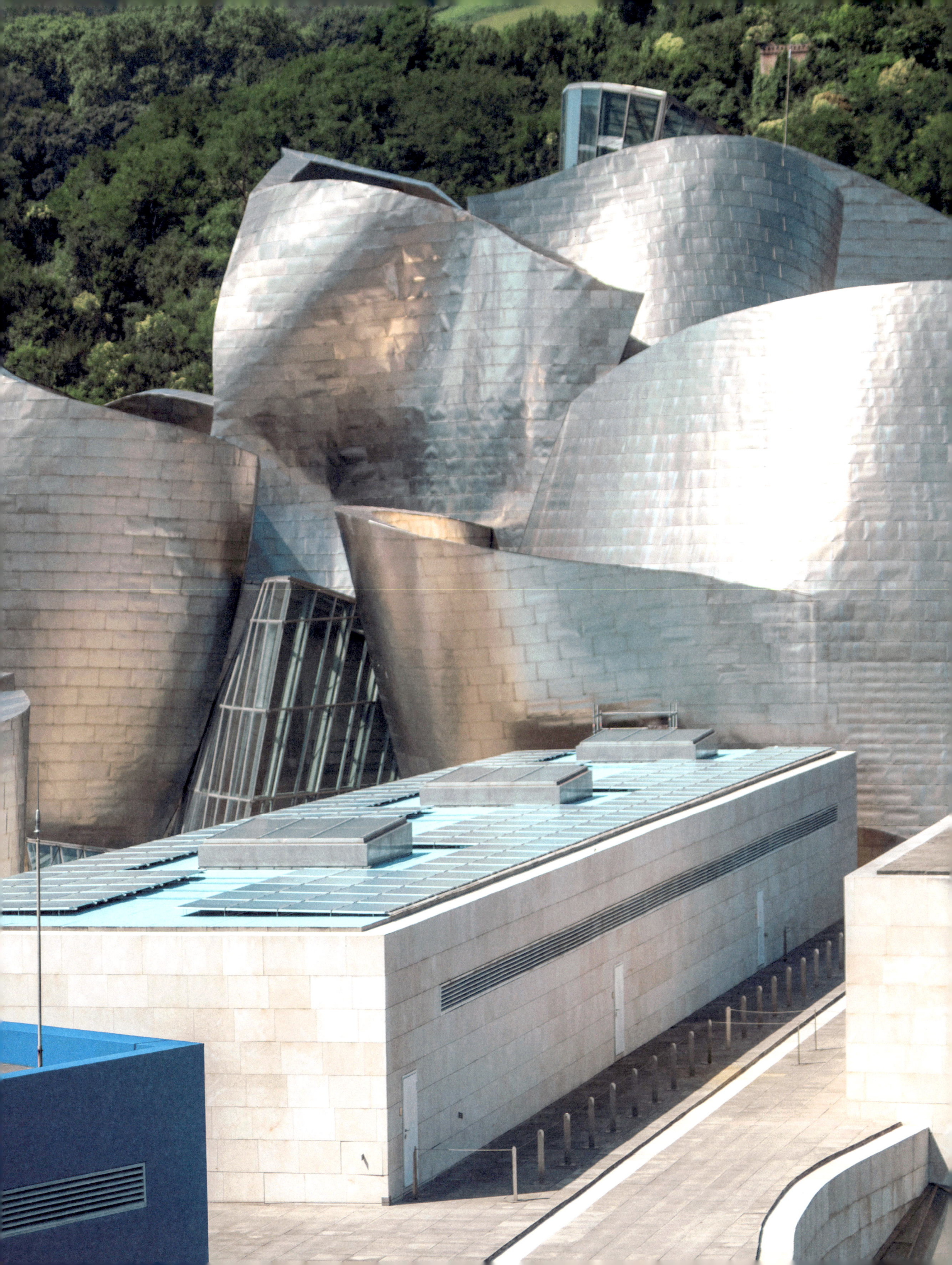

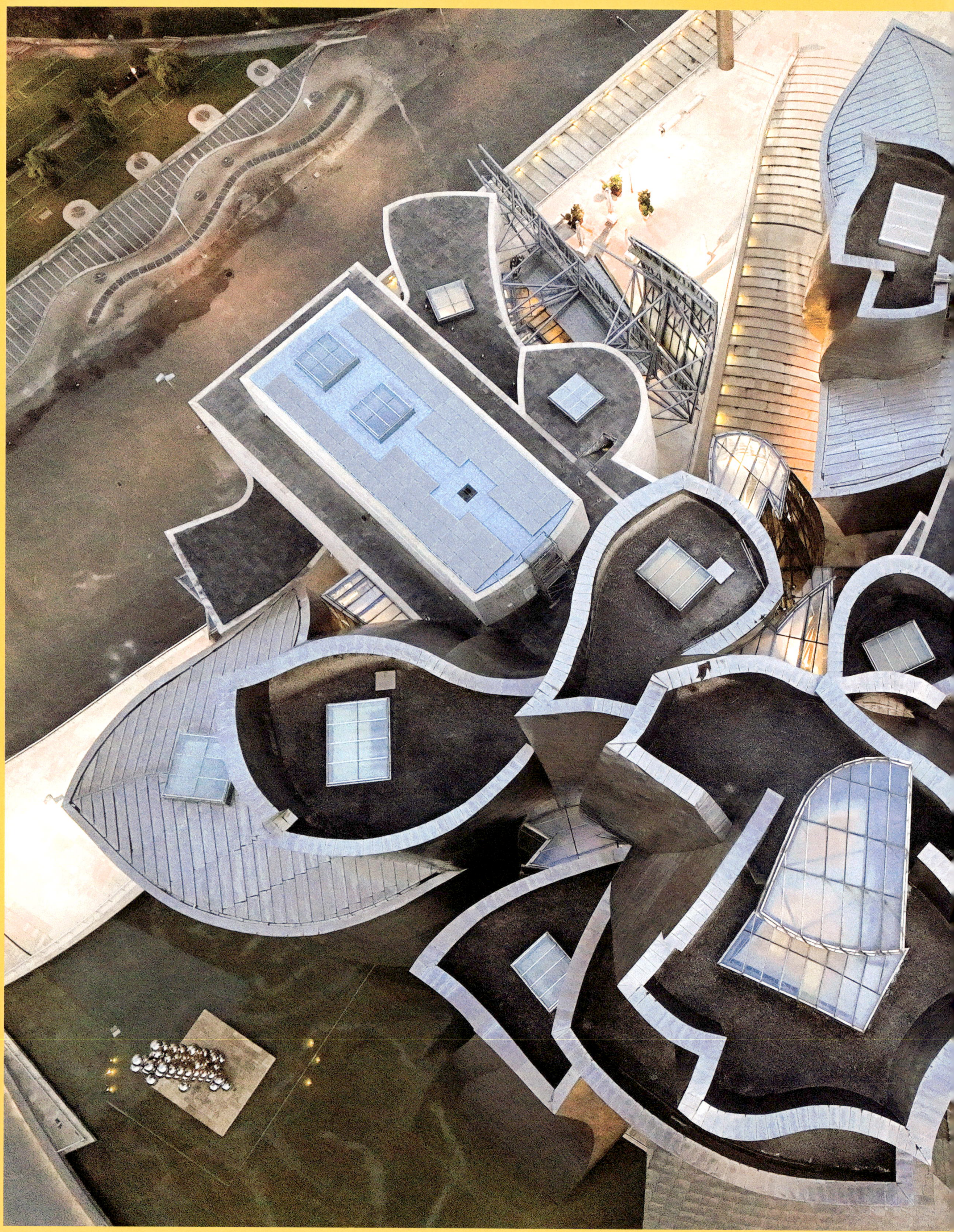

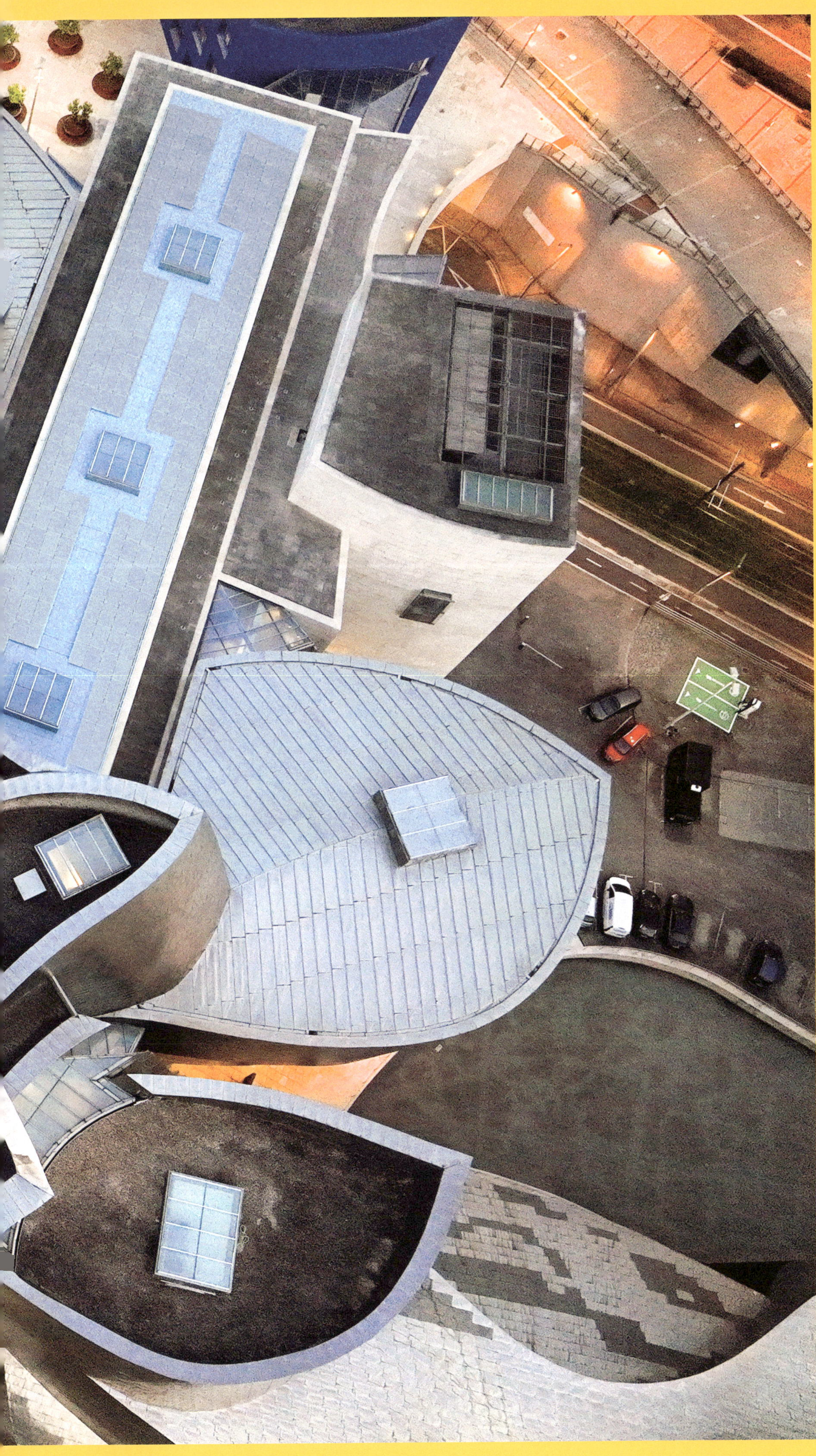

MUSEUMS WITH SIMILAR MEASURES

Australian National Maritime Museum

SIDNEY, AUSTRALIA

Installation of solar panels with an innovative design thanks to their thinness and flexibility.

Exploratorium

SAN FRANCISCO, CALIFORNIA, USA

The museum has installed photovoltaic panels that produce most of the energy required for its operations.

Field Museum

CHICAGO, ILLINOIS, USA

This museum complements its photovoltaic installation with the purchase of certified green energy to meet all its energy needs.

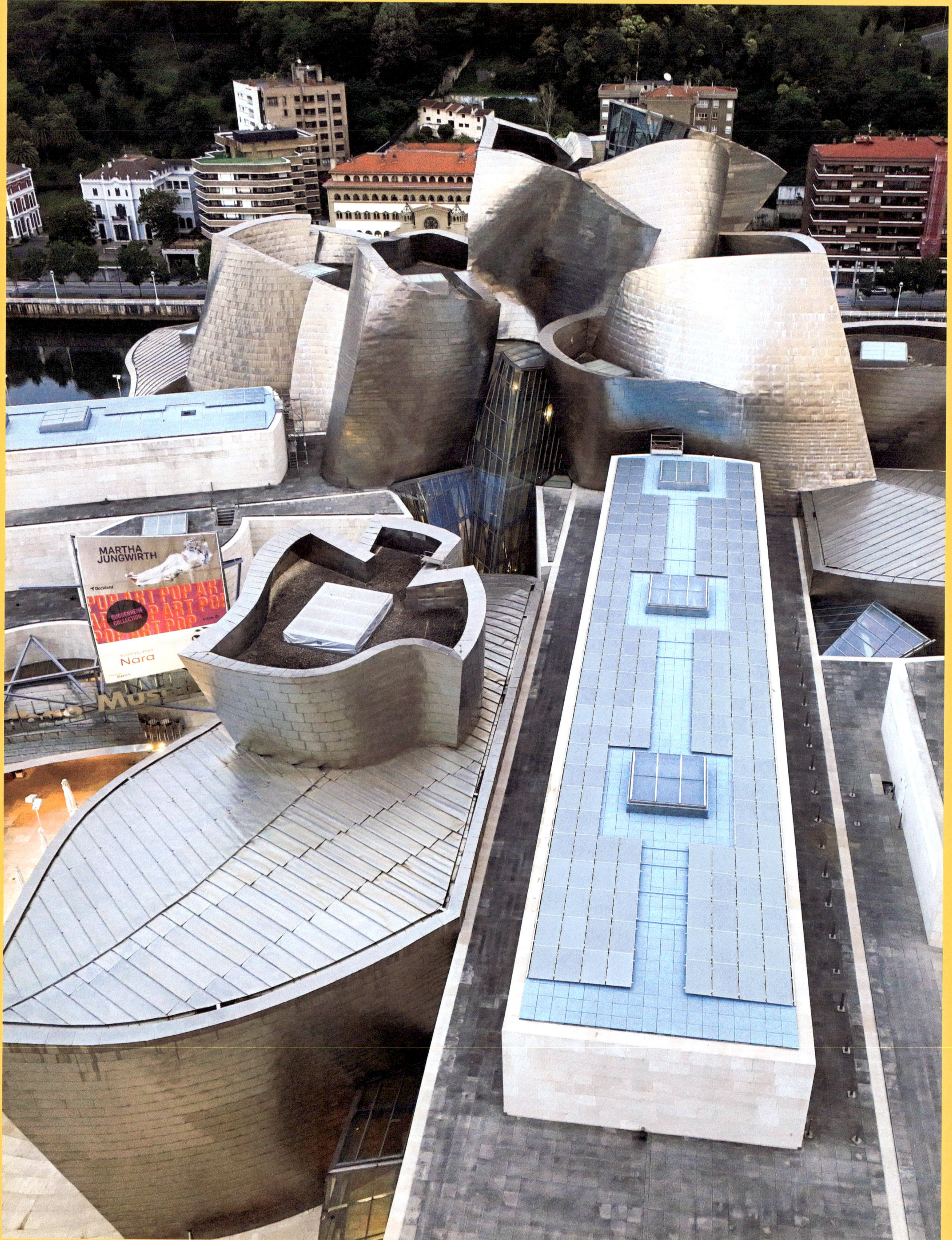
MARTHA
JUNGWIRTH
Occident
GUGGENHEIM
COLLECTION
Yoshitomo
Nara
BBVA

“The photovoltaic installation on the rooftops of the building is one of the actions included in the 2024–2025 Sustainability Plan and reinforces the museum’s firm commitment to environmental preservation.”

Guggenheim Museum Bilbao

13 GEOTHERMAL INSTALLATION FOR AIR CONDITIONING

BUILDING ENERGY EFFICIENCY SDG 7 / 9 / 11 / 13

Geothermal energy is obtained by harnessing the earth's internal heat, making it a renewable energy source. To generate geothermal electricity, wells are drilled into underground reservoirs to tap steam and hot water, which drive turbines connected to electricity generators.

The Espai Cràter in Olot has a geothermal installation for air conditioning needs. The plant features a collection field with seventeen vertical wells, each 100 meters deep, and two geothermal heat pumps, each with a capacity of 60 kWh.

Espai Cràter

FOCUS
Volcanology

LOCATION
Urban. Olot, Girona, Spain

ANNUAL VISITORS
50,000

CONSTRUCTION
2020–2021

PROJECT
BCQ Arquitectura Barcelona

SIZE
1,285 m²

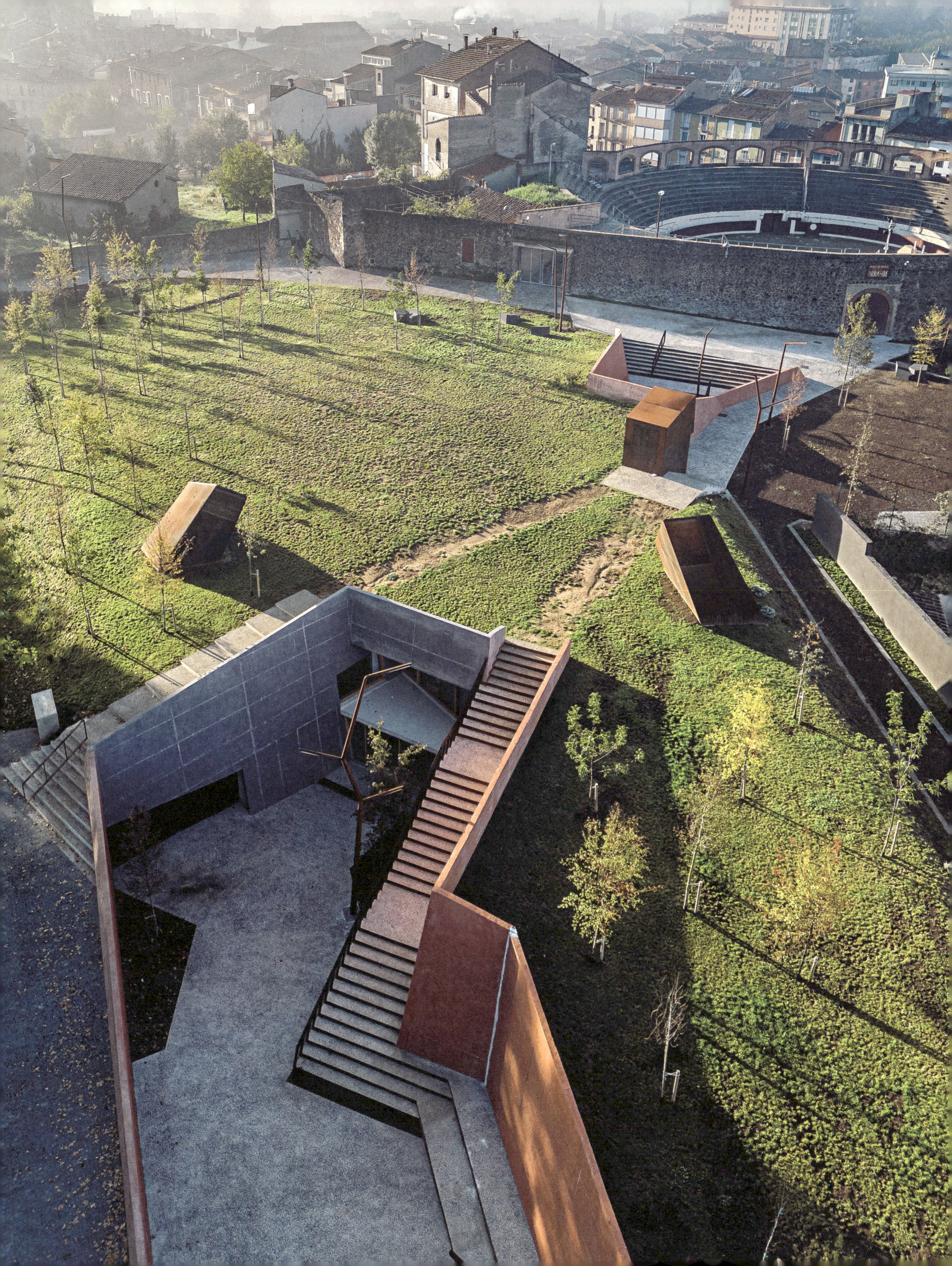

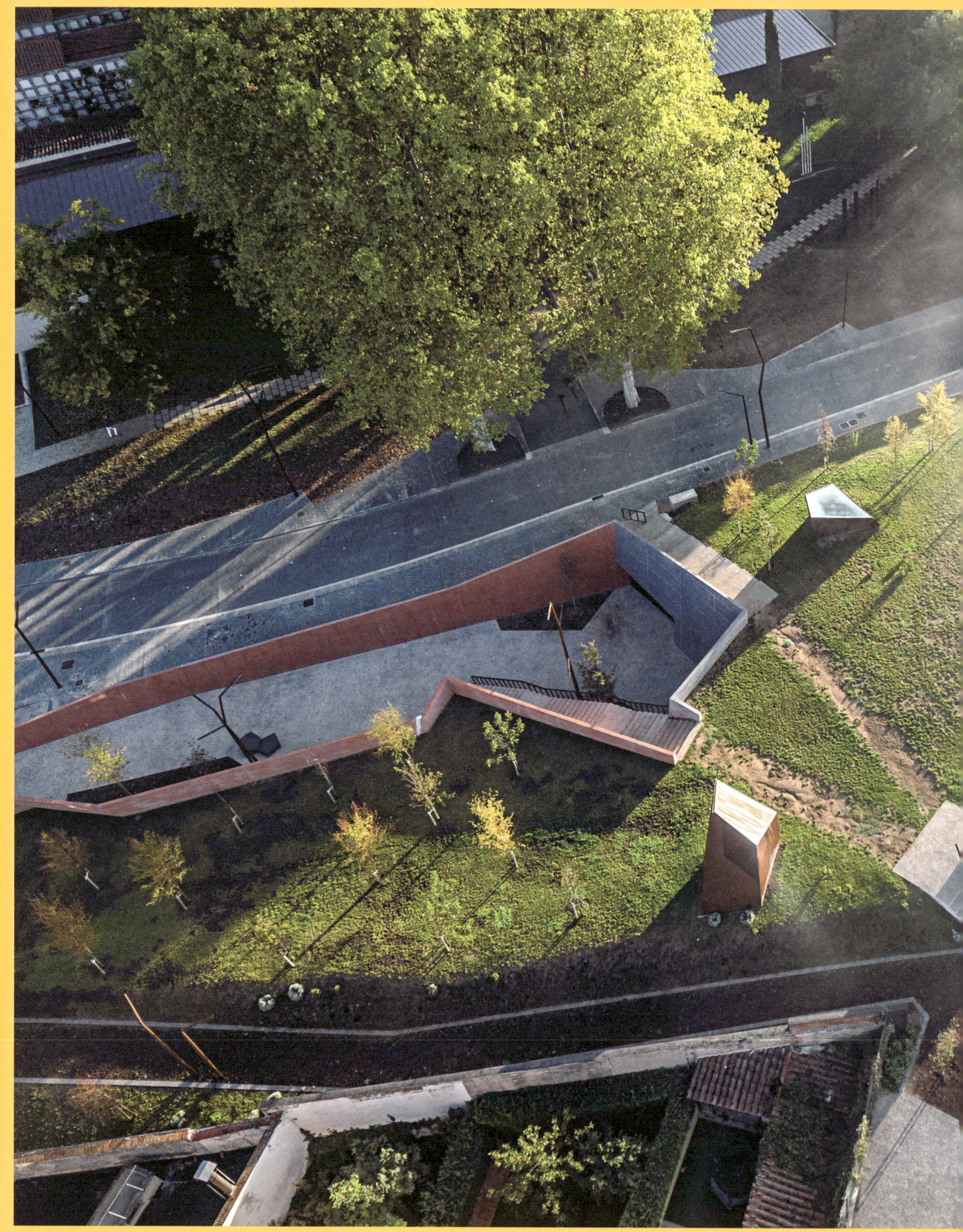

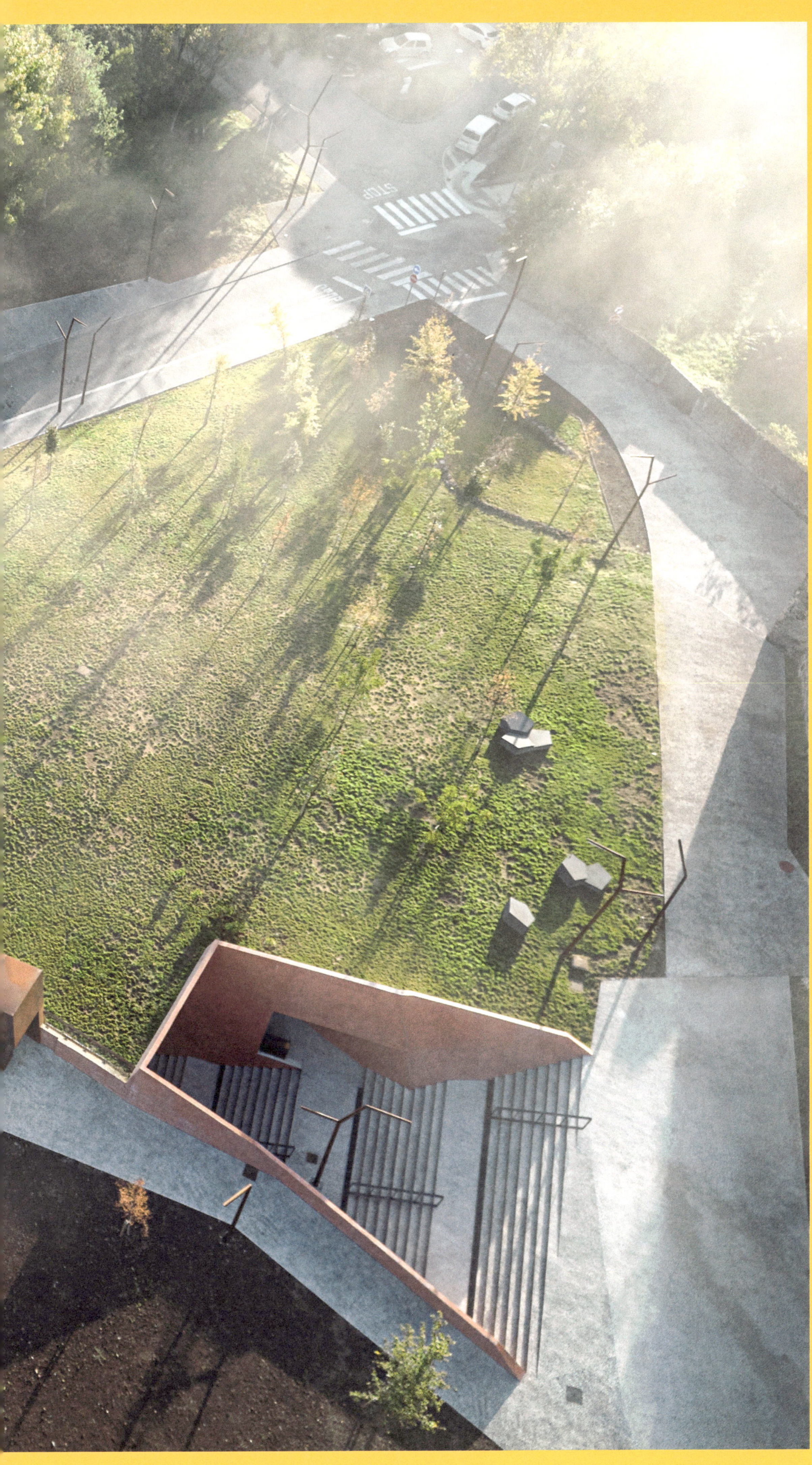

MUSEUMS WITH SIMILAR MEASURES

Museum für Naturkunde

BERLIN, GERMANY
Geothermal system in its exhibition halls.

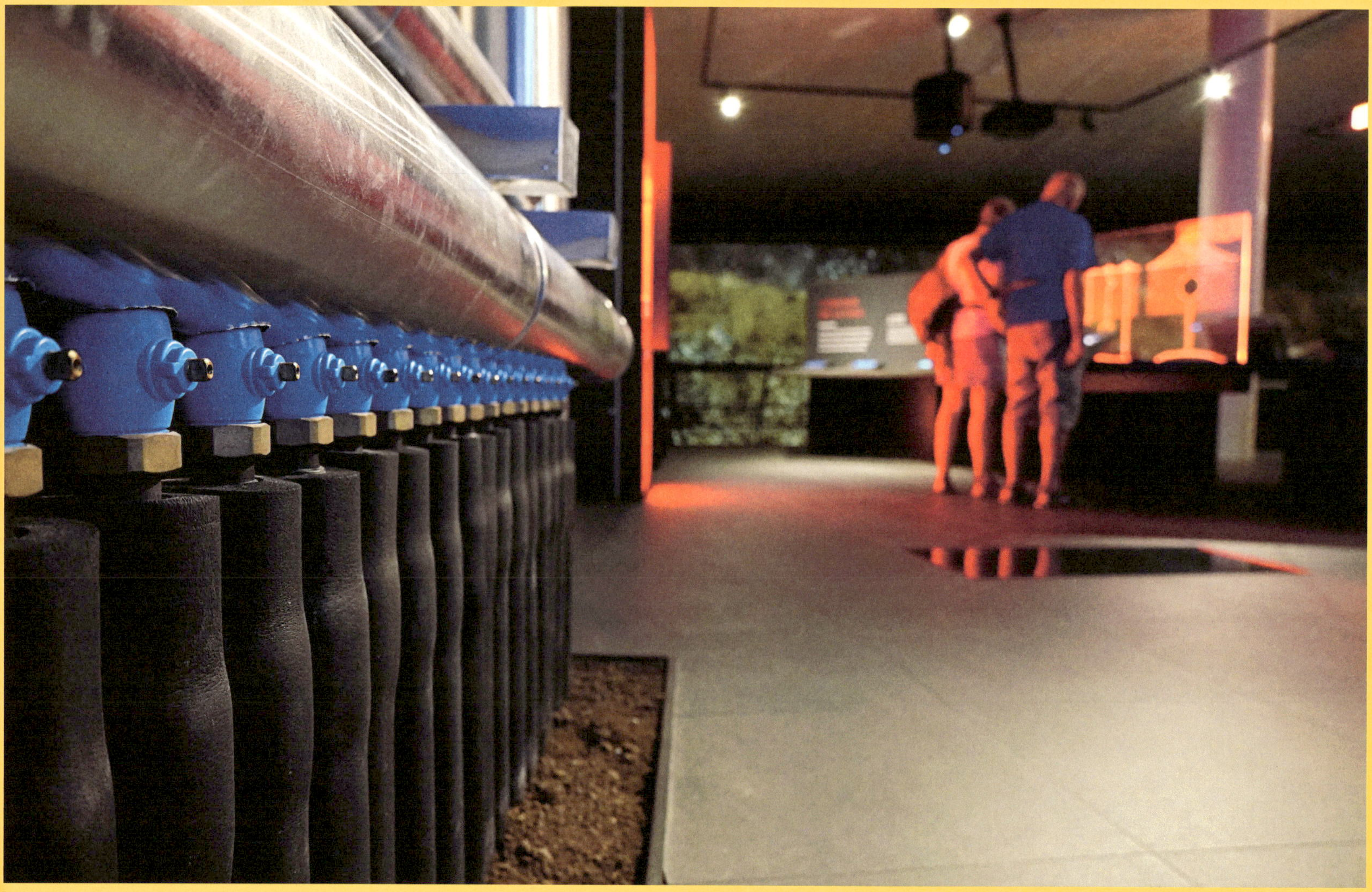

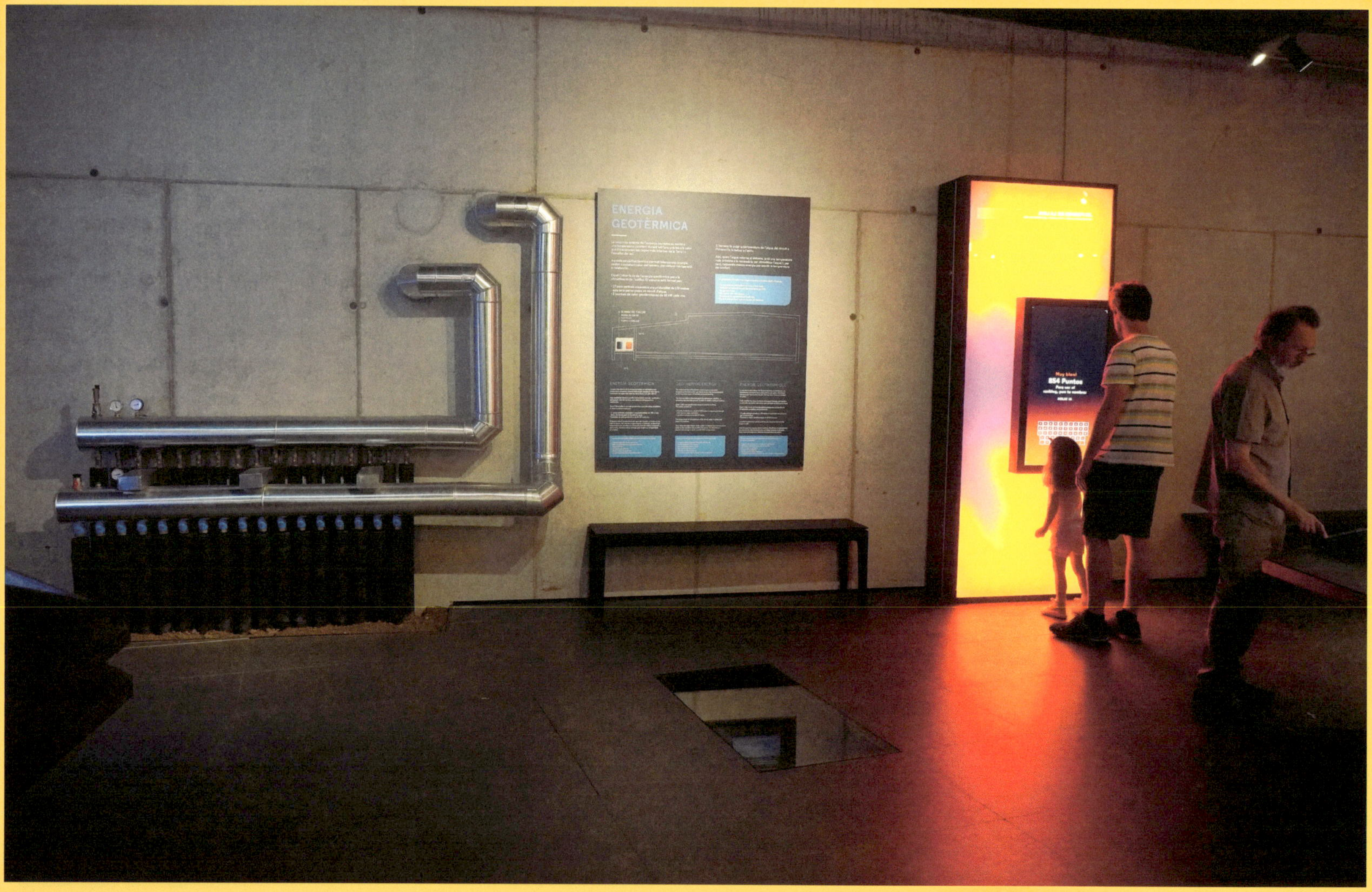

ENERGIA
GEOTÈRMICA

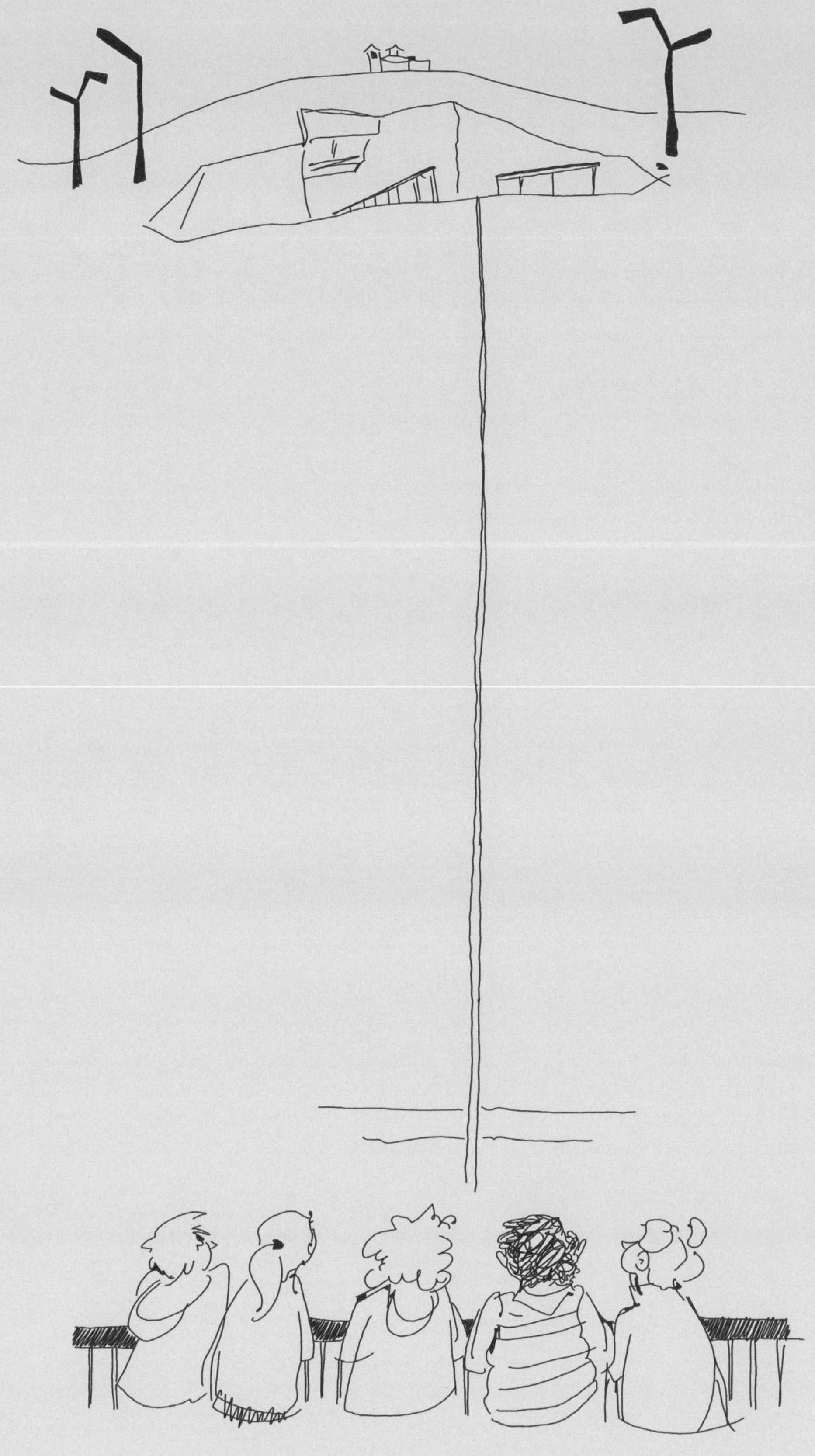

Espai Cràter, “the building that educates”.

14 LIVING MUSEUMS

PROTECTION AND PROMOTION OF BIODIVERSITY SDG 15

Botanical gardens are living museums that house diverse plant species for research, preservation, and public education. Bringing biodiversity closer to museum visitors promotes its care and fosters environmental knowledge.

The Biodiversity Park gardens of the Biomuseo Panamá (Panama Biomuseum) occupy three hectares of land around the museum, where 80% of species being endemic and native. Divided into thematic zones, the park serves as a living extension of the museum's architecture, materializing and exemplifying the concepts presented in its central exhibition.

Biomuseo Panamá

FOCUS
Natural History, Biodiversity

LOCATION
Periurban, located on the outskirts of Panama City

CONSTRUCTION
2014. Extended in 2019

PROJECT
Frank Gehry

SIZE
4,000 m².
Botanical Park: 24,000 m²

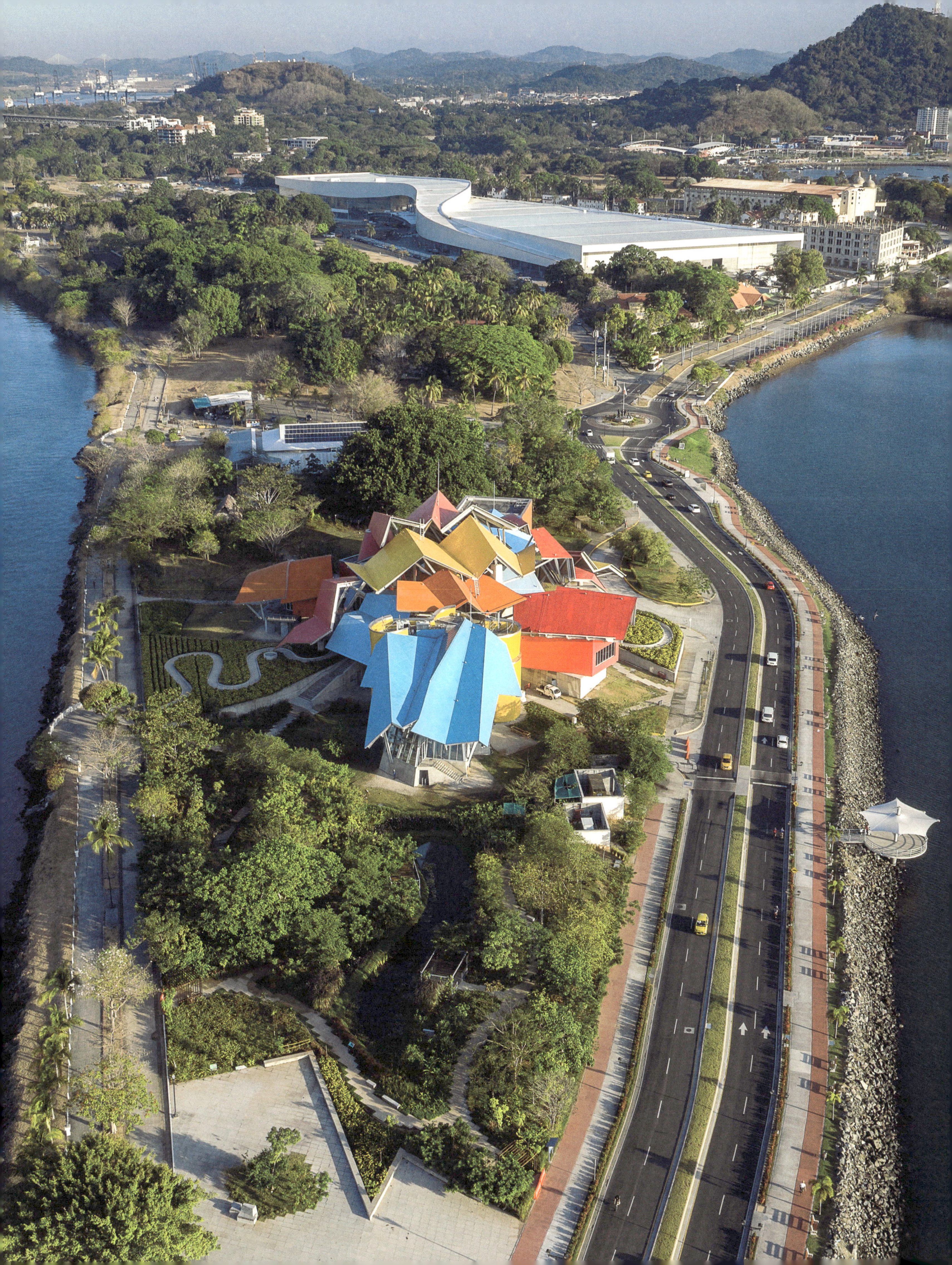

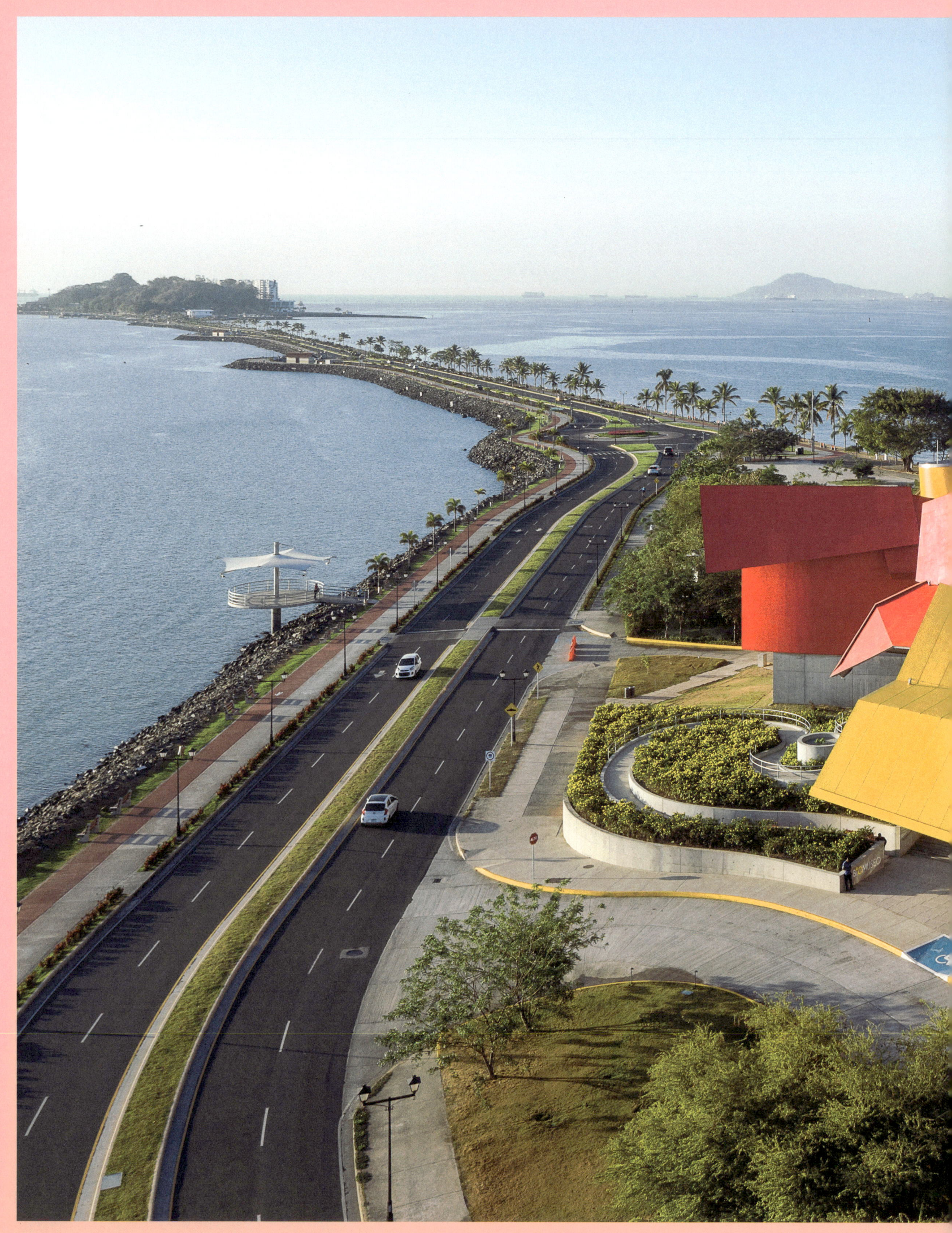

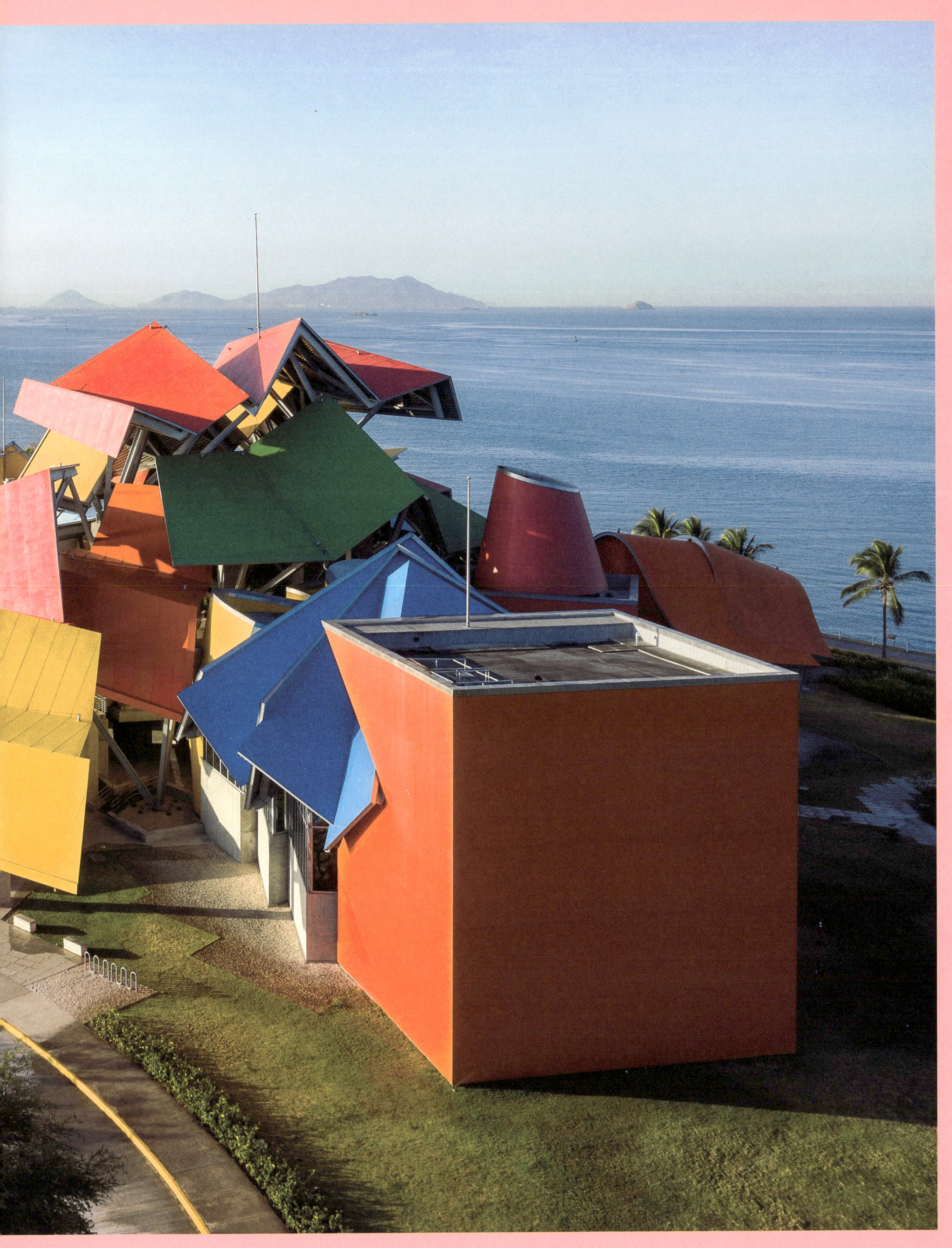

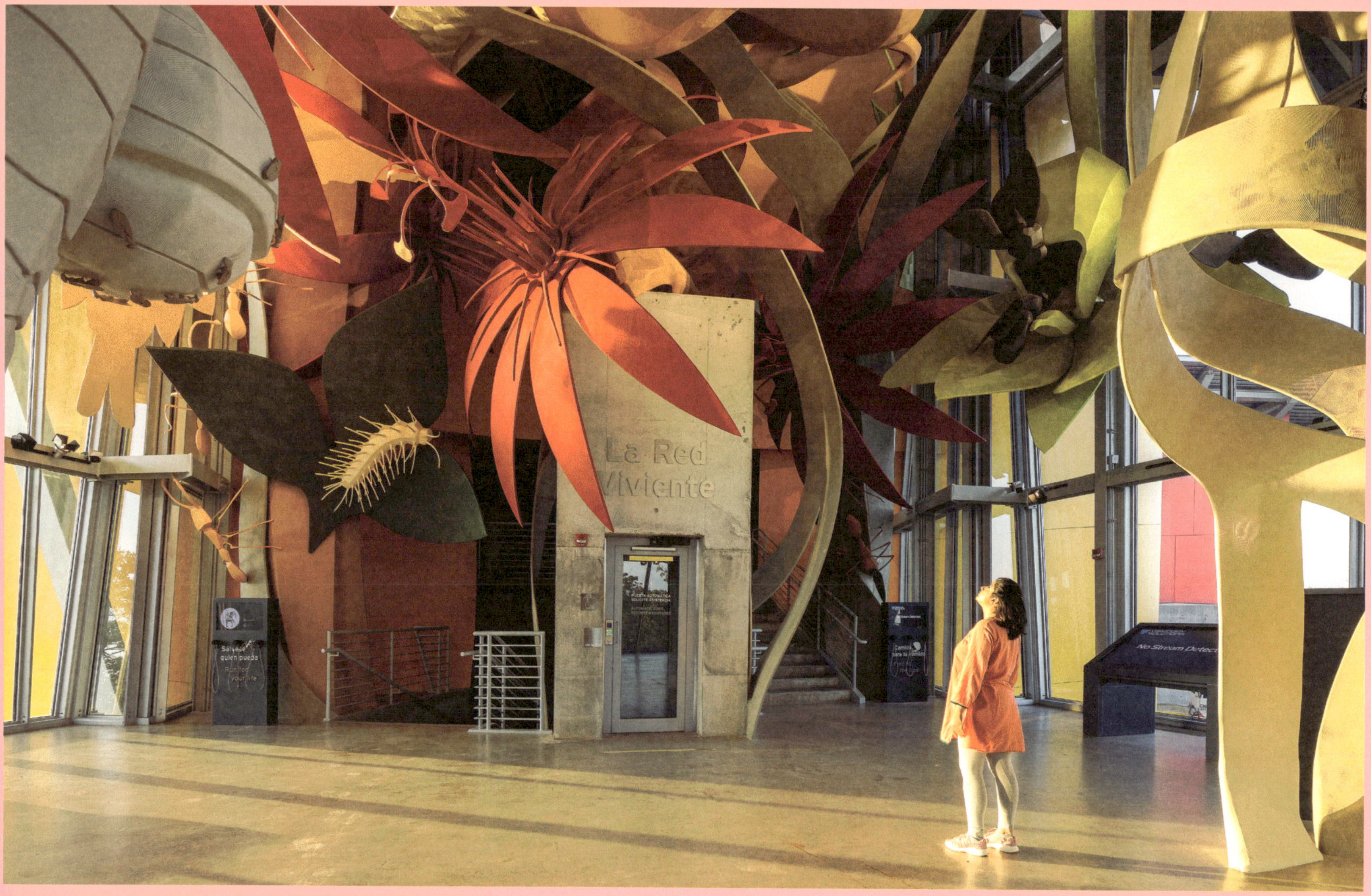

La Red
Viviente

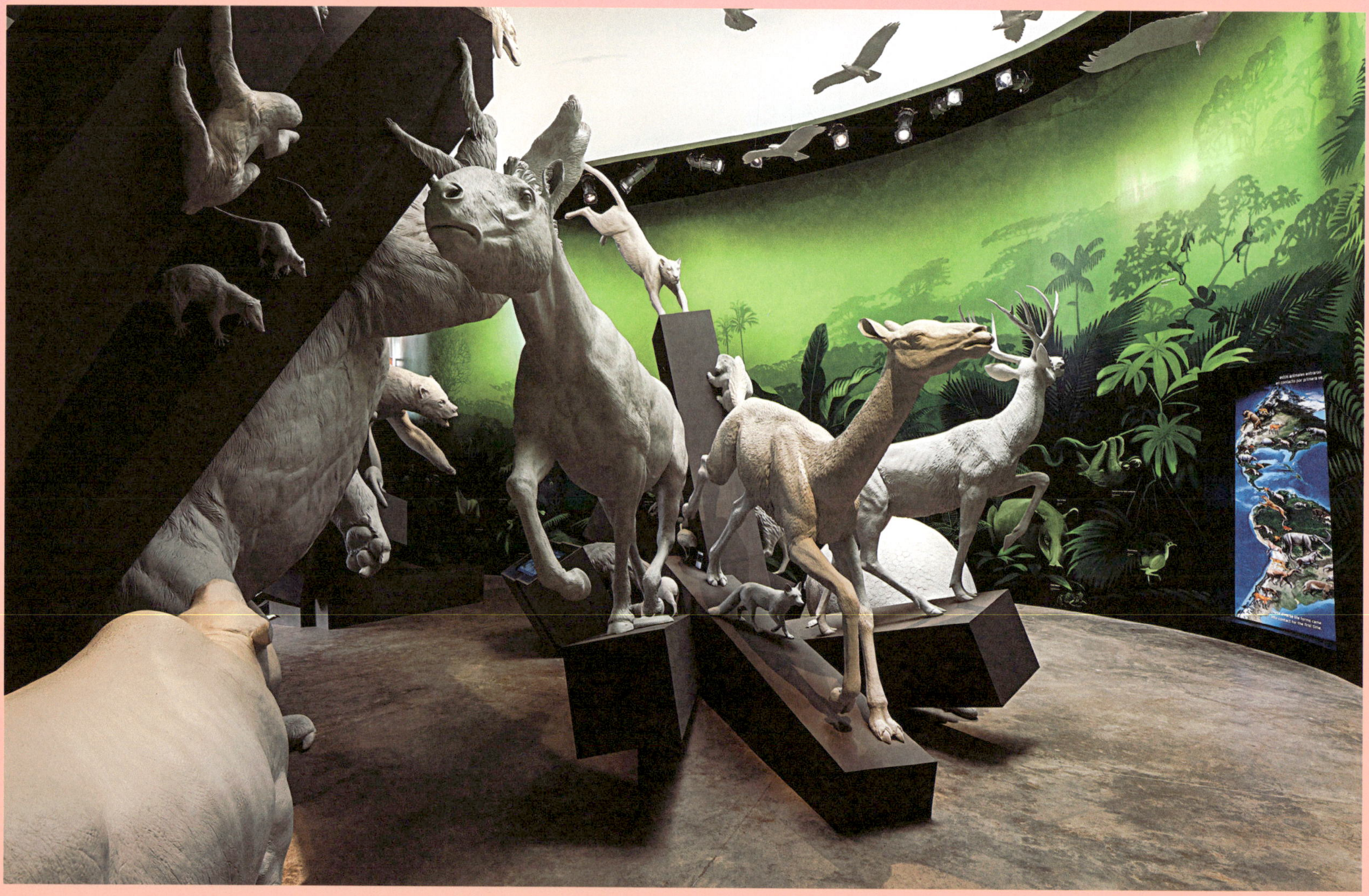

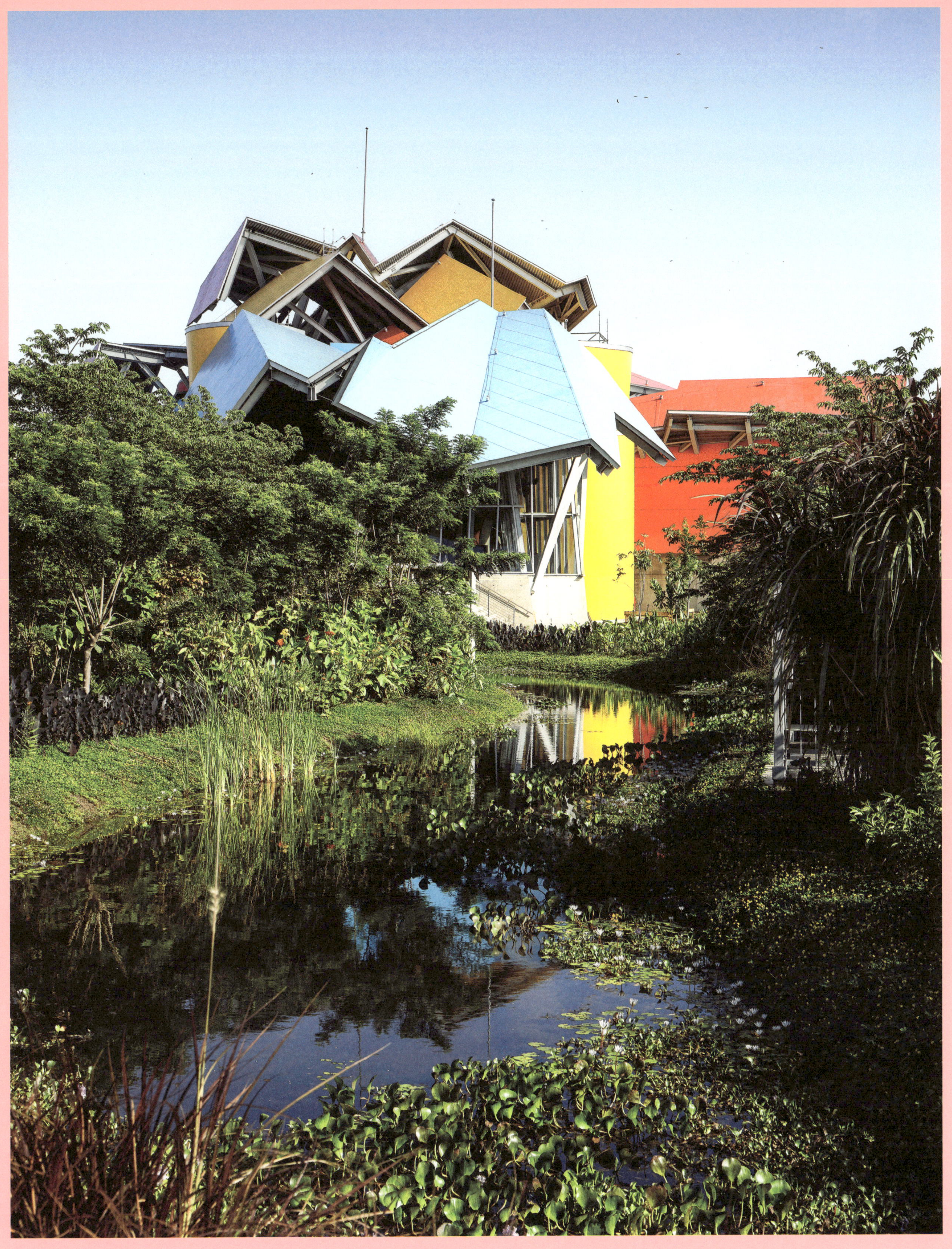

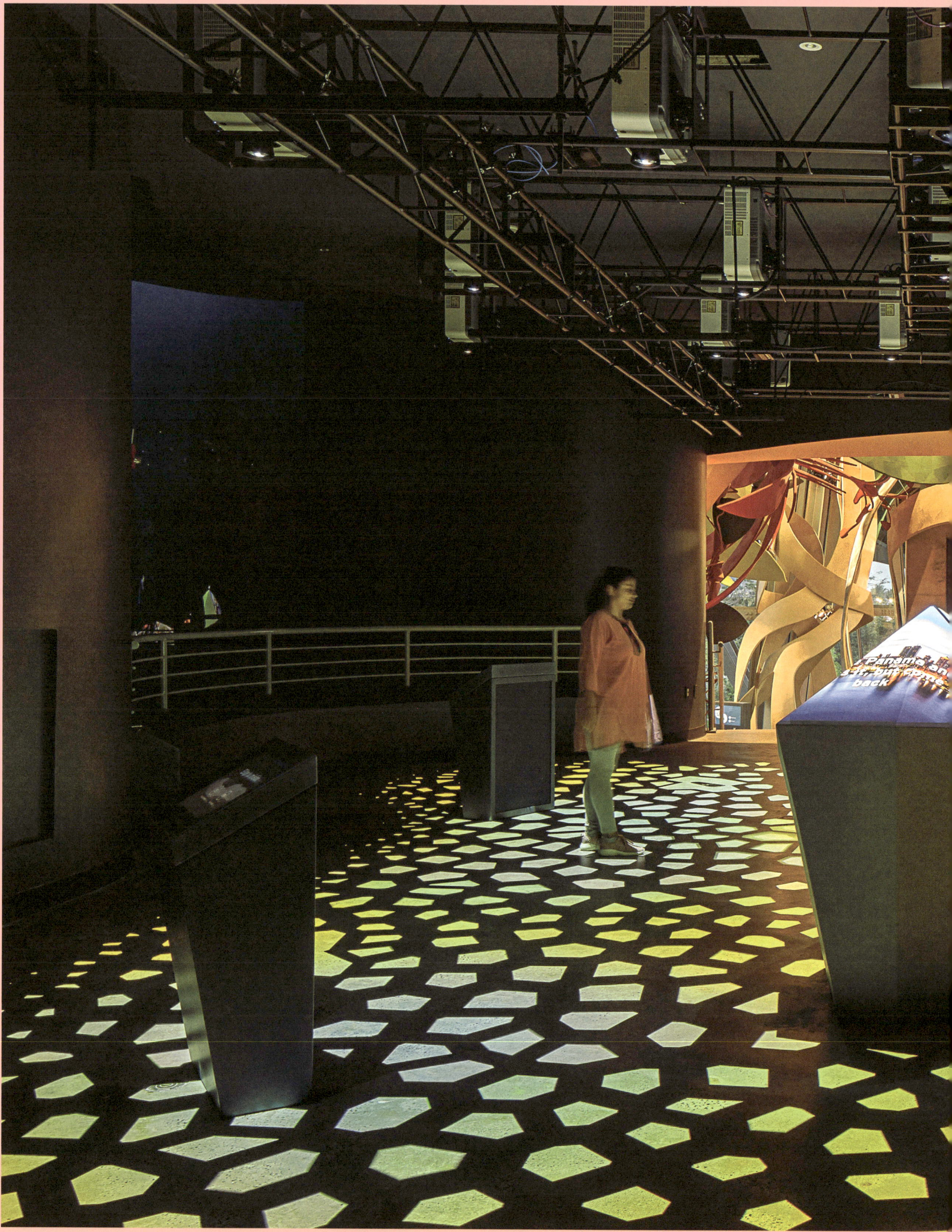

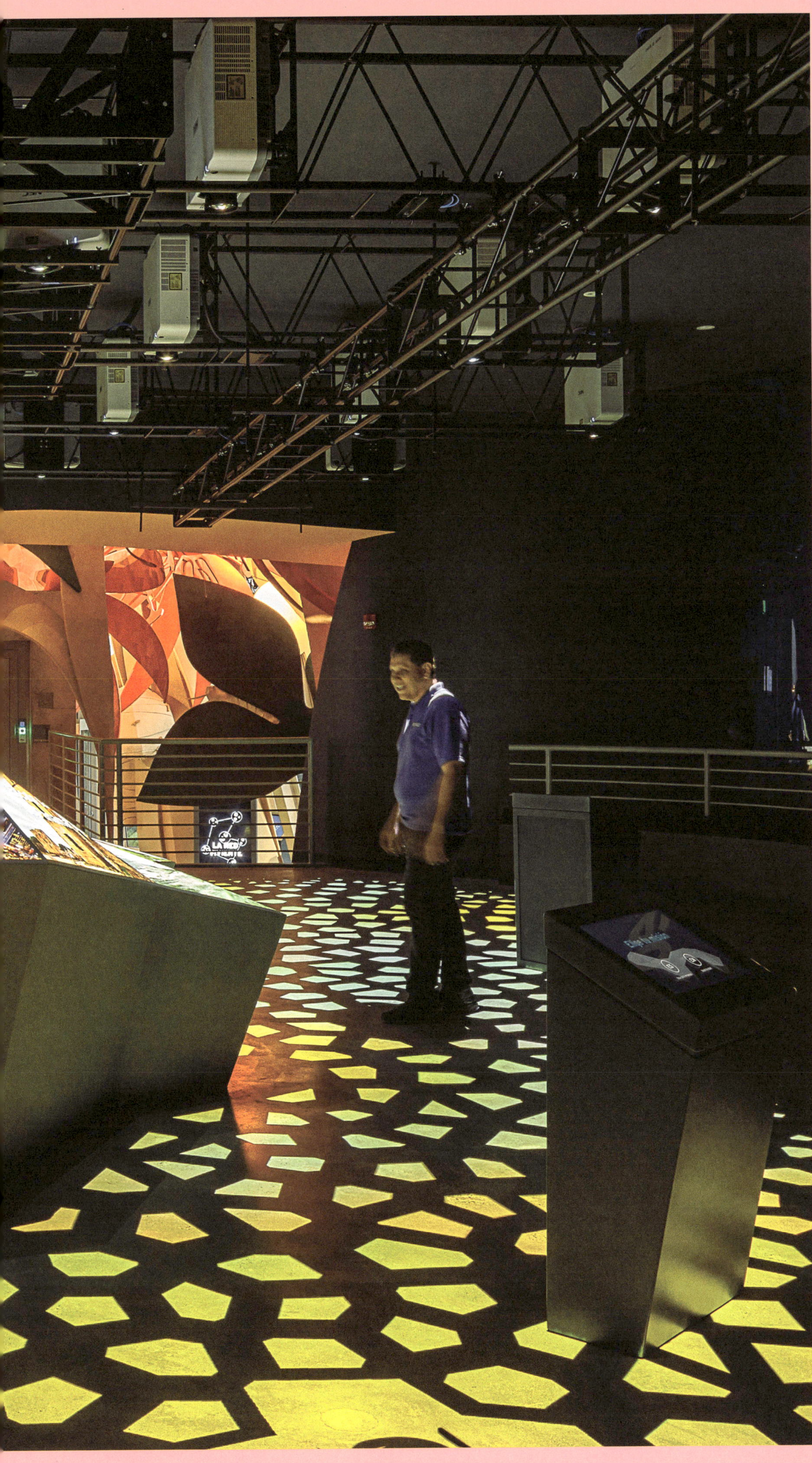

MUSEUMS WITH SIMILAR MEASURES

Instituto Inhotim

BRUMADINHO, MINAS GERAIS, BRAZIL

It maintains a protected area for the conservation of biodiversity.

Real Jardín Botánico

Madrid, Spain

The Royal Botanical Garden is a living museum in the center of Madrid, full of biodiversity, with more than 5,500 species from around the world, as well as a research center and historical archive.

Detail of *Mutisia clematis*, drawing belonging to the scientific collection Mutis. Historical Archive RJB-CSIC. Real Jardín Botánico, Madrid, Spain.

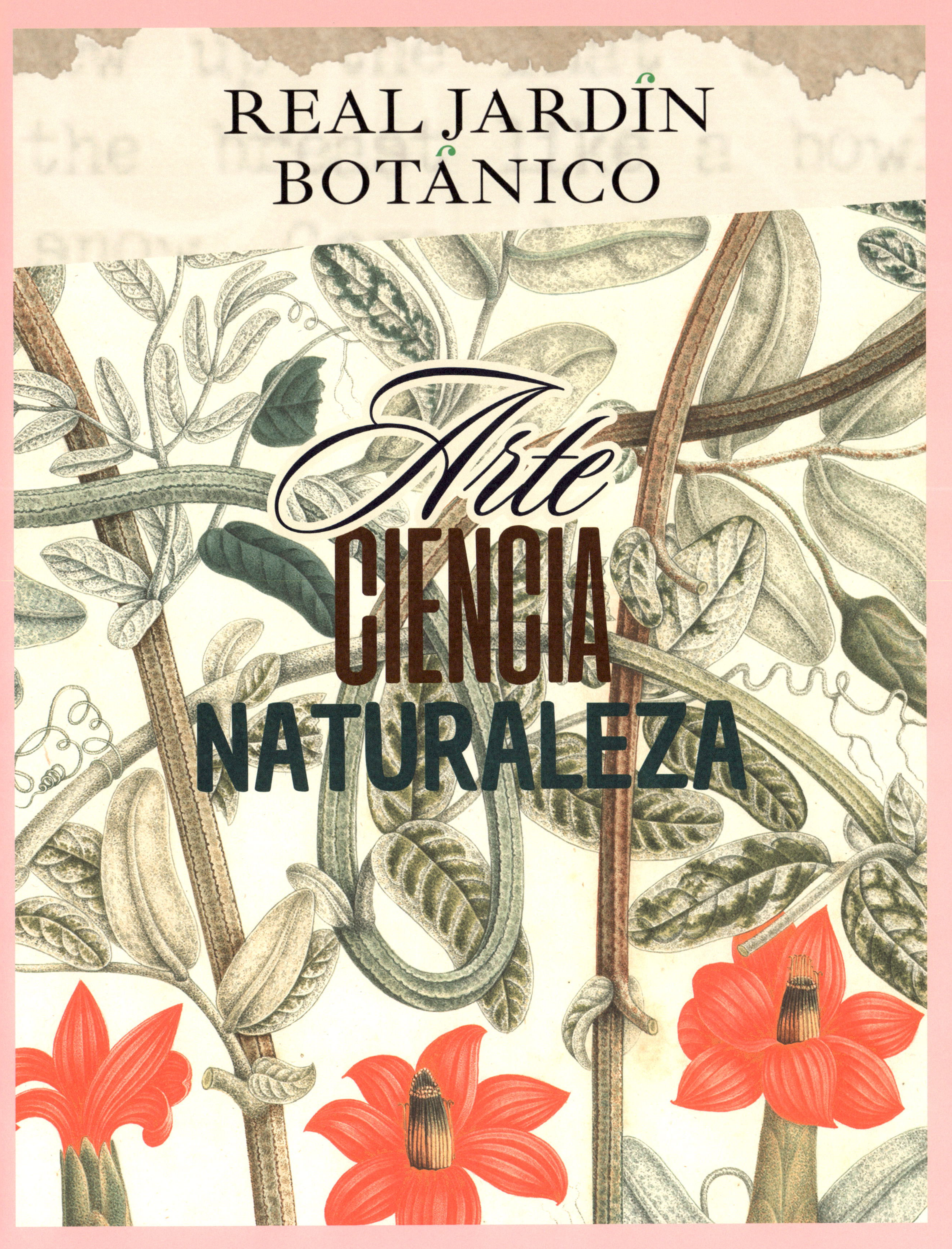
REAL JARDÍN
BOTÁNICO
Arte
CIENCIA
NATURALEZA

15 ISLANDS OF URBAN BIODIVERSITY

PROTECTION AND PROMOTION OF BIODIVERSITY SDG 11 / 13 / 15

Urban environments often prove challenging for all kinds of fauna, including pollinating insects, as traditional city layouts can lead to habitat loss and declining populations. Biodiversity islands help in the ecological restoration of green spaces, promoting the presence of fauna that are part of trophic chains and contribute to the biological control of other species. These islands are typically enhanced with native vegetation, leaf compost, decomposing wood, insect hotels, ponds, and more to support the existence of food, refuge, and nesting areas.

The Natural History Museum's Urban Biodiversity Island in London, nestled in the city center, has converted more than two hectares of its surrounding land into a freely accessible green space and biodiversity hub, incorporating grasslands, scrub, heathland, aquatic habitats, reedbeds, and hedgerows characteristic of the UK.

Natural History Museum

FOCUS
Natural History

LOCATION
Urban. London, United Kingdom

ANNUAL VISITORS
5,300,000

CONSTRUCTION
Opened in 1881.
Current remodel by Walter Lilly, J&L Gibbons, Fielden Fowles and Mace Group

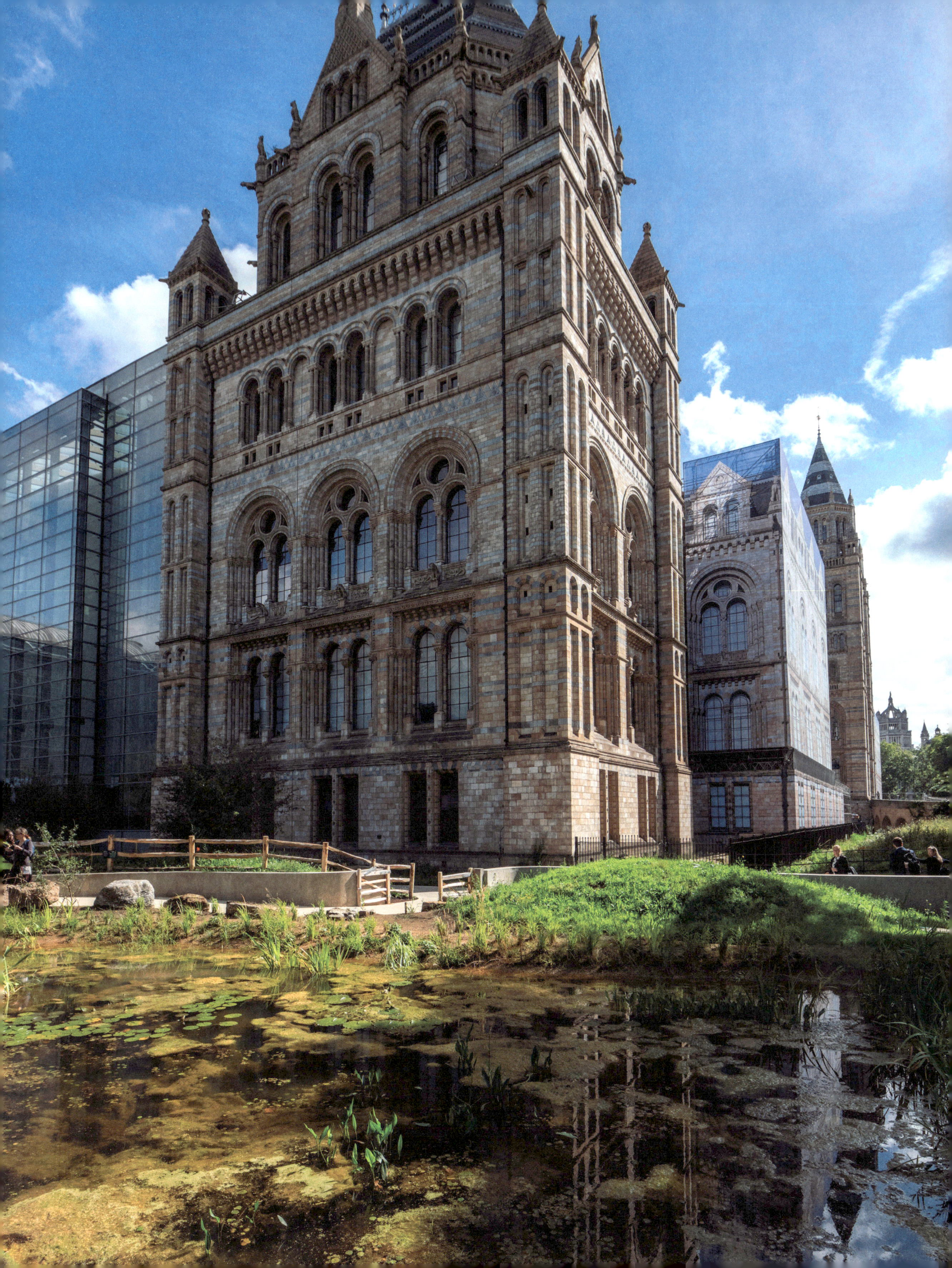

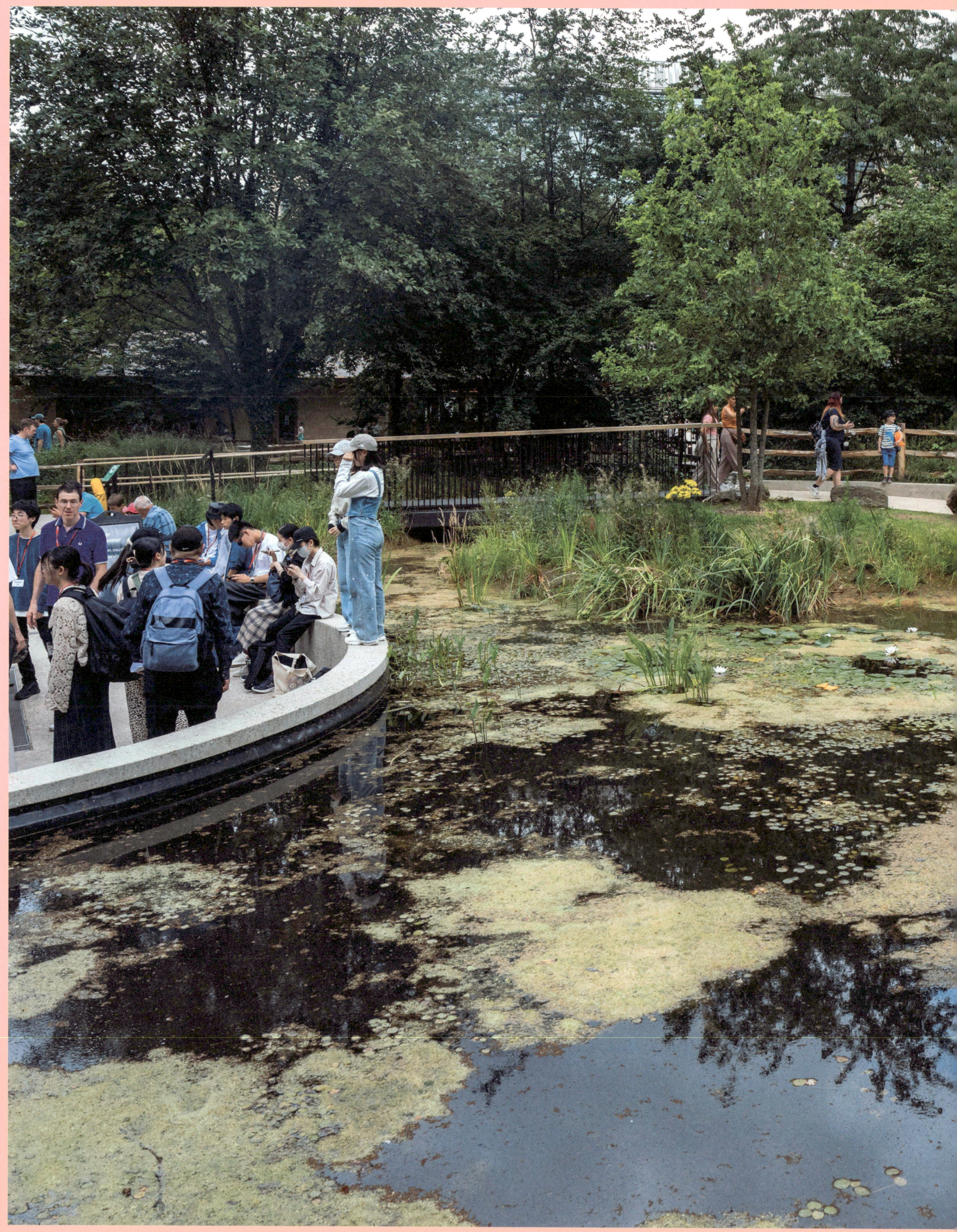

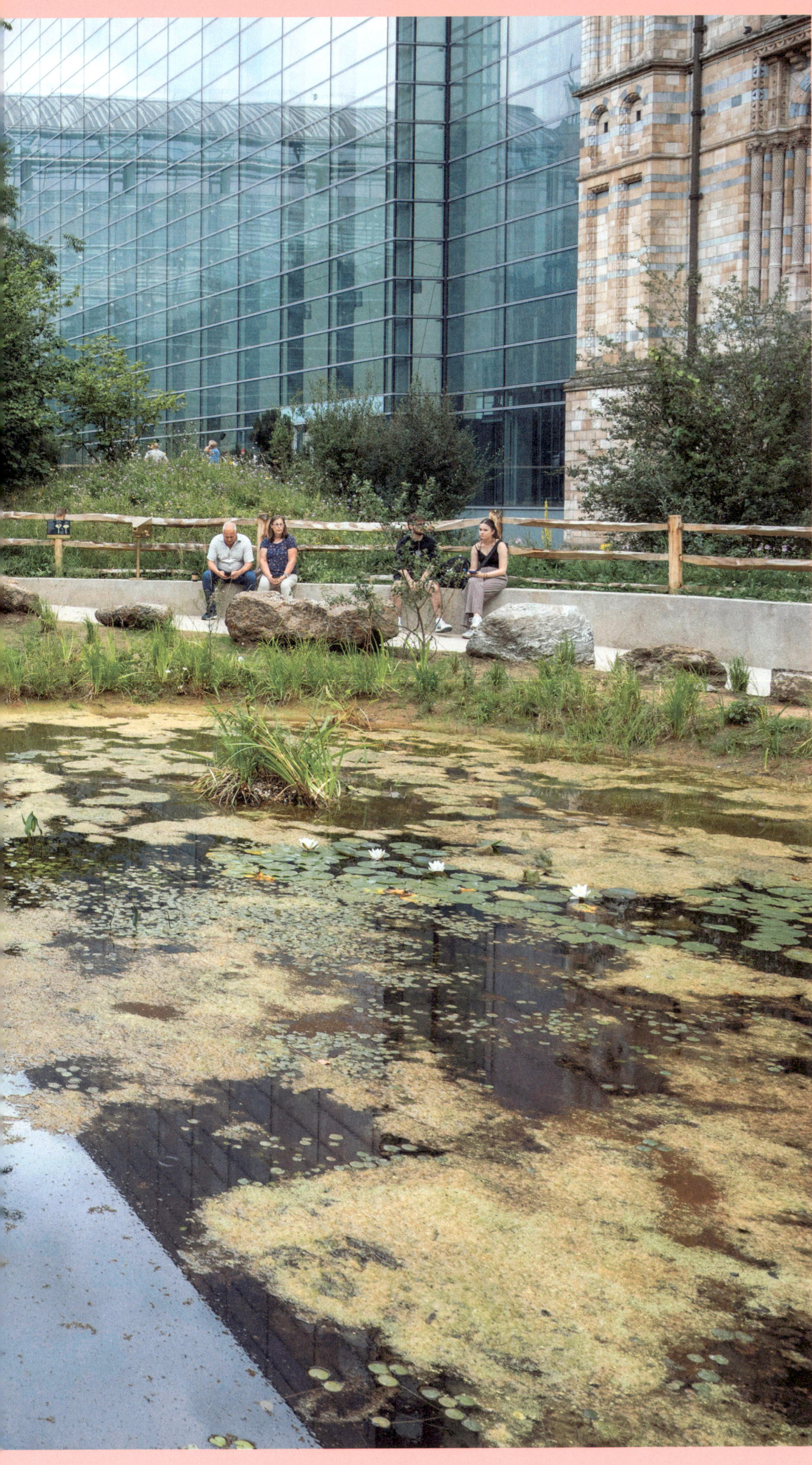

MUSEUMS WITH SIMILAR MEASURES

Horniman Museum & Gardens

LONDON, UNITED KINGDOM

The museum's gardens and green areas have been designed as a wildlife refuge.

Rijksmuseum

AMSTERDAM,
THE NETHERLANDS

It has become an urban biodiversity island thanks to the transformation of part of its land into green space.

Museo de América
Madrid, Spain

Since 2007, the Museum of America in Madrid has hosted a peregrine falcon nest in its tower, thanks to the nesting boxes installed by SEO/Birdlife. Additionally, cameras have been installed, allowing the public to follow the falcons' progress live via the museum's website.

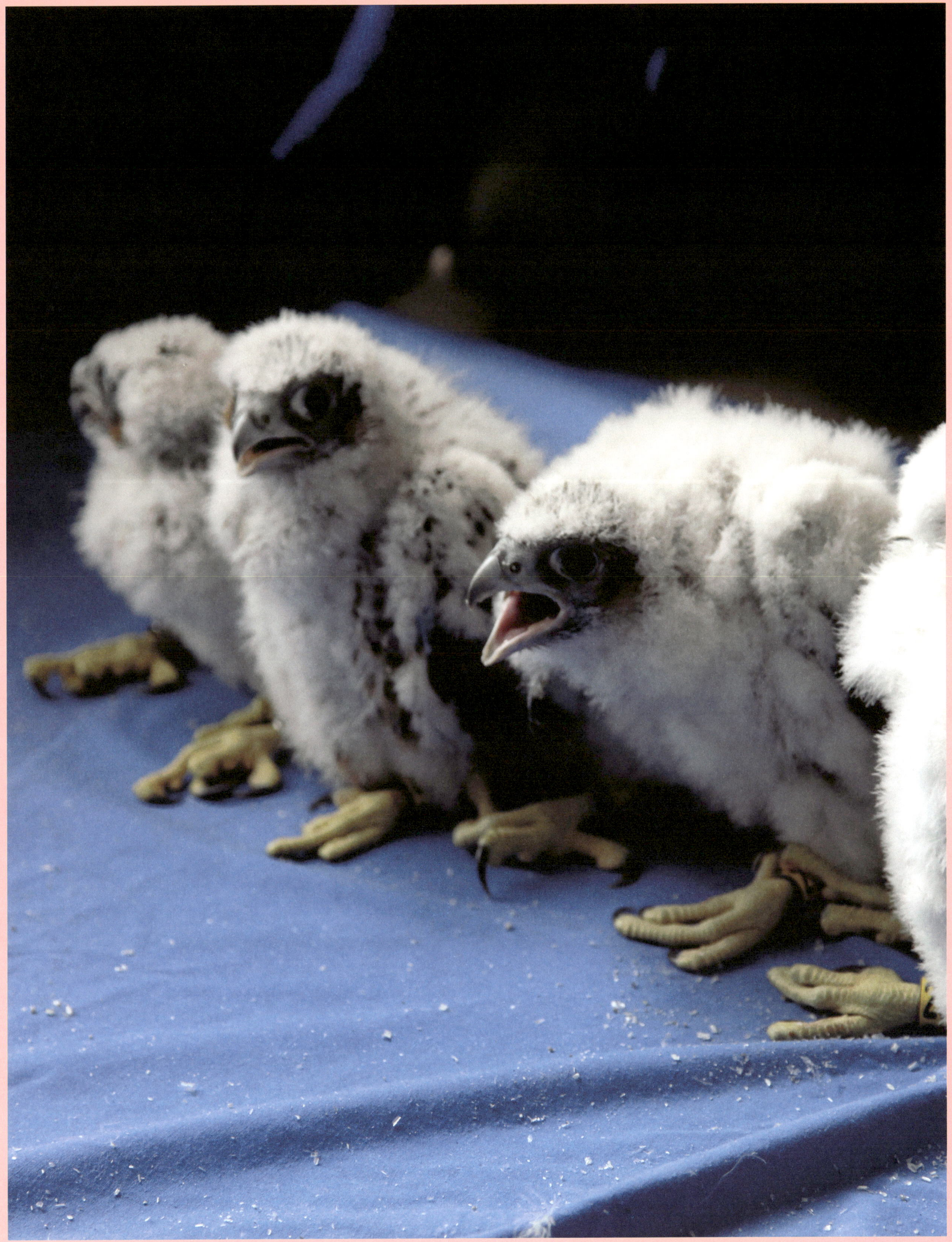

16 CIRCULARITY OF TEMPORARY EXHIBITIONS

CIRCULAR EXHIBITION DESIGN SDG 12

The circular exhibition design aims to establish a sustainable cycle of reduction, reuse, and recycling of materials to minimize waste. This approach is crucial in the design of temporary exhibitions to lessen the environmental impact due to their ephemeral nature.

The Musée du quai Branly - Jacques Chirac consistently uses the same scenographic team for successive exhibitions, enabling nearly all exhibition furniture to be reused.

Furthermore, the museum advocates for a circular economy by cataloguing objects, reusing shipping materials, and using specialized software to manage these resources. Since 2020, it has collaborated with La Réserve des Arts, a non-profit that supports the development of a circular and inclusive economy in the cultural sector.

Musée du Quai Branly - Jacques Chirac

FOCUS
Arts and Civilizations

CONSTRUCTION
2006

LOCATION
Urban. Paris, France

SIZE
5,300 m² exhibition

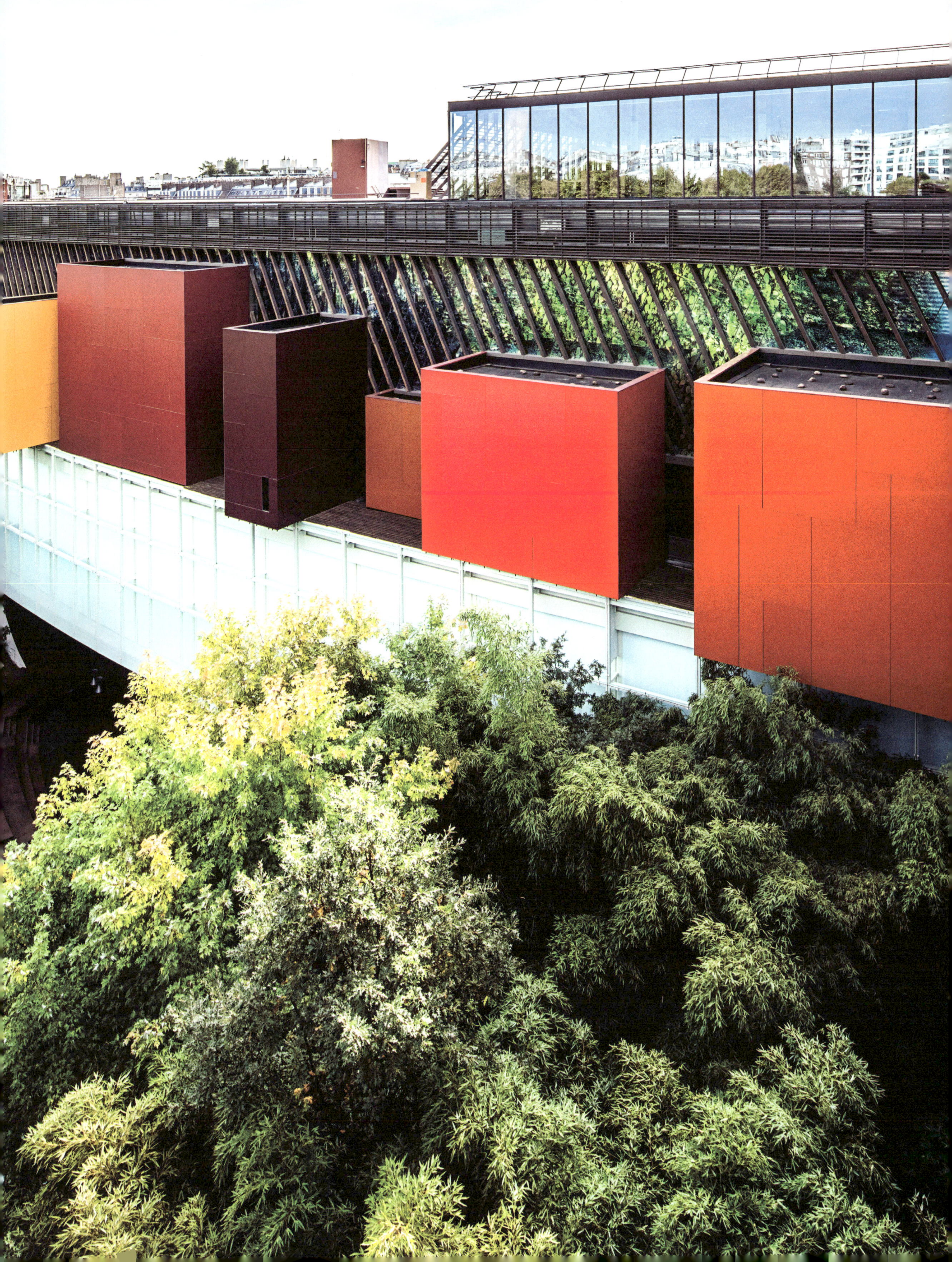

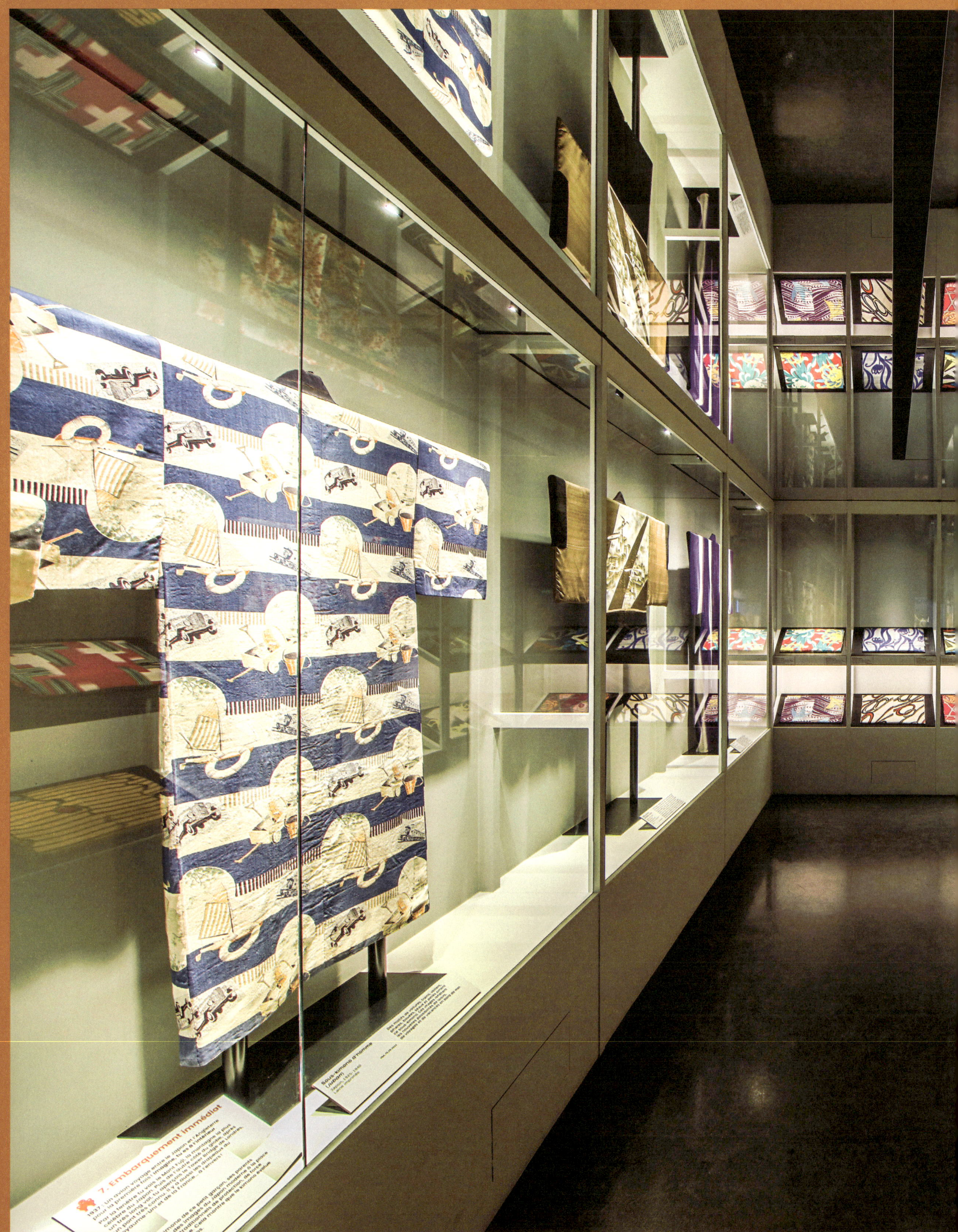
7. Embarquement immédiat
1937 : un avion voyage entre le Japon et l'Angleterre
pour la première fois ! Imagine, tu es à l'intérieur
Par la fenêtre tu vois le Mont Fuji, la montagne la plus
célèbre du Japon. Puis de l'autre côté du globe, après
un très long vol, tu aperçois le Tower Bridge de Londres,
un pont très connu. Il y a aussi les drapeaux du
Royaume-Uni et de la France... à l'envers !

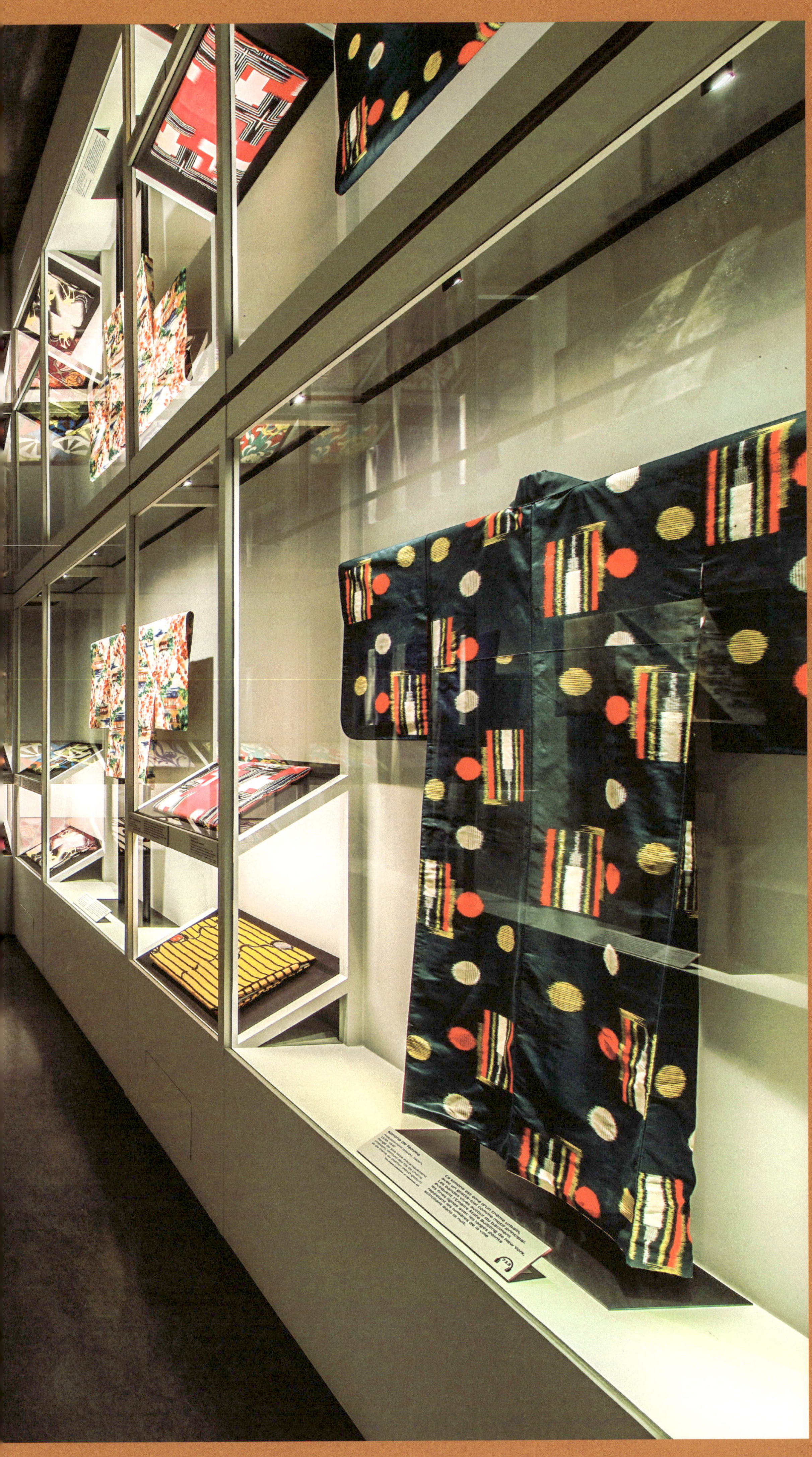

MUSEUMS WITH SIMILAR MEASURES

The Waste Museum

IBADAN, NIGERIA

Utilization of waste for the creation of facilities.

Busan Museum of Art

BUSAN, SOUTH KOREA

The *Sustainable Museum: Art and Environment* exhibition was designed to be completely reusable.

Network of CaixaForum Centers
Fundación "la Caixa", Spain

The Fundación "la Caixa" traveling exhibition program, designed with circularity and mobile format criteria, brings the best activities, exhibitions, and content to all of Spain and Portugal. The exhibitions are designed to allow for content changes throughout their lifespan. The duration of each exhibition line is estimated to be between five and ten years, with an average of about eight or nine installations per year, resulting in significant optimization of resources.

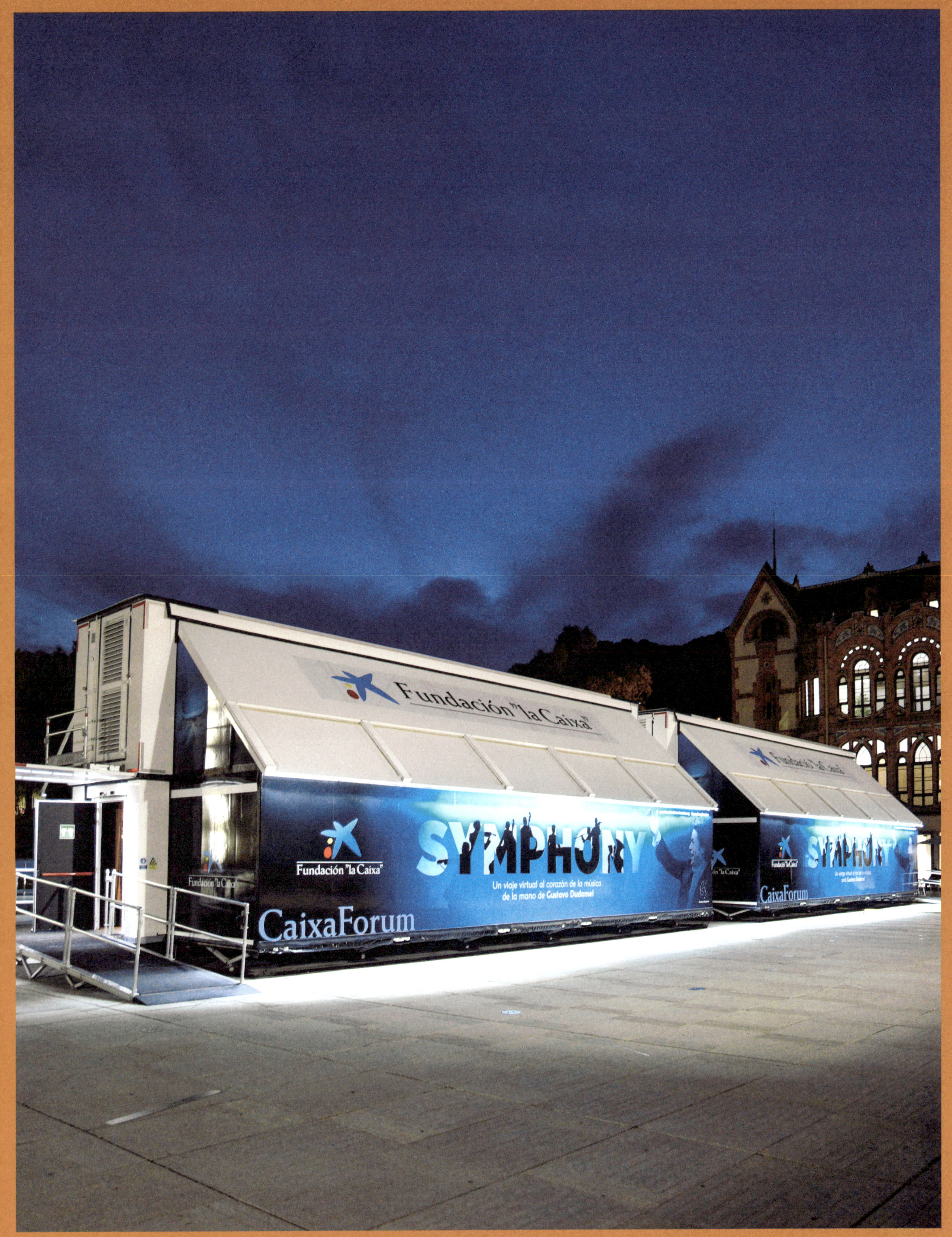
Fundación "la Caixa"
Fundación "la Caixa"
SYMPHONY
Un viaje virtual al corazón de la música
de la mano de Gustavo Dudamel
CaixaForum

17 DESIGN OF REUSABLE DISPLAY PANELS

CIRCULAR EXHIBITION DESIGN   SDG 12

Designing and using modular and reusable exhibition panels provides a sustainable alternative to traditional gallery and wall constructions, which often involve carpentry, generate more waste, and are less durable. These systems allow for the flexible manipulation of spaces to create customized exhibition routes across different shows.

For the *Net Zero* exhibition, the use of large-scale 3D printing to make the concrete walls that the show required reduced waste production by 60% in comparison to conventional machining. The result is modular, transportable, and reusable structures that are also aesthetically pleasing and adaptable to various exhibition spaces and functions.

Net Zero exhibition. ACCIONA, 2023 King Abdulaziz Center for World Culture (Ithra)

FOCUS
Arts and Civilizations

CONSTRUCTION
2018

LOCATION
Urban. Dhahran, Saudi Arabia

ANNUAL VISITORS
500,000

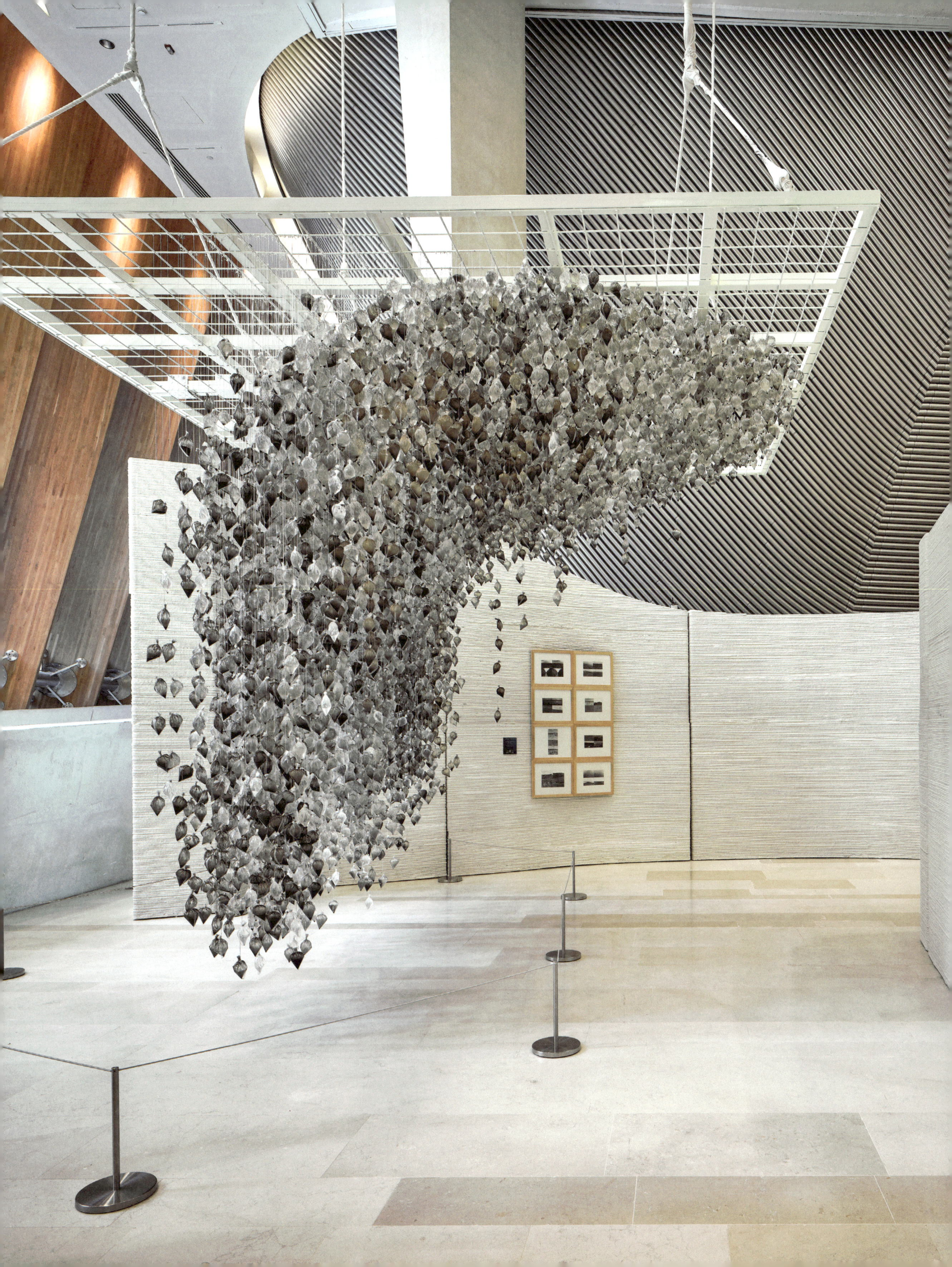

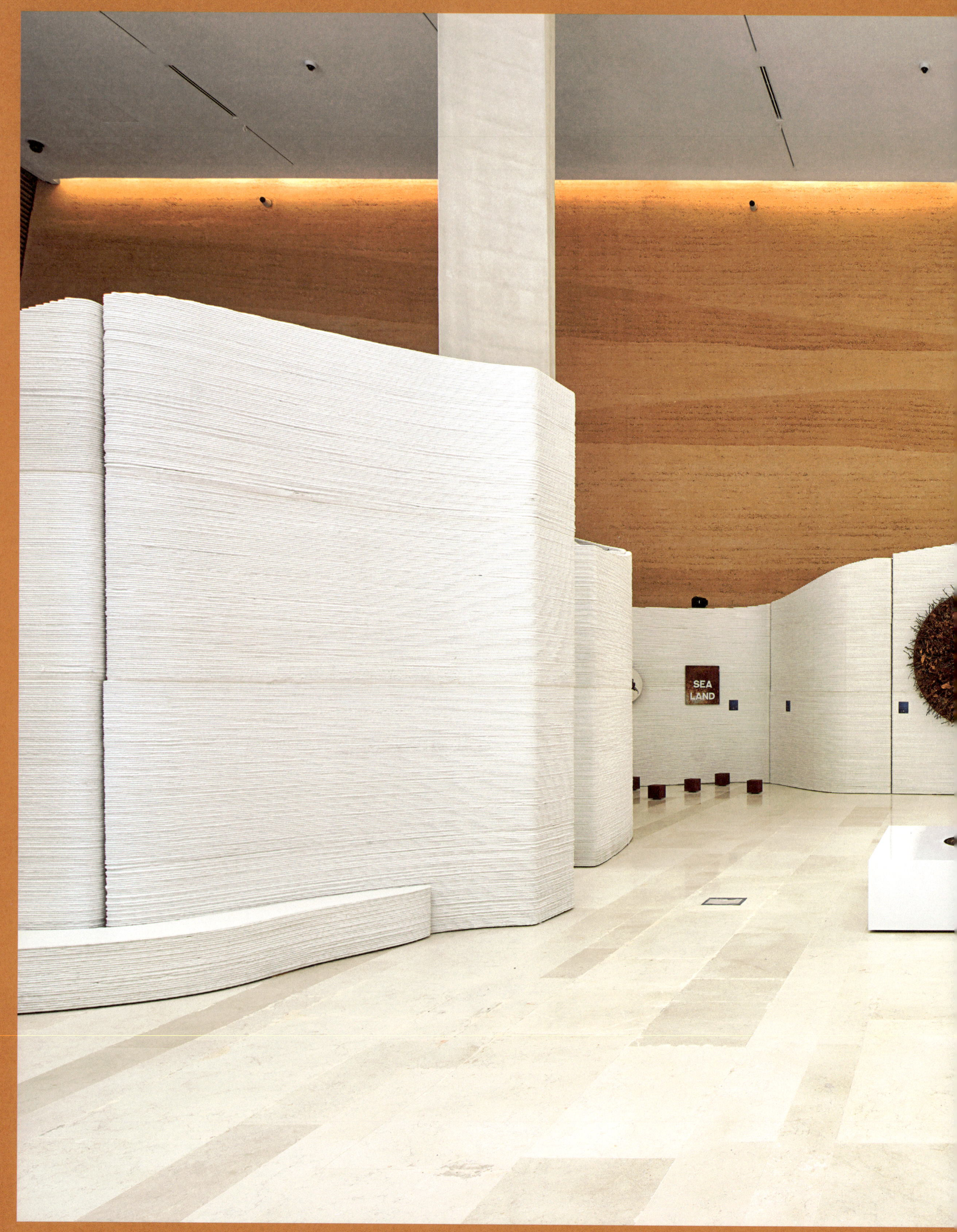
SEA
LAND

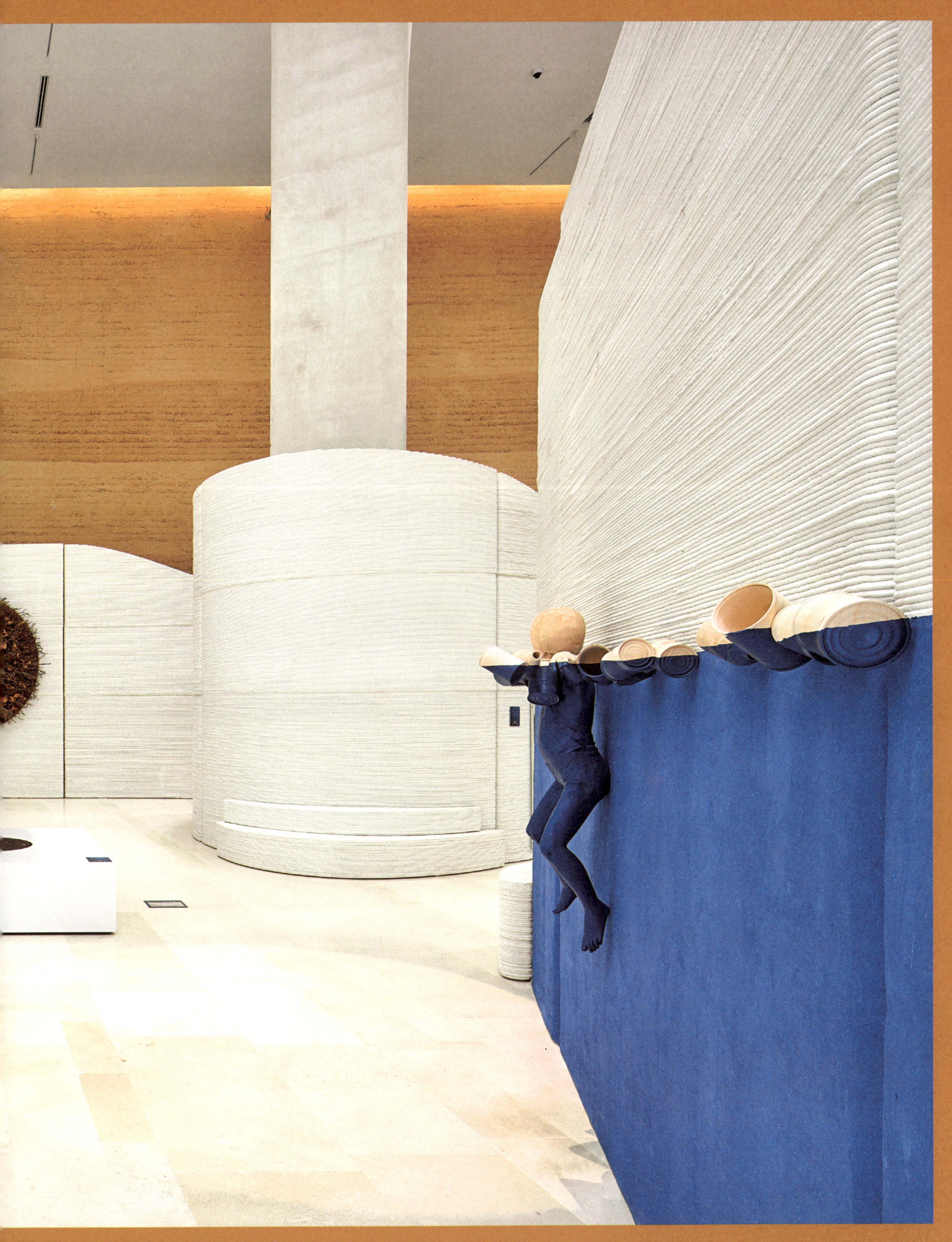

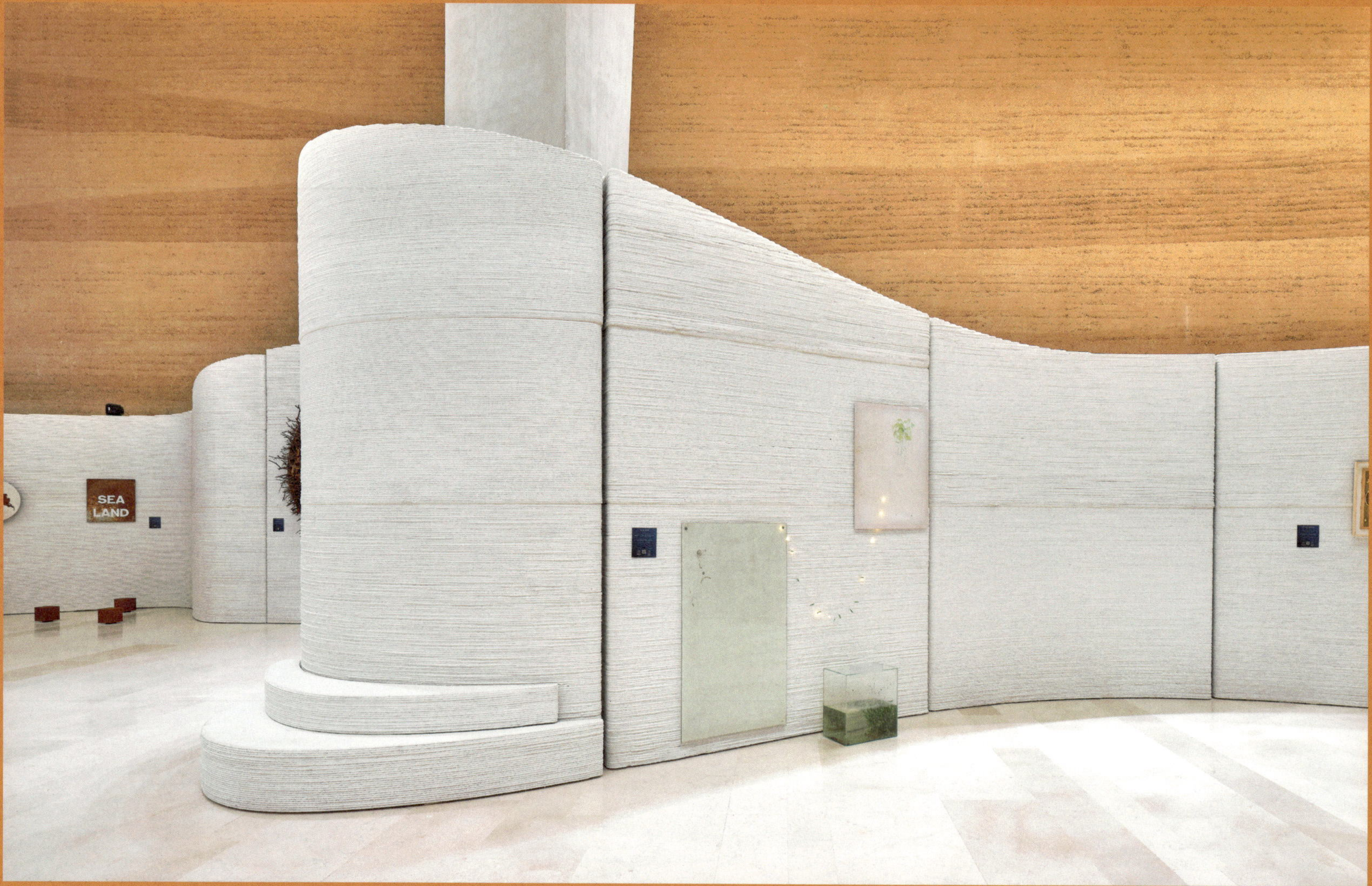

SEA
LAND

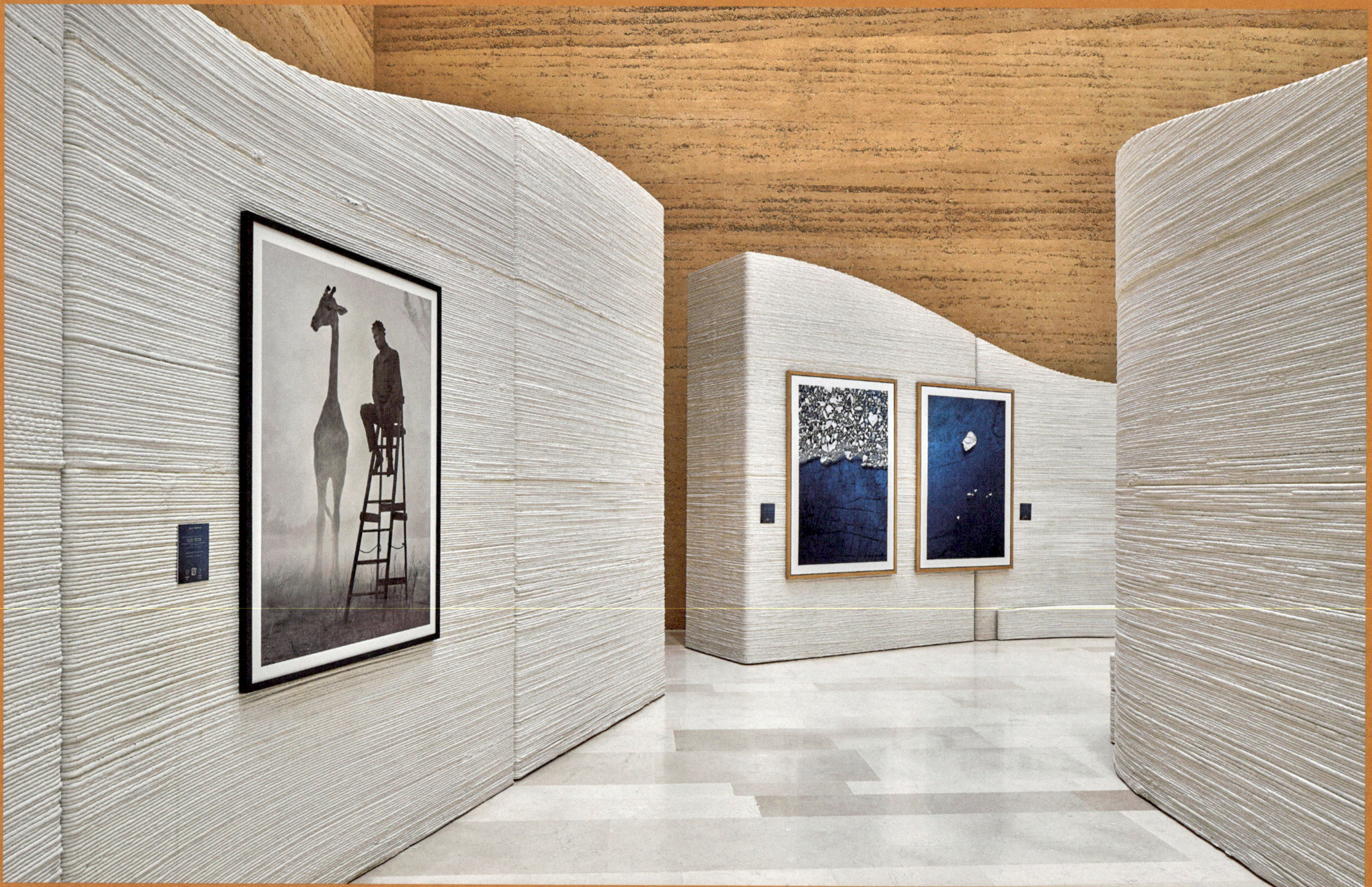

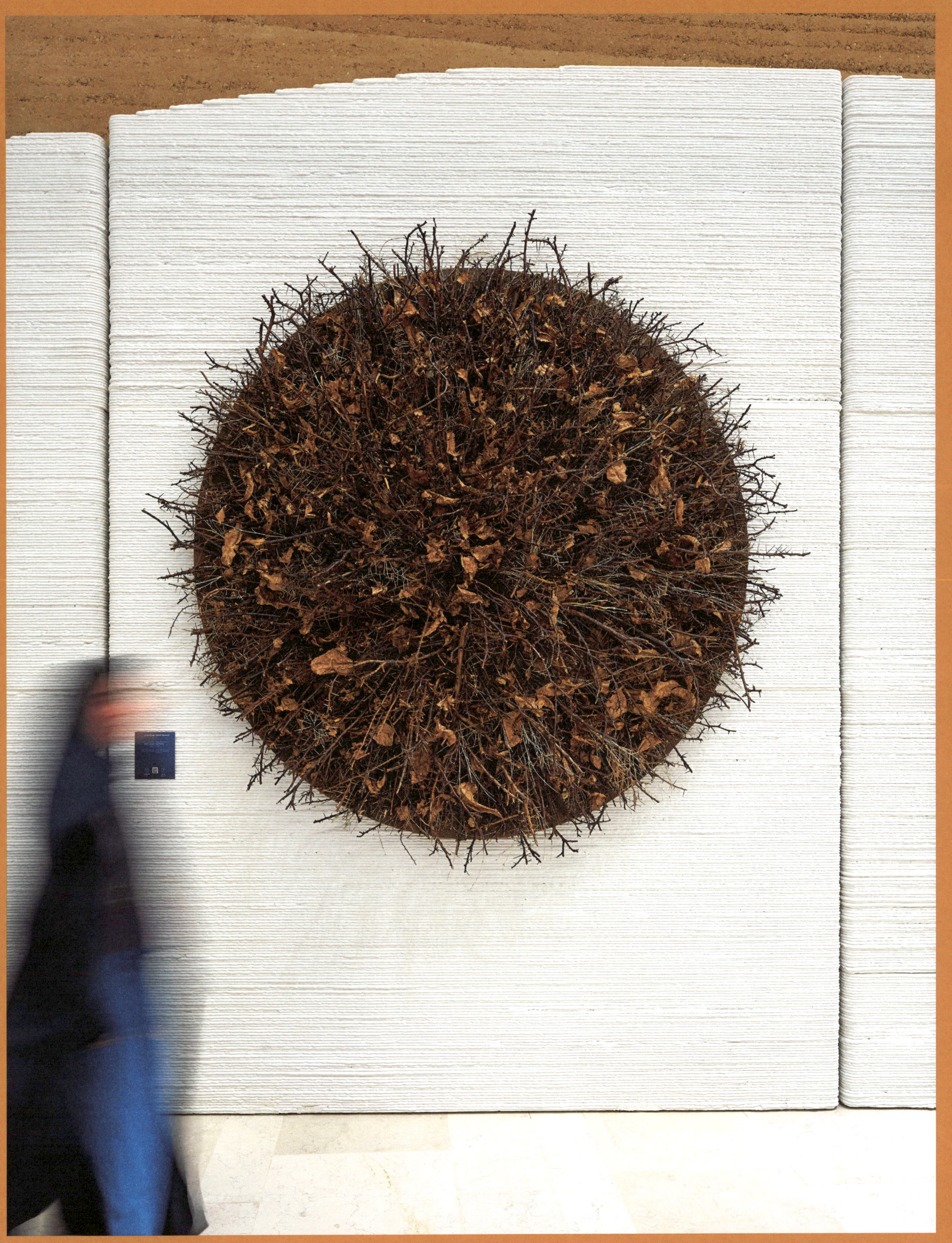

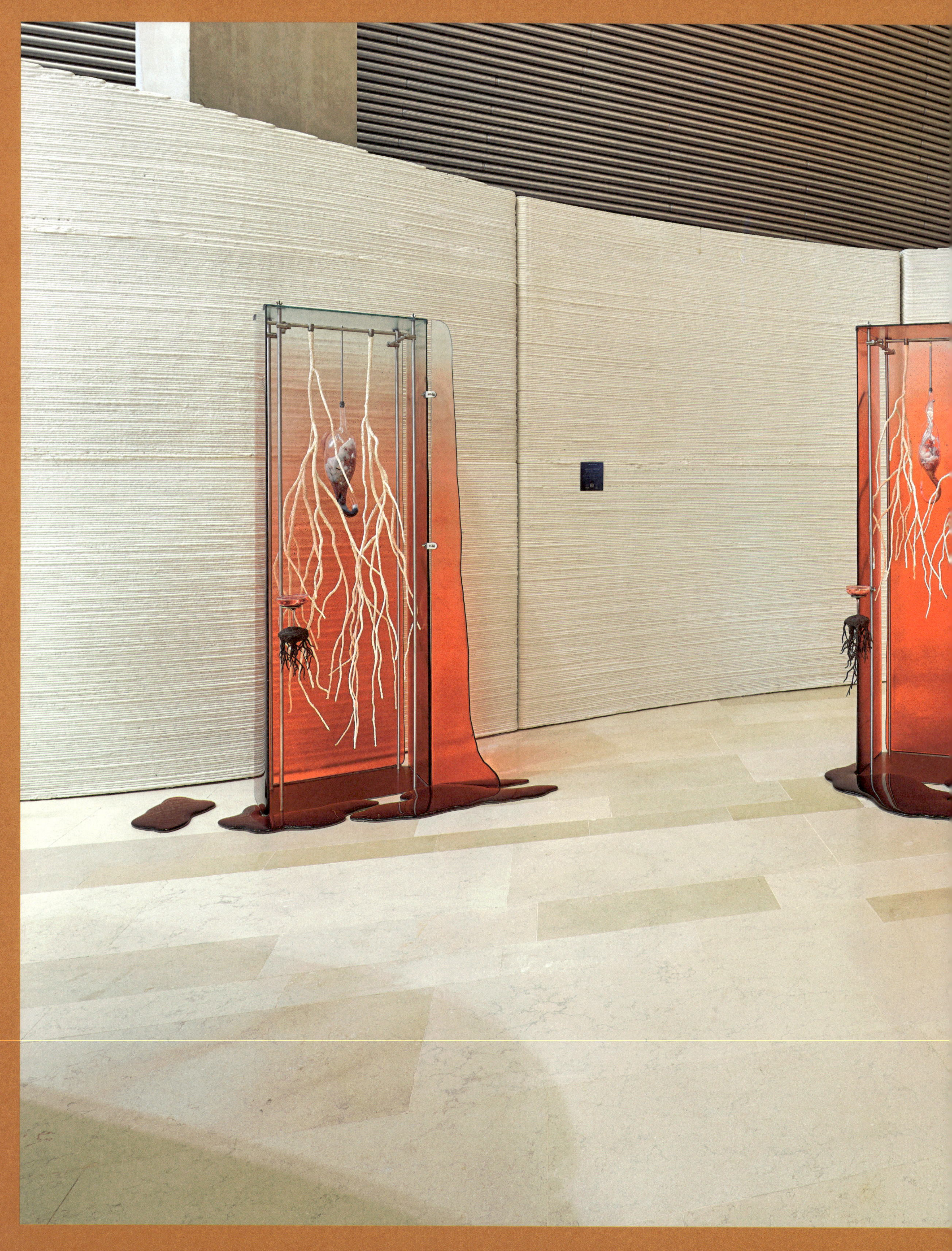

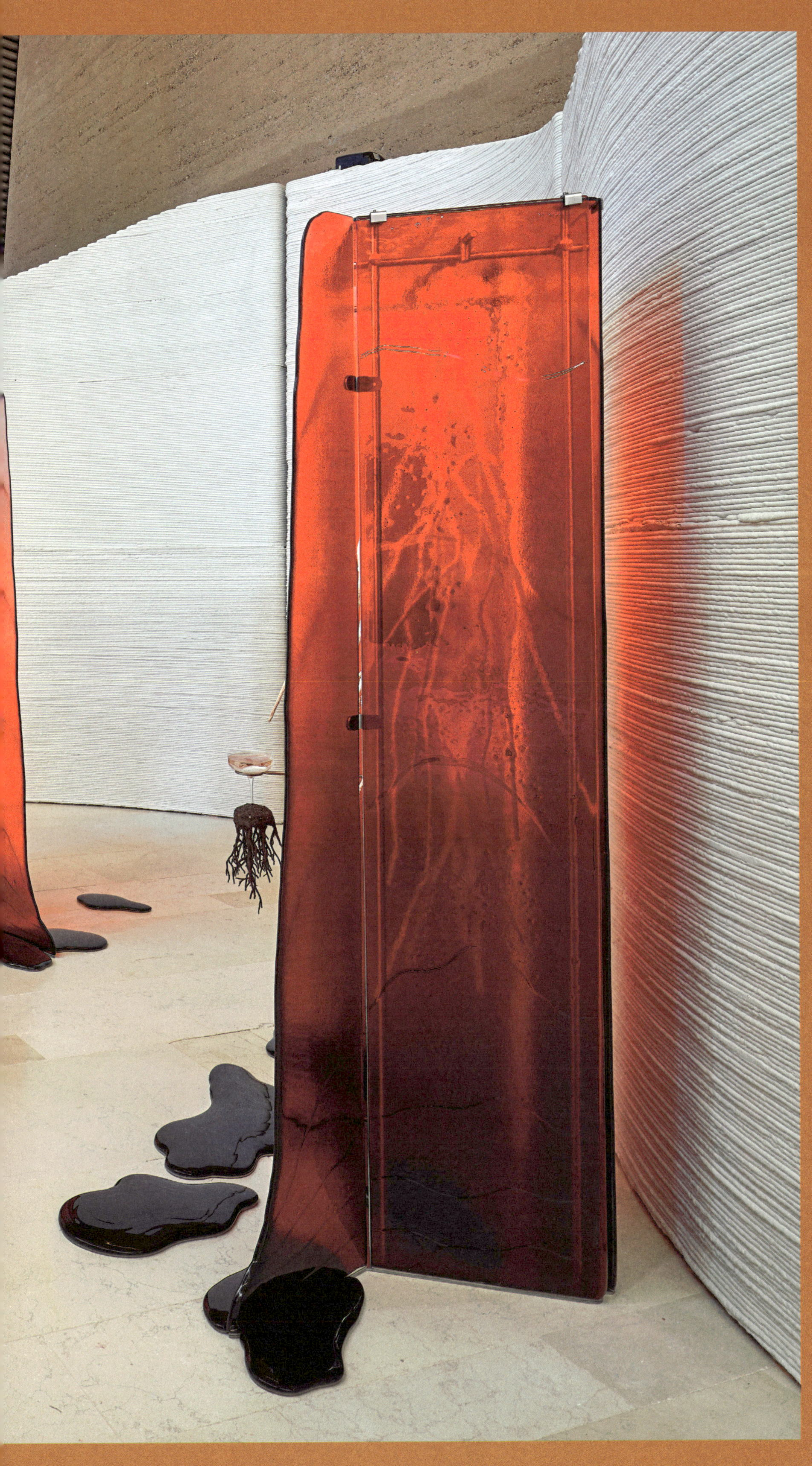

MUSEUMS WITH SIMILAR MEASURES

Fundación Telefónica. *Nikola Tesla* exhibition

MADRID, SPAIN

Comprehensive exhibition approach with a methodology that guarantees the reduction of environmental impact.

Museum Ludwig

COLOGNE, GERMANY

Green Modernism: The New View of Plants exhibition, a pilot on sustainable exhibition production.

“The *Net Zero* exhibition showcases the realities of our current environmental challenges and the hopeful visions of a better future through the work of contemporary artists.”

Candida Pestana

Curator of the *Net Zero* exhibition at the King Abdulaziz Center for World Culture (Ithra)

w e

ast

Creative design devised especially for this publication by Candida Pestana, aimed at underscoring that we are responsible for minimizing waste production.

18 ENVIRONMENTAL IMPACT ASSESSMENT MODELS

ENVIRONMENTAL IMPACT ASSESSMENT OF EXHIBITIONS SDG 11 / 12

From the design phase of an exhibition, incorporating tools to preemptively analyze potential environmental impacts—such as logistics and transport, material design and construction, communications, and energy usage—is crucial for minimizing them.

The Environmental Impact Toolkit, developed by the Design Museum of London, includes a guide for reducing the environmental impact of exhibition design and an impact model to analyze and mitigate significant contributions. The model records data to calculate the carbon footprint of exhibitions and aids decision-making during the design process. It allows the team to compare the environmental consequences of selecting different materials, for example.

Design Museum

FOCUS
Design

CONSTRUCTION
1989

LOCATION
Urban. London, United Kingdom

ANNUAL VISITORS
650,000

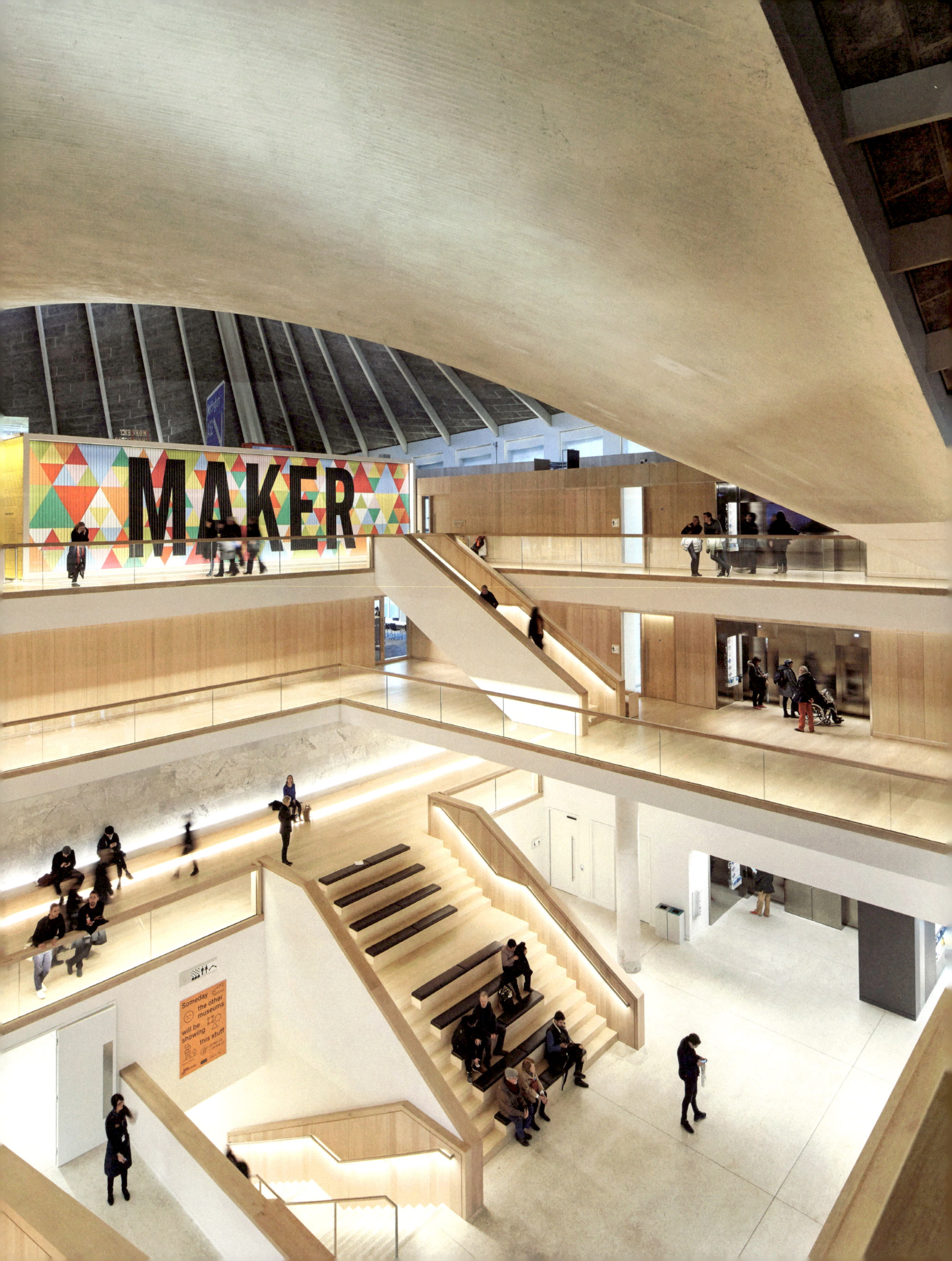
MAKER
Someday
the other museums
will be showing
this stuff

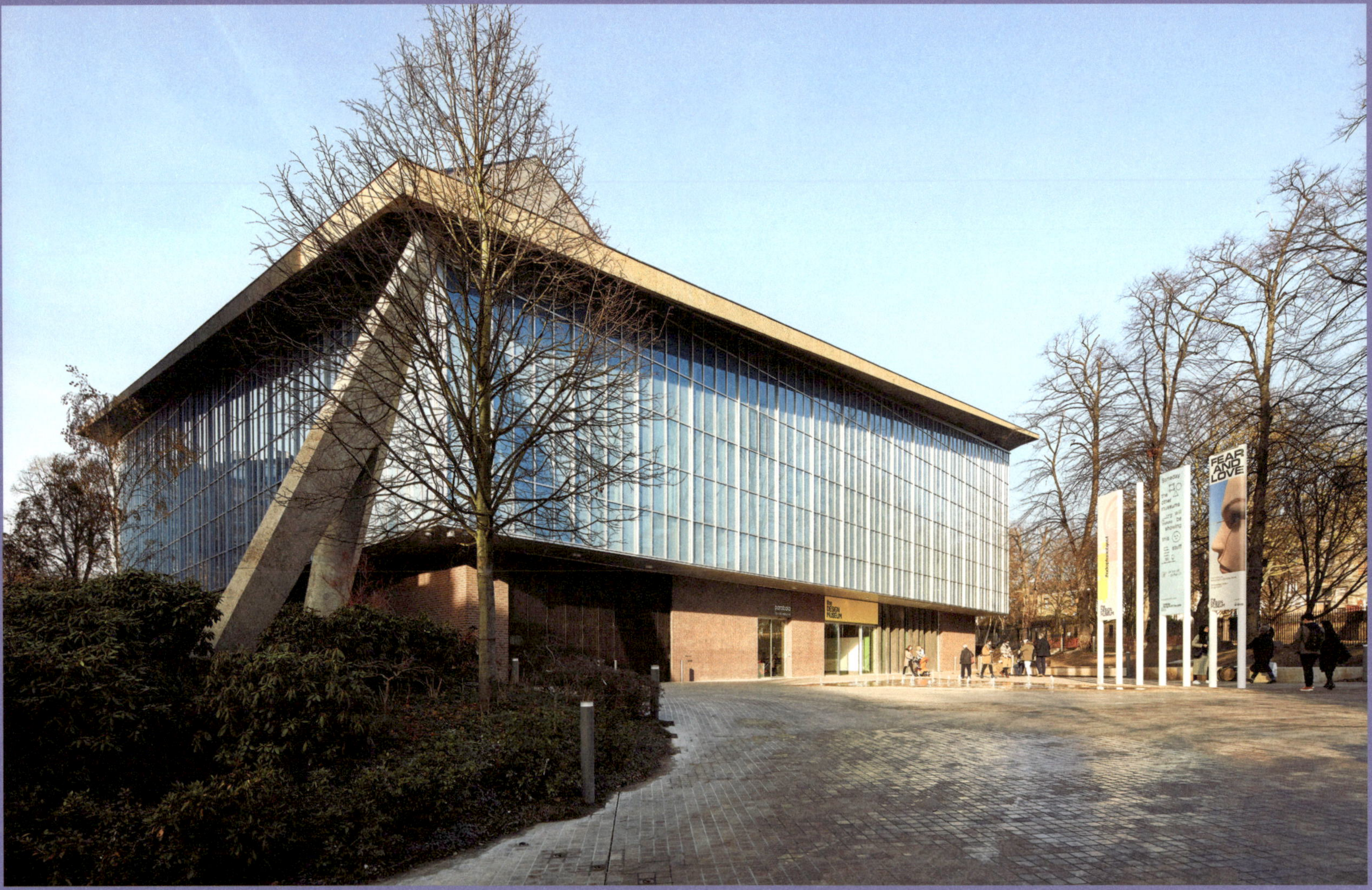

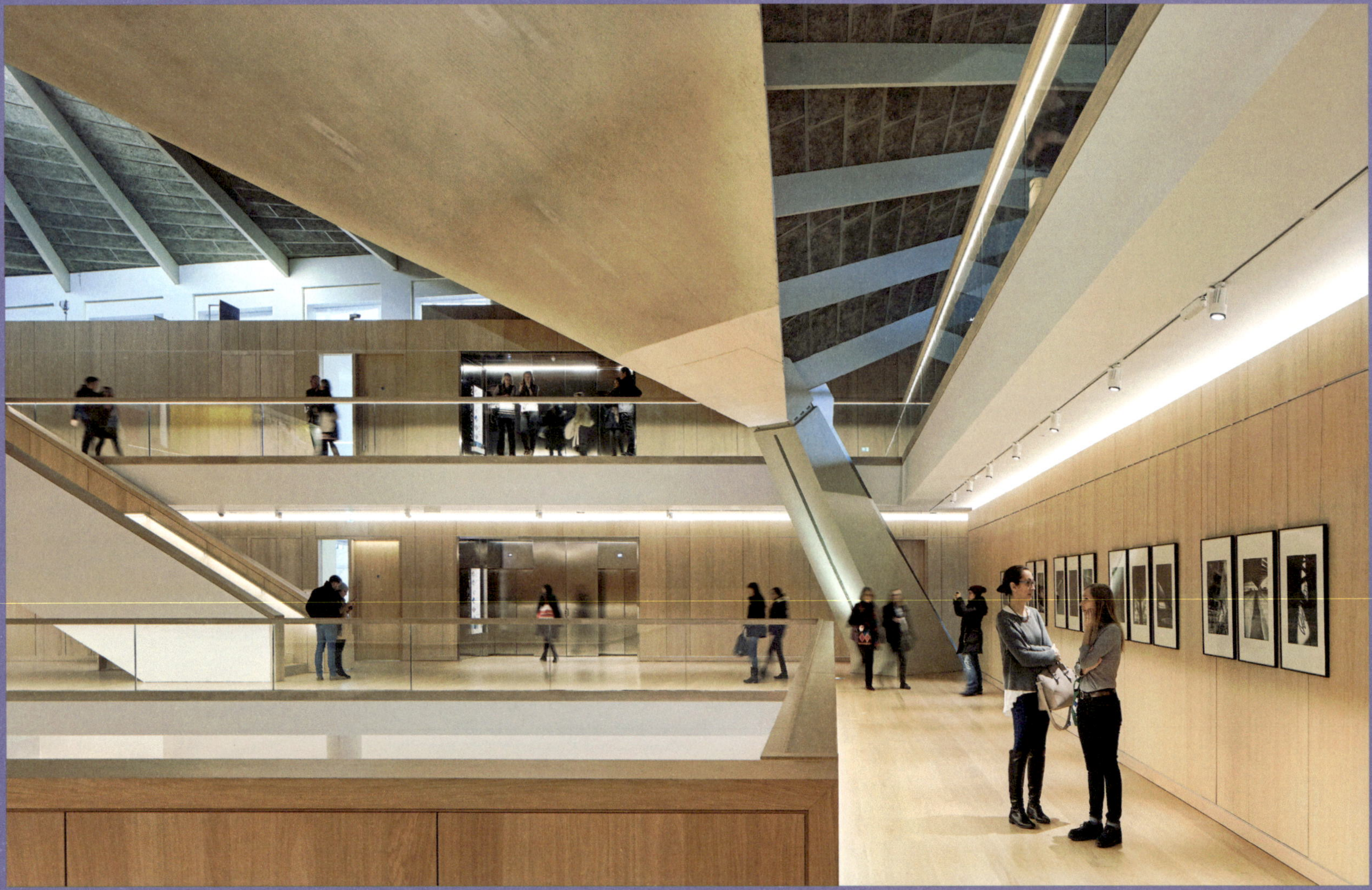

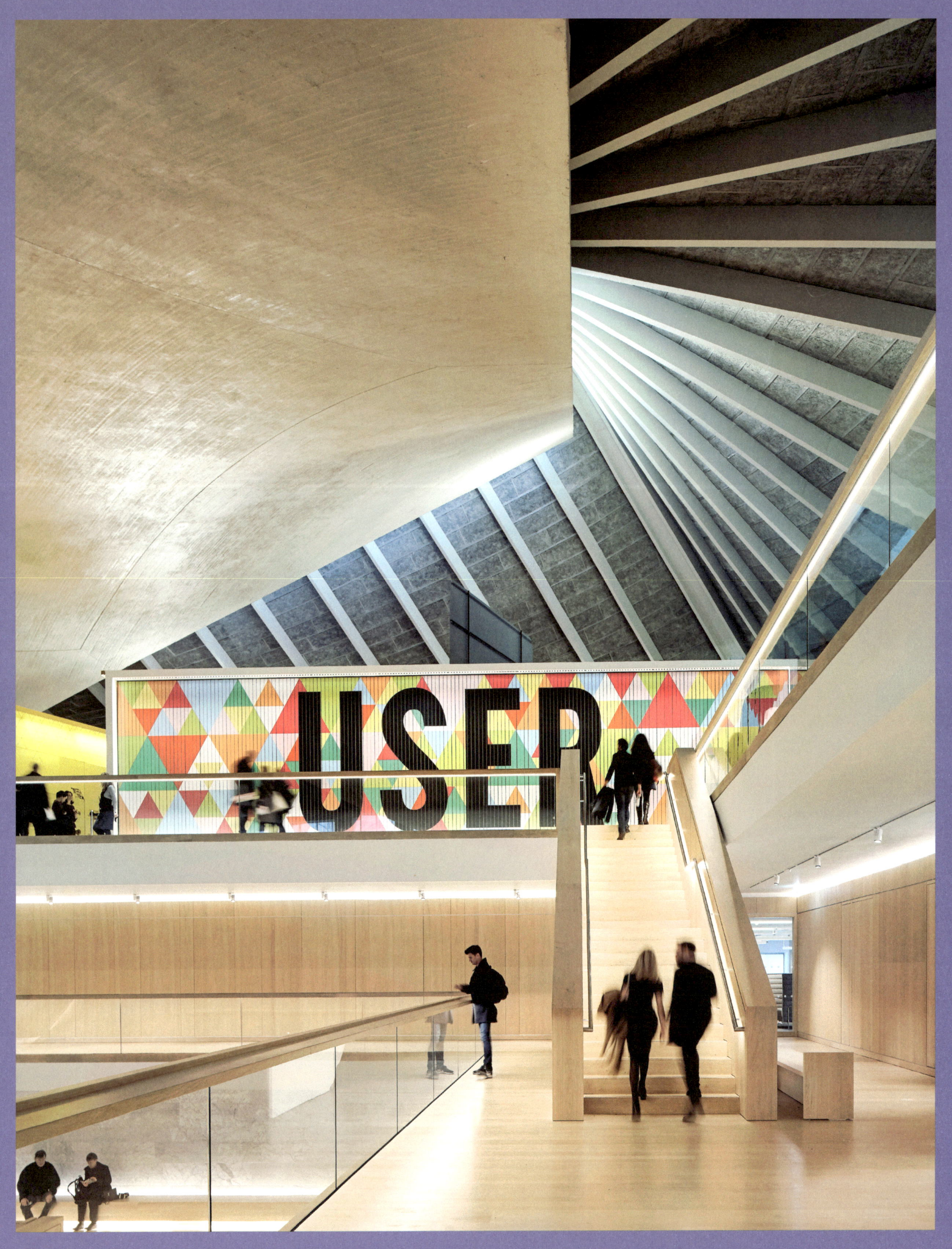
USER

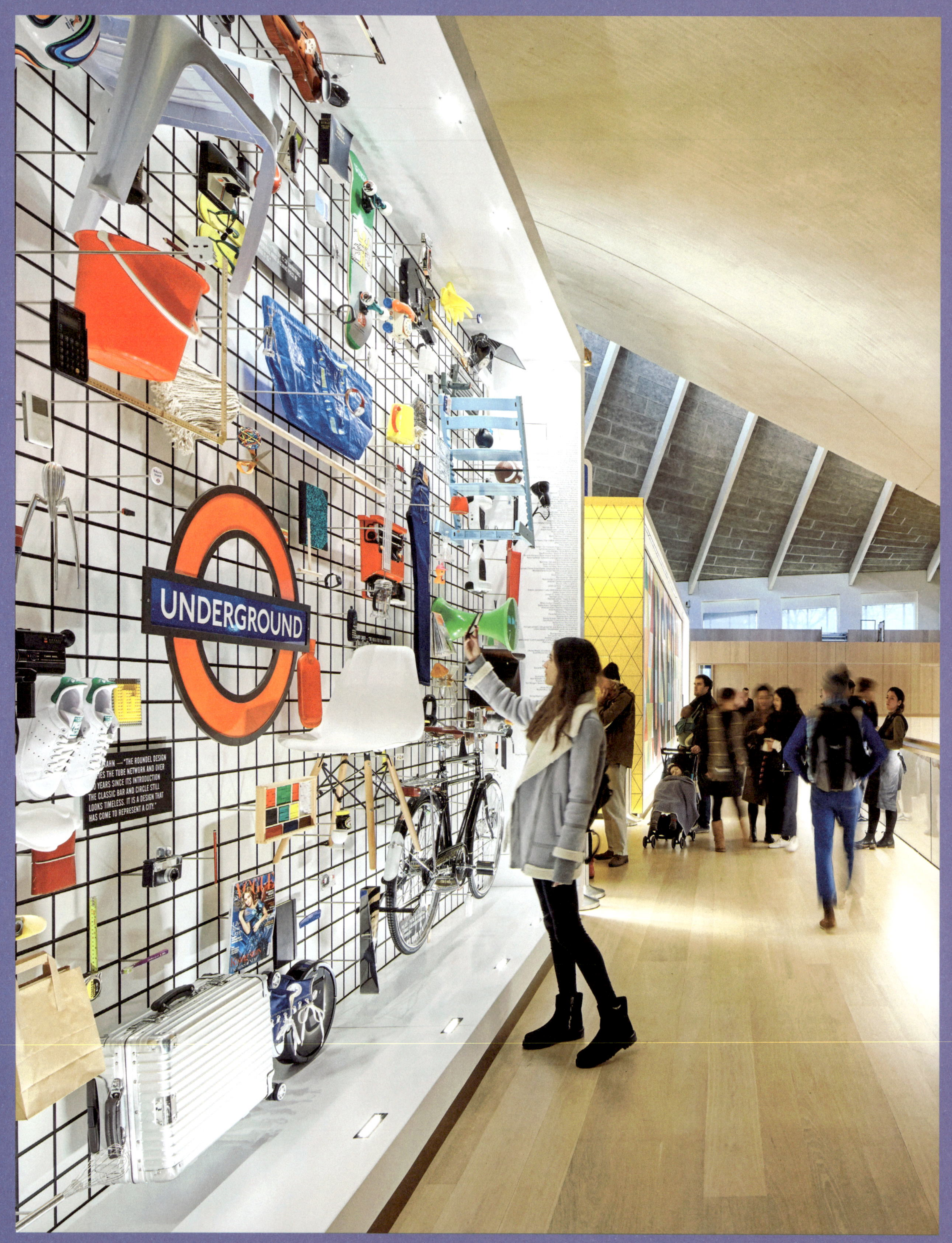
UNDERGROUND
"THE ROUNDEL DESIGN
THE TUBE NETWORK AND OVER
YEARS SINCE ITS INTRODUCTION
THE CLASSIC BAR AND CIRCLE STILL
LOOKS TIMELESS. IT IS A DESIGN THAT
HAS COME TO REPRESENT A CITY."

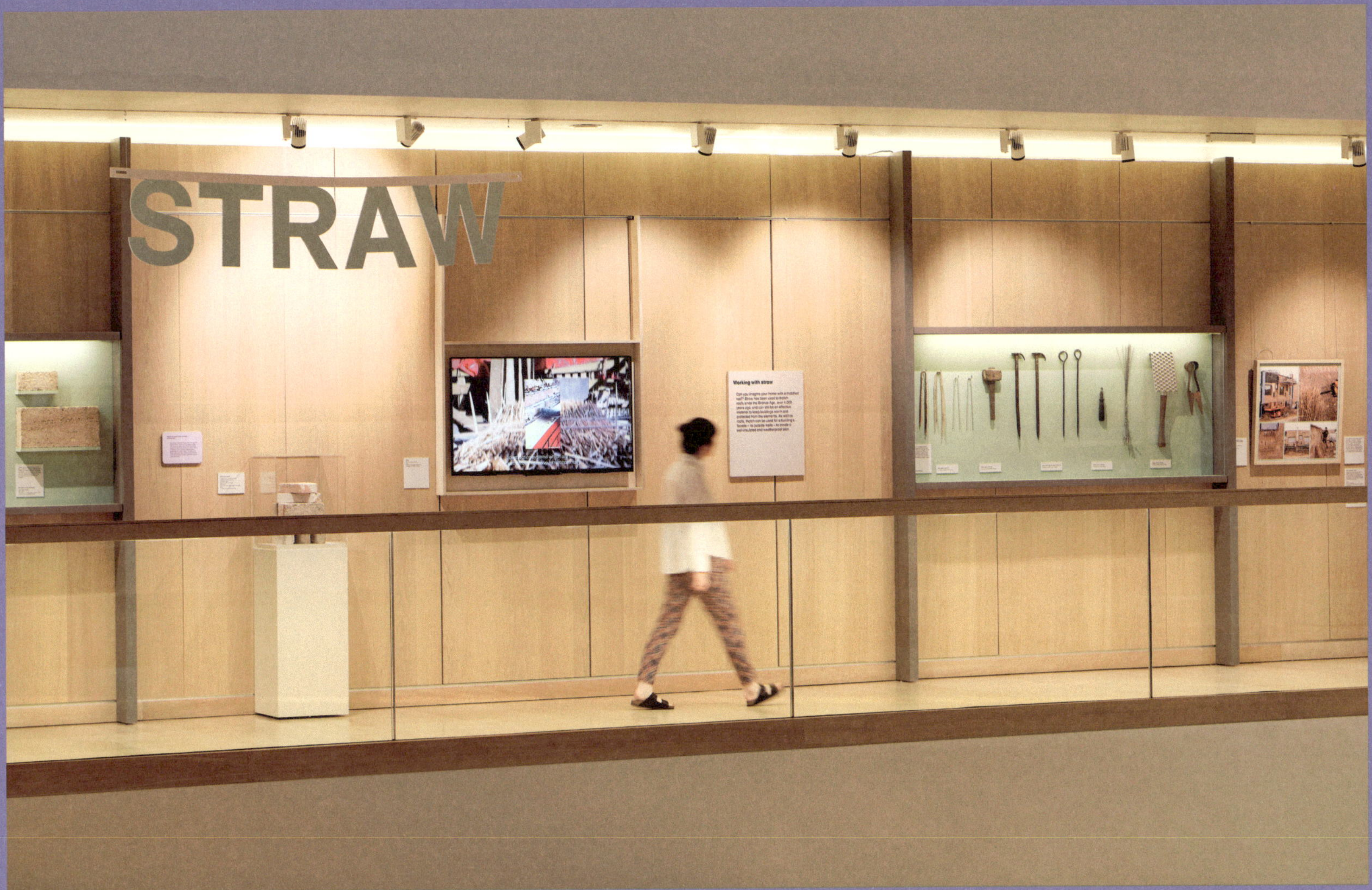

STRAW

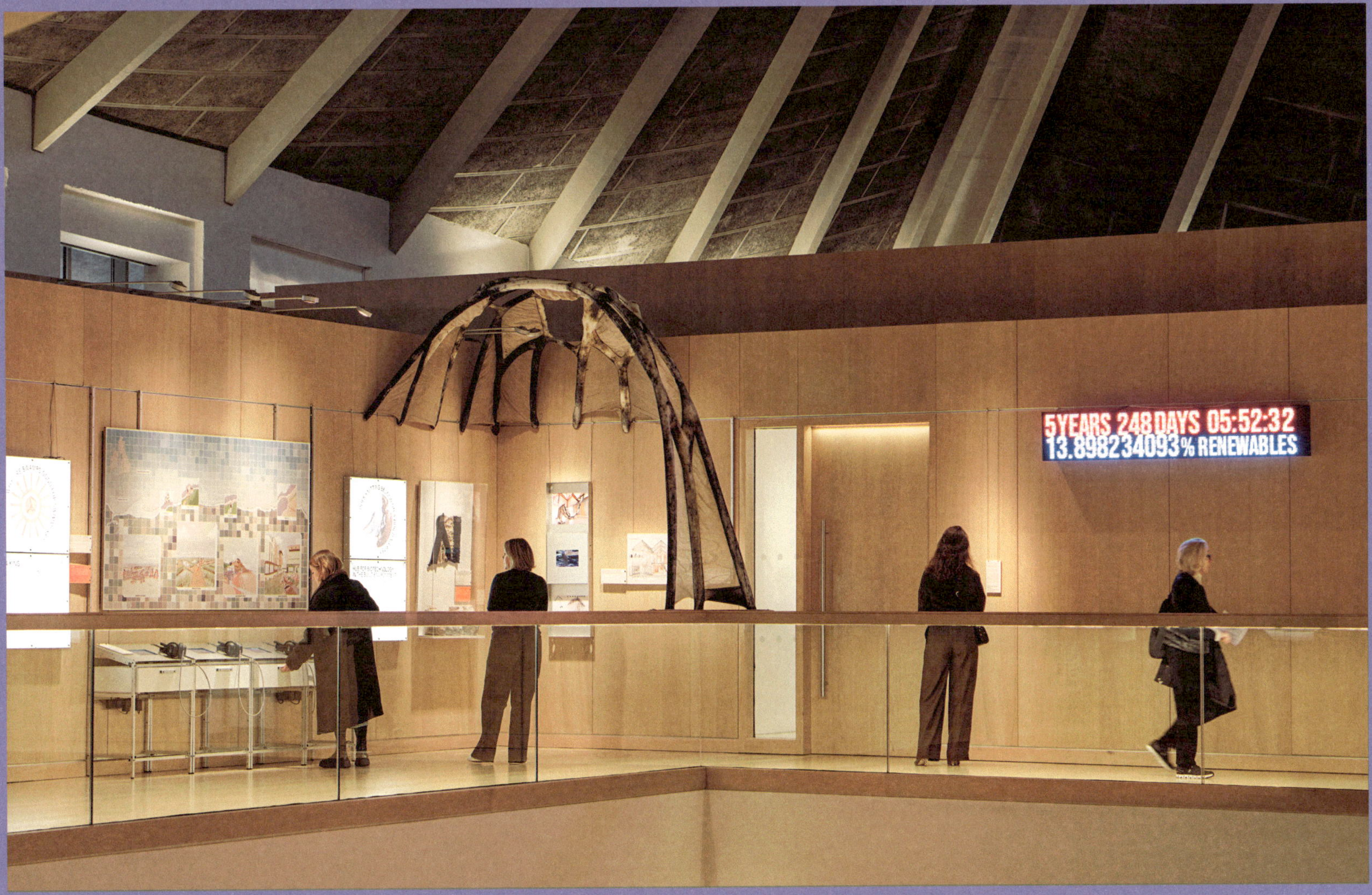

5YEARS 248DAYS 05:52:32
13.898234093% RENEWABLES

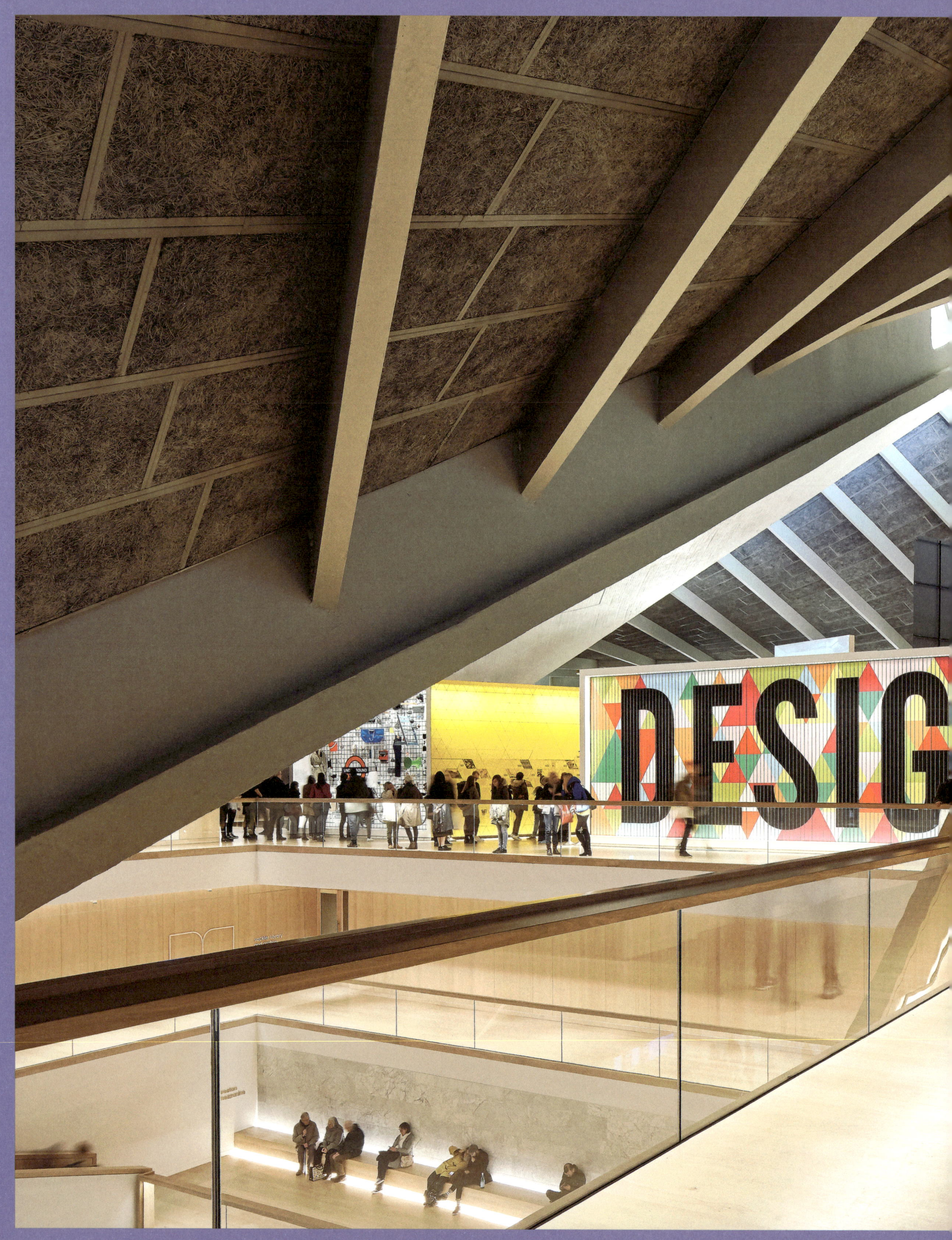
DESIG

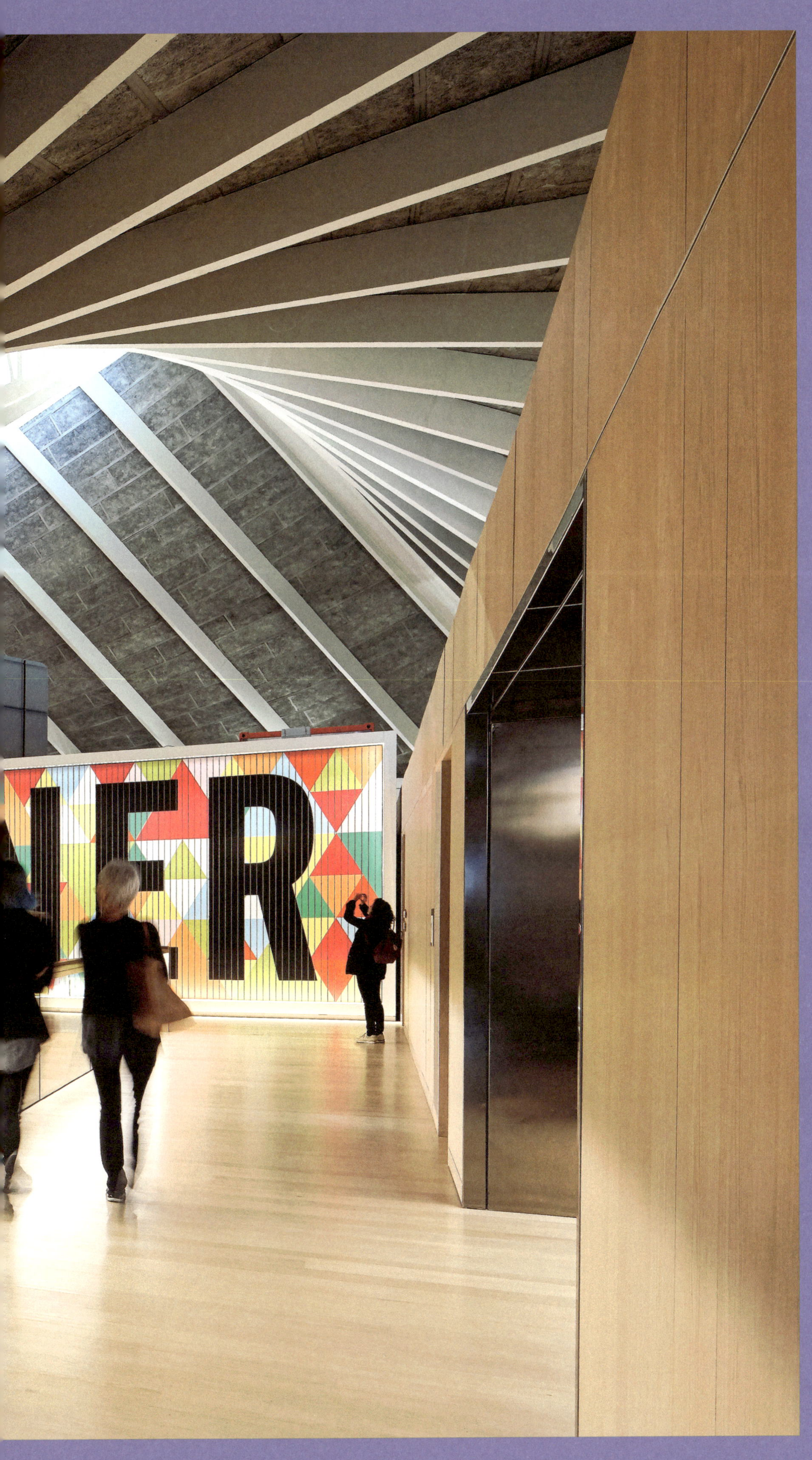

MUSEUMS WITH SIMILAR MEASURES

CINAM — International Committee for Museums and Collection of Modern Art

This international network of museums has developed the Toolkit on Sustainability in the Museum Practice.

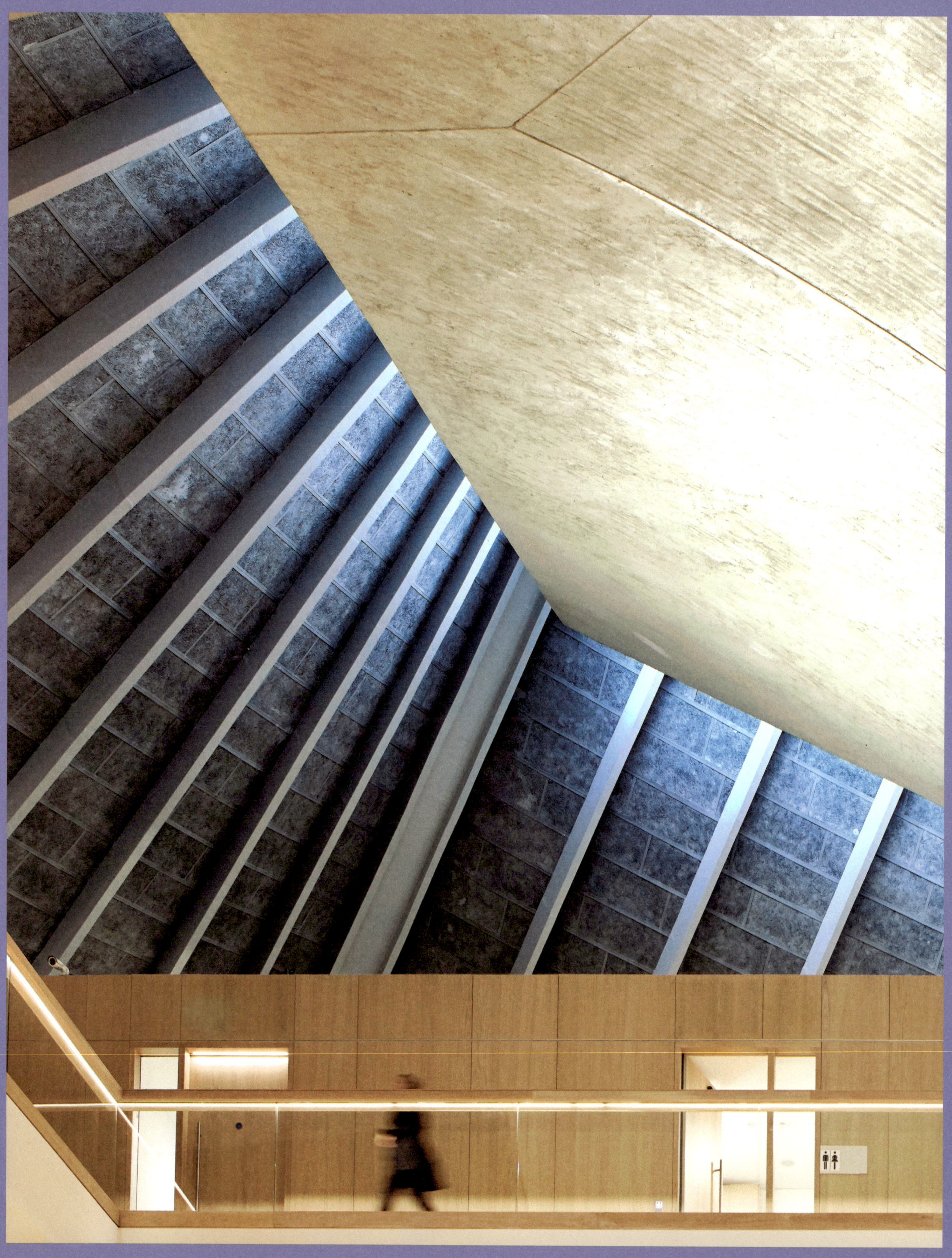

“We don’t want environmental impact to be the responsibility of just one person in the museum: it needs to be integrated into our culture.”

Design Museum of London

Exhibition Design for our Time Guide

19 LOW-IMPACT MATERIALS

EXHIBITION MATERIALS SDG 7 / 12

Building to deconstruct is a core principle in the ephemeral architecture of many exhibitions, underscoring the importance of minimizing environmental impact in the construction and interior design of museum spaces. Selecting materials free of toxic elements and those that reduce resource and energy use throughout their lifecycle is vital. Such materials should ideally come from natural or recycled sources to enhance the sustainability of any project.

The traveling exhibition *Balenciaga. La elegancia del sombrero* (*Balenciaga: The Elegance of the Hat*) exemplifies this approach by employing reusable modular walls for carpentry, paper and fabric for graphic productions instead of PVC, cardboard for direct printed posters, and 100% cotton for printed texts and images. The wood and stationery used are FSC certified, ensuring they are sourced from sustainably managed forests. Additionally, water-based paints and inks replace solvent-based options, and the exhibition employs energy-efficient LED lighting.

Balenciaga. The Elegance of the Hat exhibition

FOCUS
Fashion

LOCATION
Disseny Hub in collaboration with Museo Cristóbal Balenciaga. Guetaria, Guipúzcoa, Spain

ANNUAL VISITORS
65,000

INAUGURATION
2011

PROJECT
AV62 Arquitectos

SIZE
5,920 m² built area
(2,200 m² exhibition space)

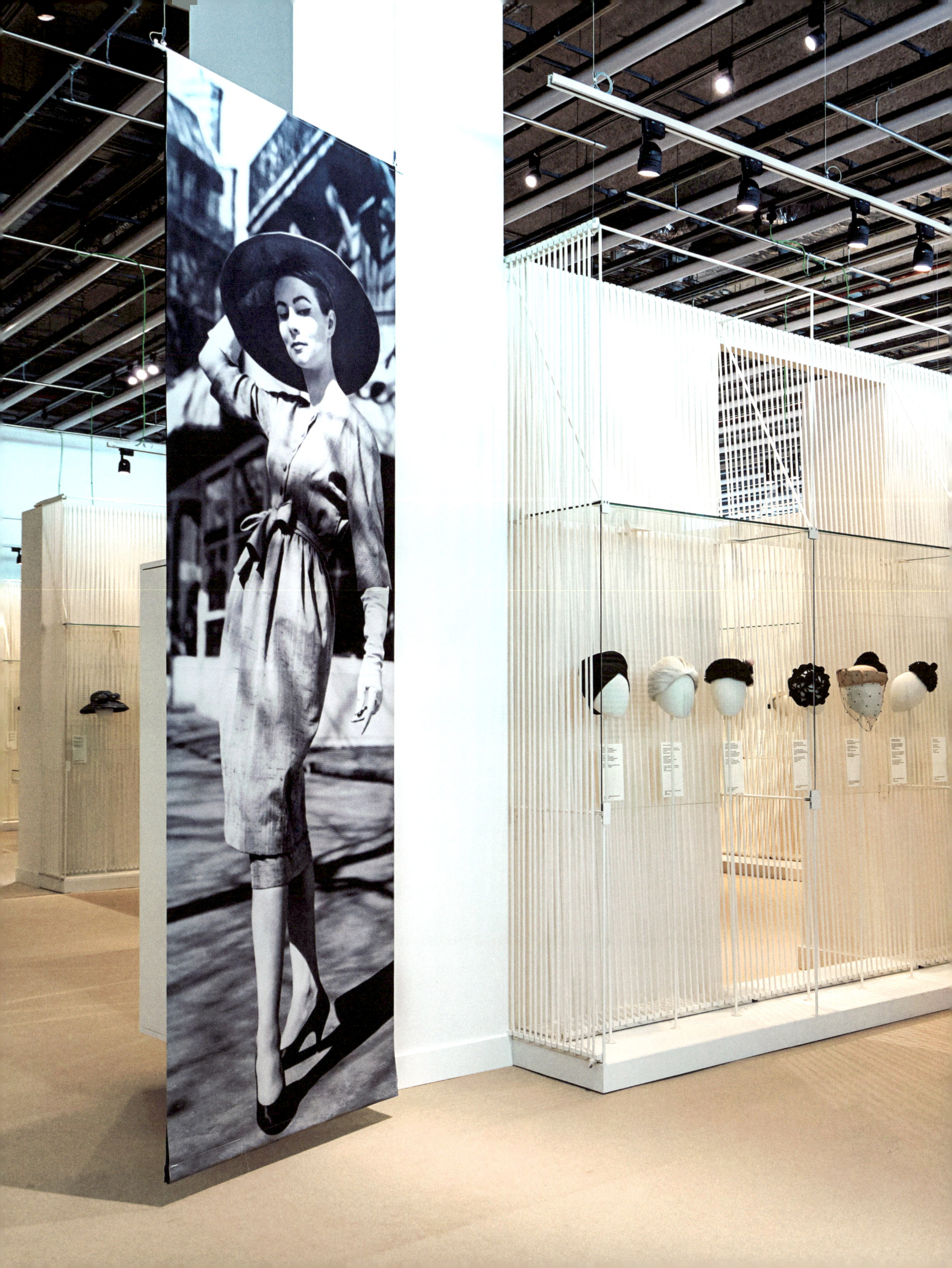

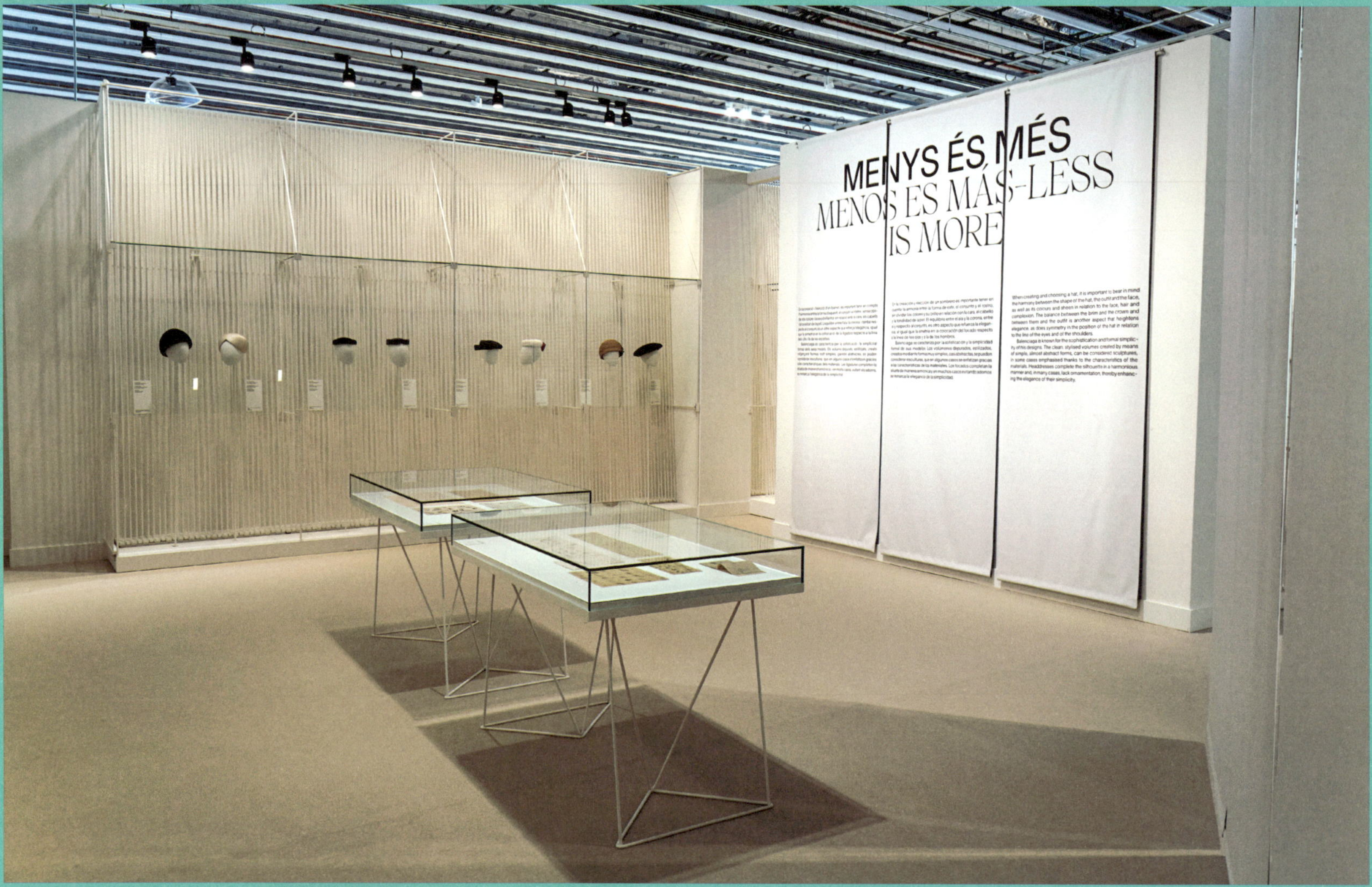

MENYS ÉS MÉS
MENOS ES MÁS-LESS IS MORE
When creating and choosing a hat, it is important to bear in mind the harmony between the shape of the hat, the outfit and the face, as well as its colours and sheen in relation to the face, hair and complexion. The balance between the brim and the crown and between them and the outfit is another aspect that heightens elegance, as does symmetry in the position of the hat in relation to the line of the eyes and of the shoulders.
Balenciaga is known for the sophistication and formal simplicity of his designs. The clean, stylised volumes created by means of simple, almost abstract forms, can be considered sculptures, in some cases emphasised thanks to the characteristics of the materials. Headdresses complete the silhouette in a harmonious manner and, in many cases, lack ornamentation, thereby enhancing the elegance of their simplicity.

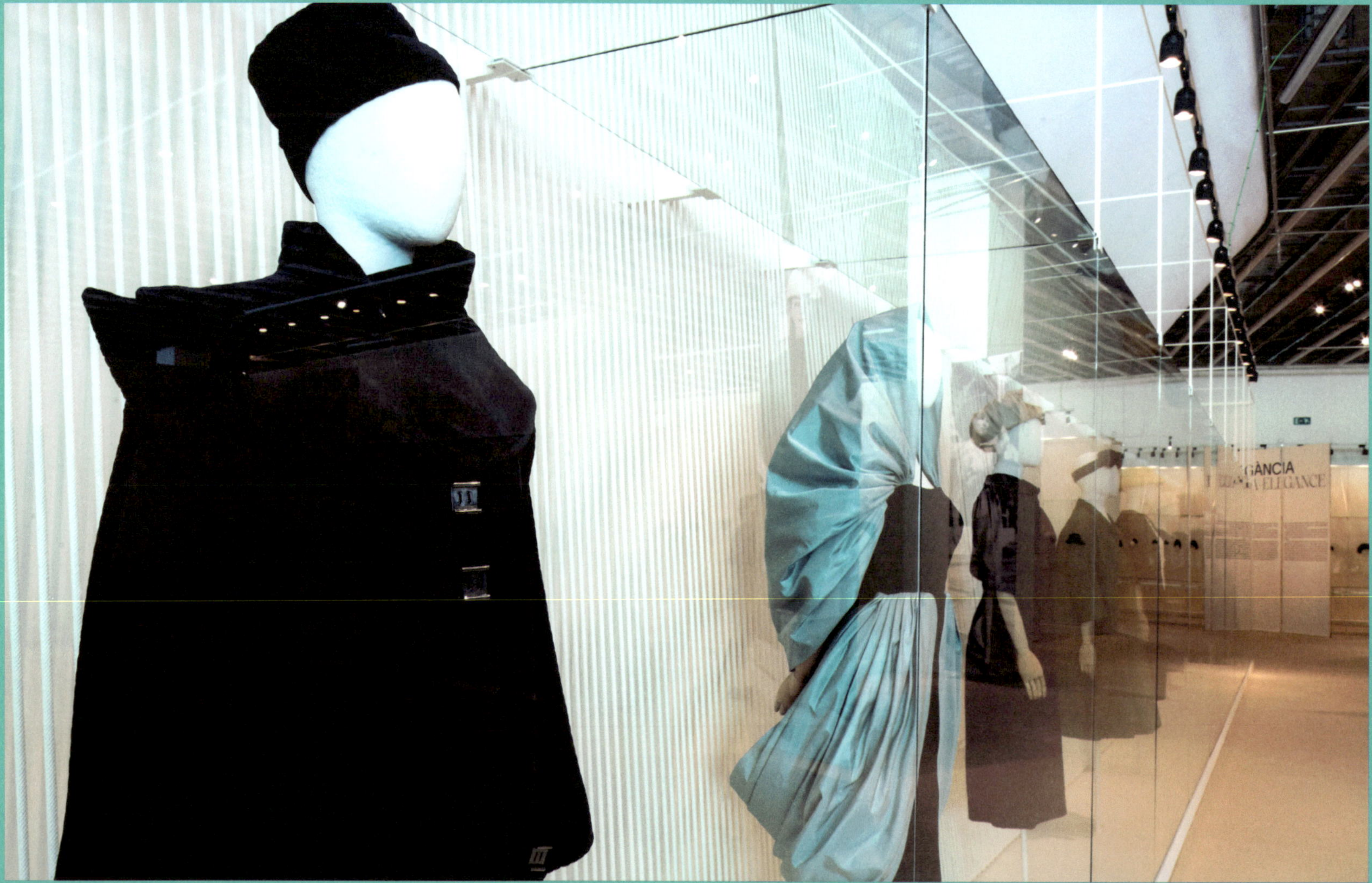

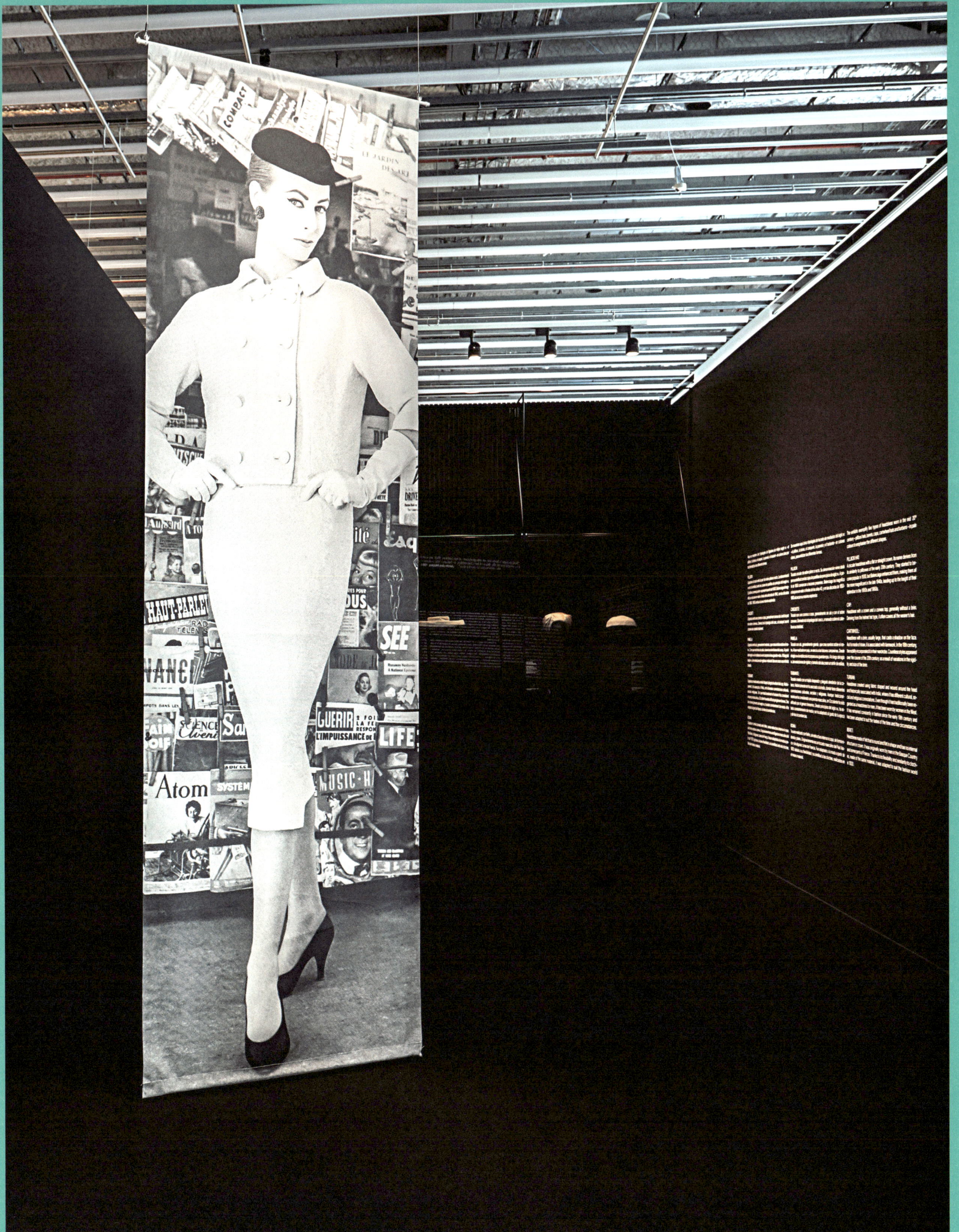
COMPACT
HAUT-PARLEU
SEE
GUERIR
L'IMPUISSANCE DE
LIFE
Atom
MUSIC-H

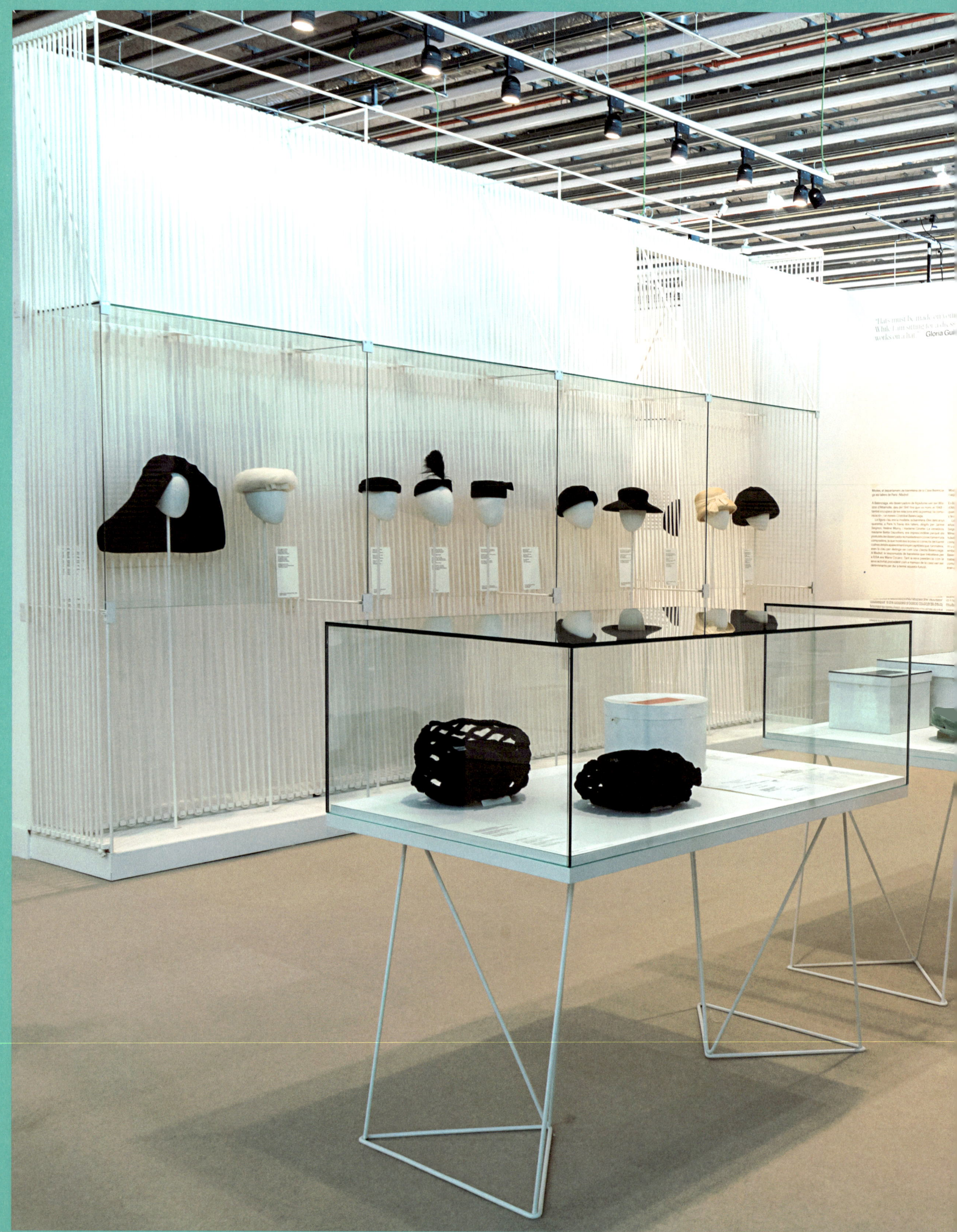
"Hats must be made on
While I am sitting for a dress
works on a hat." Gloria

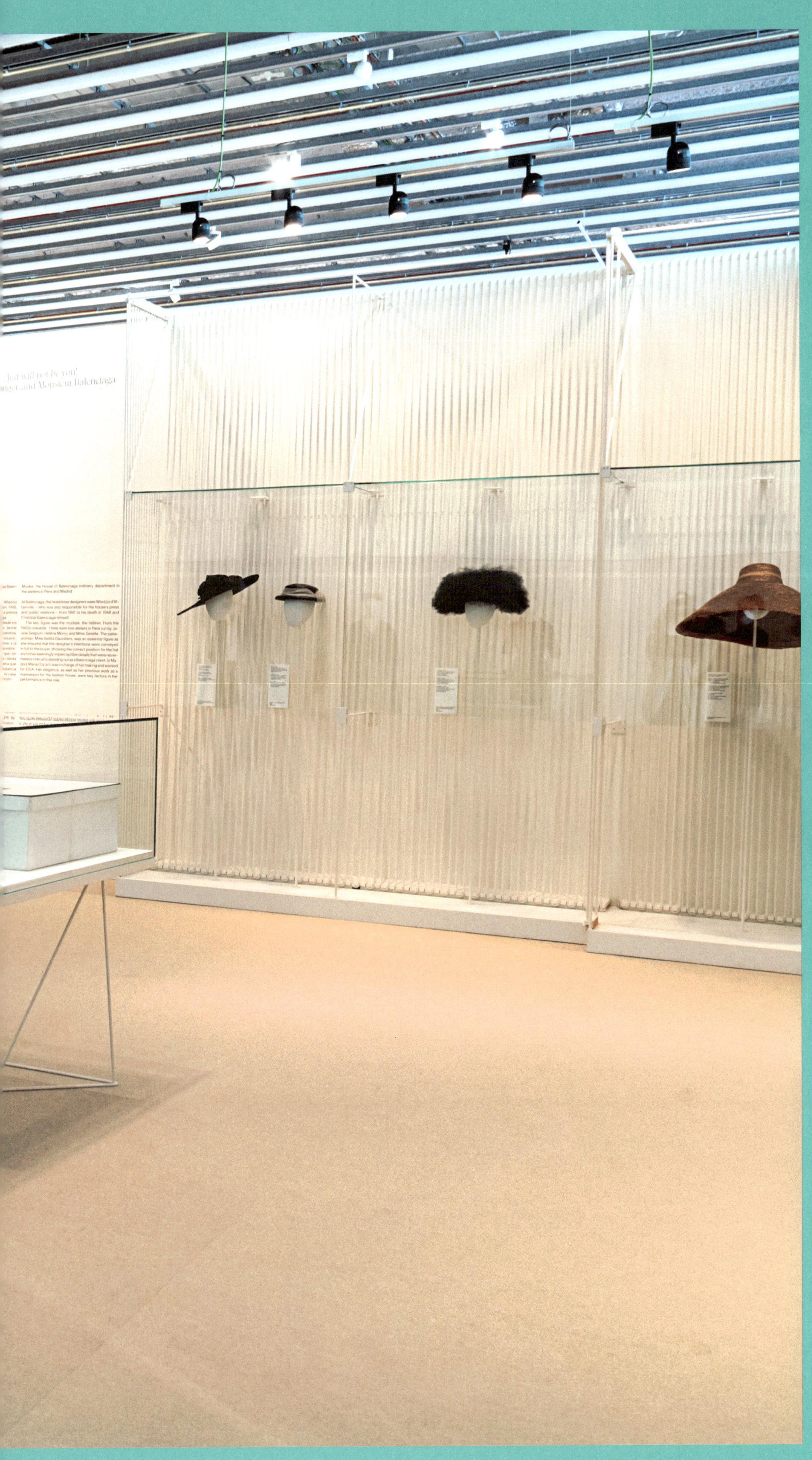

MUSEUMS WITH SIMILAR MEASURES

Leeds City Museum

LEEDS, UNITED KINGDOM

Exhibition model based on suppliers using low environmental impact materials.

“The reuse of exhibition supports, the selection of materials based on ecological criteria, and the extension of the exhibition lifecycle without sacrificing new content are essential factors that contribute to the sustainability of the center.”

Cristóbal Balenciaga Museum

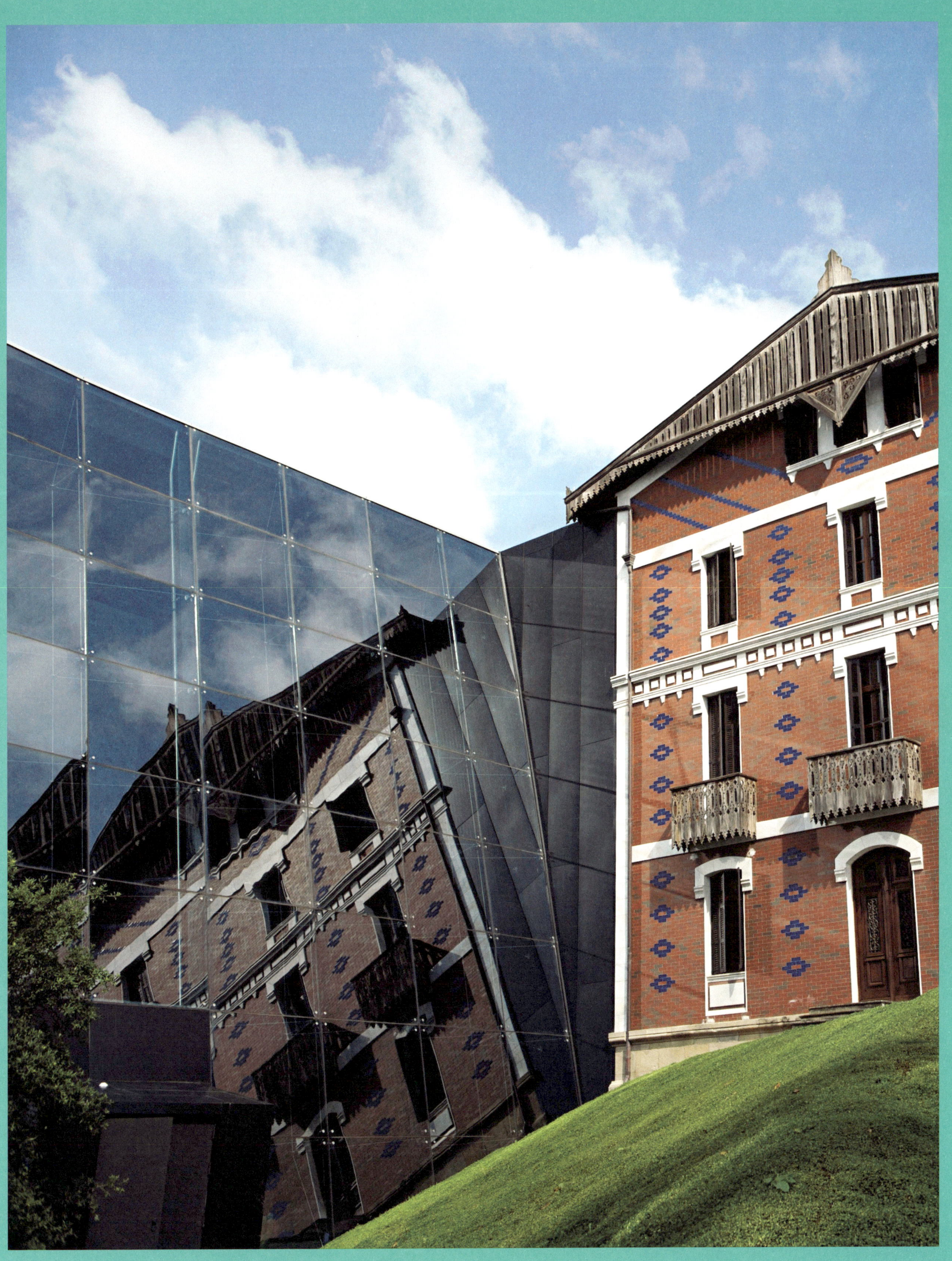

20 EXHIBITIONS WITH POSITIVE IMPACT

POSITIVE IMPACT OF EXHIBITION PROJECTS SDG 12 / 13

When designing an exhibition, it's crucial to analyze the environmental context and develop strategies aimed at leaving a positive legacy within the host community across environmental, social, and economic dimensions. This involves considering every production stage to evaluate sustainable performance, minimize negative impacts, and develop actions tailored to local needs and peculiarities.

The exhibition *Vida y obra de Frida Kahlo* (*Life and Work of Frida Kahlo*) is a prime example, utilizing materials chosen through life cycle analysis. This immersive traveling exhibition minimizes greenhouse gas emissions and calculates and offsets those that couldn't be avoided by planting trees as part of reforestation projects in Spain and Mexico.

Life and Work of Frida Kahlo exhibition
ACCIONA

FOCUS
Traveling exhibition

LOCATION
Instante Theater, Madrid, Spain

OPENING
2022. Currently touring.
It is the most awarded immersive cultural work in the world

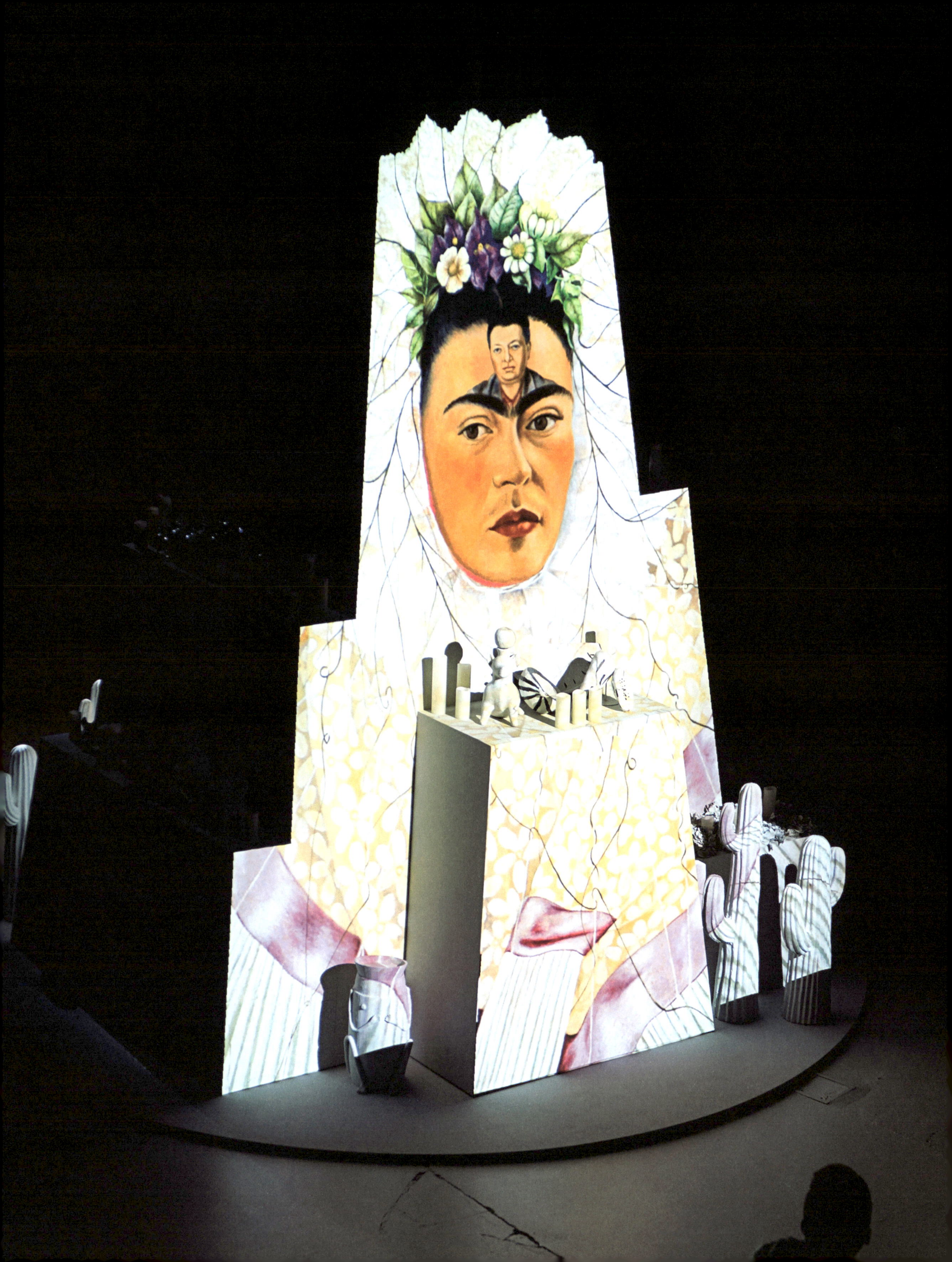

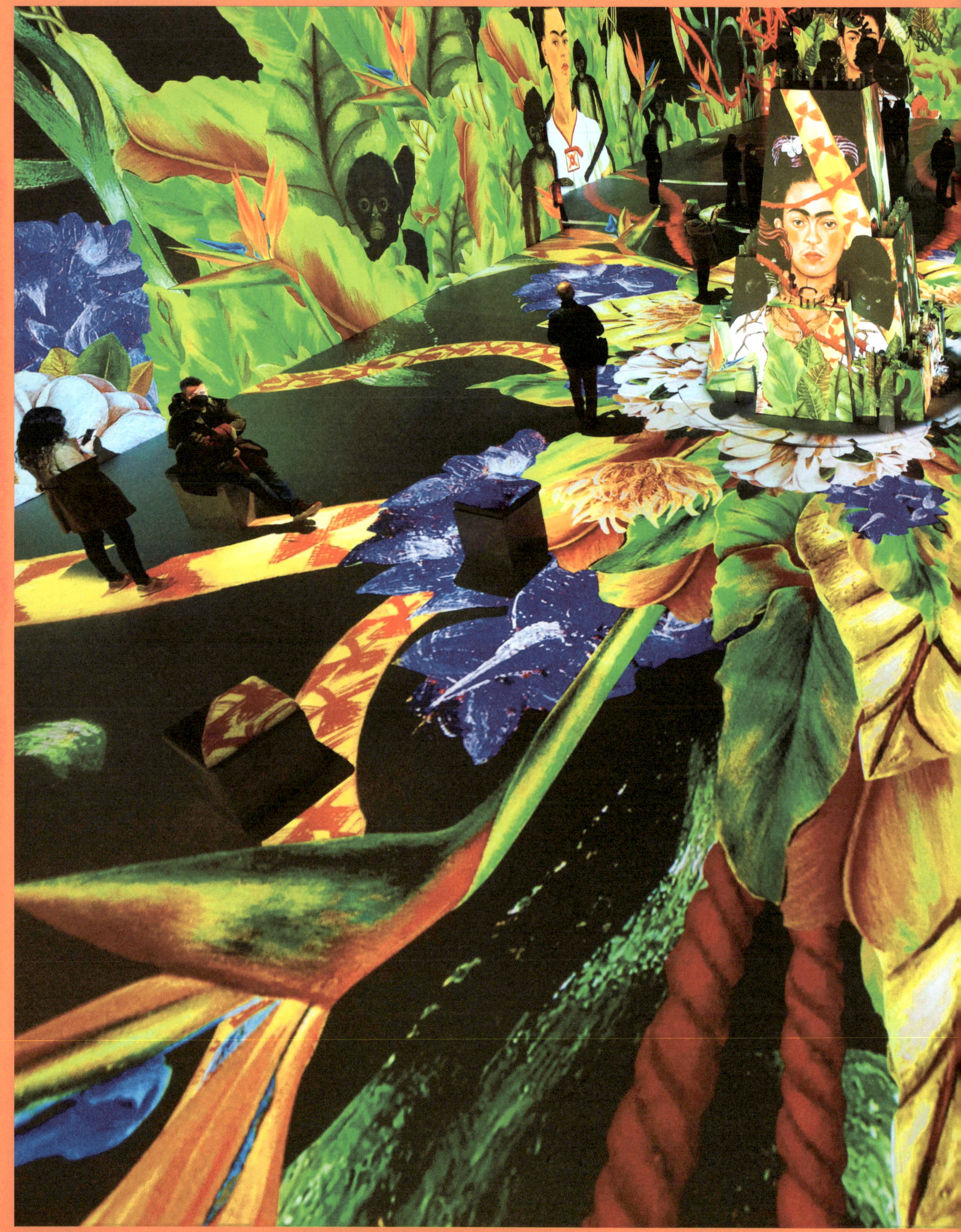

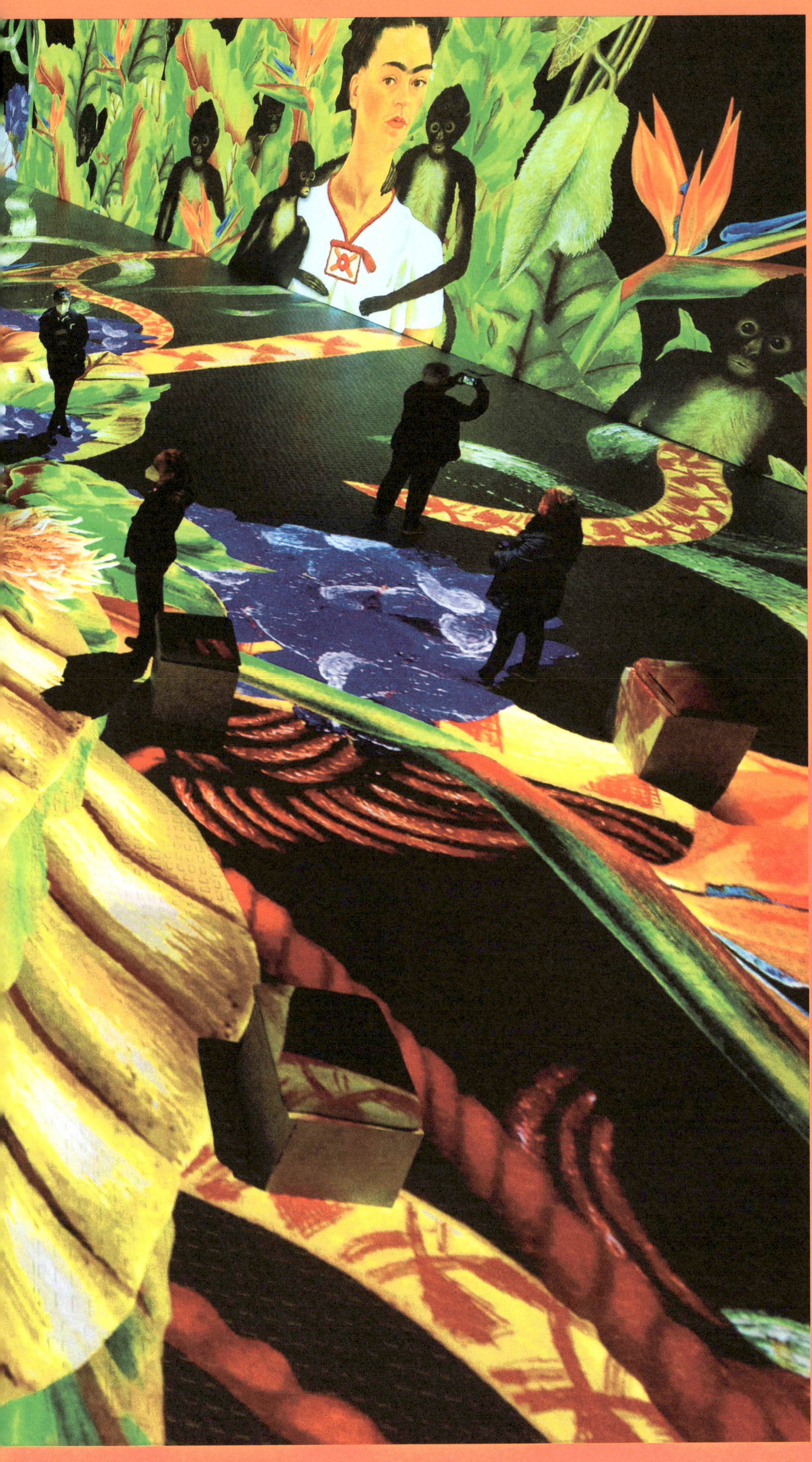

MUSEUMS WITH SIMILAR MEASURES

Science Museum Group

LONDON, UNITED KINGDOM

Production of exhibition plans for third parties with criteria of replicability and sustainability.

“Nothing is absolute. Everything changes, everything moves, everything turns, everything flies and disappears.”

Frida Kahlo

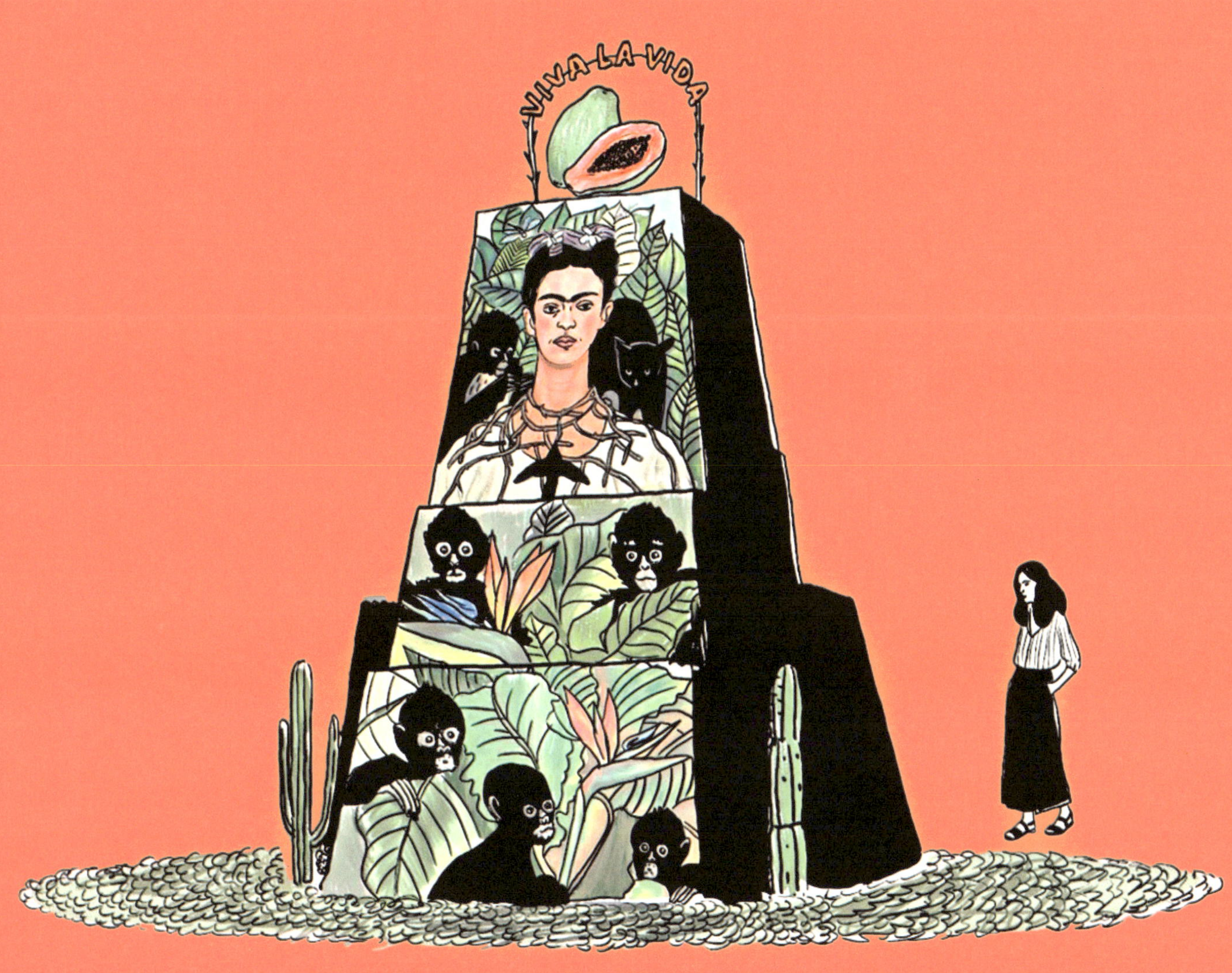

Conceptual sketch of the exhibition *Life and Work of Frida Kahlo.*
ACCIONA.

21 ACCESSIBILITY IN MUSEUMS AND EXHIBITIONS

ACCESSIBILITY, INCLUSION, AND DIVERSITY SDG 10 / 16

Ensuring accessibility in museums requires different technical solutions to meet the needs of diverse audiences. The goal is to make the museum's physical spaces and exhibited contents accessible to people with mobility, comprehension, or communication challenges. An accessible museum promotes the social inclusion and integration of persons with disabilities by adapting its facilities and contents, improving its equipment and services, and guaranteeing their right to experience it just like everyone else, so that all visitors can have hassle-free access to culture.

Being Human, the Wellcome Collection Museum's permanent exhibition on health and wellness, incorporates several accessibility features: tactile floor marking systems for the visually impaired, display cases at wheelchair-accessible heights, Braille-labeled signage, audio guides, a digital interpretation system into British Sign Language (BSL), multisensory works that visitors can touch or smell, rooms equipped with magnetic loops, and exits that are clearly visible, accessible, and marked throughout to aid visitors with intellectual disabilities.

Wellcome Collection

FOCUS
Science and Contemporary Art

CONSTRUCTION
2007. Extension: 2015

LOCATION
Urban. London, United Kingdom

PROJECT
WilkinsonEyre Architects

ANNUAL VISITORS
260,000

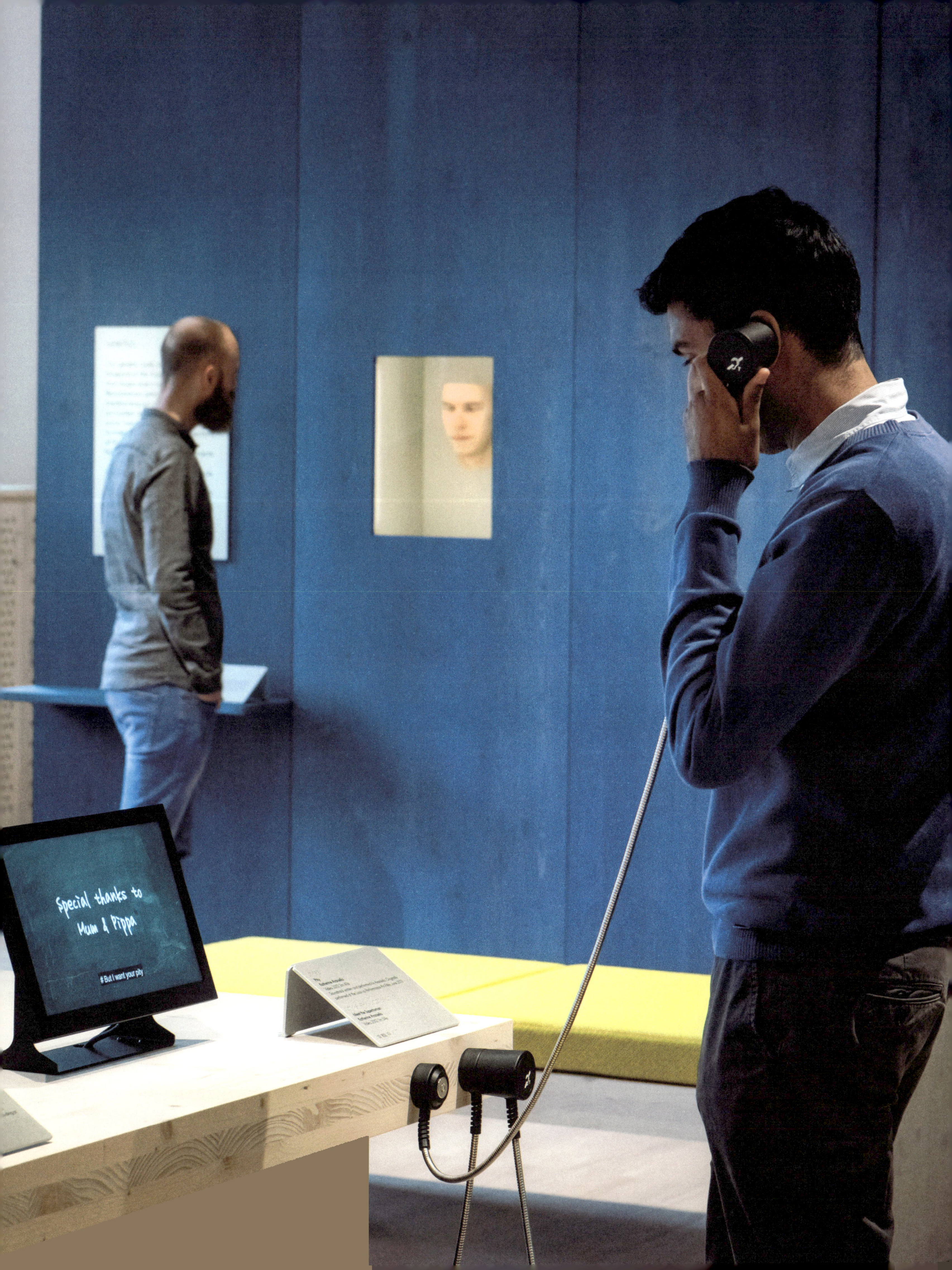
Special thanks to
Mum & Pippa
But I want your pity

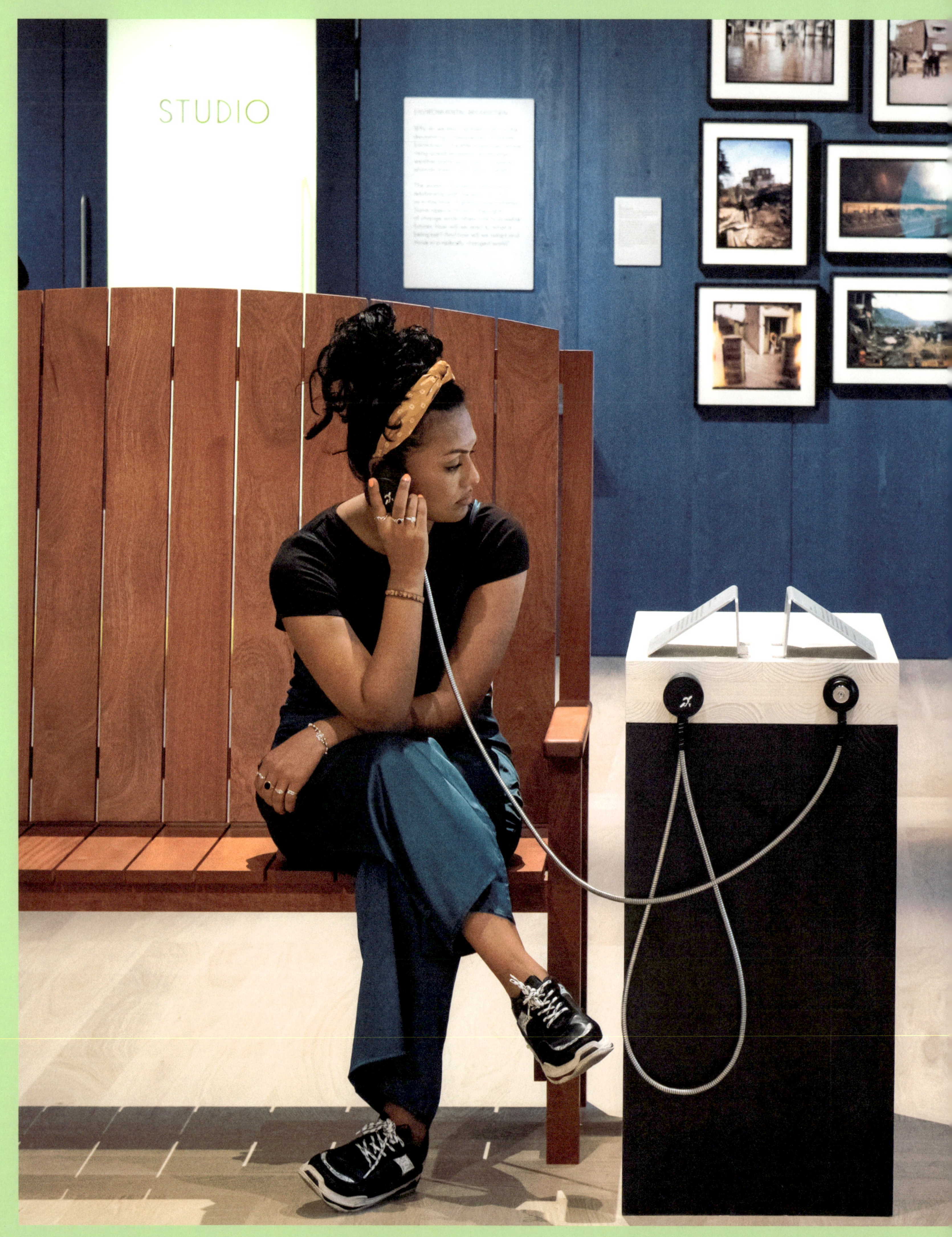
STUDIO

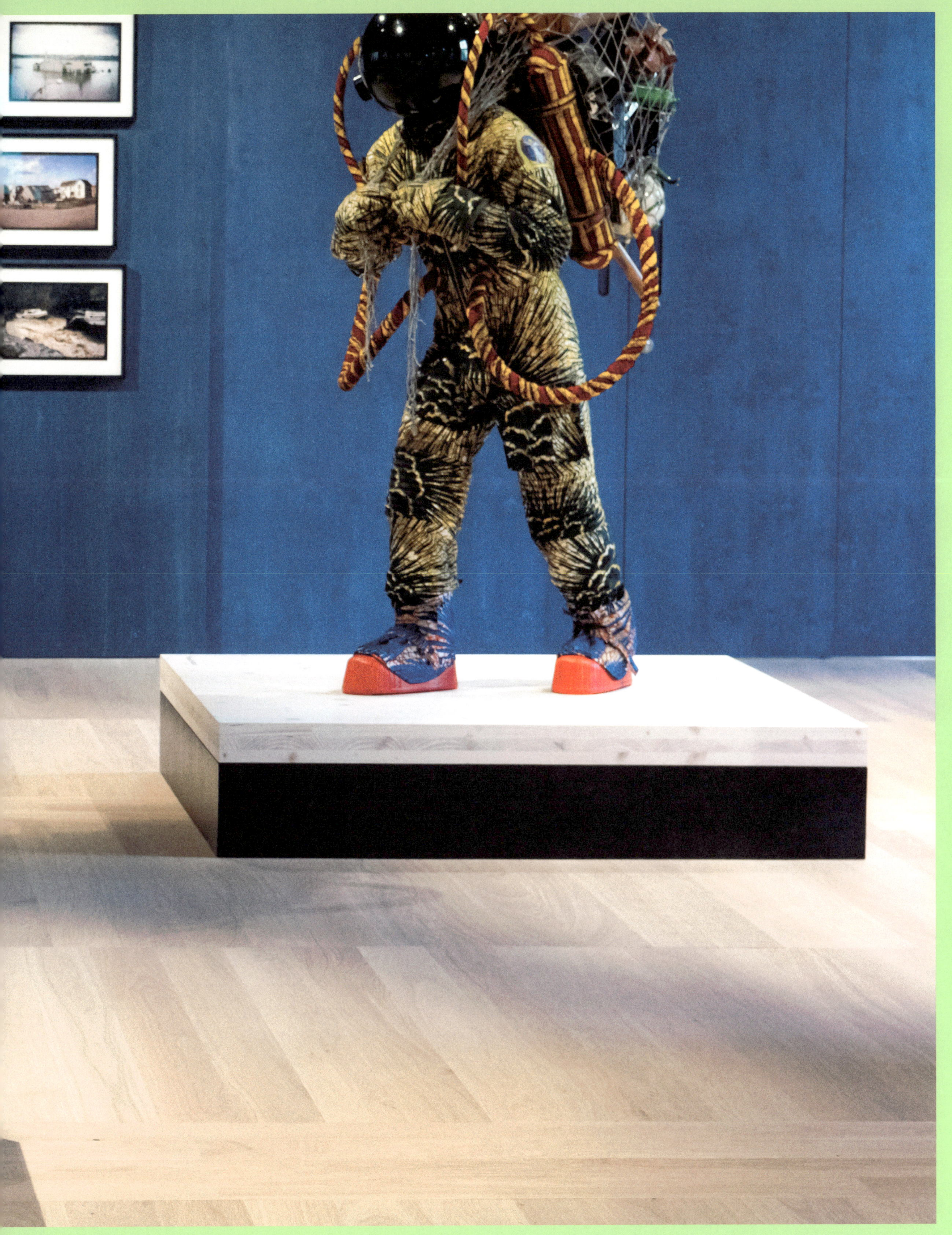

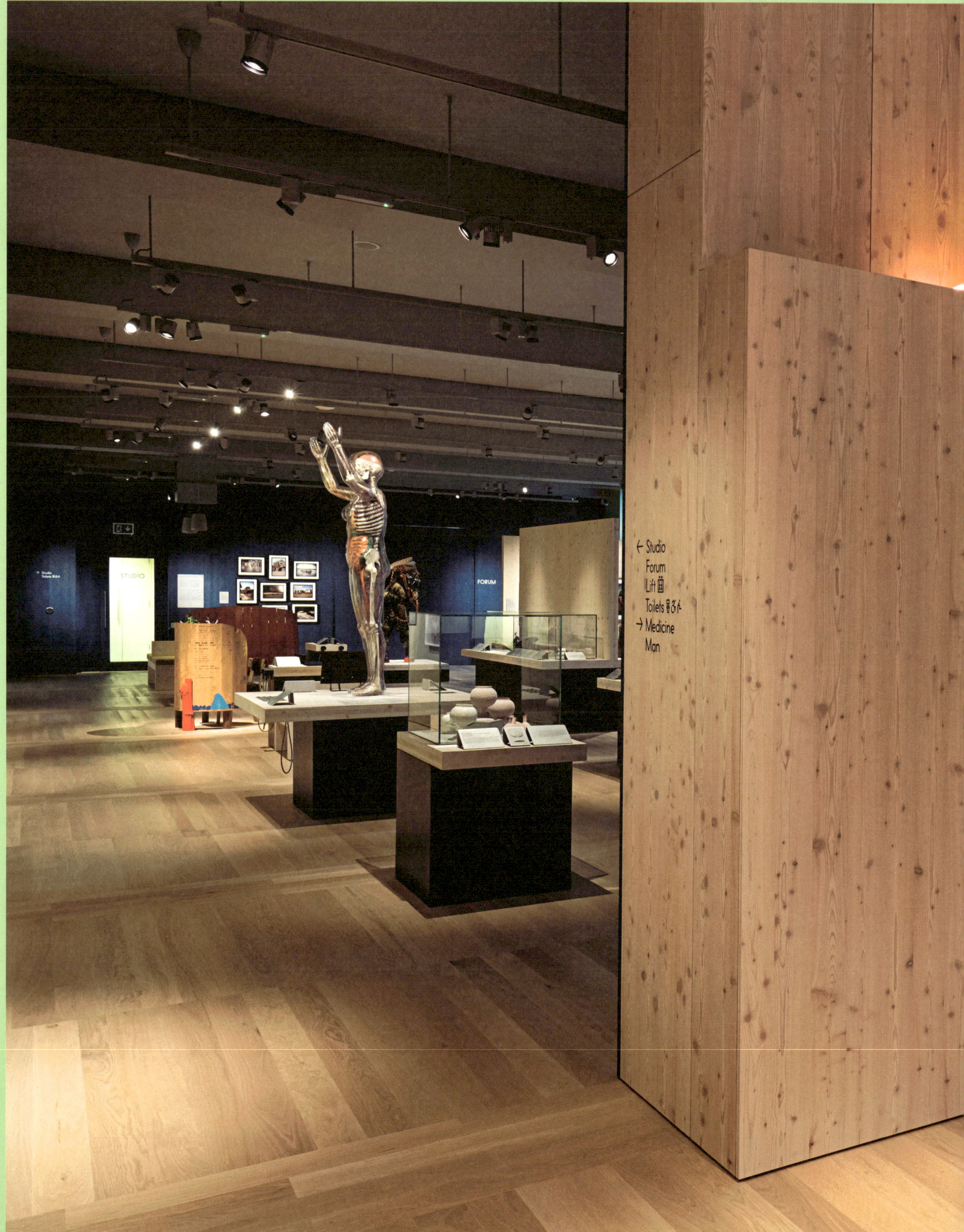

← Studio
Forum
Lift
Toilets
→ Medicine
Man
STUDIO
FORUM

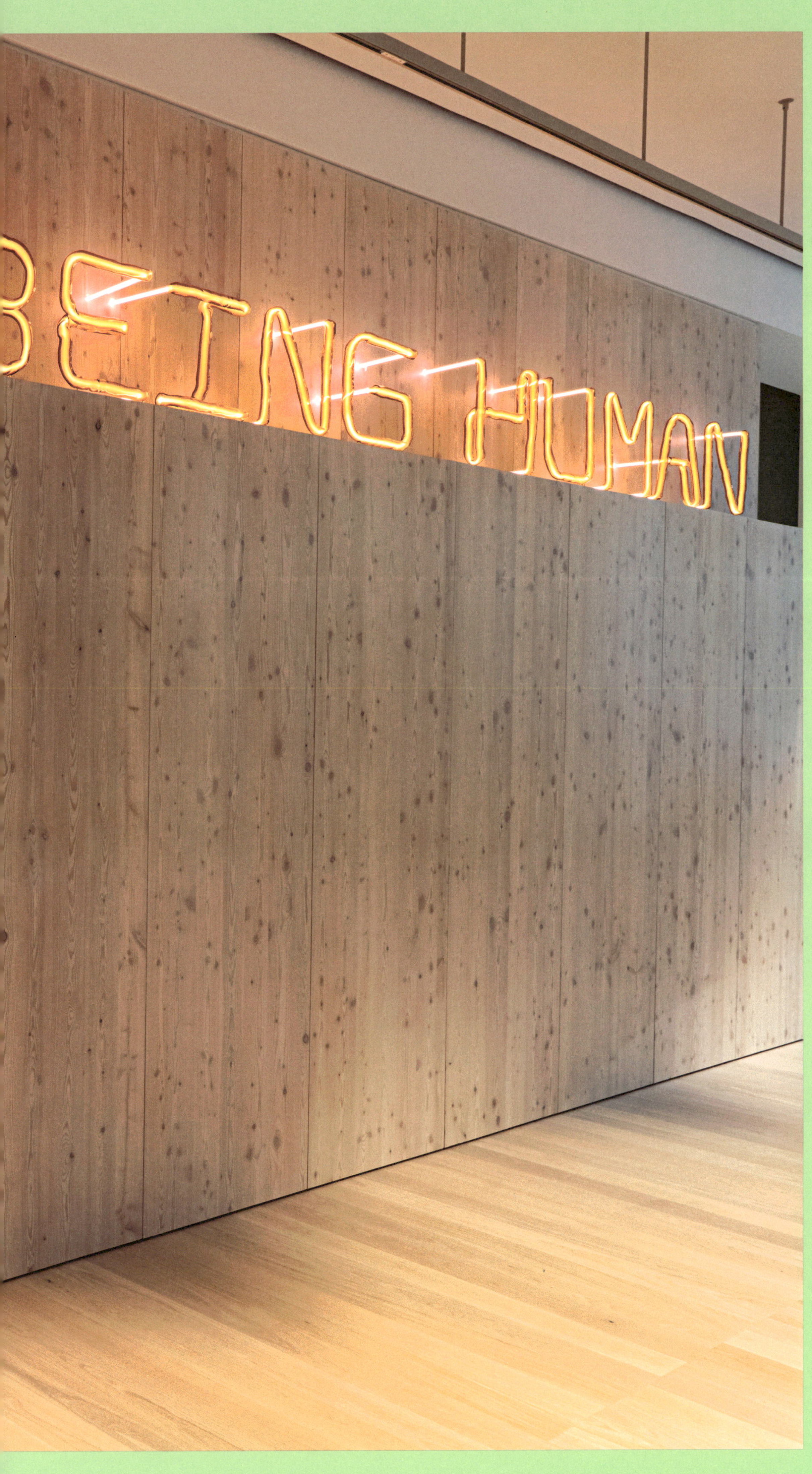

MUSEUMS WITH SIMILAR MEASURES

Young At Art Museum

PLANTATION, FLORIDA, USA

Initiatives for integrating vulnerable groups.

Museo Tiflológico de la ONCE

MADRID, SPAIN

Universally accessible museum, an example of sensory adaptation.

Guggenheim Museum Bilbao

BILBAO, SPAIN

Accessibility guide of the museum available to visitors.

Museo Moderno

BUENOS AIRES, ARGENTINA

Inclusive accessibility plan incorporating multiple workshops and adapted materials.

Musée du Quai Branly - Jacques Chirac

PARIS, FRANCE

Collaboration for the social integration of at-risk individuals or persons with disabilities.

Dallas Museum of Art
Dallas, Texas, USA

The Speechless: Different by Design exhibition explores interactive and multisensory participation, especially for people with disabilities.

“I imagined that we would create immersive spaces within the museum gallery setting that allow people to explore the senses and think about how objects can be experienced without using text as a mediator.”

Sarah Schleuning

Curator of the exhibition *Speechless: Different by Design*
American Alliance of Museums blog

22 TACTILE PERCEPTION OF ARTWORKS

ACCESSIBILITY, INCLUSION, AND DIVERSITY SDG 10 / 16

The prohibition of touching artworks in museums and galleries often means that they can only be appreciated visually. This presents an accessibility issue for people with visual impairments. Tactile perception allows individuals to experience the reality of the represented artworks and mentally reconstruct them in their entirety.

The exhibition *Hoy toca el Prado* presents six representative works from various genres in the Museo del Prado that can be touched to achieve an emotional perception of the artwork. Through a relief reproduction technique, which applies different textures and volumes to create tactile reproductions, people with visual impairments can enjoy a greater artistic experience.

Museo del Prado
Hoy toca el Prado exhibition

FOCUS
Art

ANNUAL VISITORS
3.3 million

LOCATION
Urban. Madrid, Spain

CONSTRUCTION
Original structure built in 1795.
Opened in 1819

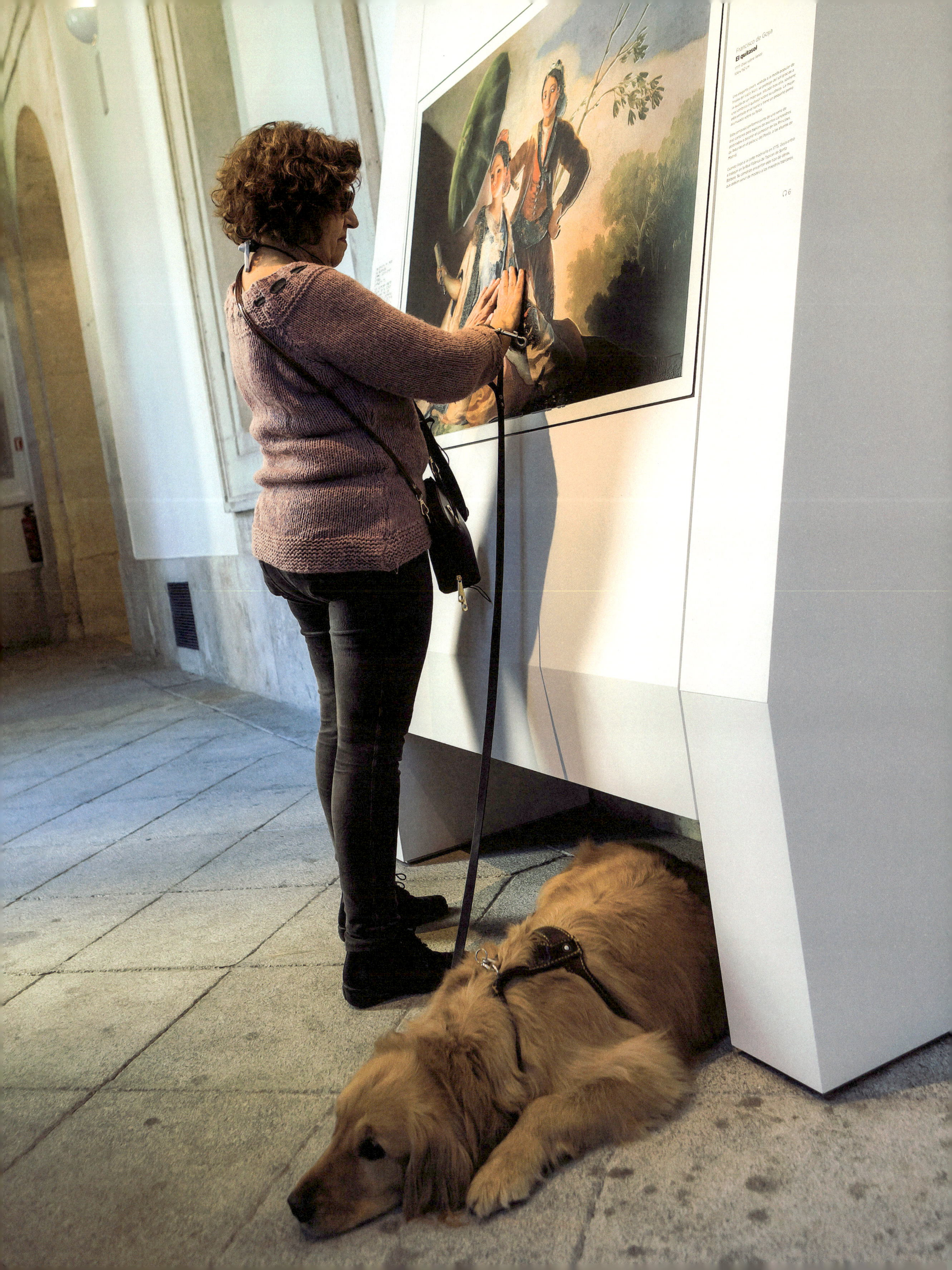

Francisco de Goya
El quitasol

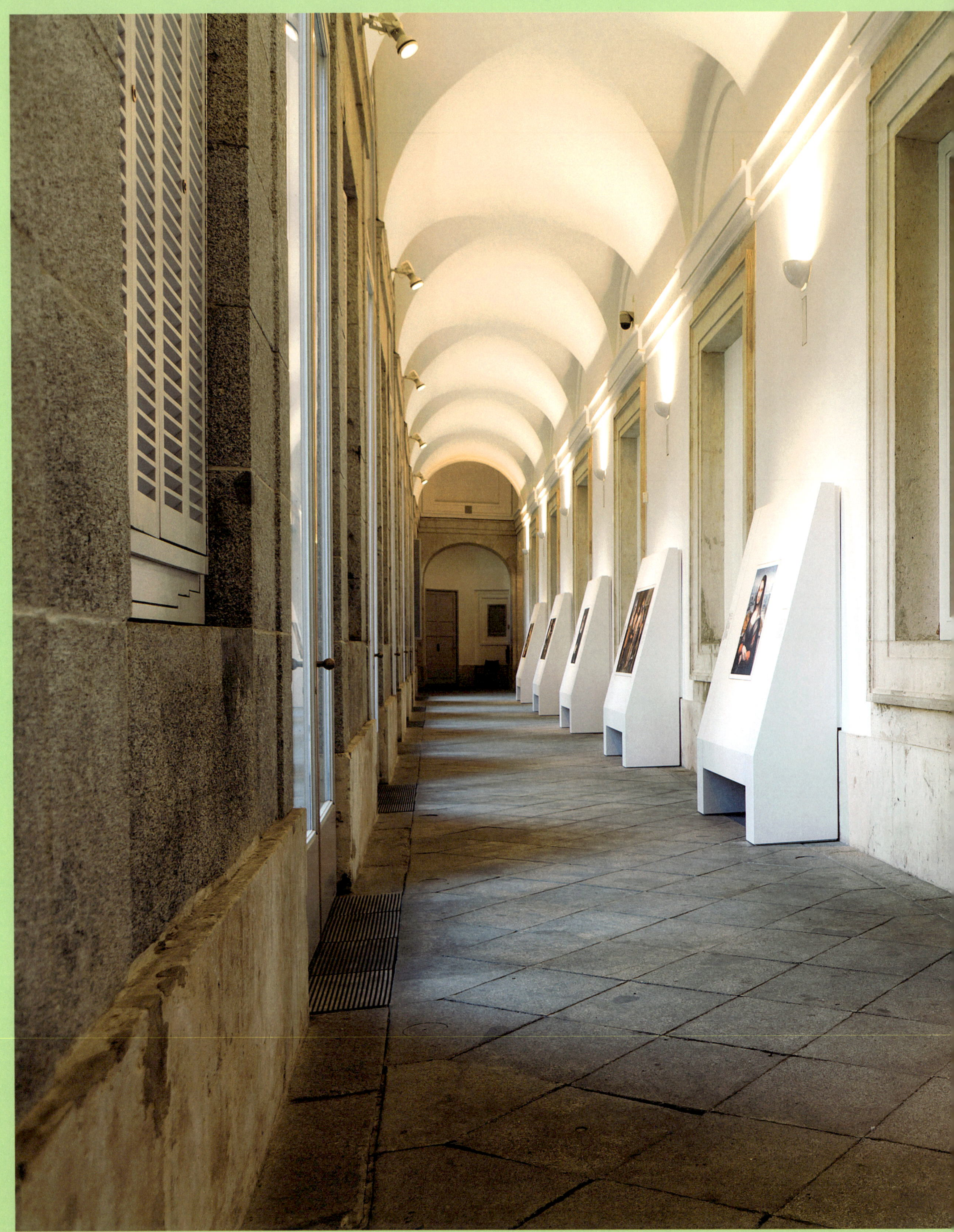

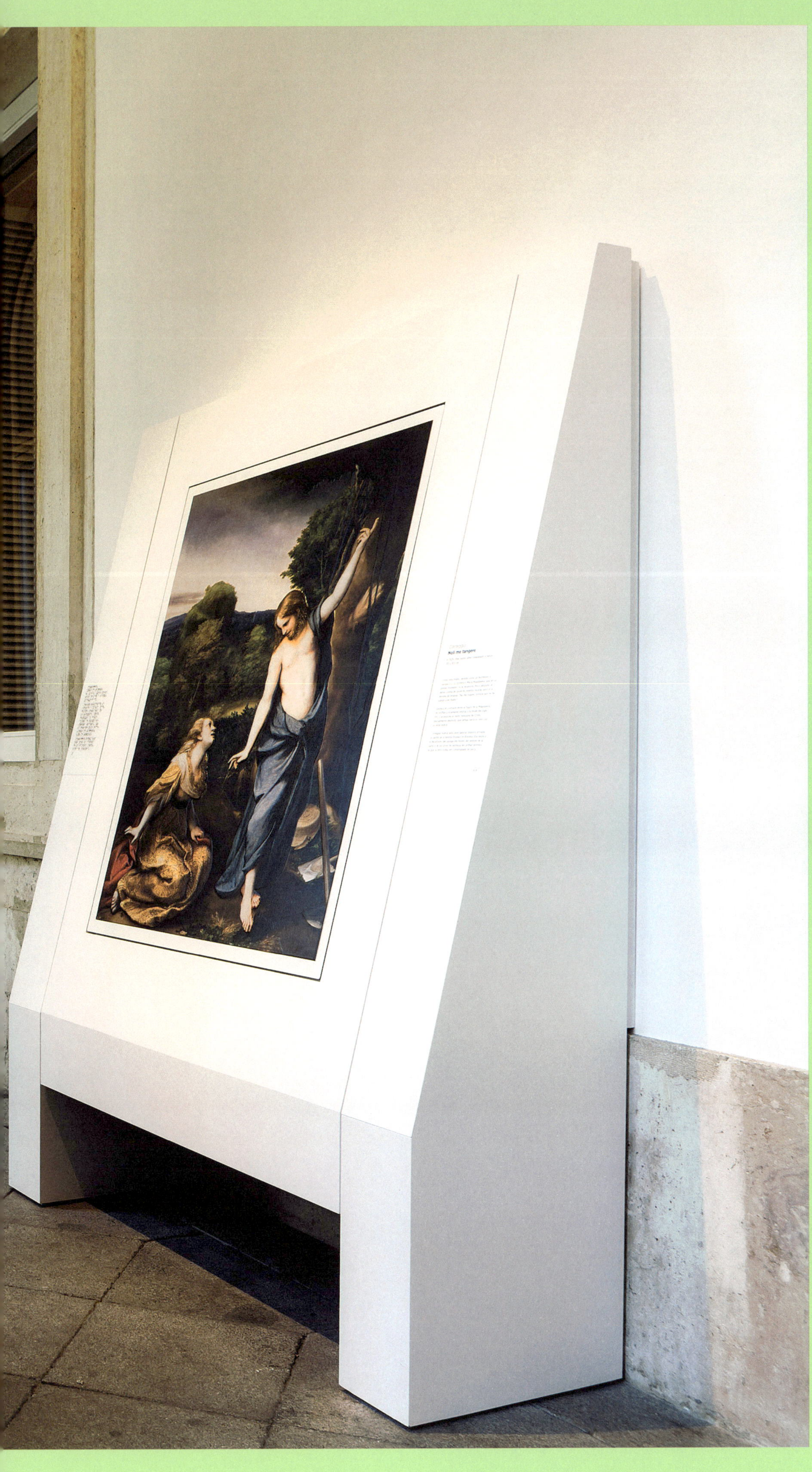

MUSEUMS WITH SIMILAR MEASURES

Museo Nacional de Ciencias Naturales

MADRID, SPAIN

Wide variety of 3D reproductions and relief models.

The Metropolitan Museum of Art (MET)

NEW YORK, USA

Tactile tours for the visually impaired.

Smithsonian American Art Museum

WASHINGTON, D.C., USA

Special tours for visually impaired visitors, including verbal descriptions, sensory experiences, and tactile tour components.

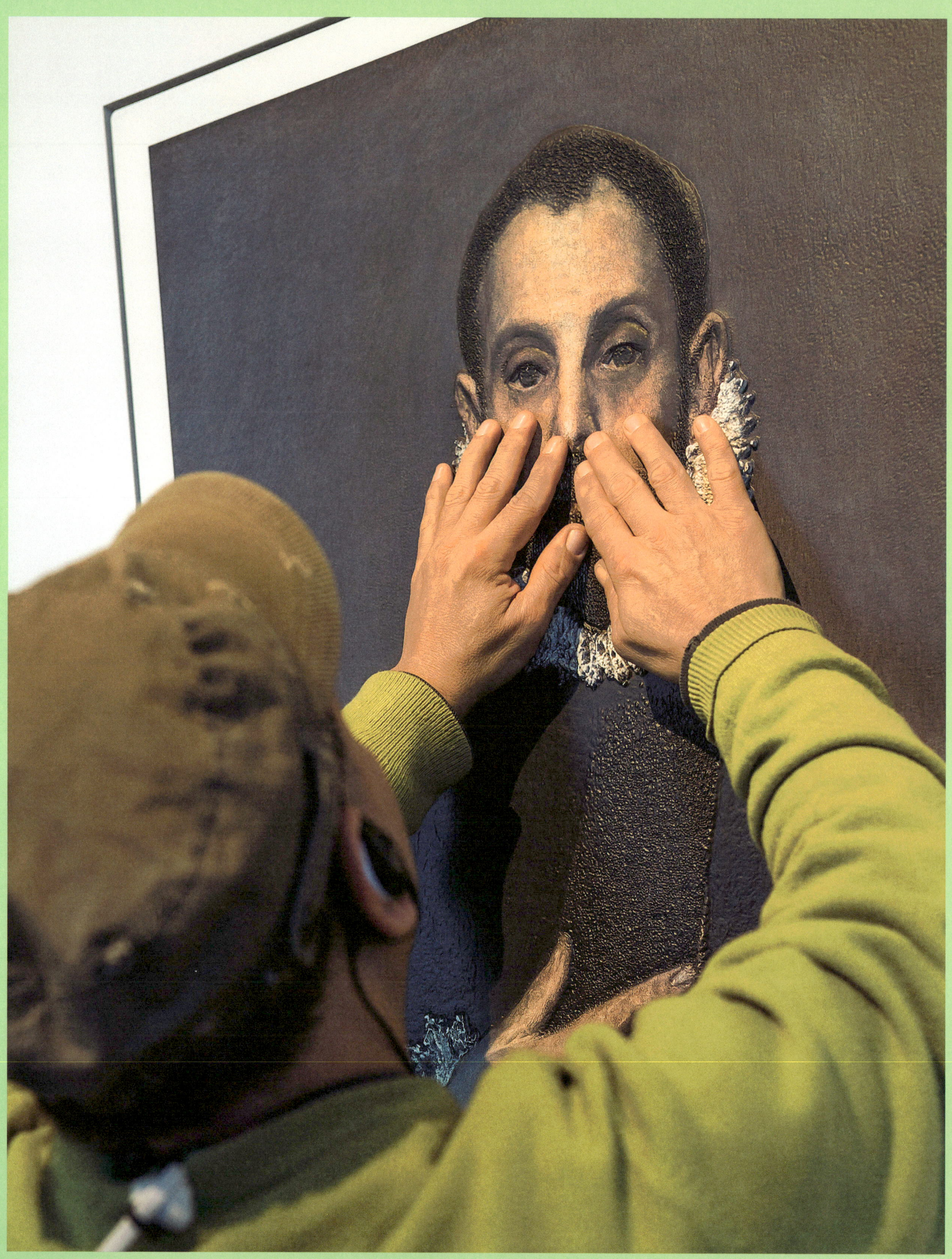

PLEASE
DO TOUCH

23 EMPLOYEE TRAINING

TRAINING OF EMPLOYEES AND WORK TEAMS SDG 13

Training is crucial for addressing the challenges set by the Sustainable Development Goals, aiming to transform museum employees into active agents of change. Their involvement and commitment are vital for the success of sustainability programs, as they play a significant role in implementing initiatives. Additionally, equipped with the necessary knowledge, employees can bring innovative perspectives that help identify opportunities for improvement and develop more effective solutions.

The Manchester Museum was the first in the world to implement the Carbon Literacy project, a nonprofit training program designed to educate about carbon footprint and climate change mitigation at the individual, community, and organizational levels. The museum staff receive certified training through this program and participate in internal environmental action and social justice groups to help achieve the set goals.

Manchester Museum

FOCUS
University Museum, Archaeological Museum

LOCATION
Urban. Manchester, United Kingdom

ANNUAL VISITORS
500,000

CONSTRUCTION
Original neo-Gothic building founded in 1821. Renovation: 2003

PROJECT
Project: Purcell | Architects, Studio C102, Mobile Studio Architects

CERTIFICATION
BREEAM

SIZE
New extension of the museum: 1,272 m²

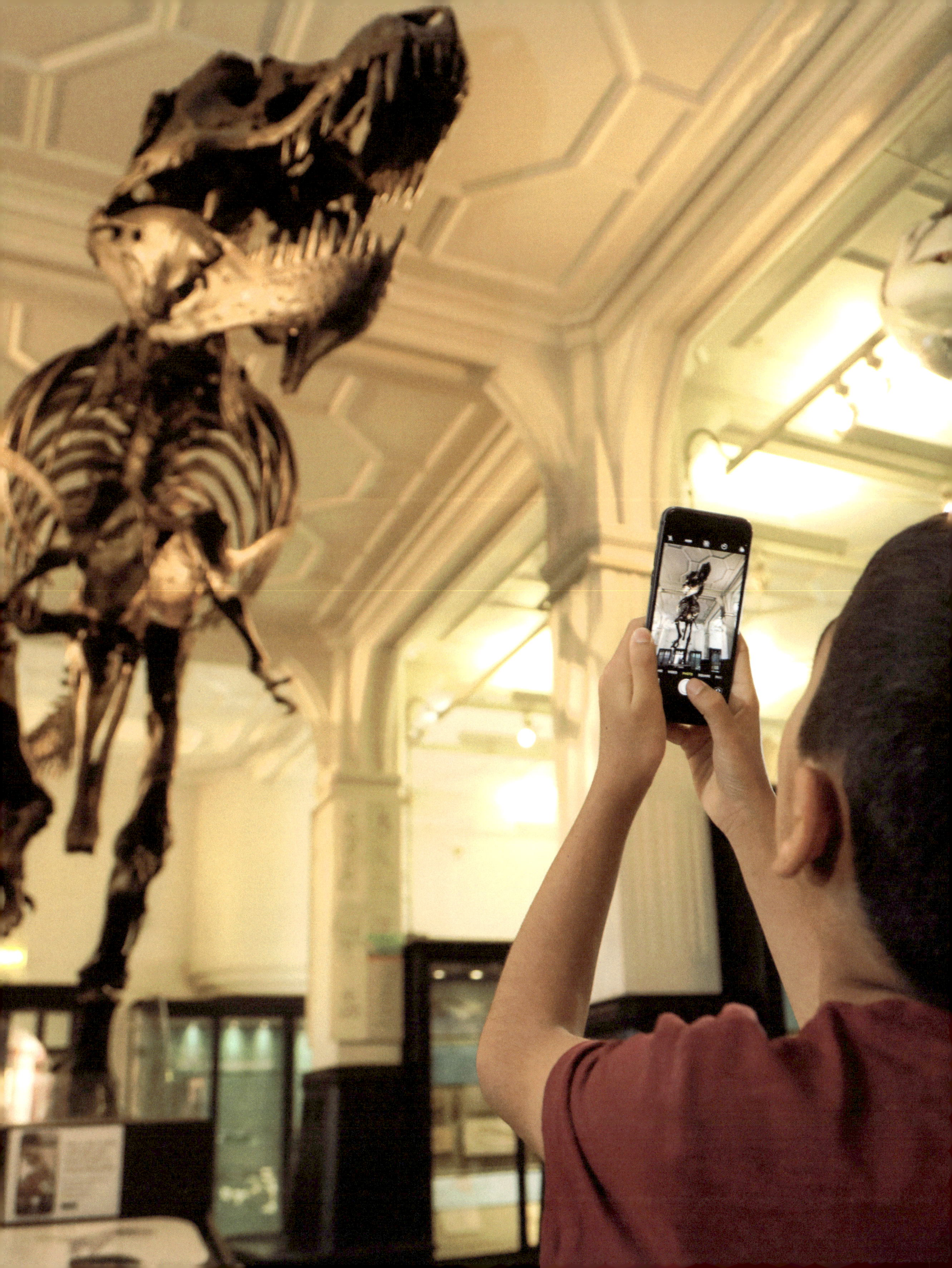

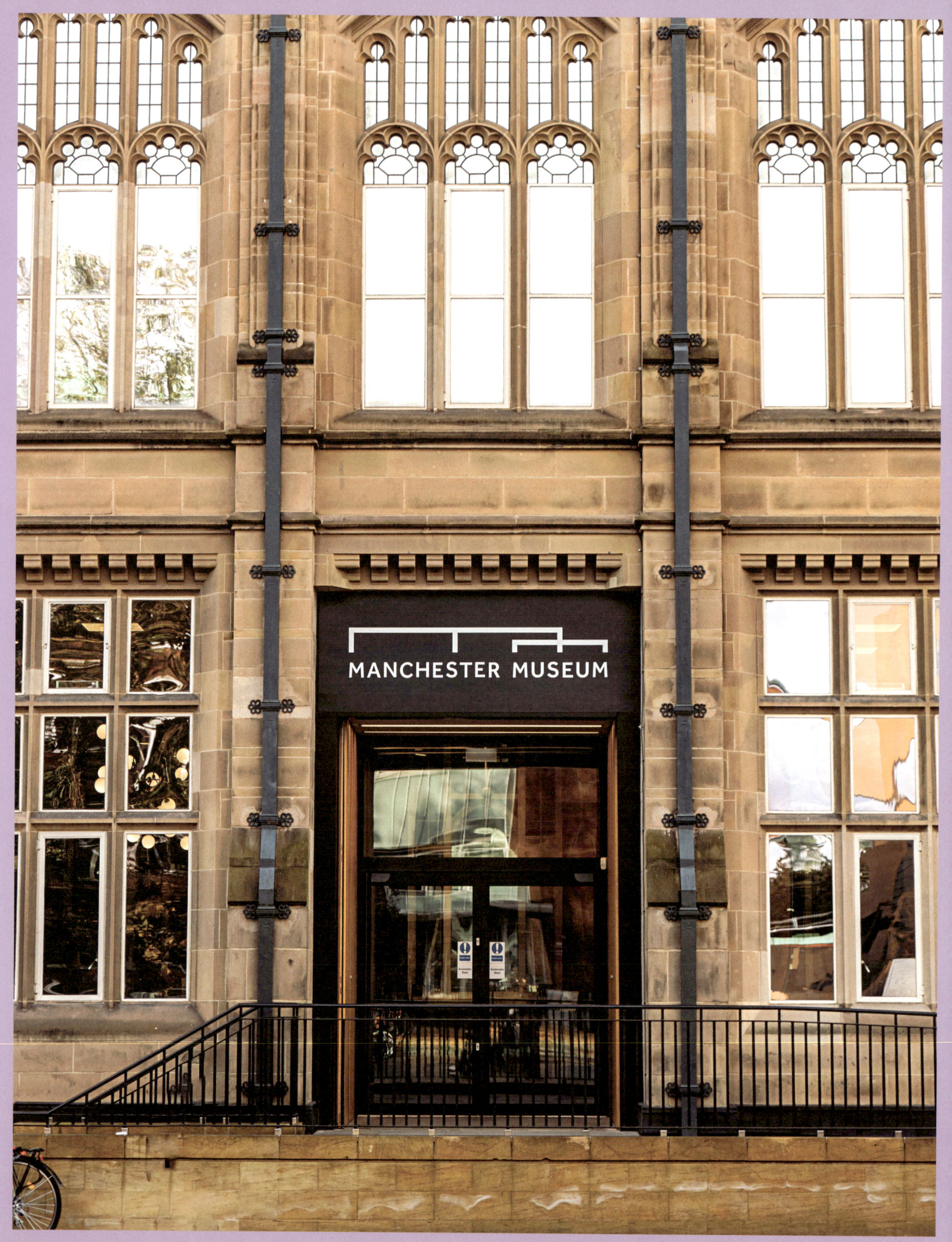
MANCHESTER MUSEUM

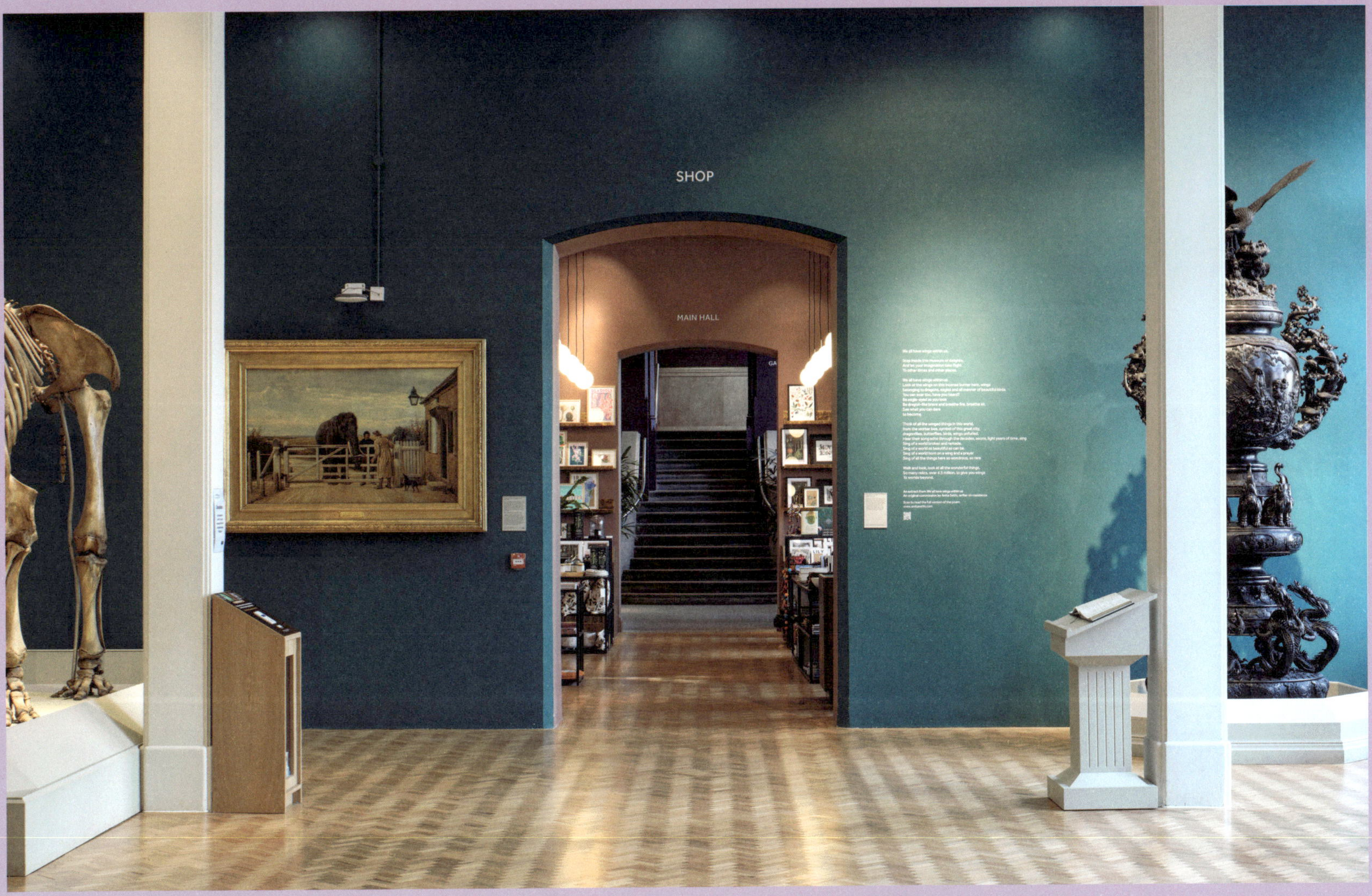

SHOP

MAIN HALL

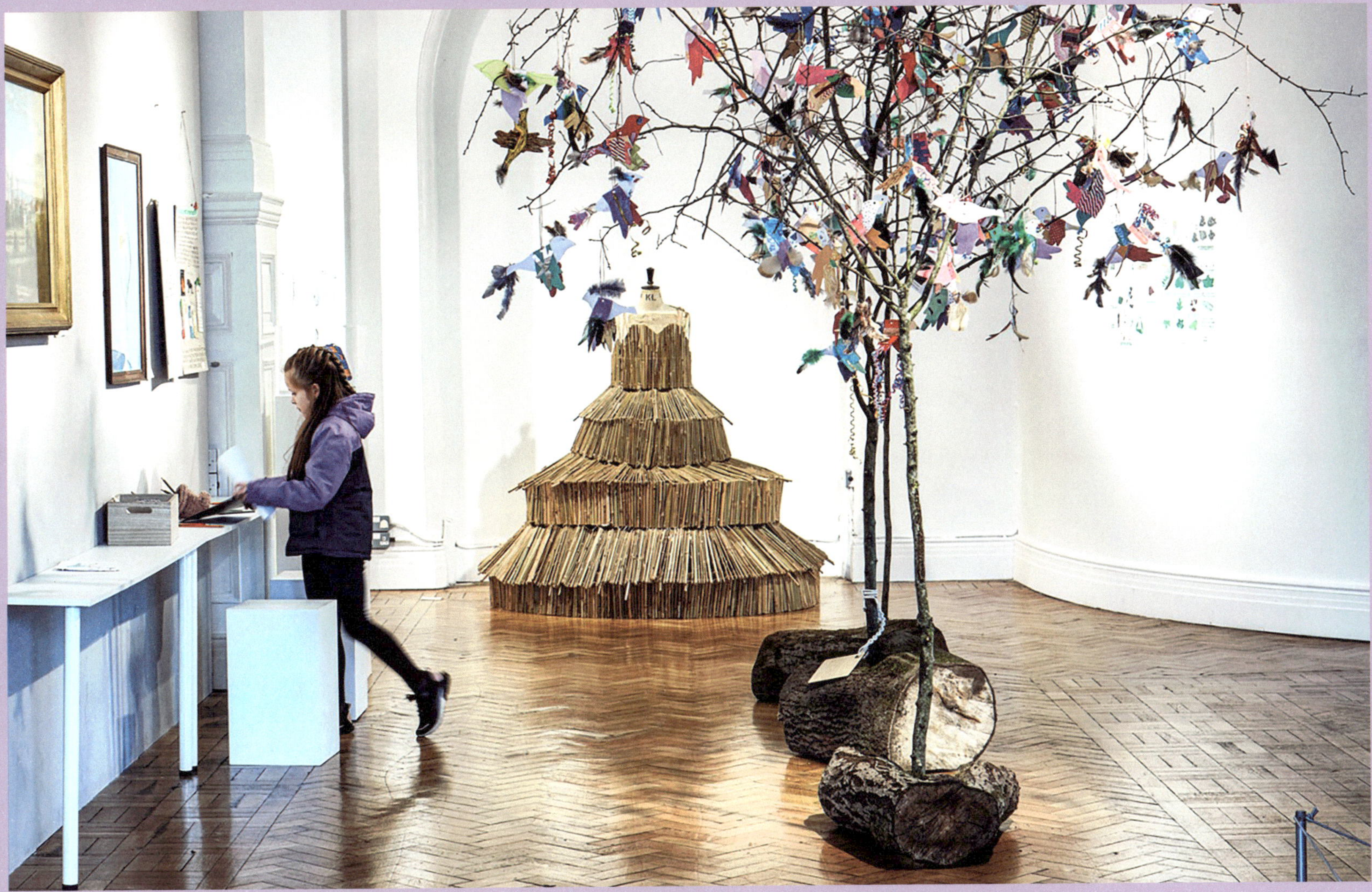

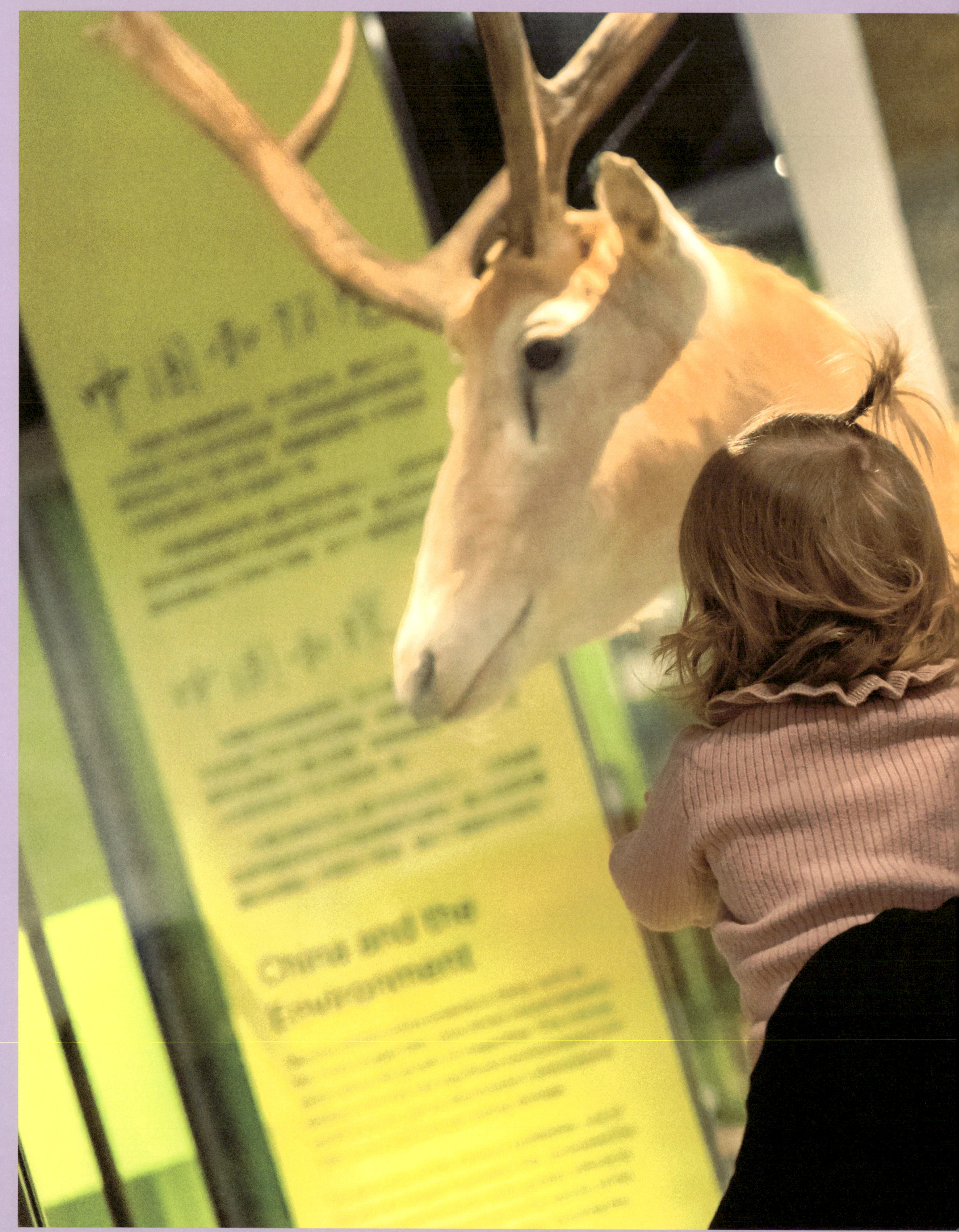
China and the
Environment

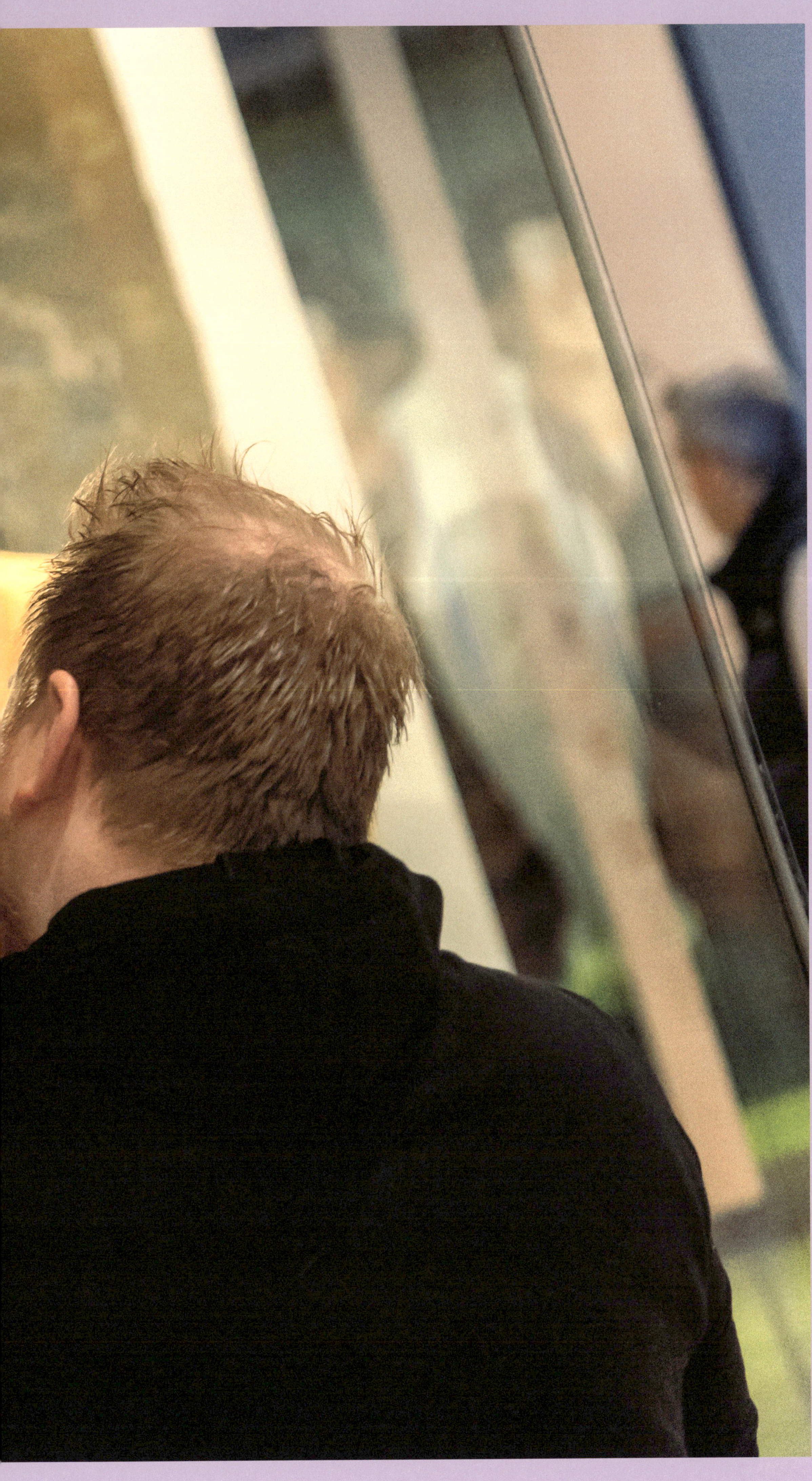

MUSEUMS WITH SIMILAR MEASURES

Victoria & Albert Museum

LONDON, UNITED KINGDOM

Employee development and learning program focused on sustainability.

Museu Nacional d'Art de Catalunya

BARCELONA, SPAIN

Dissemination of "information capsules" on the museum's intranet with practical sustainability tips for employees.

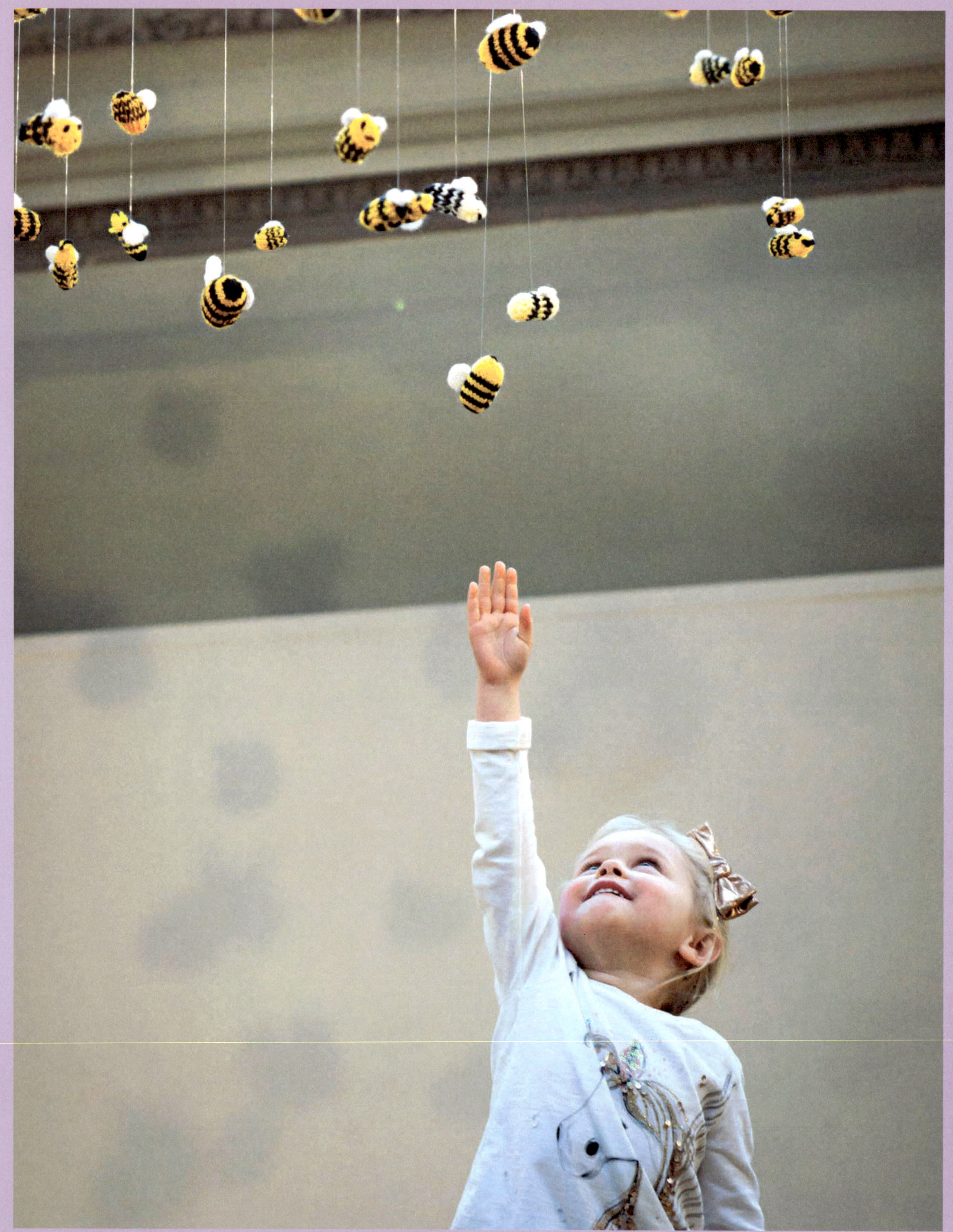

“Upskilling for activism.”

Hannah Hartley

Environmental Action Manager
Manchester Museum

24 SUSTAINABILITY GOVERNANCE BODIES

TRAINING OF EMPLOYEES AND WORK TEAMS   SDG 11 / 13

Governance, as the backbone of an institution or company, facilitates the environmental and social objectives set by museums and promotes long-term growth and sustainability. Creating governing bodies for sustainability inserts this variable in decision-making processes and facilitates the integration of sustainable development aspects in the museum's daily management.

In 2020, MOCA (Los Angeles) announced the creation of an environmental council, the first for a major US museum. Its goal is to harness art's transformative power to protect the planet and the museum for future generations. Major initiatives include green funding commitments, greenhouse gas emission reduction goals, renewable energy use, and environmentally focused exhibitions and educational programming. MOCA publicly shares the efforts and progress of its environmental council as a platform for public dialogue and engagement.

The Museum of Contemporary Art (MOCA)

FOCUS
Contemporary Art

VISITORS
236,104 (2010)

LOCATION
Urban. Los Angeles, California, USA

CONSTRUCTION
Established in 1979. Opened in 1983

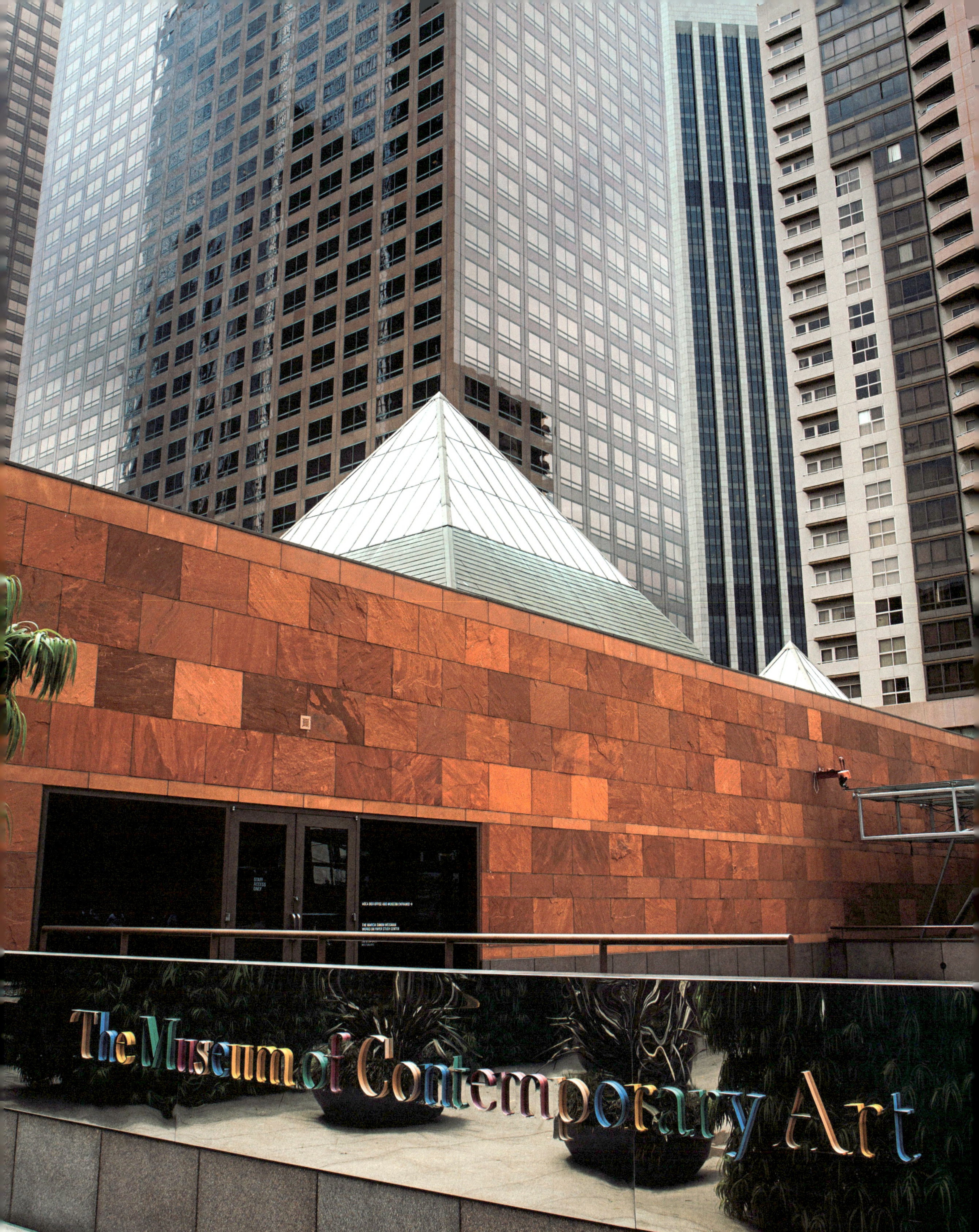
The Museum of Contemporary Art

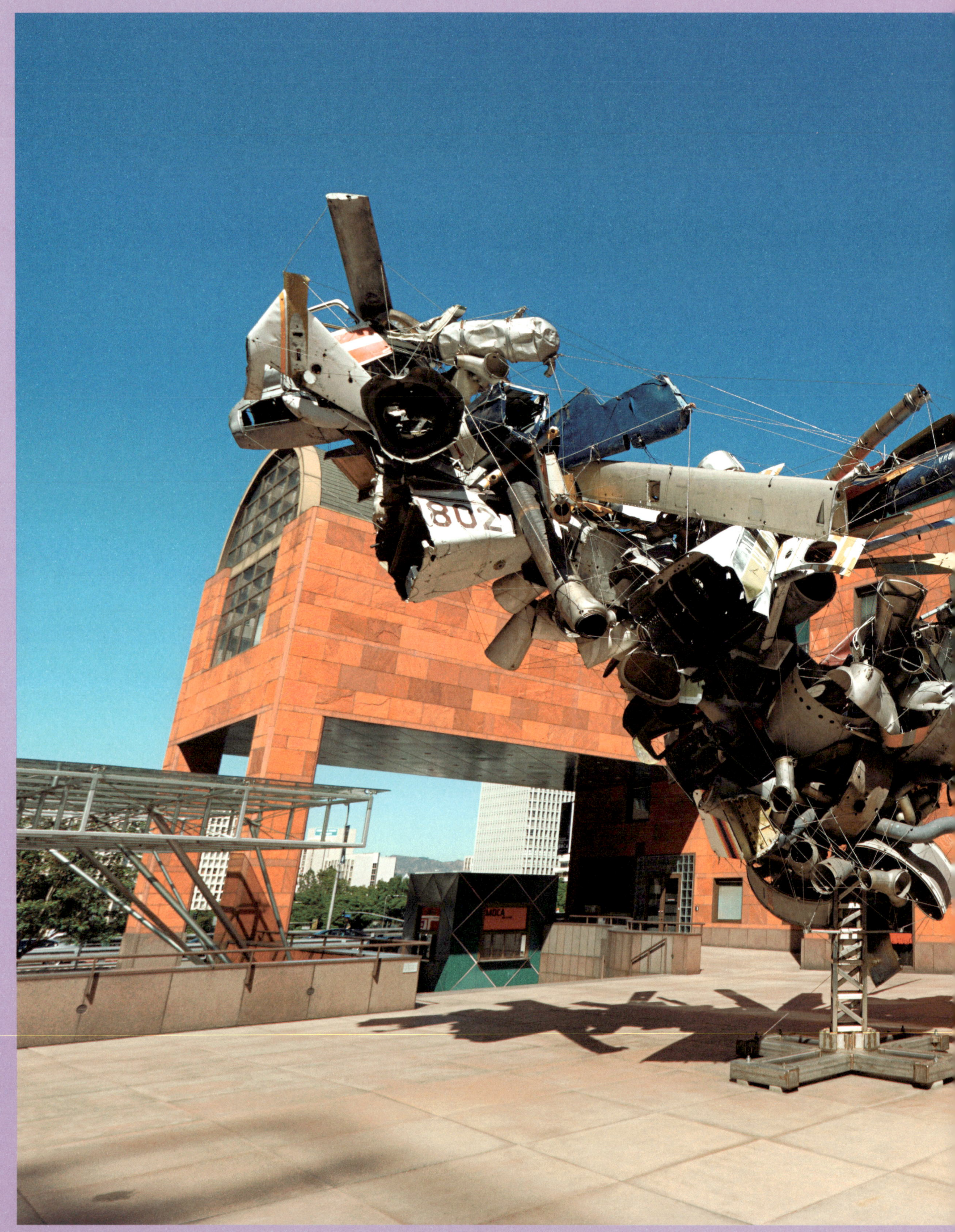
802

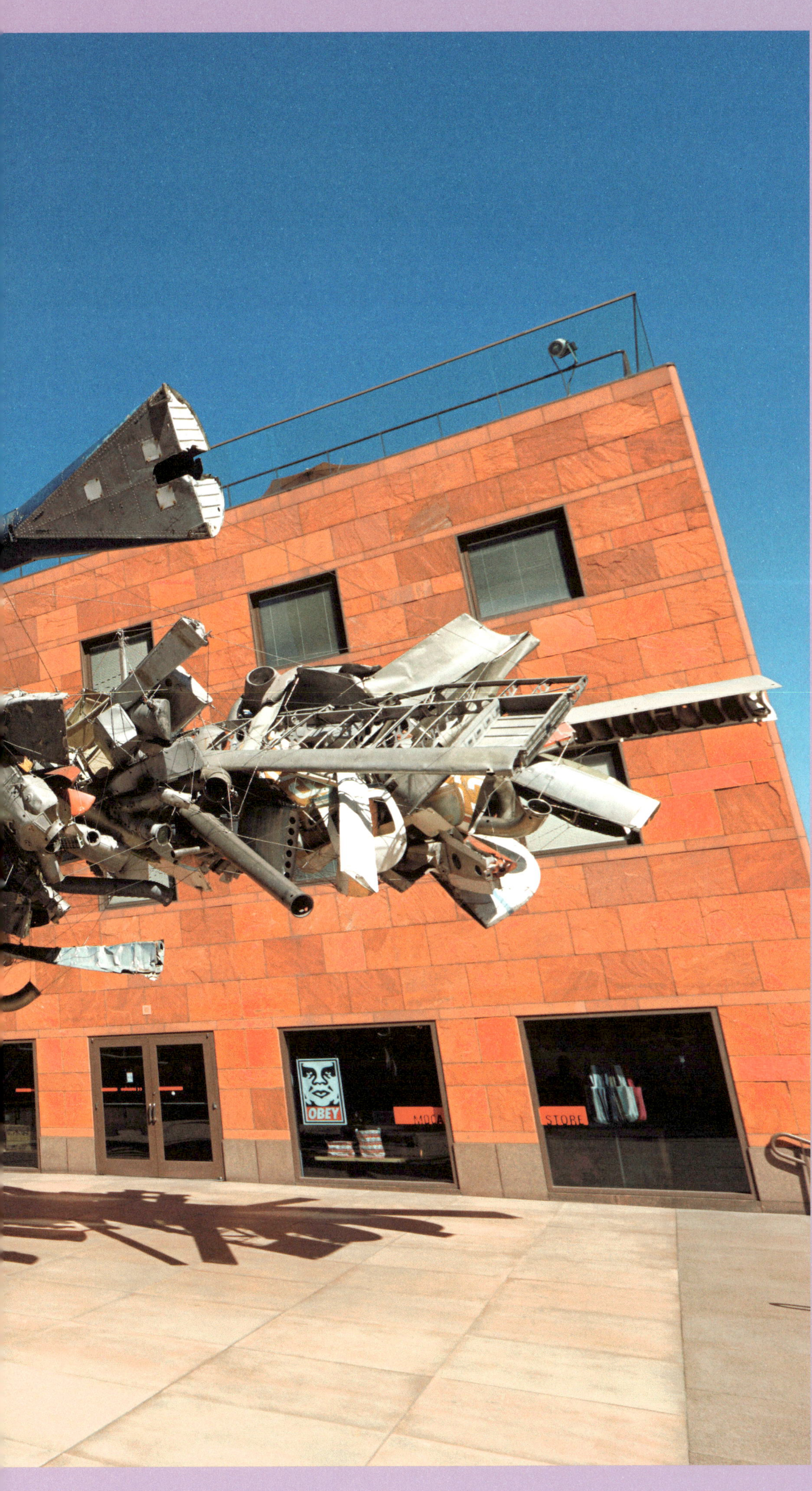

MUSEUMS WITH SIMILAR MEASURES

Royal Ontario Museum

TORONTO, CANADA

New climate change curator profile dedicated to building global partnerships and projects, combining research, programming, and community education.

Museo Lázaro Galdiano

MADRID, SPAIN

Creation of a working group to promote responsible consumption by employees and visitors, and launch of a newsletter with initiatives carried out at the museum.

High Museum of Art

ATLANTA, GEORGIA, USA

Creation of a "green" working group in the museum.

Guggenheim Museum Bilbao

BILBAO, SPAIN

Specific interdepartmental group (Gu-Zero) to inform and involve the workforce, suppliers, and social agents in sustainability initiatives.

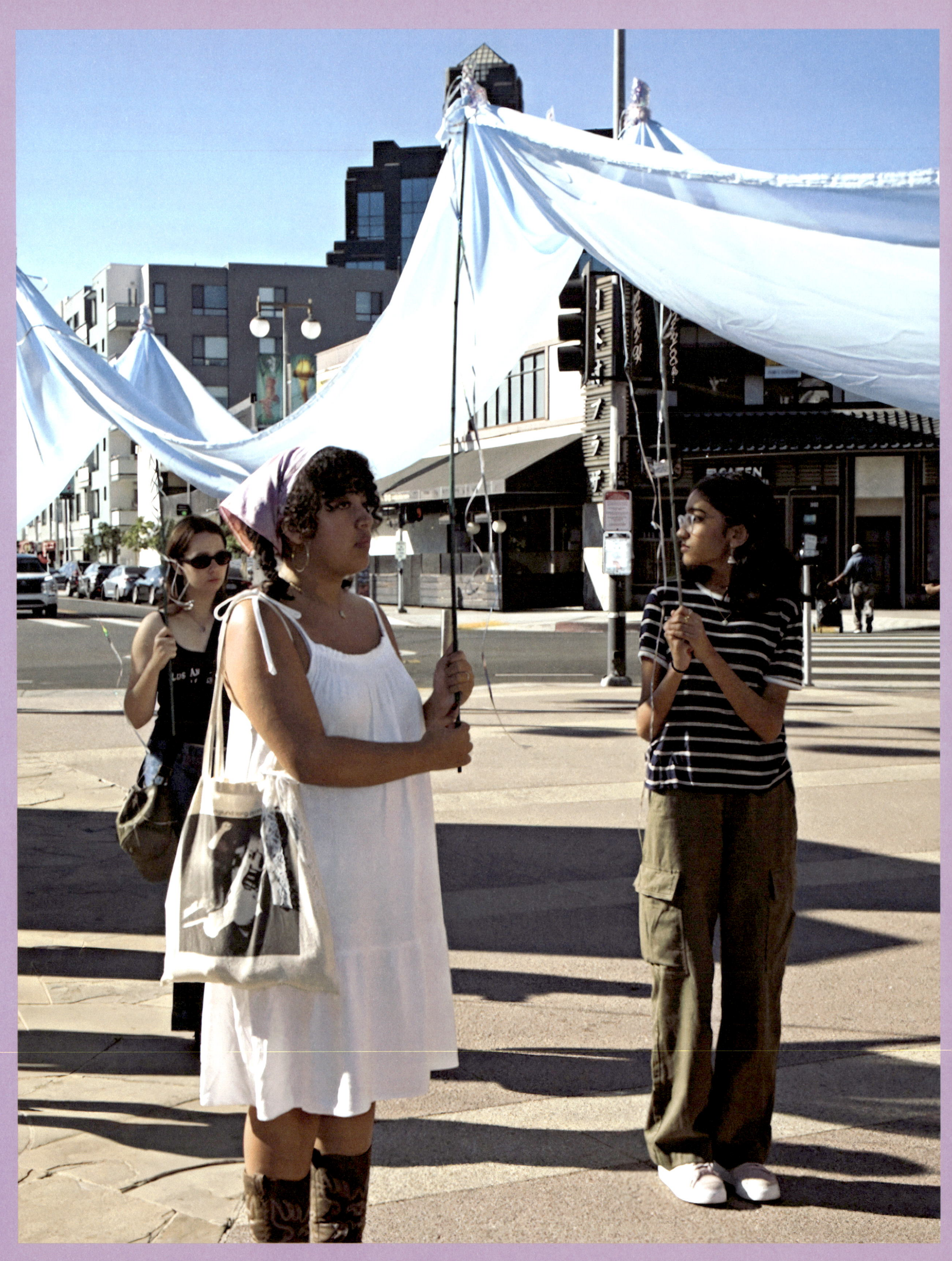

“A sustainable present ensures a better future.”
MOCA Environmental Council

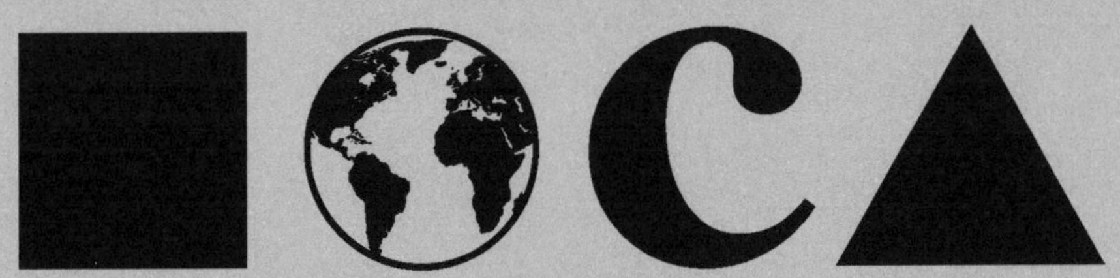

25 PREPARATION FOR ENVIRONMENTAL EMERGENCIES

ENVIRONMENTAL EMERGENCIES SDG 9 / 11 / 12

In a context where extreme weather events are becoming increasingly frequent, the implementation of measures to minimize potential adverse environmental impacts caused by these events becomes indispensable.

The geographic area of Florida is prone to being affected by cyclones. For this reason, The Dalí Museum in Florida has been designed as a hurricane-resistant building. Its walls, constructed of thick reinforced concrete, are capable of withstanding Category 5 hurricanes. To protect the artworks, they have been located starting from the third floor, always above the floodplain.

The Dalí Museum

FOCUS
Contemporary Art

LOCATION
Urban. St. Petersburg, Florida, USA

CONSTRUCTION
1982–2011

PROJECT
HOK Architecture

SIZE
6,317 m²

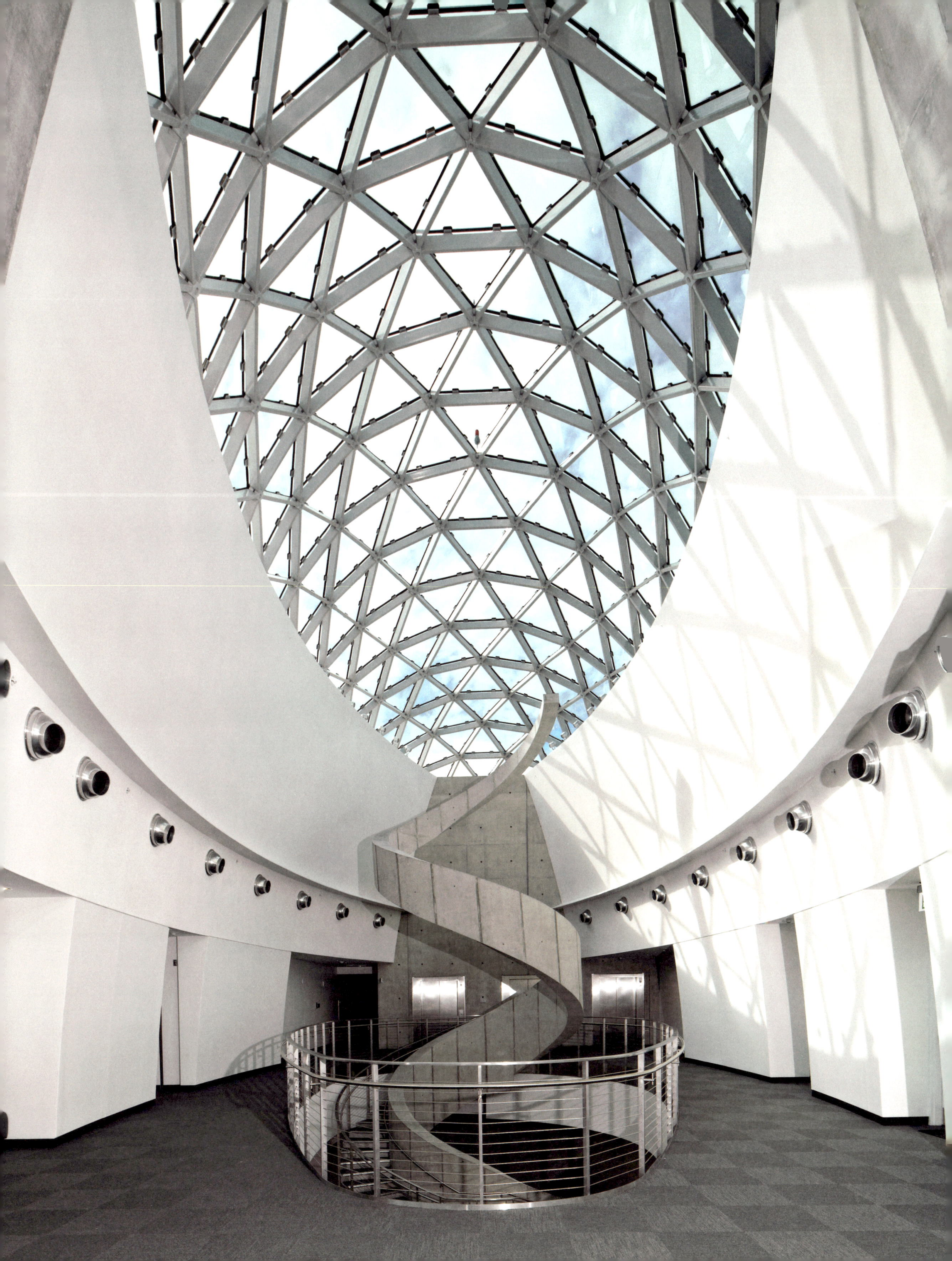

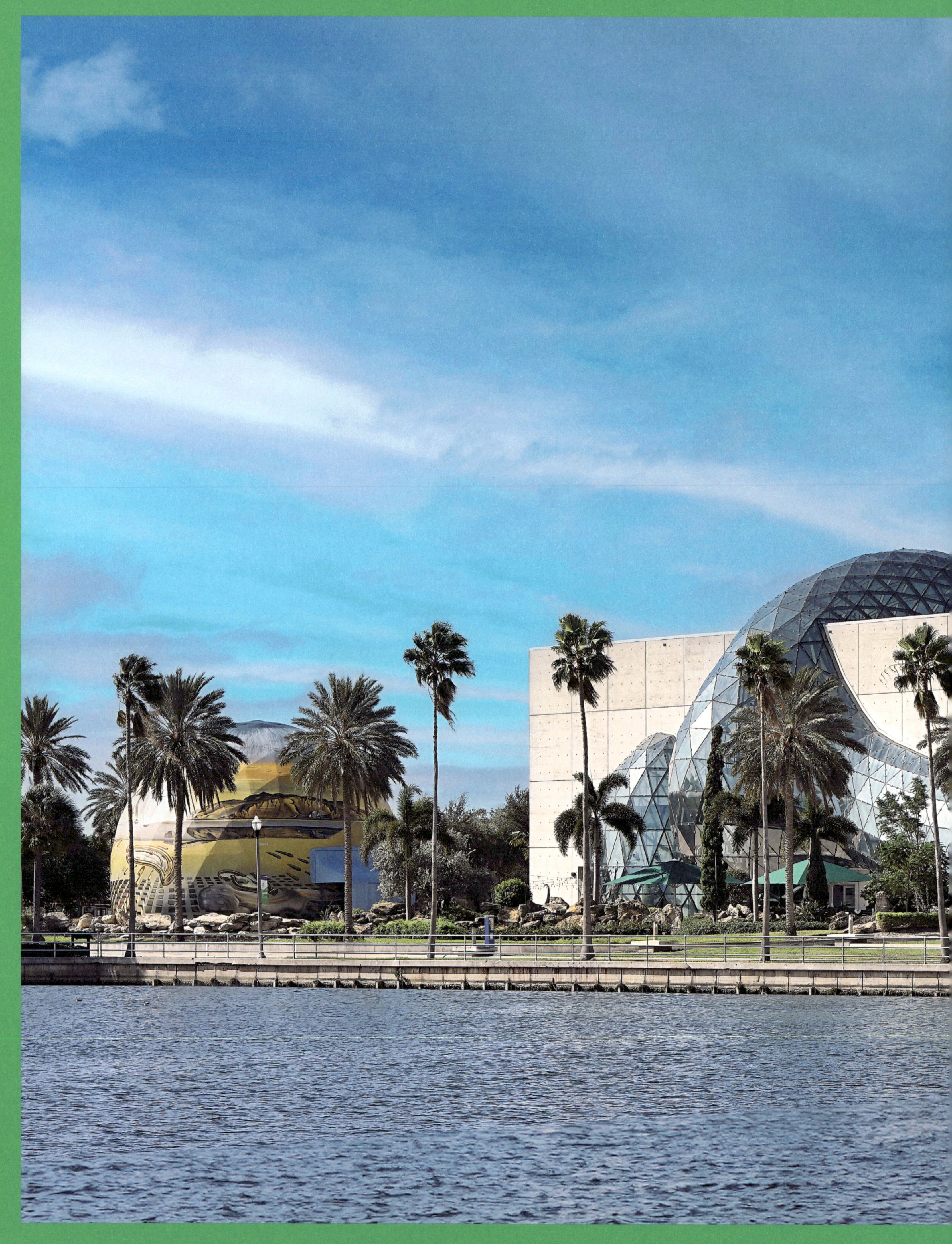

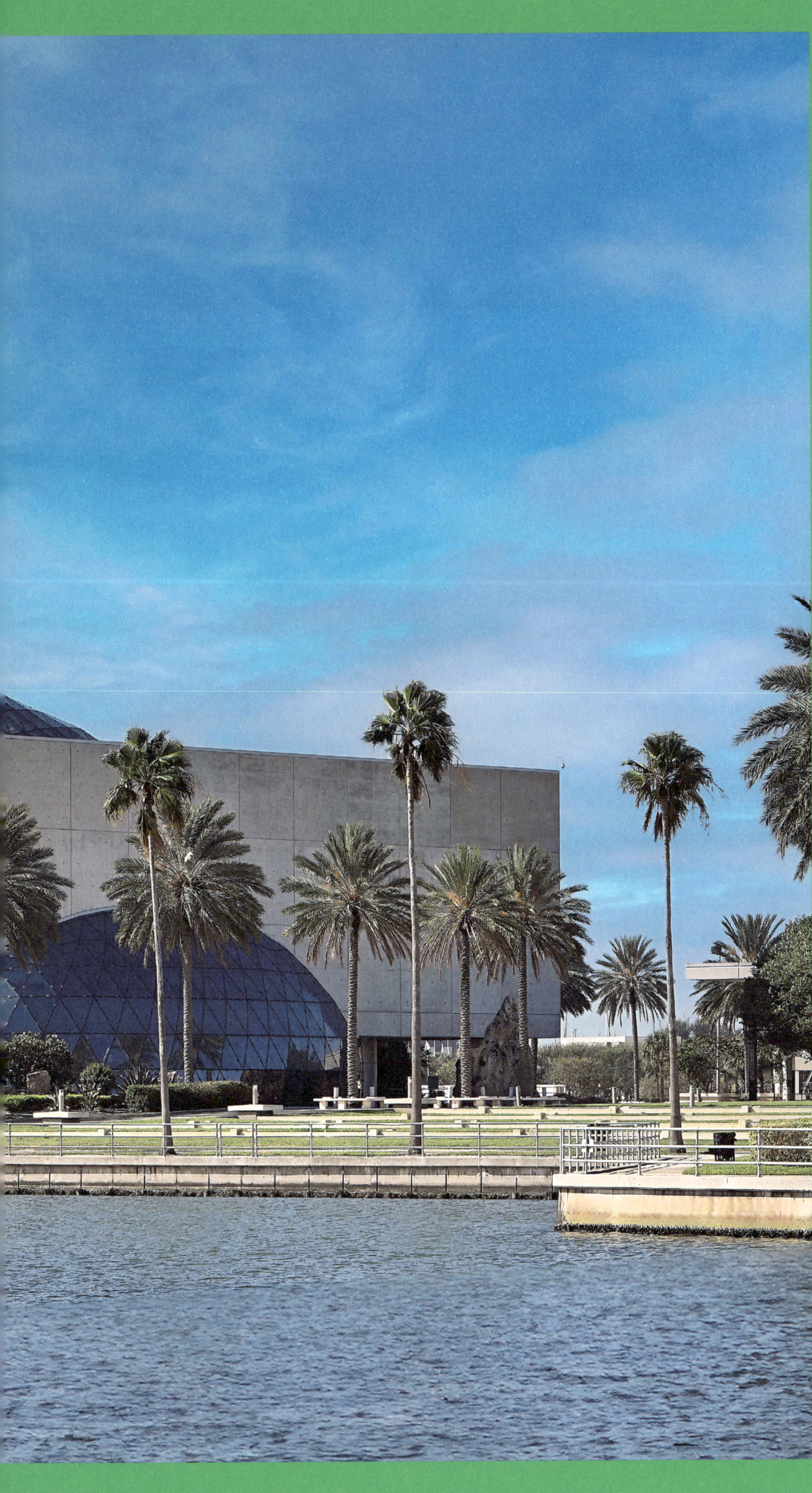

MUSEUMS WITH SIMILAR MEASURES

Pérez Art Museum Miami

MIAMI, FLORIDA, USA

Construction of a new building with climate-resistant materials.

The National Museum of Western Art

TOKYO, JAPAN

Seismic isolation technology that absorbs movements caused by earthquakes.

Earthquake Memorial Museum

WENCHUAN, CHINA

This memorial museum honoring the victims of the 2008 Sichaun earthquake is equipped with an effective seismic system based on rubber dampers.

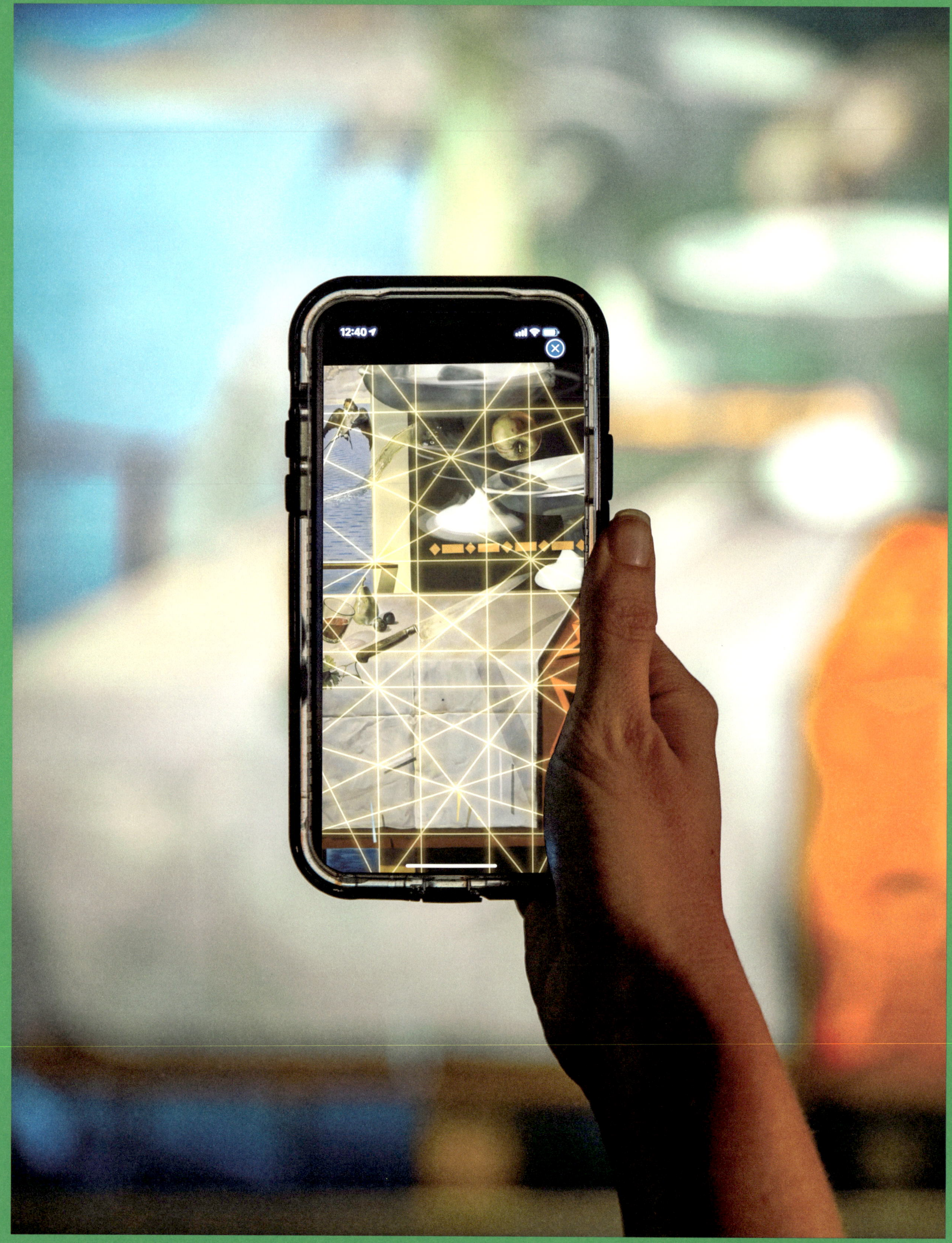
12:40

"We exposed the bare faces of concrete to reduce maintenance and turn them into a durable and natural layer, contrasted with the more refined precision of Enigma glass. This contrast between the rational world of the conscious and the more intuitive, surprising natural world is a constant in Dalí's work."

Yann Weymouth

Architect, designer of The Dalí Museum

26 PROMOTION OF SUSTAINABLE MOBILITY

SUSTAINABLE MOBILITY SDG 7 / 13

The new model of city requires other ways of getting around that meet residents' needs while minimizing environmental impact. Museums should offer visitors every possible facility to promote more sustainable ways of getting to them, such as public transportation, cycling, walking, or zero-emission vehicles.

The Horniman Museum & Gardens in London periodically runs information campaigns to promote sustainable transportation among employees and visitors, with a focus on cycling. They provide details on the best bicycle routes via segregated lanes and offer specific bicycle parking facilities. Additionally, the museum's website provides information on being a climate-friendly visitor, including the best public transportation options for getting to the museum, the best walking routes, and other details.

Horniman Museum & Gardens

FOCUS
Natural History

ANNUAL VISITORS
950,000

LOCATION
Urban. London, United Kingdom

CONSTRUCTION
Built in 1898.
Opened in 1901

SIZE
The gardens occupy 65,000 m²

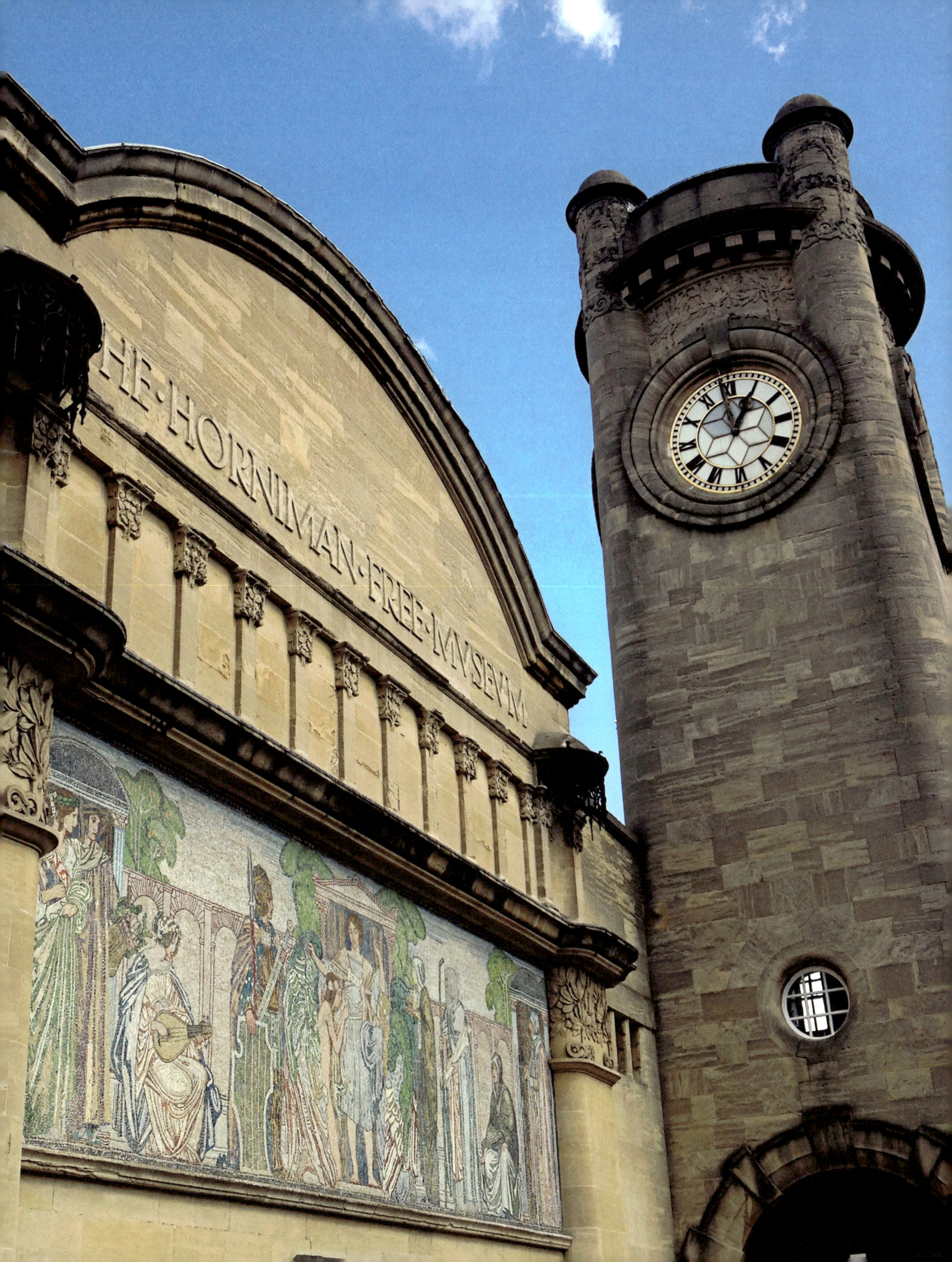
HE·HORNIMAN·FREE·MVSEVM

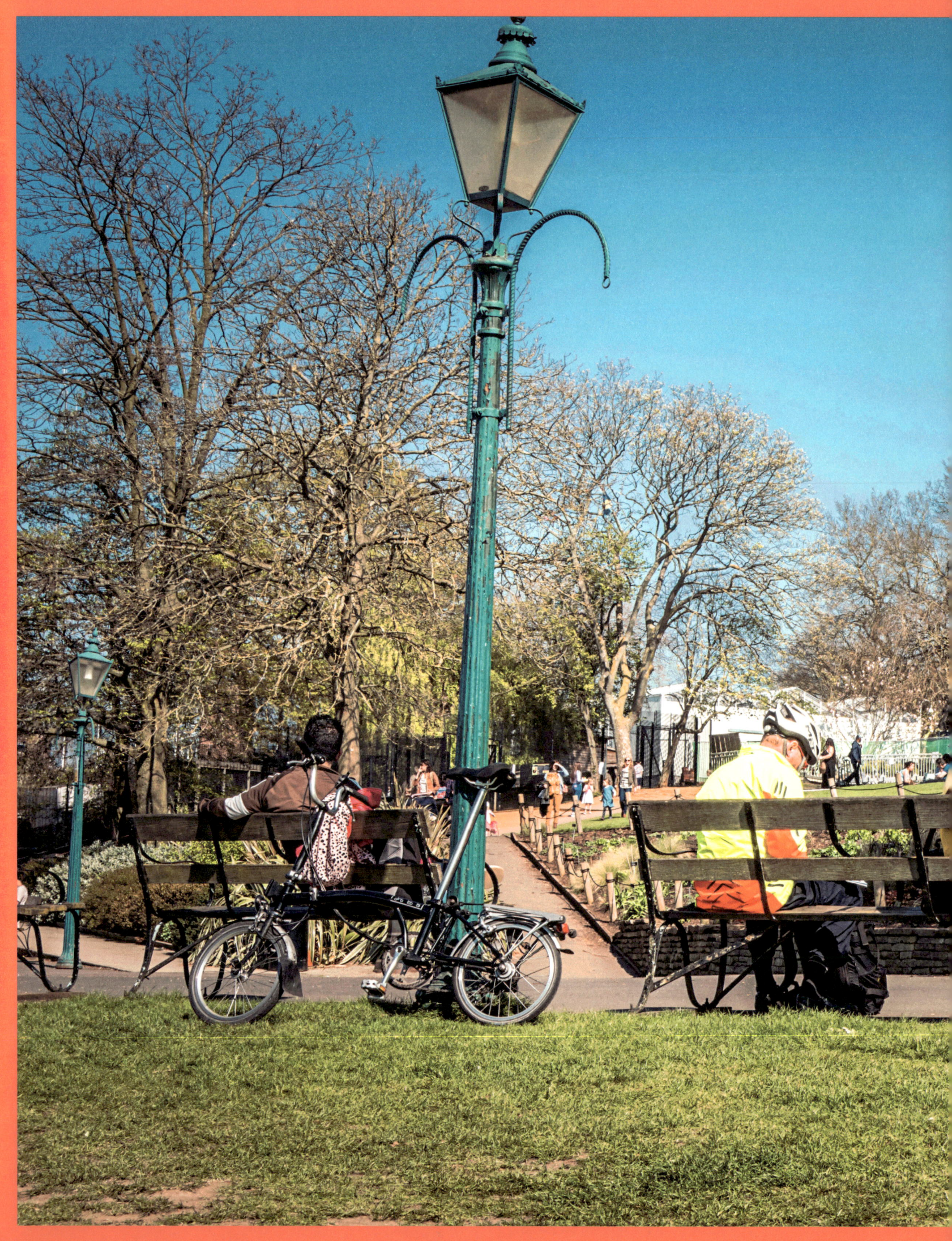

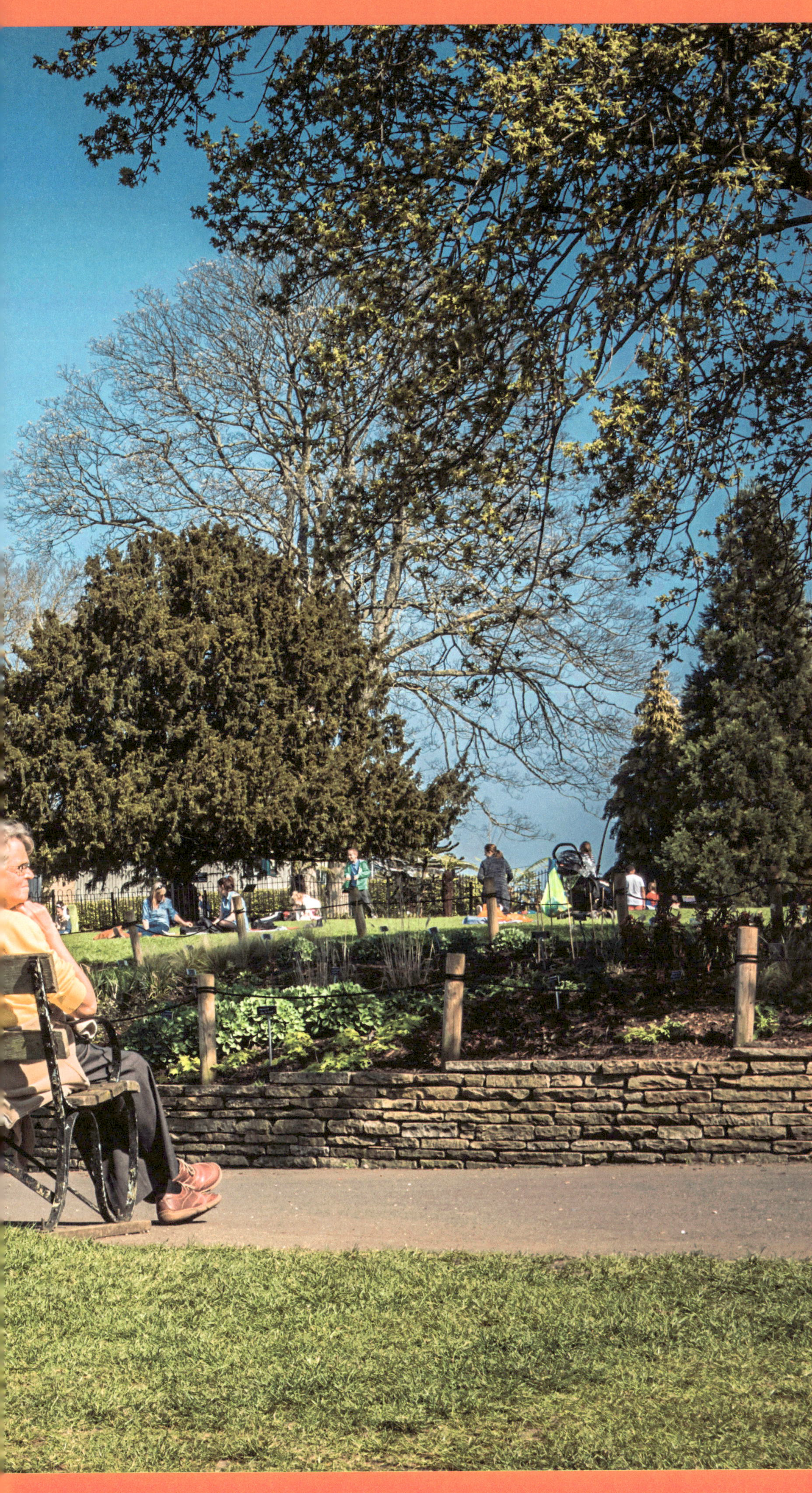

MUSEUMS WITH SIMILAR MEASURES

Cincinnati Museum Center

CINCINNATI, OHIO, USA

It has electric vehicle charging stations, allowing visitors to recharge their vehicles while visiting the museum.

Brunel Museum

LONDON, UNITED KINGDOM

Employee benefit program for avoiding the use of airplanes during vacations.

Museu Marítim de Barcelona
Barcelona, Spain

Comprehensive sustainable mobility plan
for employees and visitors.

“The main goal of the plan is to optimize mobility, emphasizing the promotion of public transportation, the rationalization of private vehicle use, and the encouragement of carpooling and non-motorized vehicles among both staff and collaborators, as well as visitors.”

Sustainable Mobility Plan of the Museu Marítim de Barcelona

27 CALCULATION OF THE CARBON FOOTPRINT

GREENHOUSE GASES SDG 7 / 12 / 13

The carbon footprint represents the total volume of greenhouse gases produced by an activity or facility. Measuring this footprint in terms of tons of CO_2 emitted is crucial for implementing specific measures and initiatives to begin the decarbonization process in museums.

The Museu do Amanhã (Museum of Tomorrow) in Rio de Janeiro tracks and calculates its greenhouse gas emissions following the GHG protocol, the most widely used international tool for calculating and reporting emissions. The museum accounts for its own direct emissions as well as for indirect emissions from suppliers and subcontractors. Furthermore, it has established a compensation mechanism by purchasing emission rights on the voluntary market, which finances the shift to renewable fuels in the kilns of local ceramic manufacturers.

Museu do Amanhã

FOCUS
Applied Sciences

LOCATION
Urban, Maua Pier,
Rio de Janeiro, Brazil

ANNUAL VISITORS
366,045

CONSTRUCTION
2015

PROJECT
Santiago Calatrava

CERTIFICATION
LEED Gold

SIZE
15,000 m²

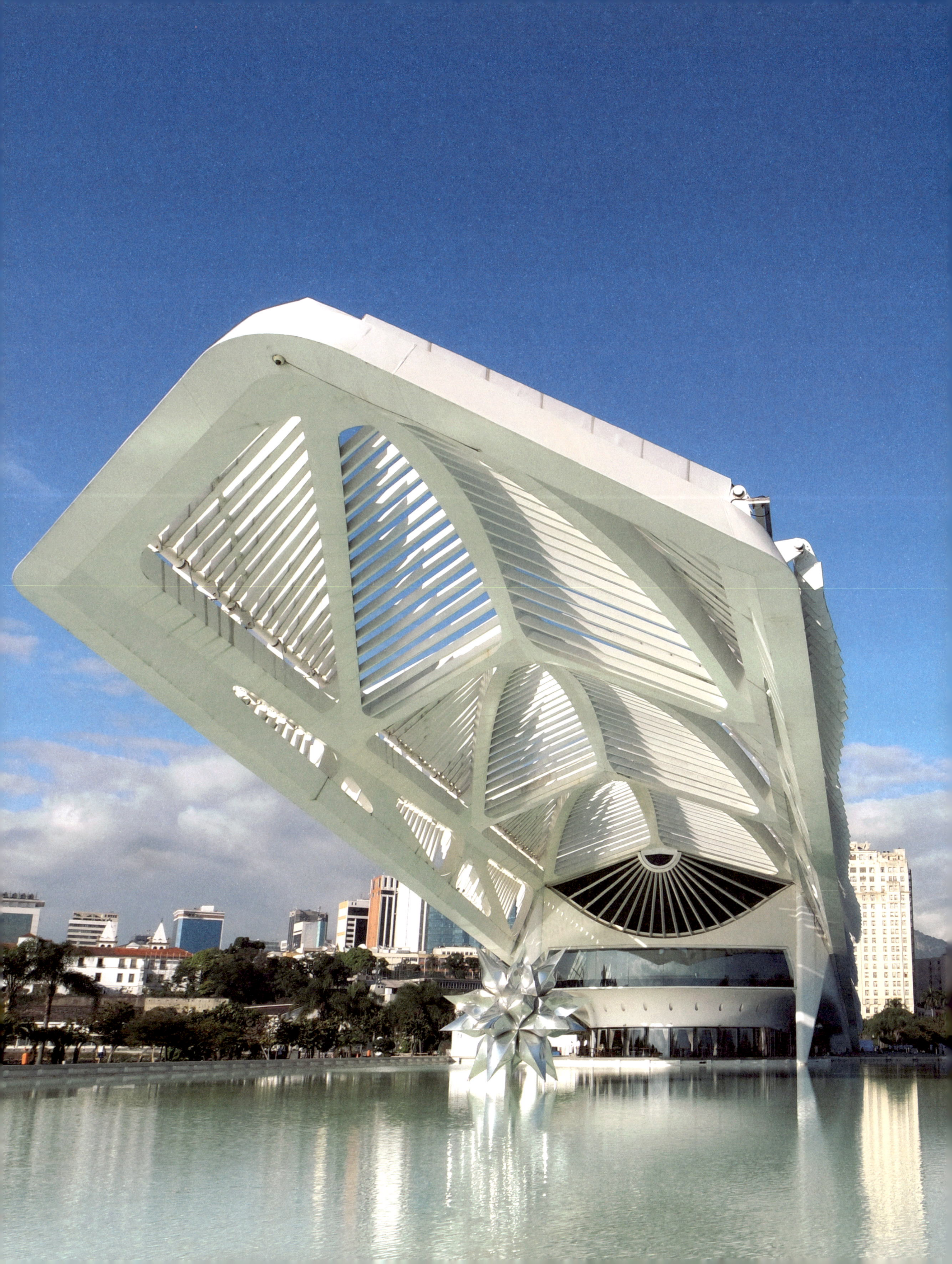

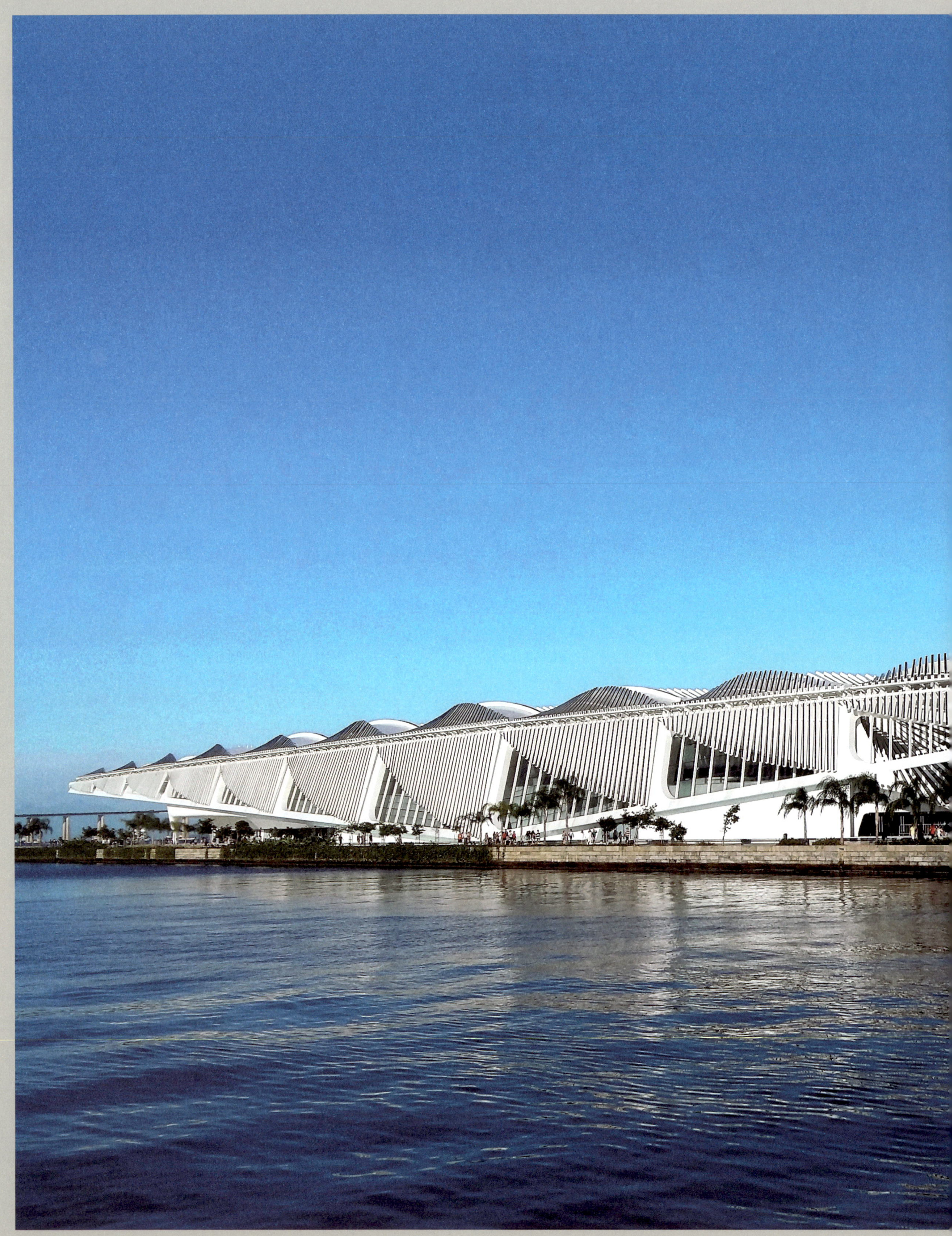

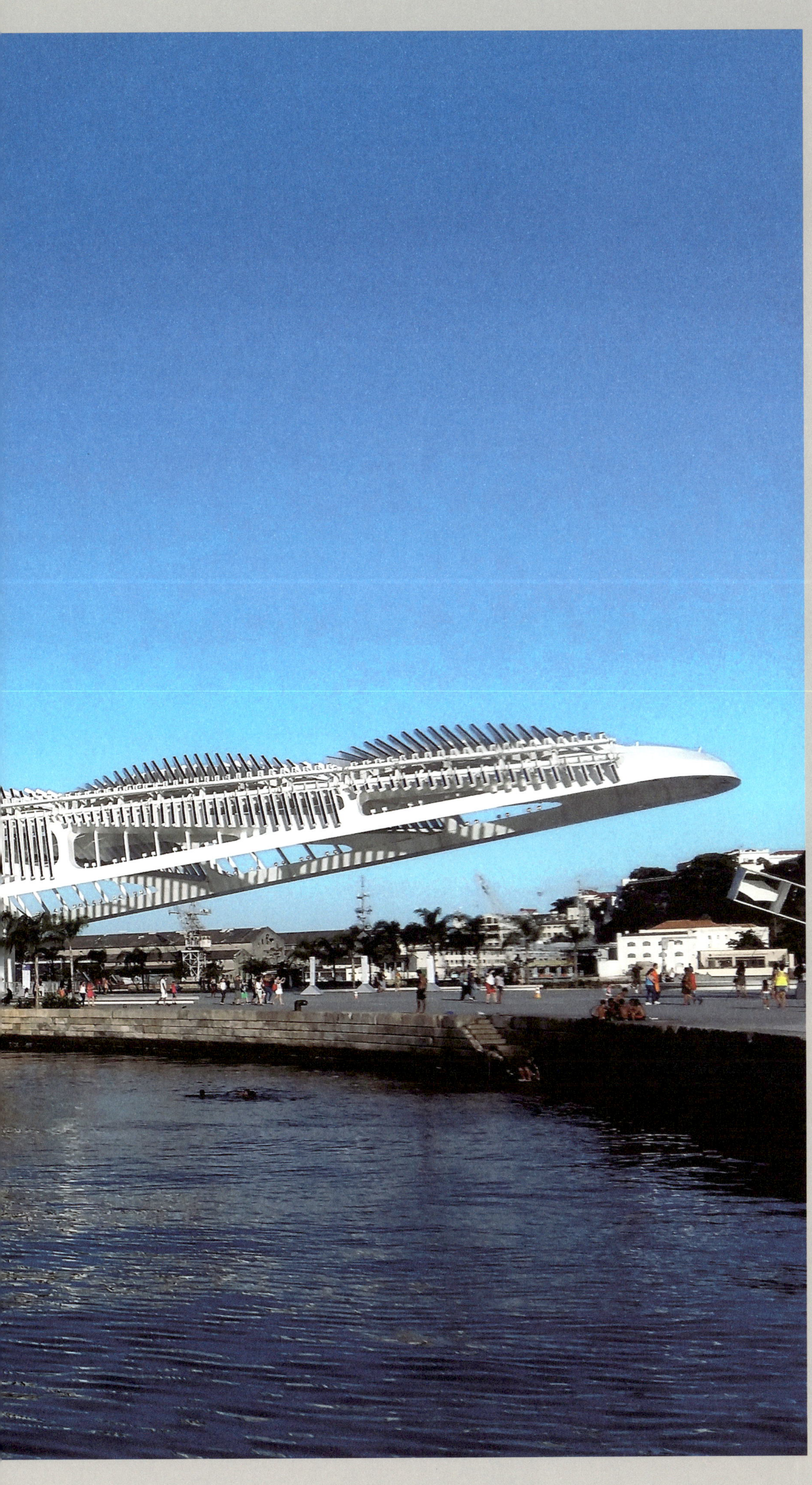

MUSEUMS WITH SIMILAR MEASURES

Discovery Museum

MASSACHUSETTS, USA

Employee and visitor emissions measurement and carbon footprint offsetting systems for visitors.

Museo de Arte Contemporáneo Helga de Alvear

CÁCERES, SPAIN

Measuring and reducing emissions through renewable energy and energy efficiency measures.

Tate Modern

LONDON, UNITED KINGDOM

Calculation of the carbon footprint and specific recommendations for reducing it.

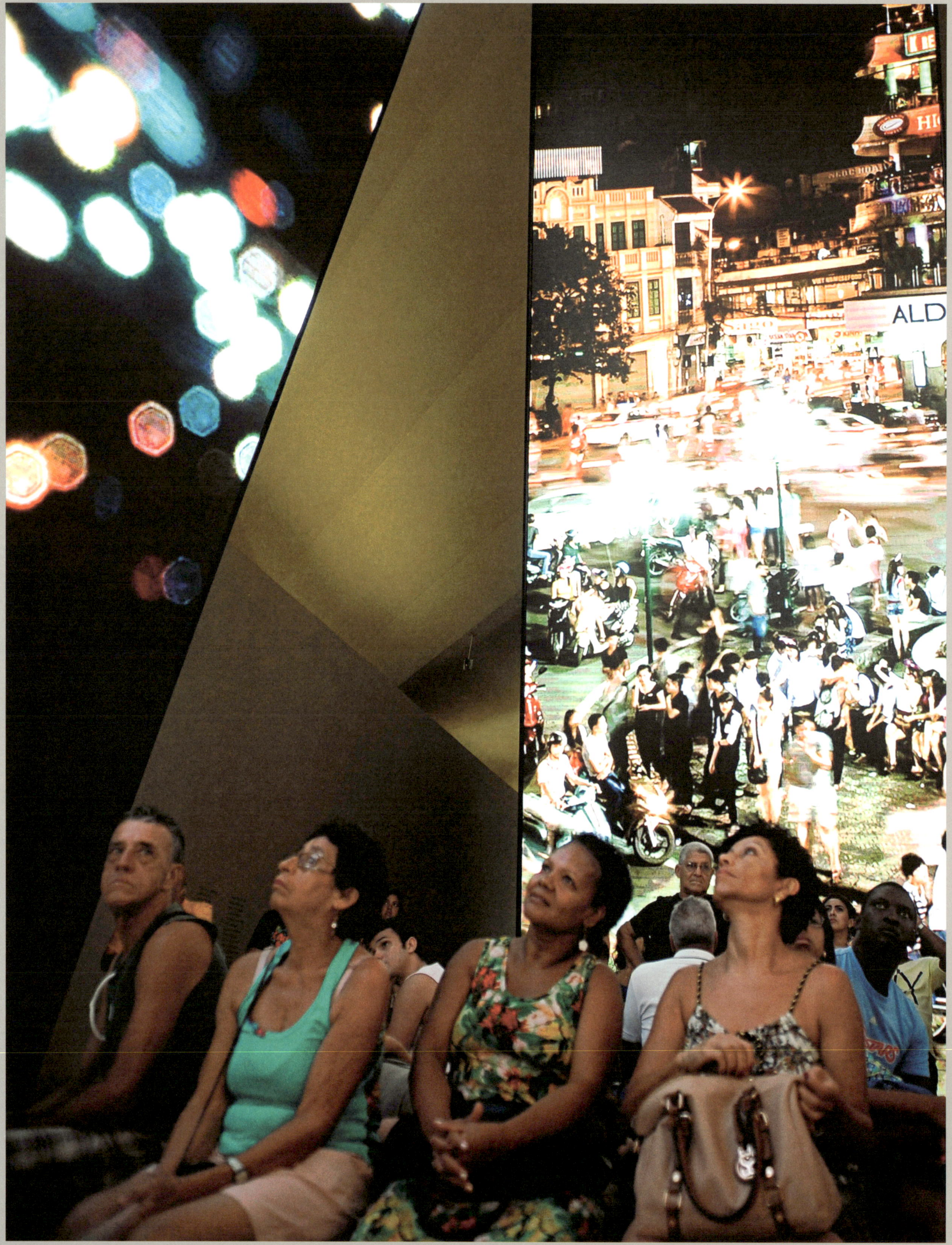

“When preparing an exhibition, it is just as important to think about how it will be dismantled as how it will be set up.”

Futuring Toolkit from the BIO27 Design Biennial for Sustainable Cultural Production

28 EXHIBITION SPACES DEDICATED TO SUSTAINABILITY

VISITOR EDUCATION AND AWARENESS SDG 4 / 13

Museums have a unique role in using their expertise, perspectives, and reputations to inspire visitors to engage in the fight against climate change and shift towards more sustainable lifestyles. Culture serves as a catalyst for change, with museums acting as hubs for generating knowledge, fostering conversation, and encouraging critical thinking.

The Climate House at the Natural History Museum in Oslo is an exhibition space focused on climate change and environmental issues. Through interactive exhibitions and immersive experiences, the institution invites visitors to reflect and take action for a more sustainable future by explaining the different natural and human factors that influence climate change and the consequences of various future scenarios. Visitors also receive information about what they can do to reduce their greenhouse gas emissions and the role they can play in the fight against climate change.

Natural History Museum

FOCUS
Natural History

LOCATION
Urban. Oslo, Norway

CONSTRUCTION
Built in 1814.
Renovated in 2022

ANNUAL VISITORS
366,045

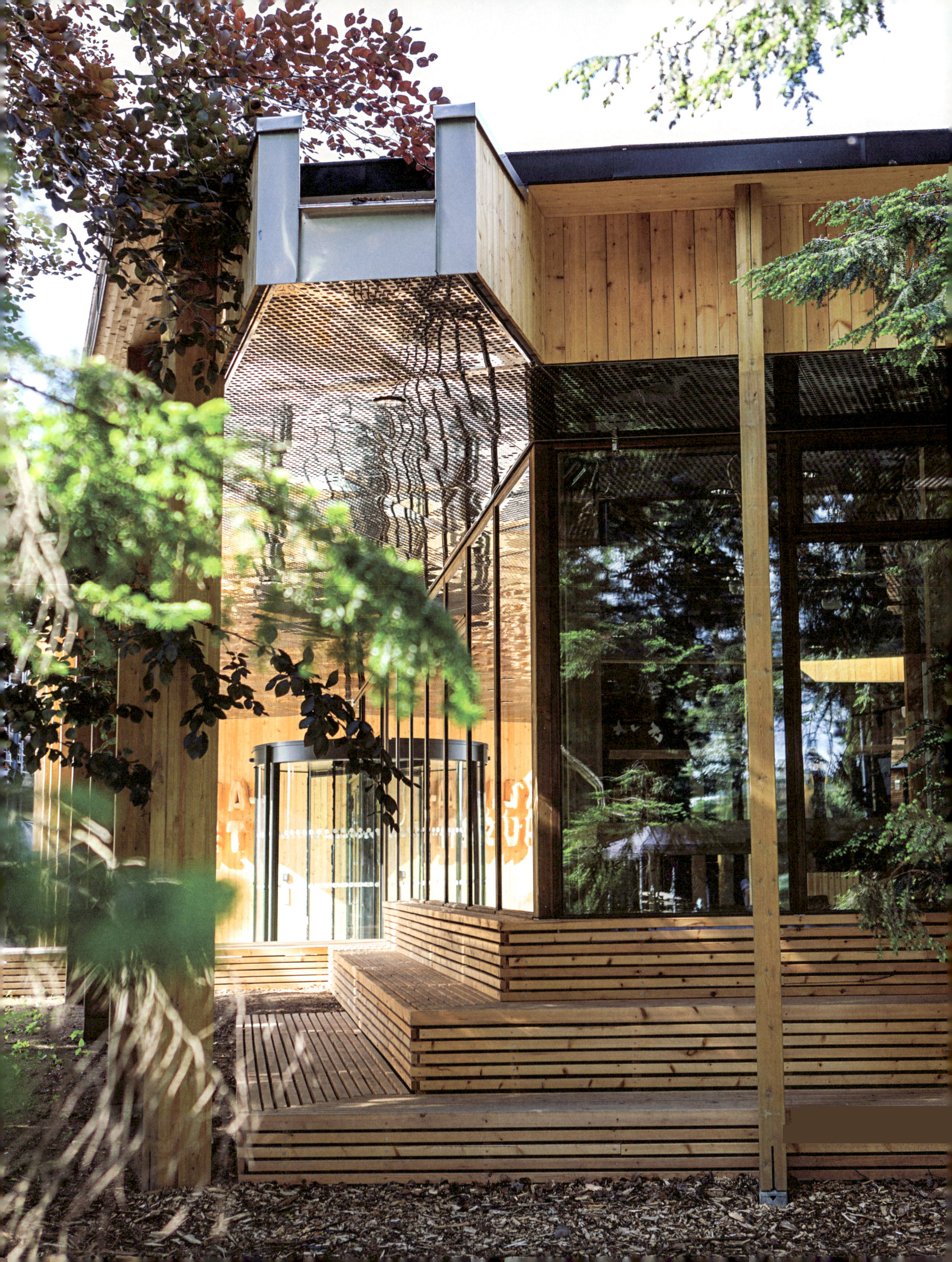

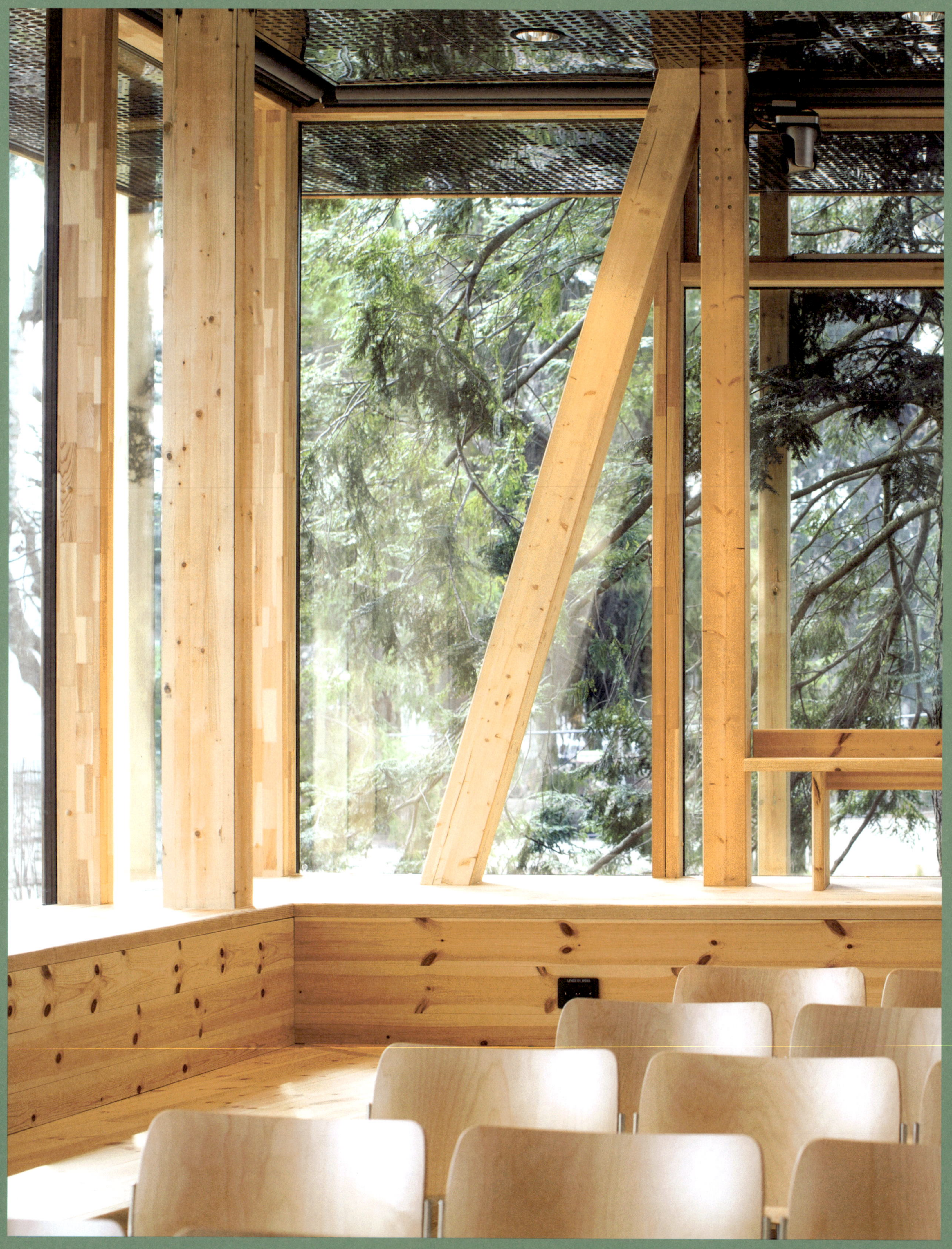

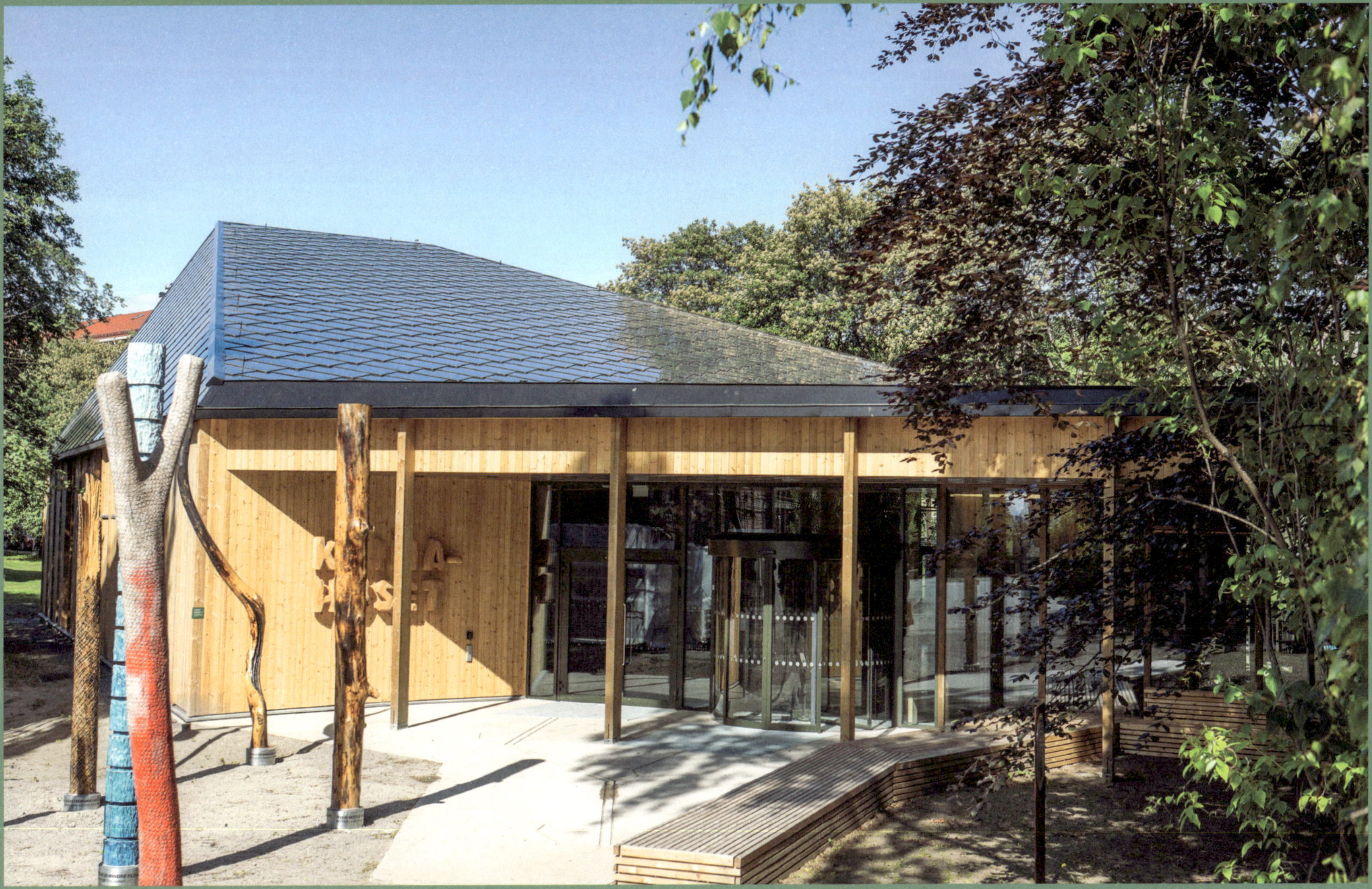

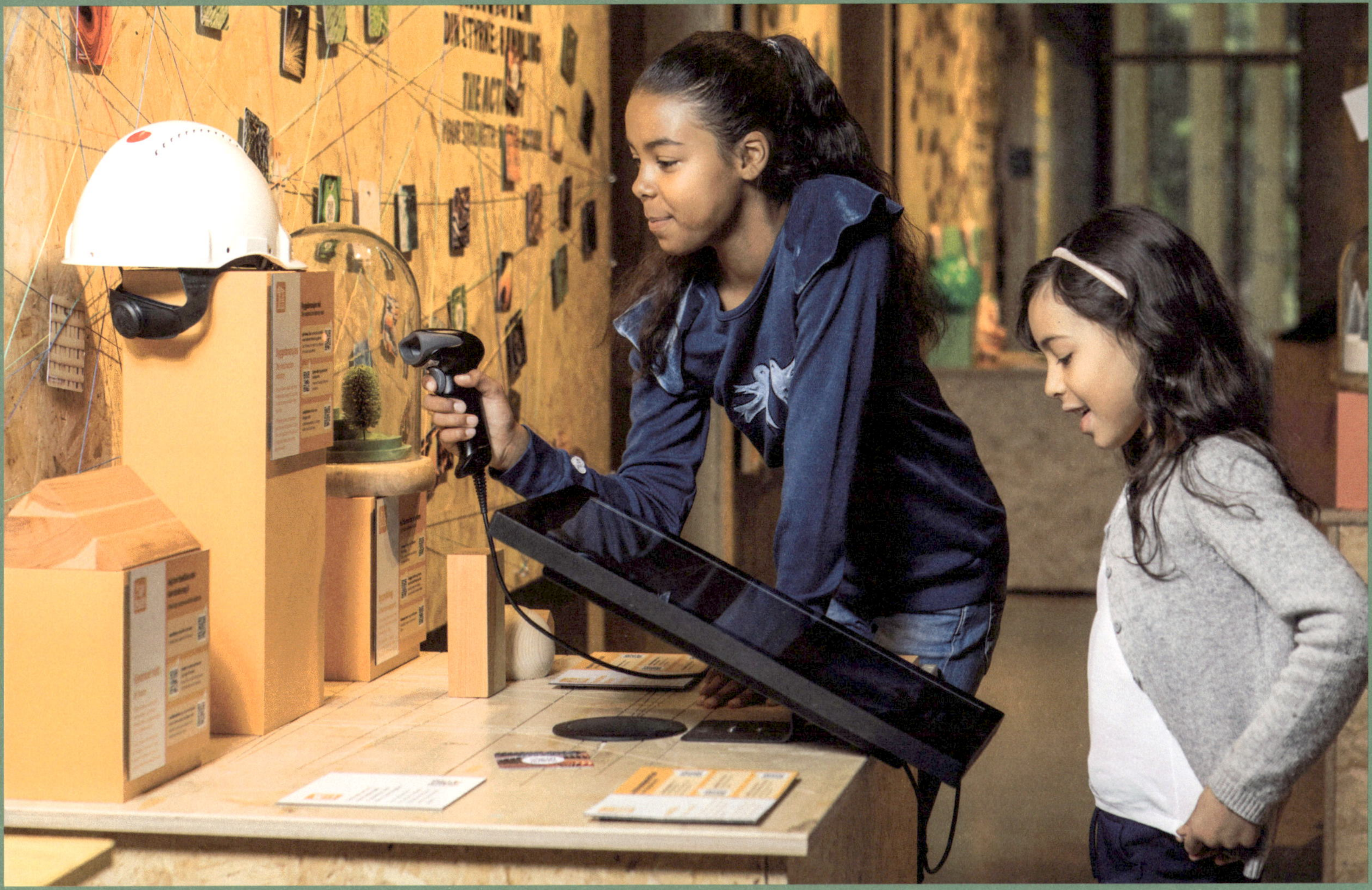

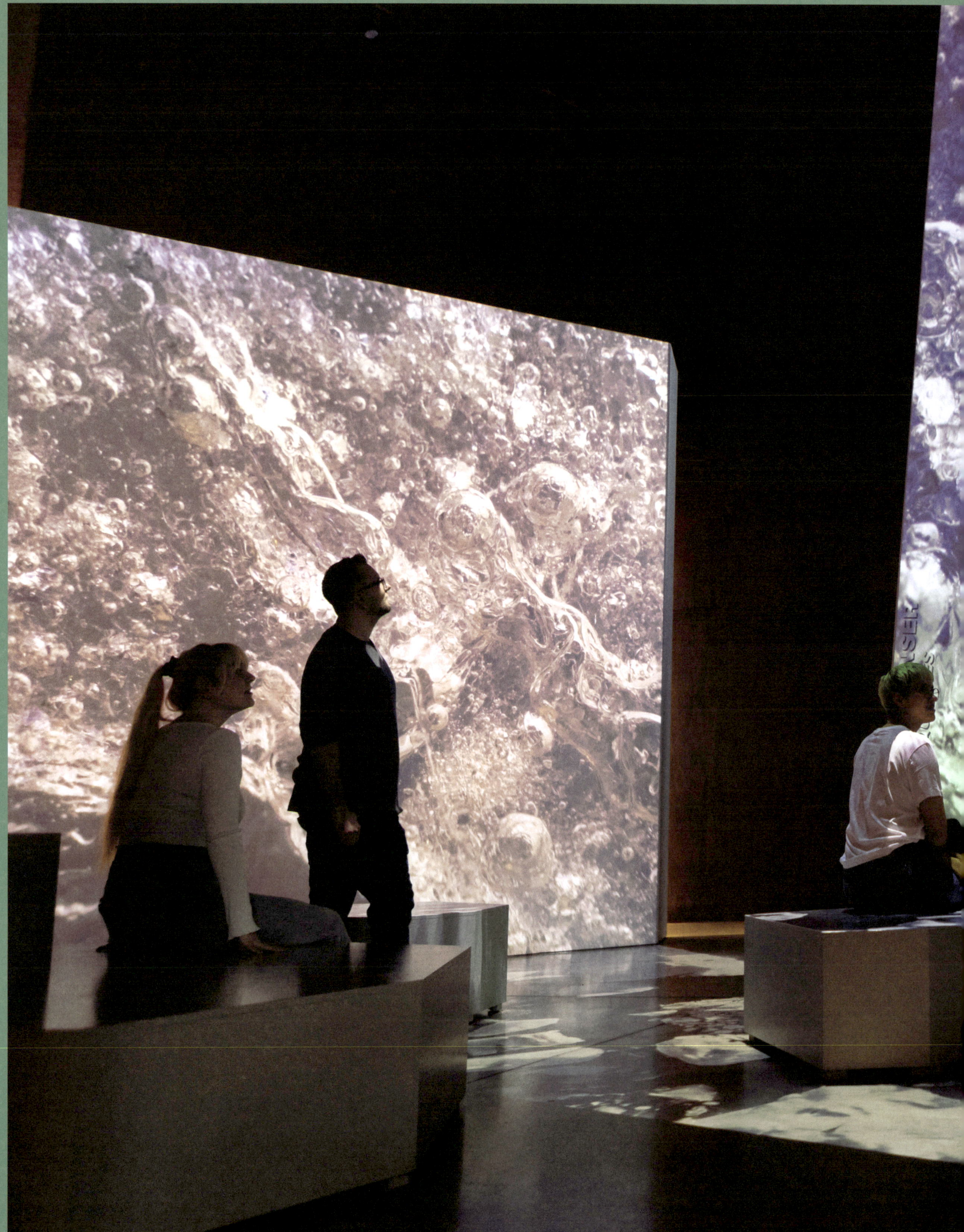

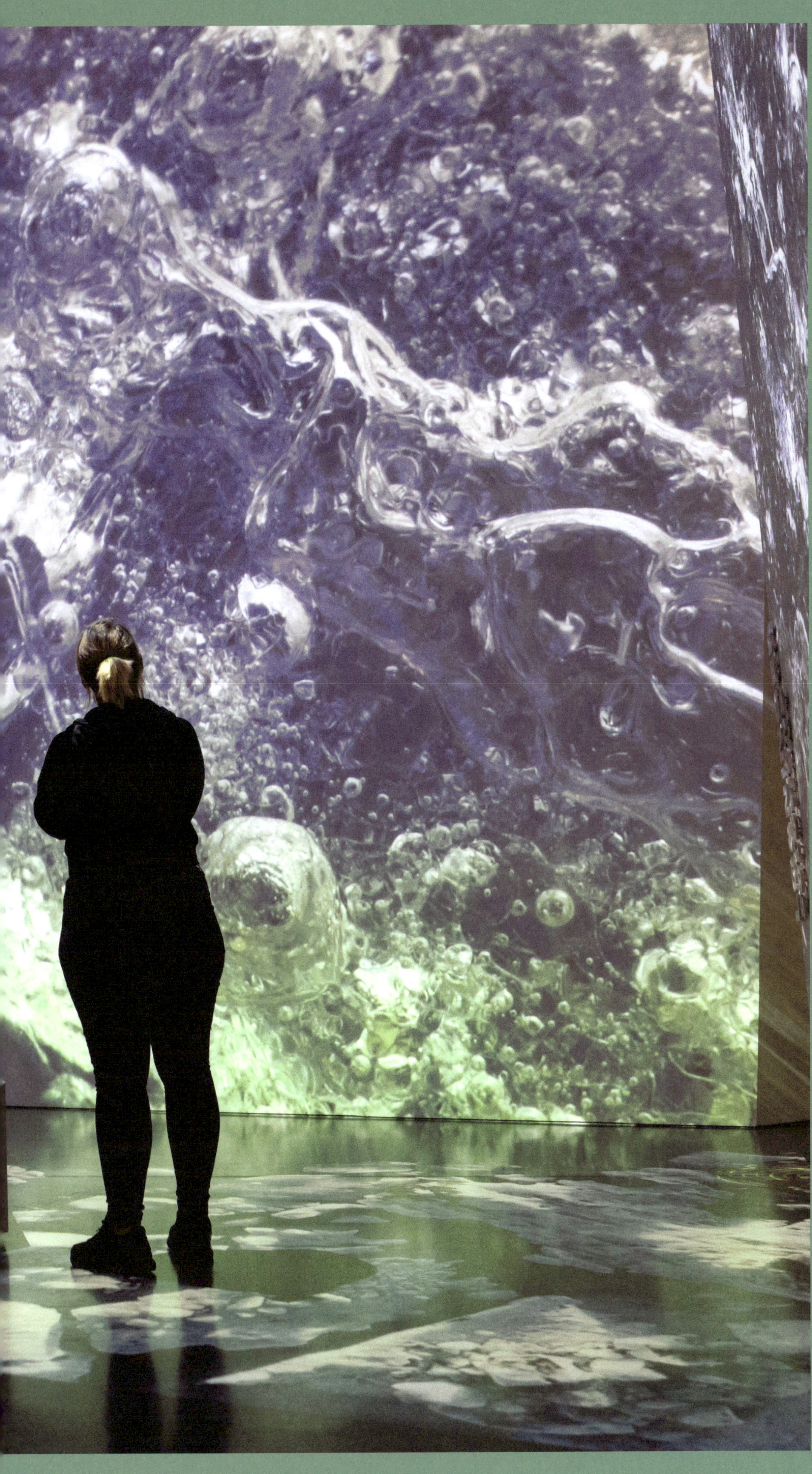

MUSEUMS WITH SIMILAR MEASURES

Tate Modern, *The Weather Project*, 2003

LONDON, UNITED KINGDOM

Art installation that marks the first step toward new climate awareness.

Spark - Australian Museum

SIDNEY, AUSTRALIA

An exhibition space dedicated to innovative projects that combat climate change.

The Climate Museum

NEW YORK, USA

This museum's mission is to mitigate climate change through artistic and cultural programming, connecting people and promoting equitable solutions.

Jockey Club Museum of Climate Change

HONG KONG, CHINA

It launched the *Net Zero The Hero* program, a challenge to reduce the carbon footprint of the community's daily habits.

Sustainability Pavilion
Expo 2020 Dubai
Dubai, United Arab Emirates

The pavilion took visitors on an exciting journey to understand our relationship with nature and the impact we have on it.

Axonometry of gallery 3
Under the forest
Sustainability Pavilion
Expo 2020 Dubai
ACCIONA

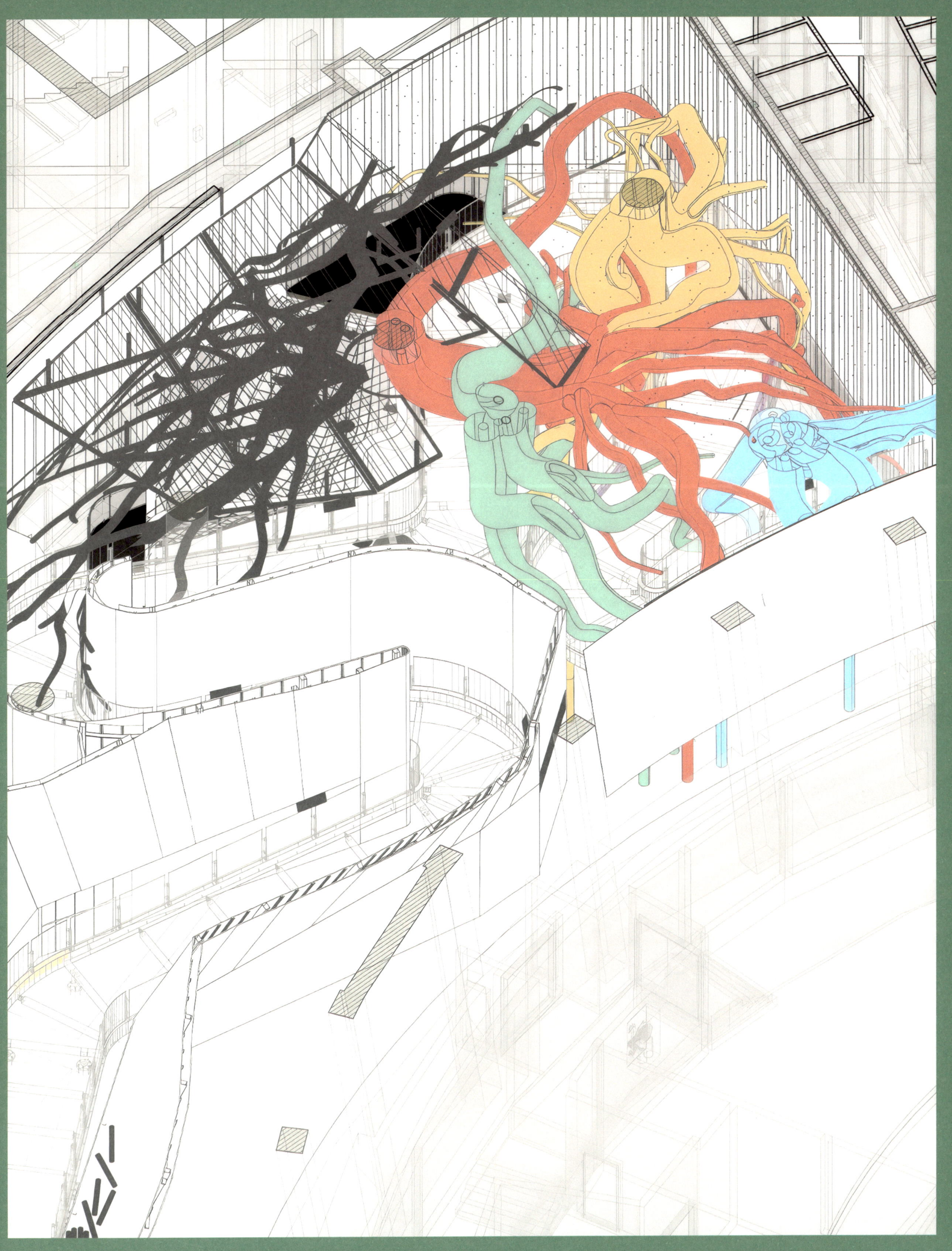

29 GAMIFICATION

VISITOR EDUCATION AND AWARENESS SDG 4 / 13

Gamification is a technique that applies the principles and elements of games to a learning environment with the aim of influencing the subjects' behavior, boosting their motivation, and encouraging them to participate. Using educational apps or video games as incentives that prompt museum-goers to be more sustainable in their daily lives seems to be an effective way to raise awareness.

World Future Lab is a game in which visitors to the Klimahaus museum, in the German city of Bremerhaven, have to make decisions and devise strategies in order to overcome different challenges related to climate change. Each challenge is linked to scenarios such as saving an island from rising sea levels, sustainable coffee production, or ethical smartphone manufacturing. The game can be played individually or in groups.

Klimahaus Bremerhaven

FOCUS
Science

LOCATION
Urban. Port area,
Bremerhaven, Germany

CONSTRUCTION
2009

PROJECT
Thomas Klumpp

SIZE
18,000 m²

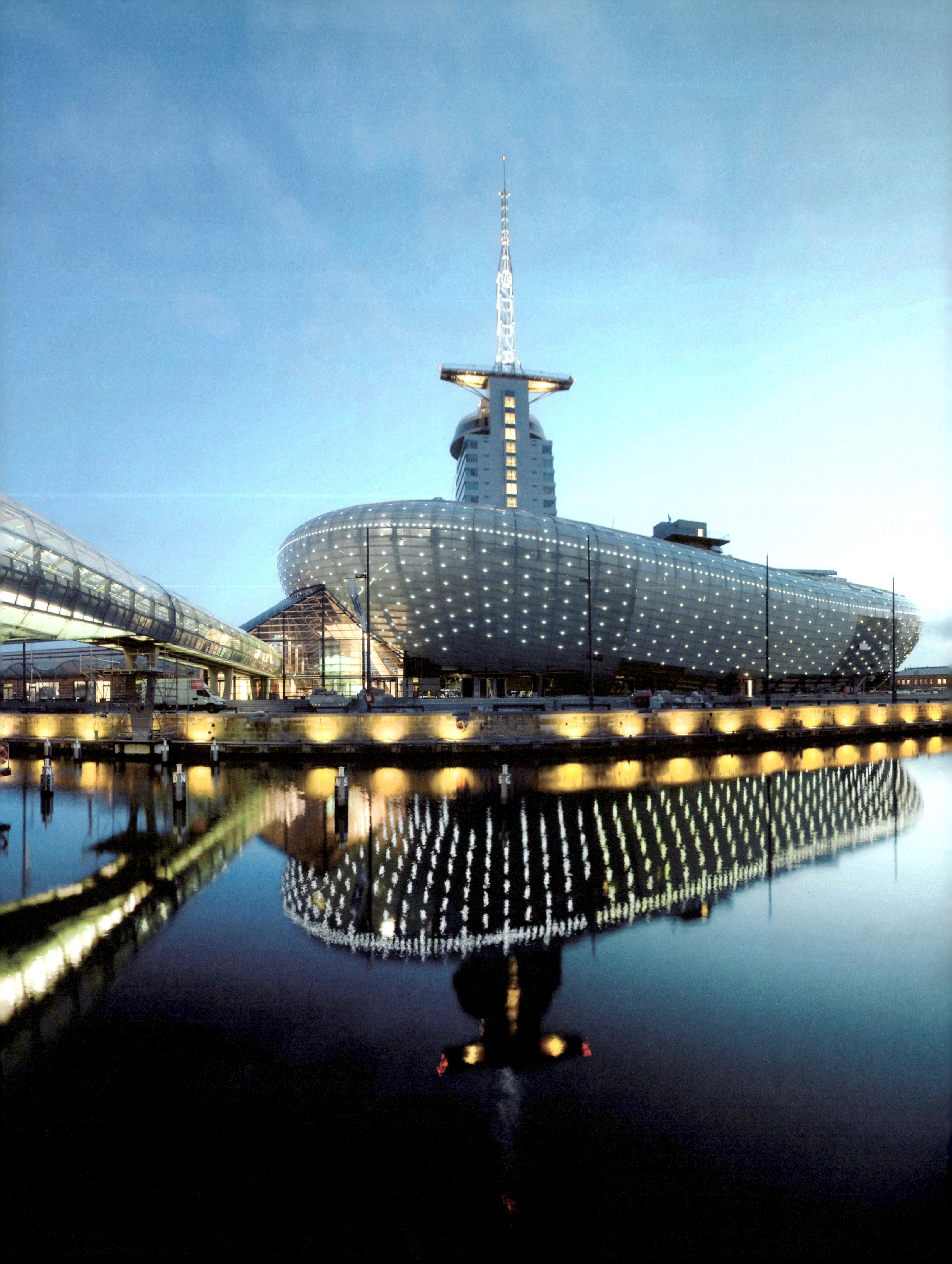

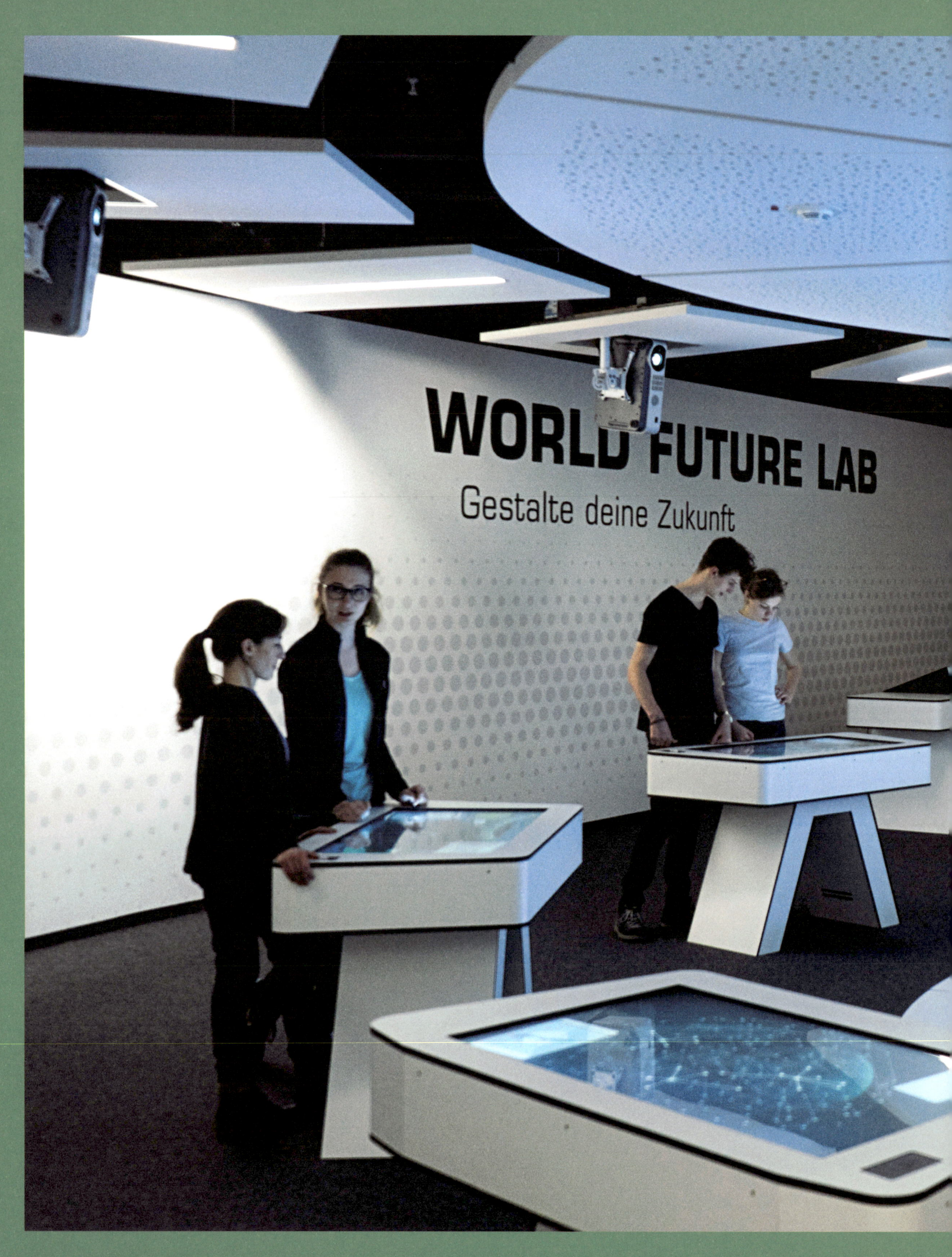
WORLD FUTURE LAB
Gestalte deine Zukunft

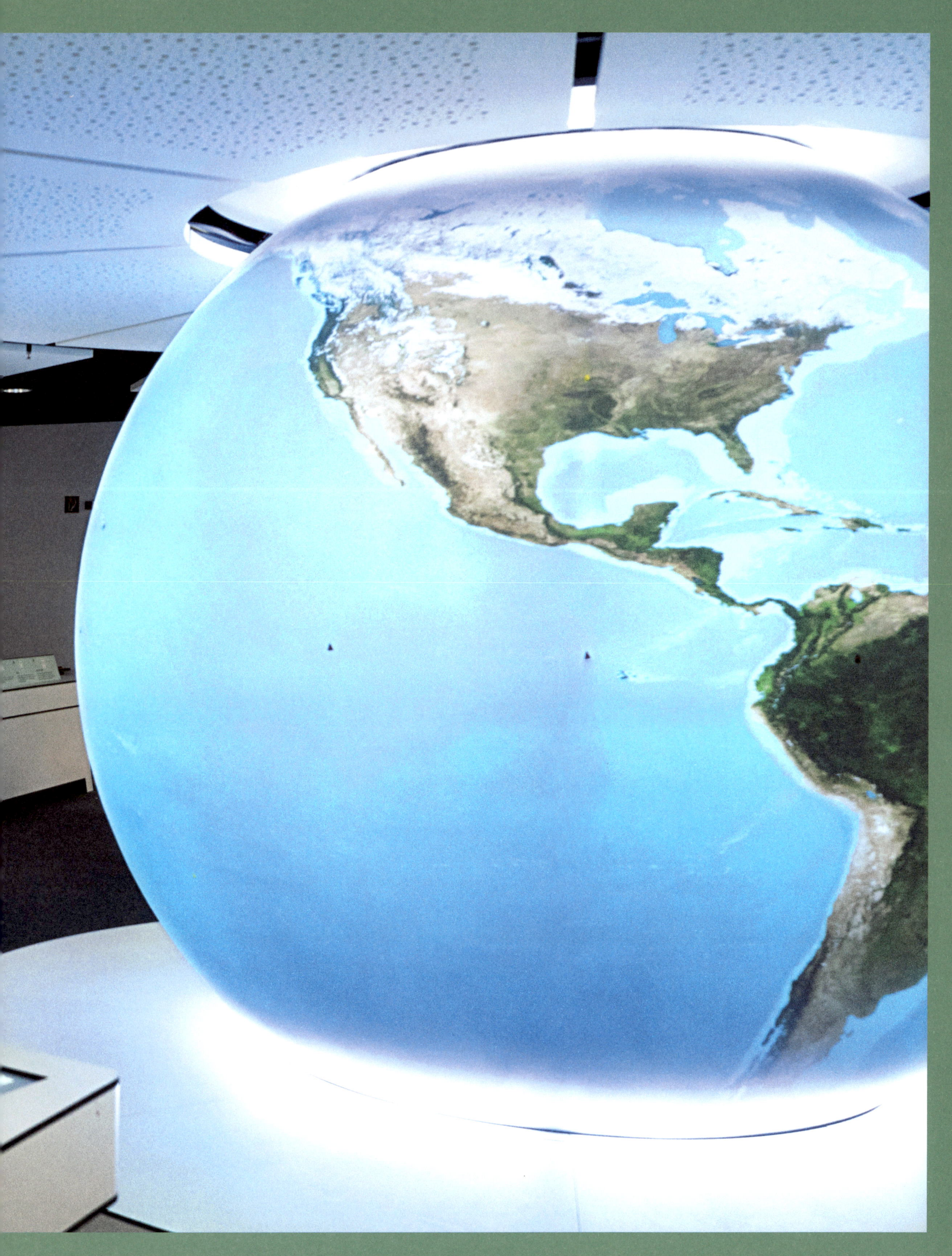

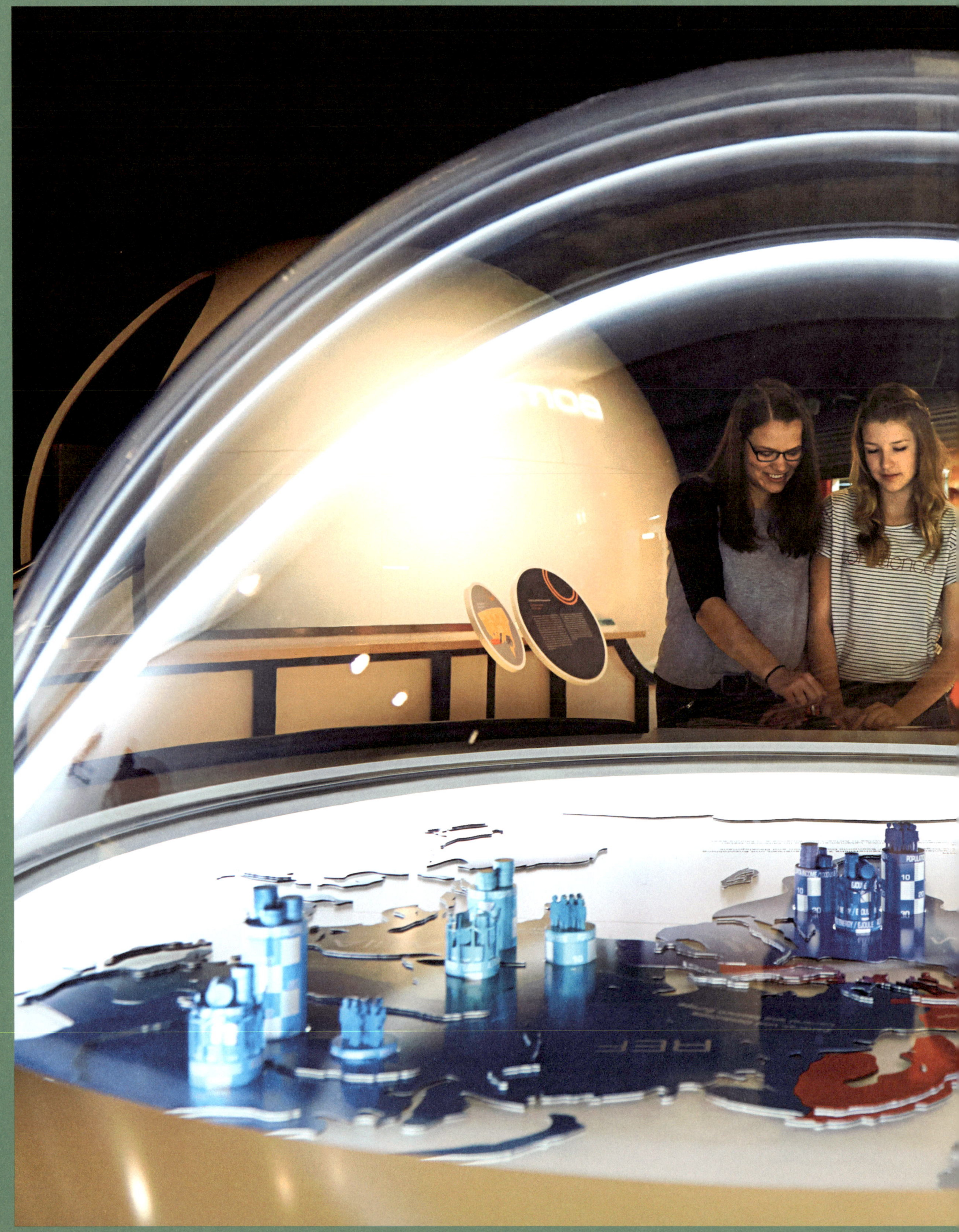

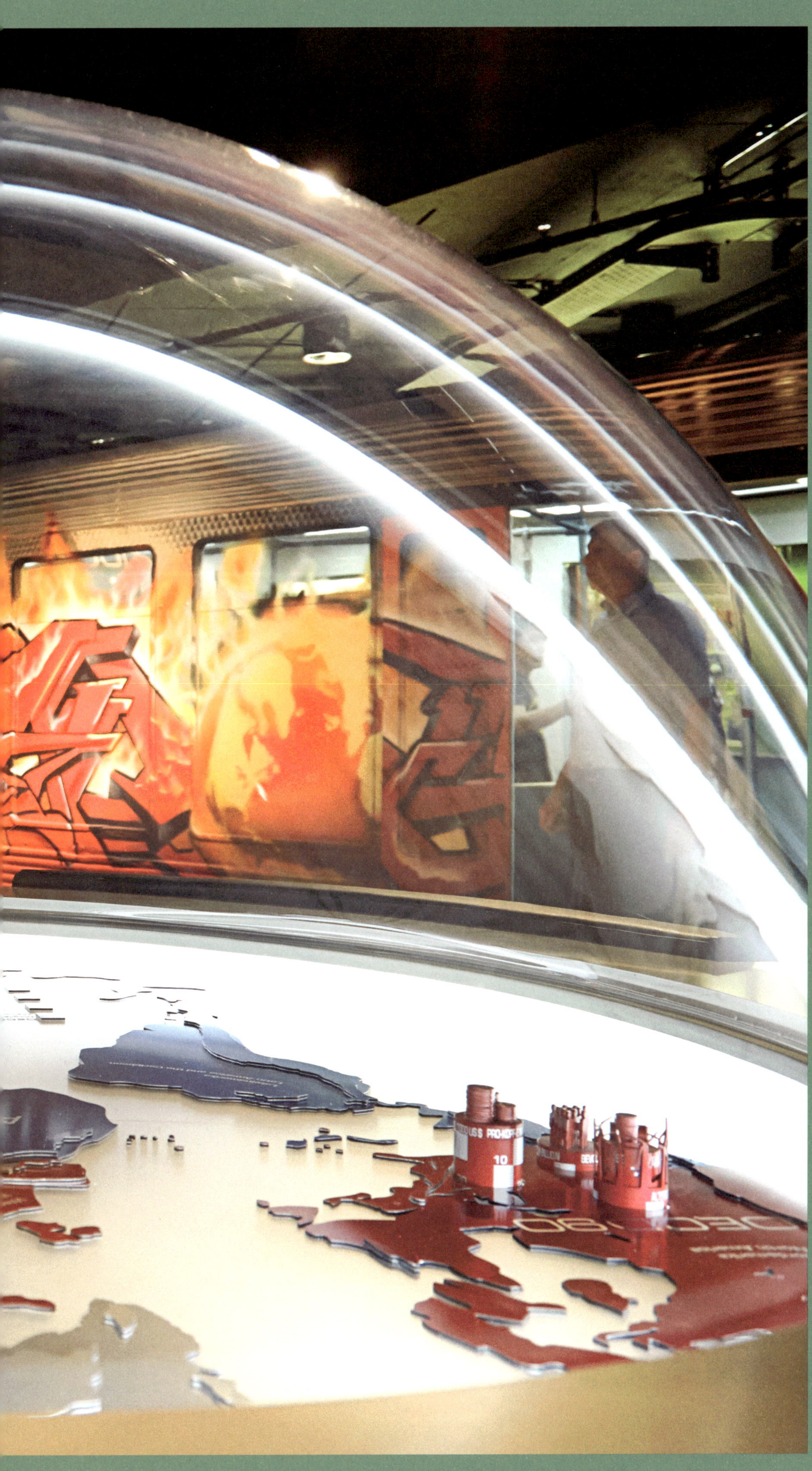

MUSEUMS WITH SIMILAR MEASURES

Natural History Museum of Utah

SALT LAKE CITY, UTAH, USA

Utah Climate Challenge: multiplayer game that encourages young visitors to tackle the climate crisis together.

The National Museum

OSLO, NORWAY

Primeval Forest Silva: interactive and immersive game that promotes children's environmental responsibility.

Museu Terra

L'ESPLUGA DE FRANCOLÍ, TARRAGONA, SPAIN

Educational proposal with games and museum materials about the SDGs.

Papalote Museo del Niño
Monterrey, Mexico

This museum presents a wide variety of thematic areas to raise environmental awareness through games for young children.

"Touch, play, and learn" is the motto of the Papalote Museo del Niño in Mexico.

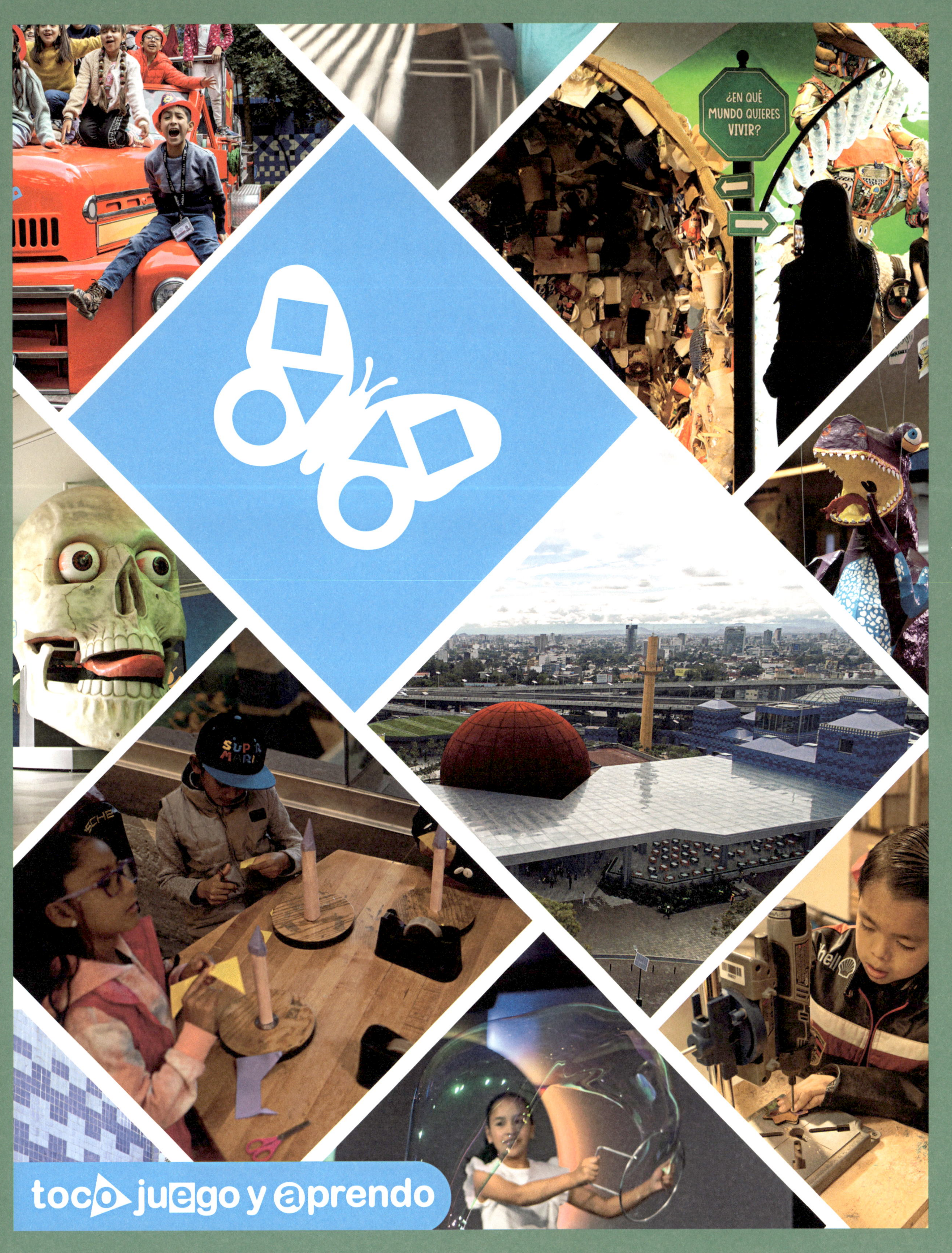
¿EN QUÉ
MUNDO QUIERES
VIVIR?
toco juego y aprendo

30 COMMUNITY DEVELOPMENT PROGRAM

INTEGRATION OF MUSEUMS IN THE COMMUNITY SDG 4 / 10 / 17

Museums should be seen as local development drivers within the communities they serve. Culture should be viewed as a factor in the development of the service sector, a dynamic and innovative force for cities, and as a value that enhances local identity and promotes the city's image. Ultimately, culture should be regarded as a key element in enhancing the quality of life in urban areas.

Brooklyn Children's Museum exemplifies this by integrating its programs with the local environment and social identity, fostering self-identity and a sense of community among residents.

The museum collaborates with local schools to enhance student achievement and bridge cultural gaps through free, in-person after-school programs. It also creates spaces for students and hosts thirteen annual cultural festivals that celebrate and connect with the diverse communities of Brooklyn. Additionally, the museum organizes community working, learning, focus, and conversation groups that contribute to the development of specific local programs.

Brooklyn Children's Museum

FOCUS
Visual Arts, Science and Technology, Children

LOCATION
Urban. New York, USA

ANNUAL VISITORS
365,000

CONSTRUCTION
1899. Remodeled in 2008

PROJECT
Rafael Viñoly

CERTIFICATION
LEED Silver

SIZE
9,500 m^2

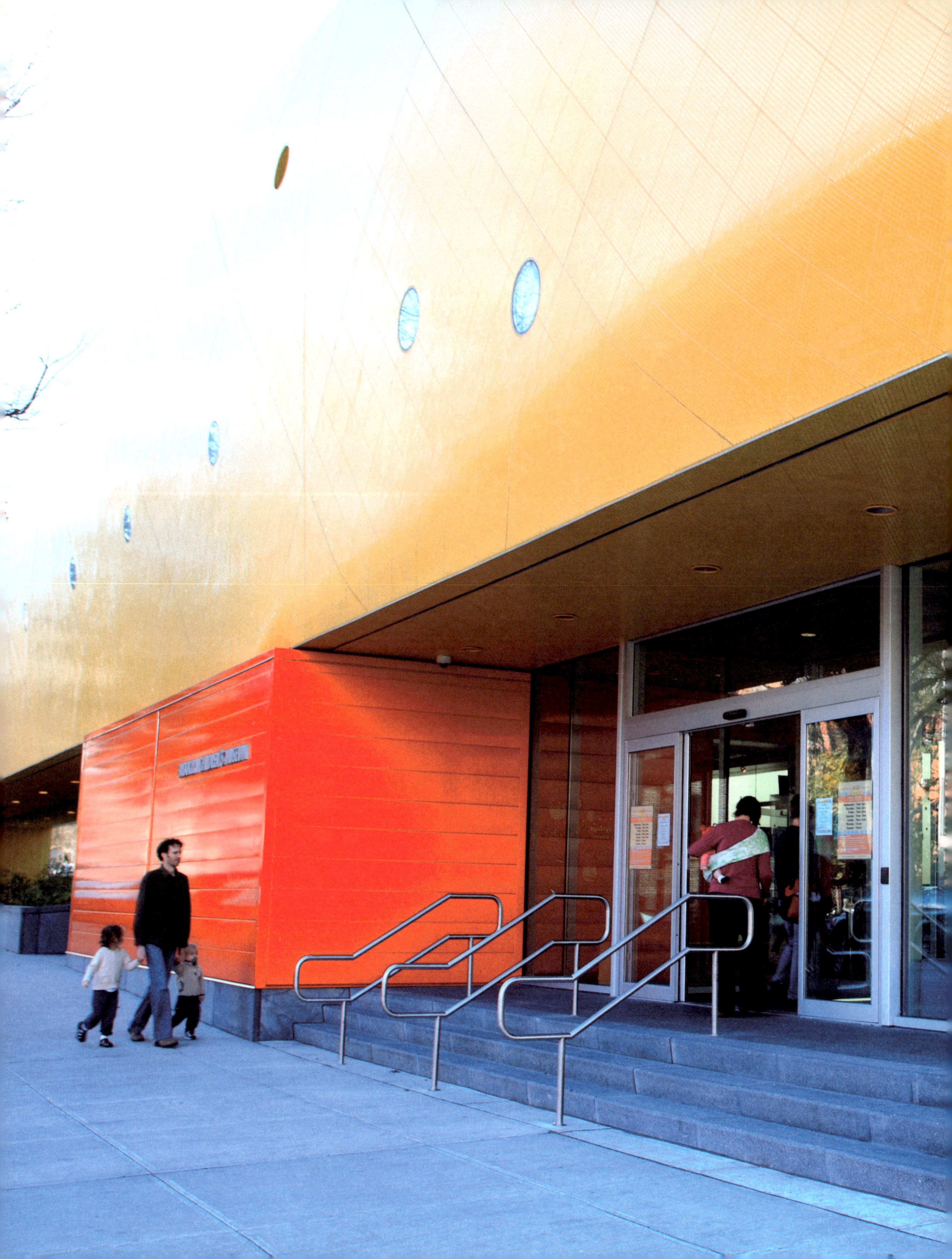

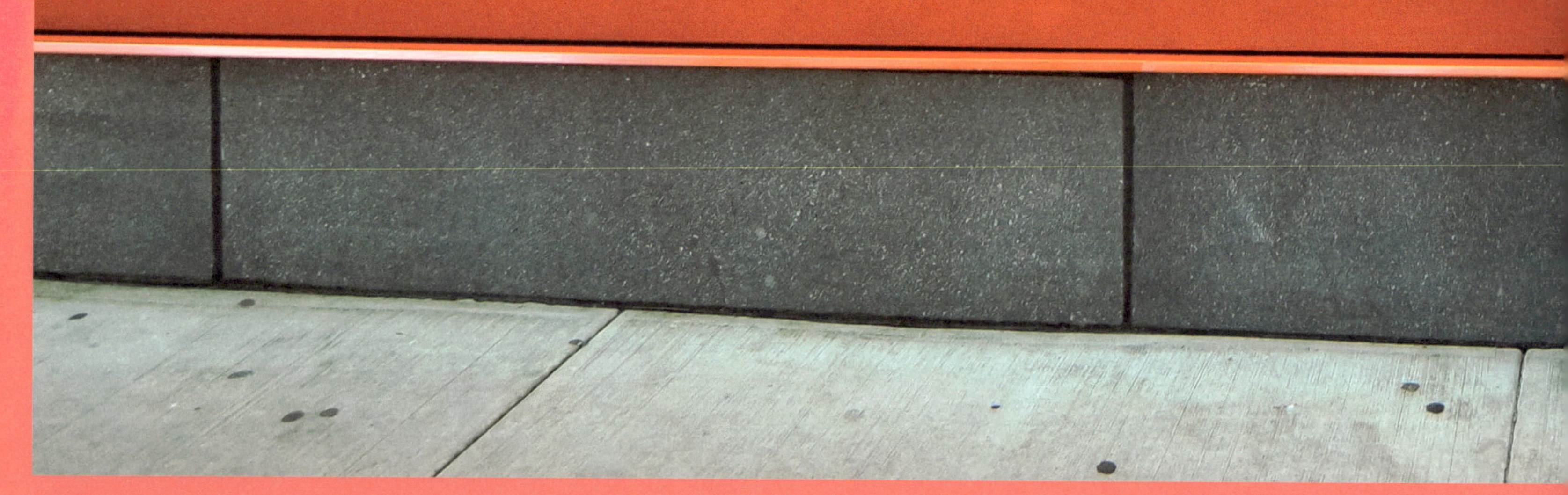
BROOKLYN CHIL

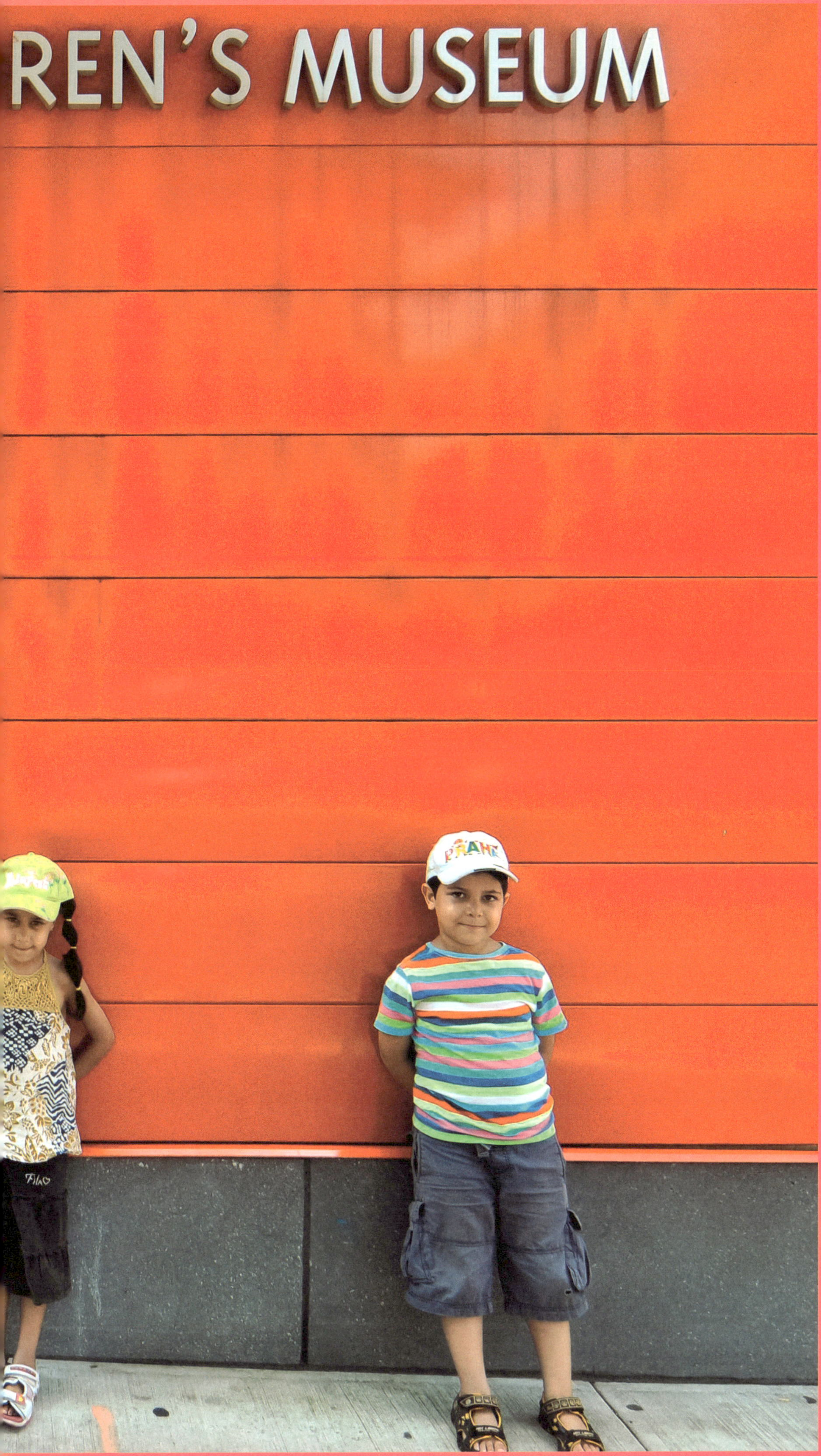

MUSEUMS WITH SIMILAR MEASURES

Haggerty Museum of Art

MILWAUKEE, WISCONSIN, USA

Its museum program acts as a catalyst of the local community and its memory.

Museo de Educación Ambiental

PAMPLONA, SPAIN

The museum's facilities are open to socio-environmental community projects.

Phipps Conservatory and Botanical Gardens

PITTSBURGH, PENNSYLVANIA, USA

It offers a promotional program for museum visitors to switch their electricity provider to renewable energy.

Museum of the Moving Image
New York, USA

"The Museum of the Moving Image is the only museum in North America dedicated to the art, history, technology, and future of media and the moving image. Community is at the heart of everything we do, serving one of the most diverse and creative neighborhoods in the United States, if not the world. Each year, an average of 70,000 students embark on a journey of discovery through our media education programs."

Aziz Isham

Executive Director of the Museum of the Moving Image, New York, USA.

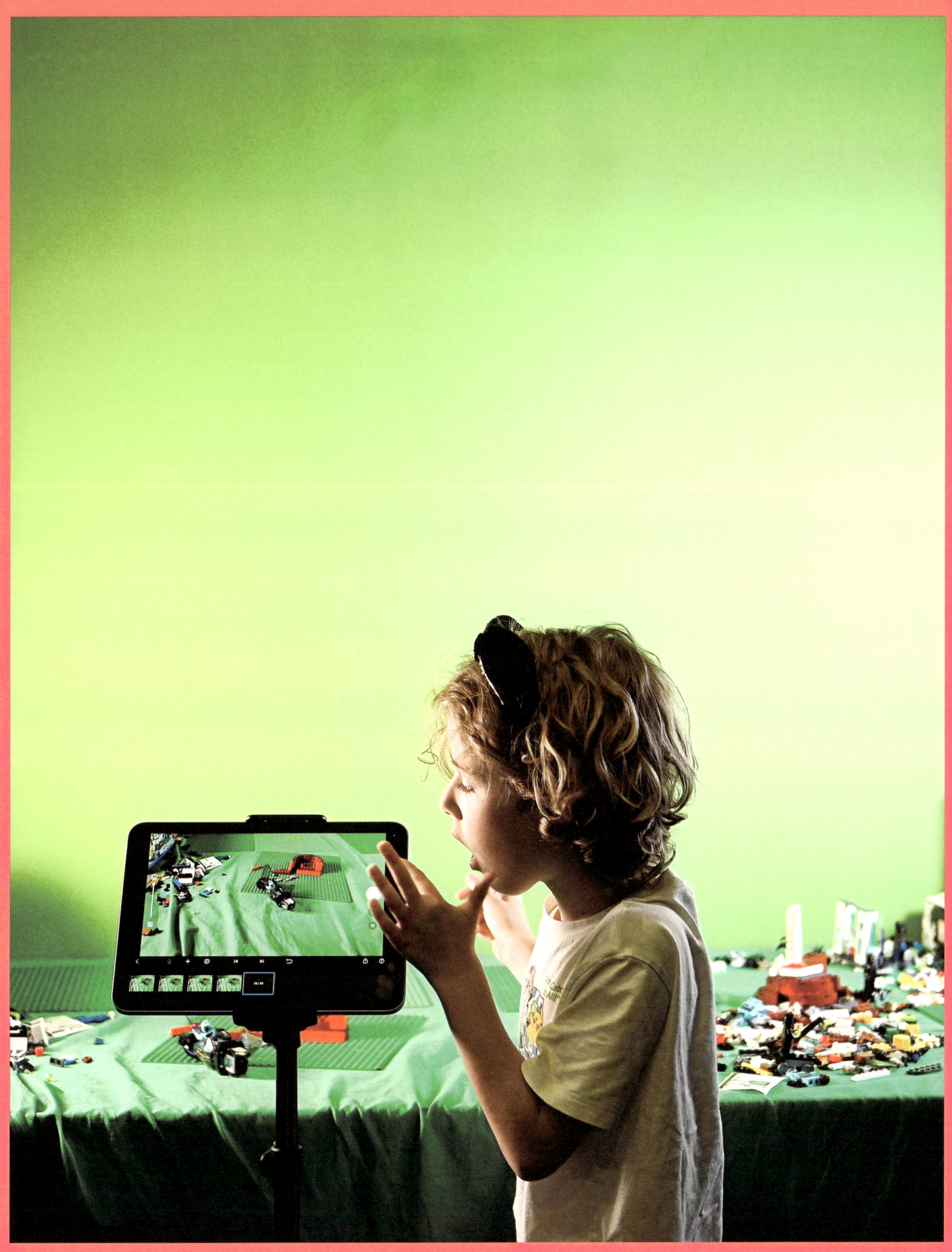

31 COMMUNITY REVITALIZATION

INTEGRATION OF MUSEUMS IN THE COMMUNITY SDG 8 / 10 / 11

Cultural facilities play a fundamental role in urban regeneration. Their integration into cities aims to create dynamics that promote urban cohesion, both in urban planning and social and economic aspects.

CaixaForum Sevilla was conceived by Fundación "la Caixa" with the aim of revitalizing the Puerta Triana area on the Isla de la Cartuja, which hosted the 1992 World's Fair. After the exhibition, the area experienced some degradation and a worrying state of neglect. Fundación "la Caixa"'s commitment to promoting culture and science as agents of social improvement has resulted in CaixaForum, a unique and well-regarded project by the people of Seville, serving as a connecting point between the city center, the revitalized Isla de la Cartuja, and the popular Triana neighborhood.

CaixaForum Sevilla

FOCUS
Science and Culture

LOCATION
Urban. Seville, Spain

ANNUAL VISITORS
324,000

CONSTRUCTION
2017

SIZE
8,100 m²

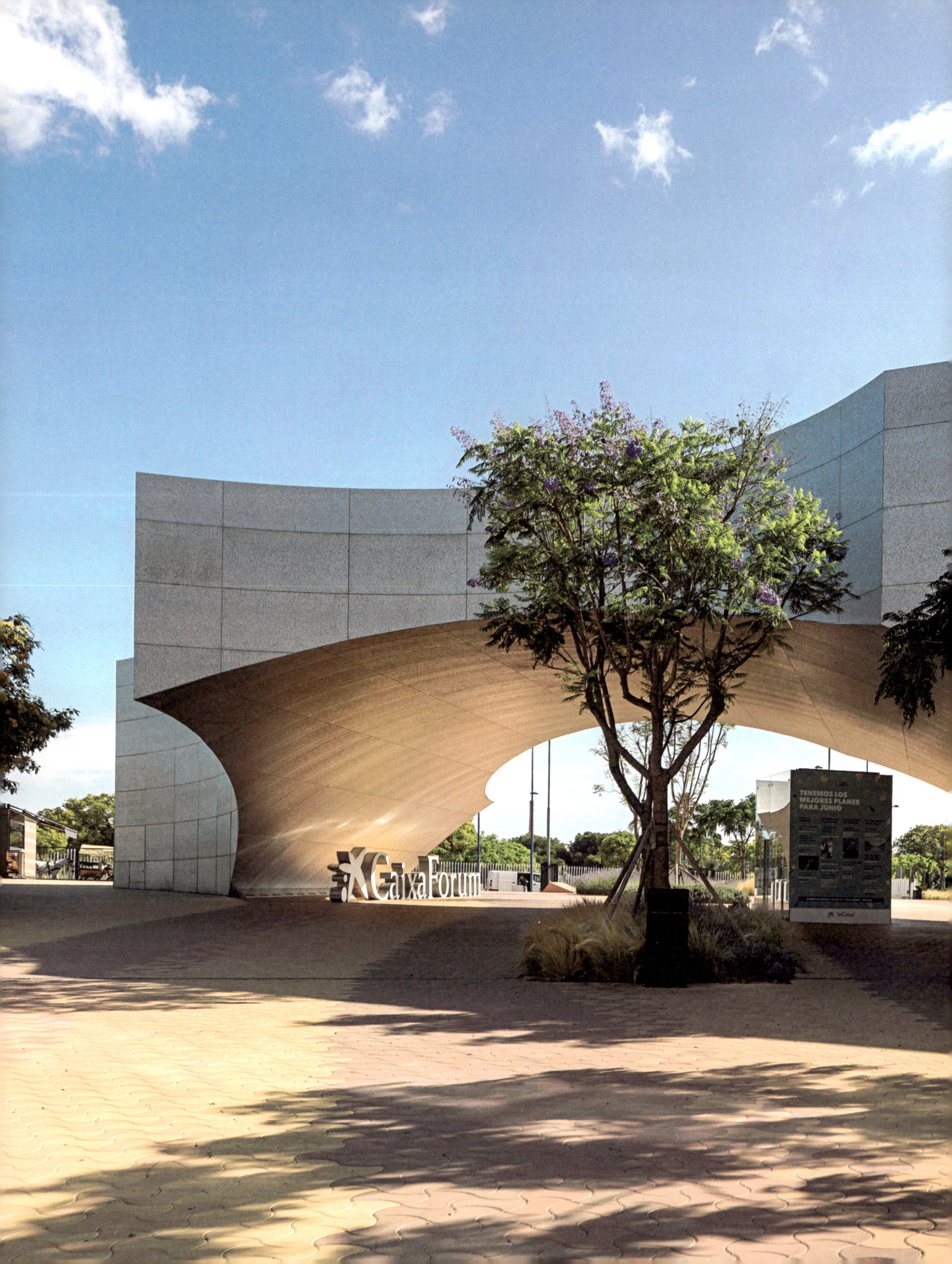
CaixaForum
TENEMOS LOS
MEJORES PLANES
PARA JUNIO
"la Caixa"

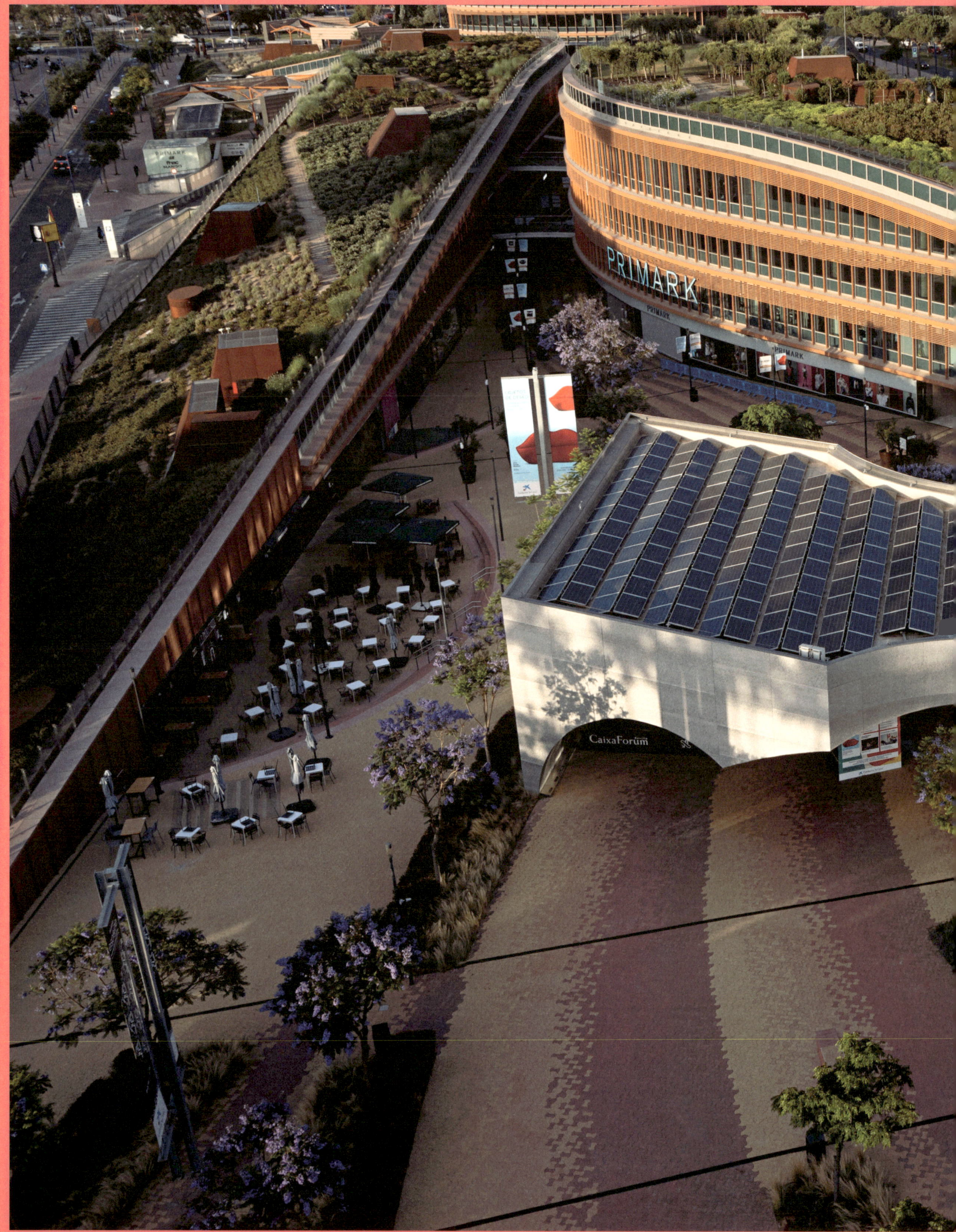
PRIMARK
CaixaForum

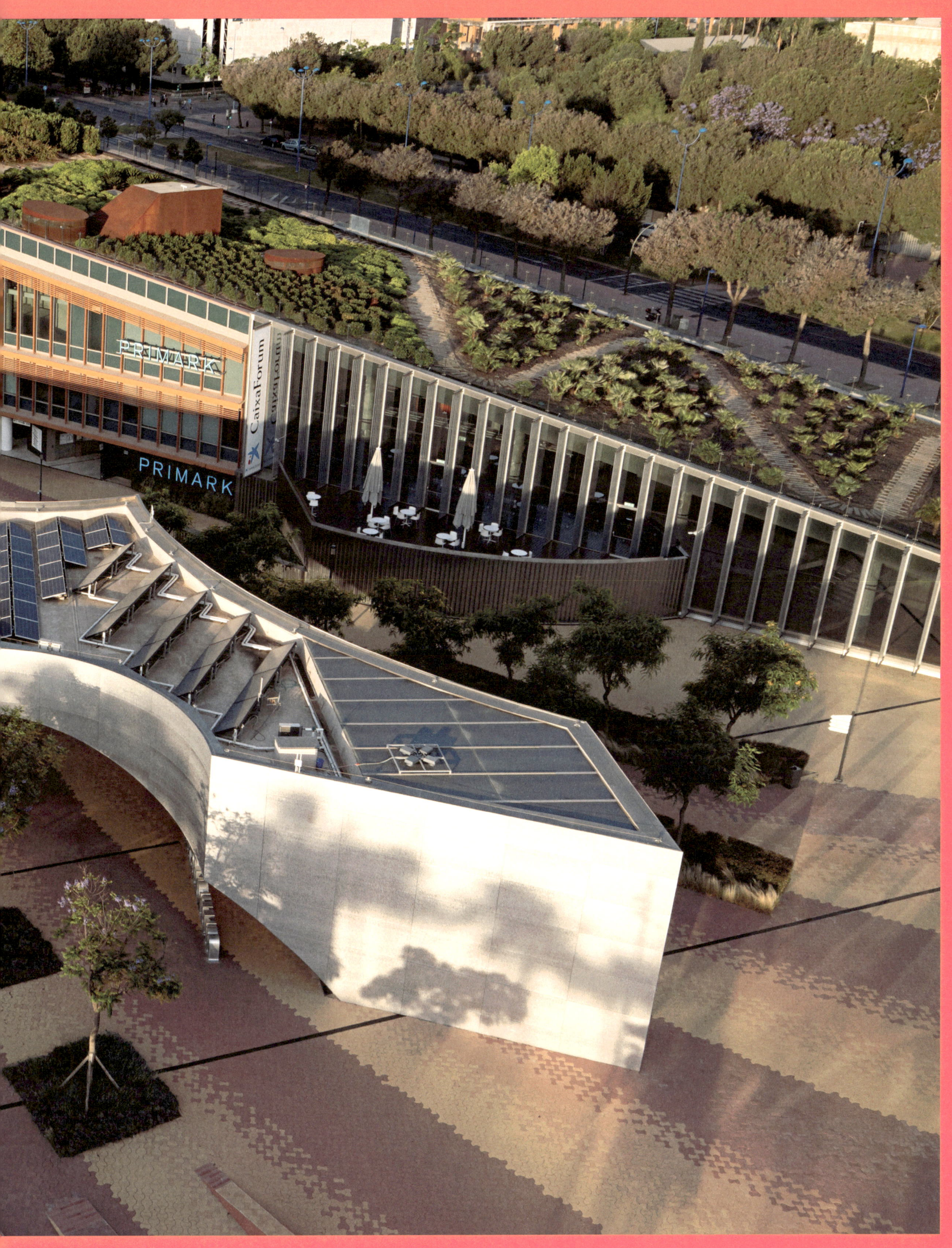
PRIMARK
PRIMARK
CaixaForum

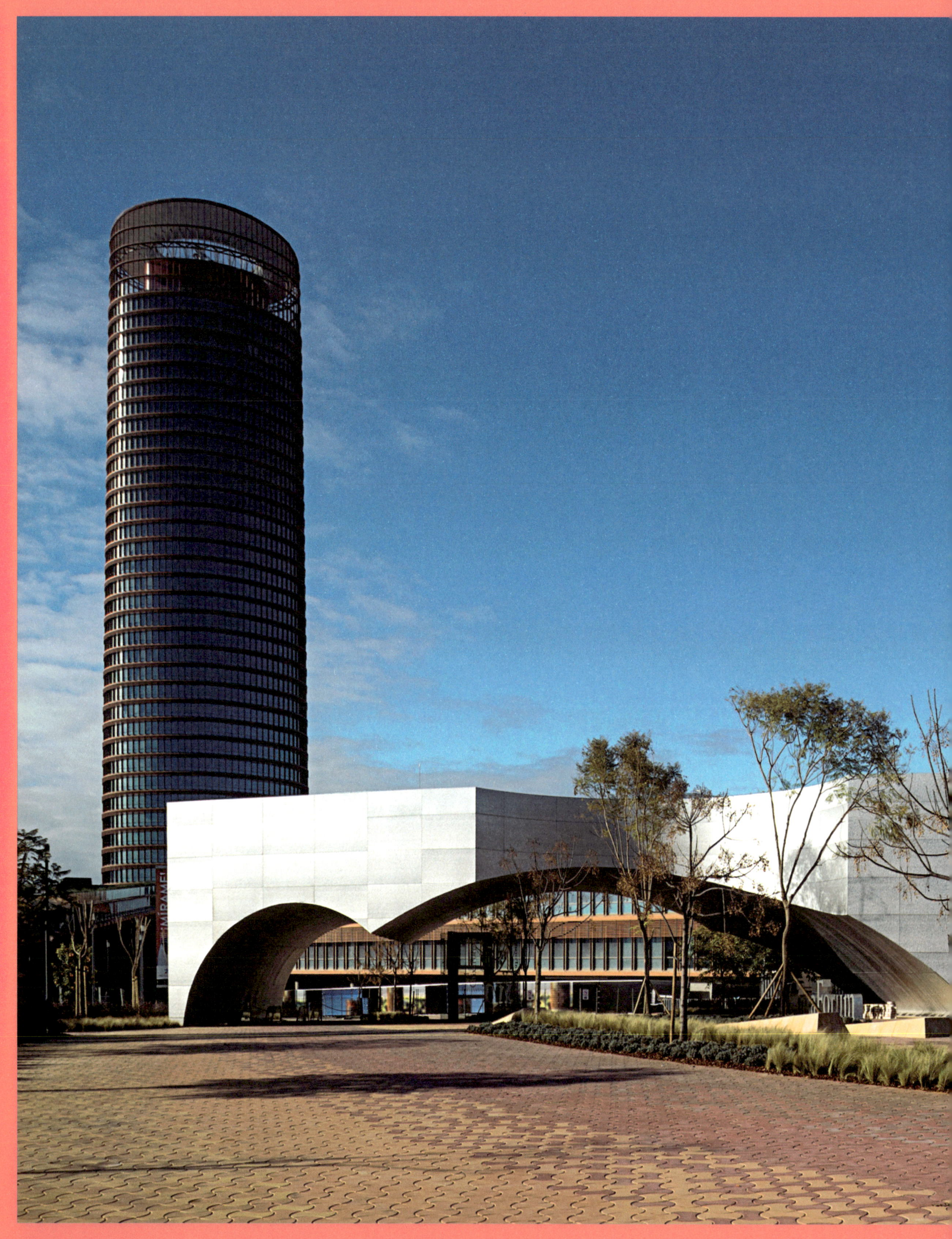
MÍRAME!
Forum

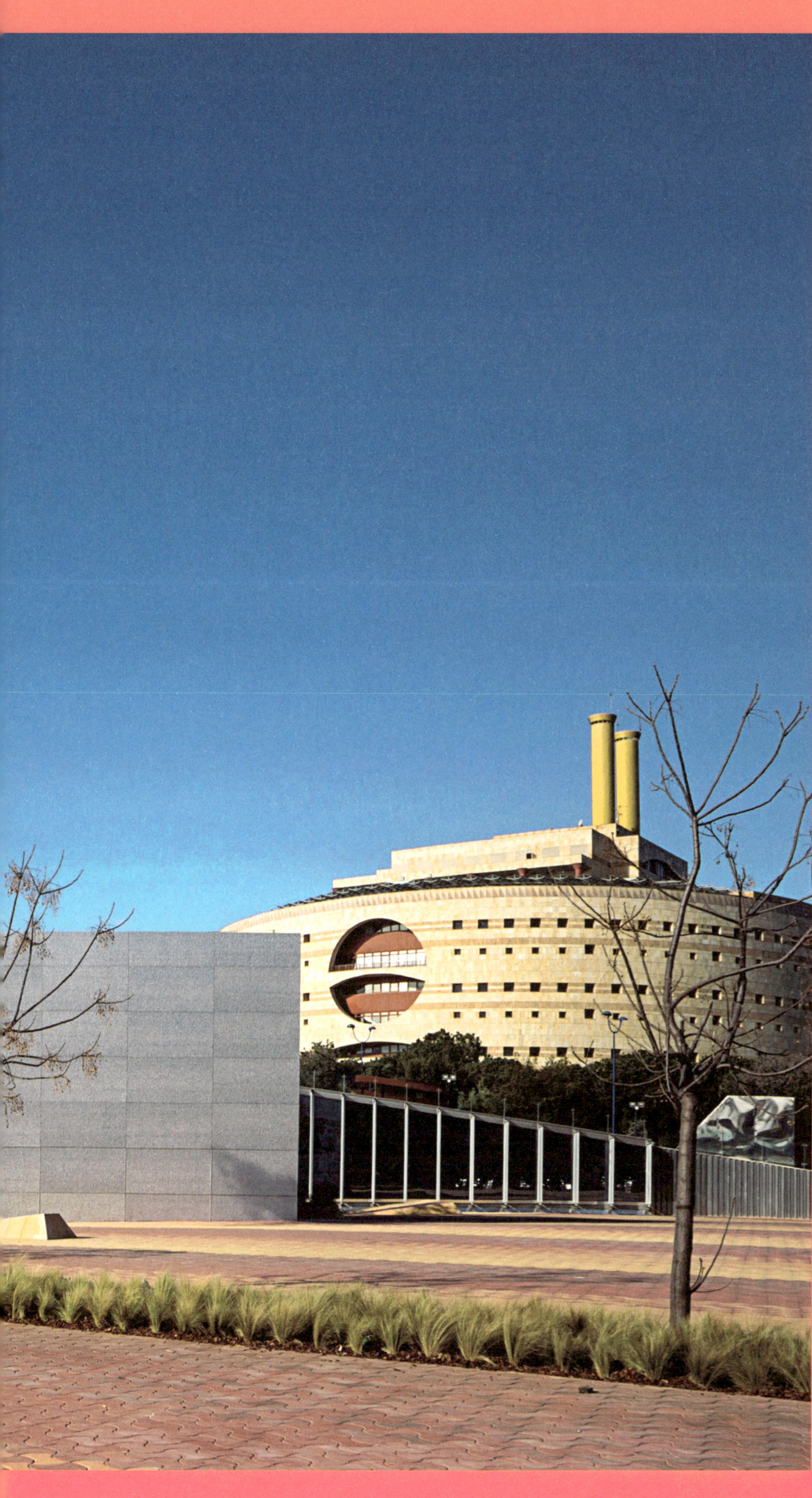

MUSEUMS WITH SIMILAR MEASURES

Museo Universitario del Chopo

MEXICO CITY, MEXICO

Program to strengthen the social structure and economy of neighborhoods near the museum.

Museo de Antioquia

MEDELLÍN, COLOMBIA

Transformation of the museum into a reference point for the city and a catalyst for the development of its surroundings.

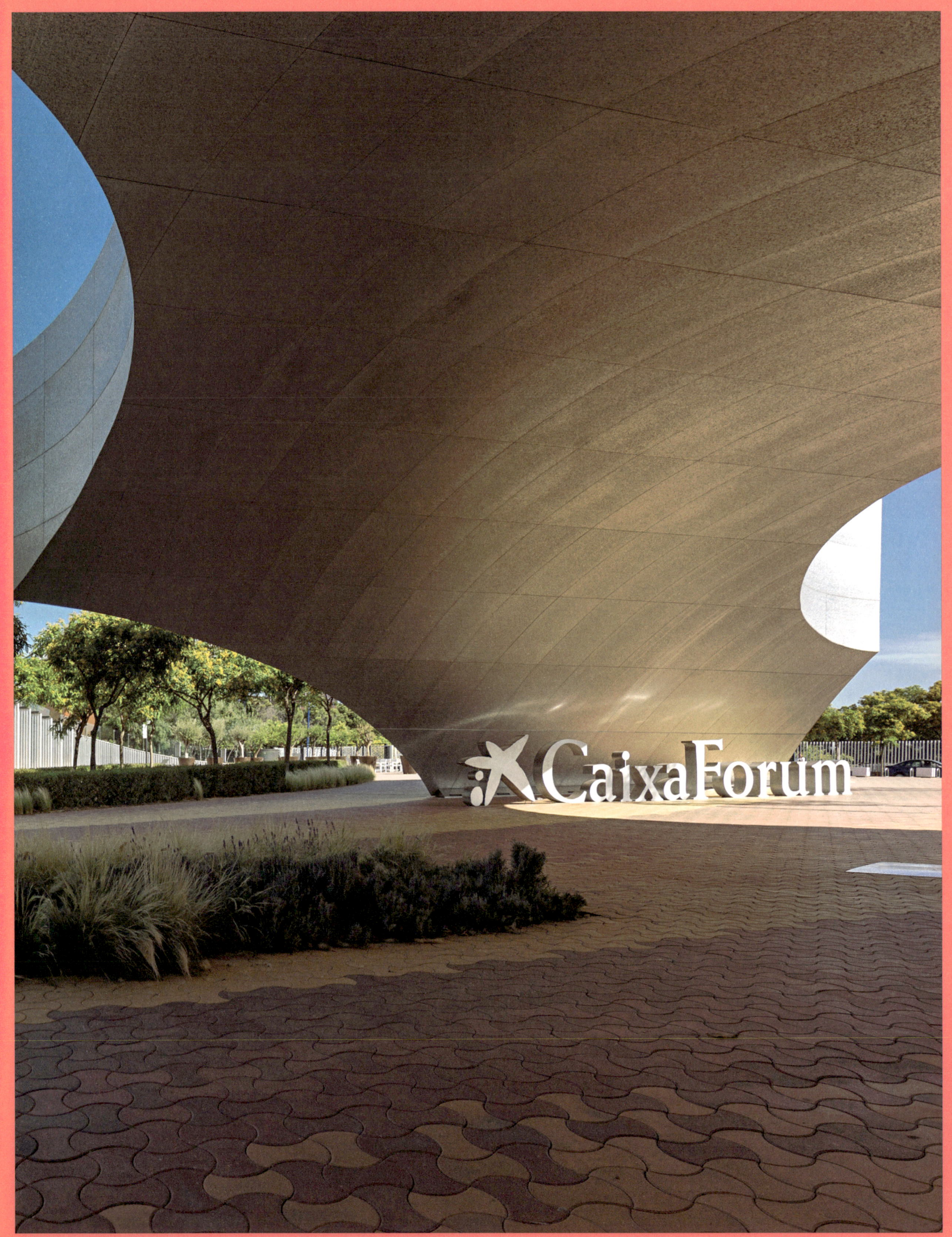
CaixaForum

“We need physical spaces for cultural conversation.”

Charles Landry

Author of *The Creative City: A Toolkit for Urban Innovators*

32 PRESERVATION OF CULTURAL HERITAGE

PRESERVATION OF MEMORY AND HERITAGE SDG 10 / 11

Museums play a crucial role in safeguarding natural, cultural, and scientific heritage through the preservation and enhancement of their collections. Over time, the process of preserving memory has evolved, with museum objects shifting from a static existence to serving as dynamic tools or media. This transformation also extends to the roles of individuals—visitors or agents—whose active participation and decision-making influence contemporary museology.

The Great Egyptian Museum (GEM) presents an exhaustive survey of the history of ancient Egypt, being the largest archaeological museum globally dedicated to a single civilization. Besides its exhibition spaces, GEM features a significant conservation and restoration center aimed at promoting and enhancing the value of Egyptian history for a global audience.

Grand Egyptian Museum

FOCUS
Archaeology

ANNUAL VISITORS
5 million (expected)

LOCATION
Cairo, Egypt

CONSTRUCTION
Due to open in 2025

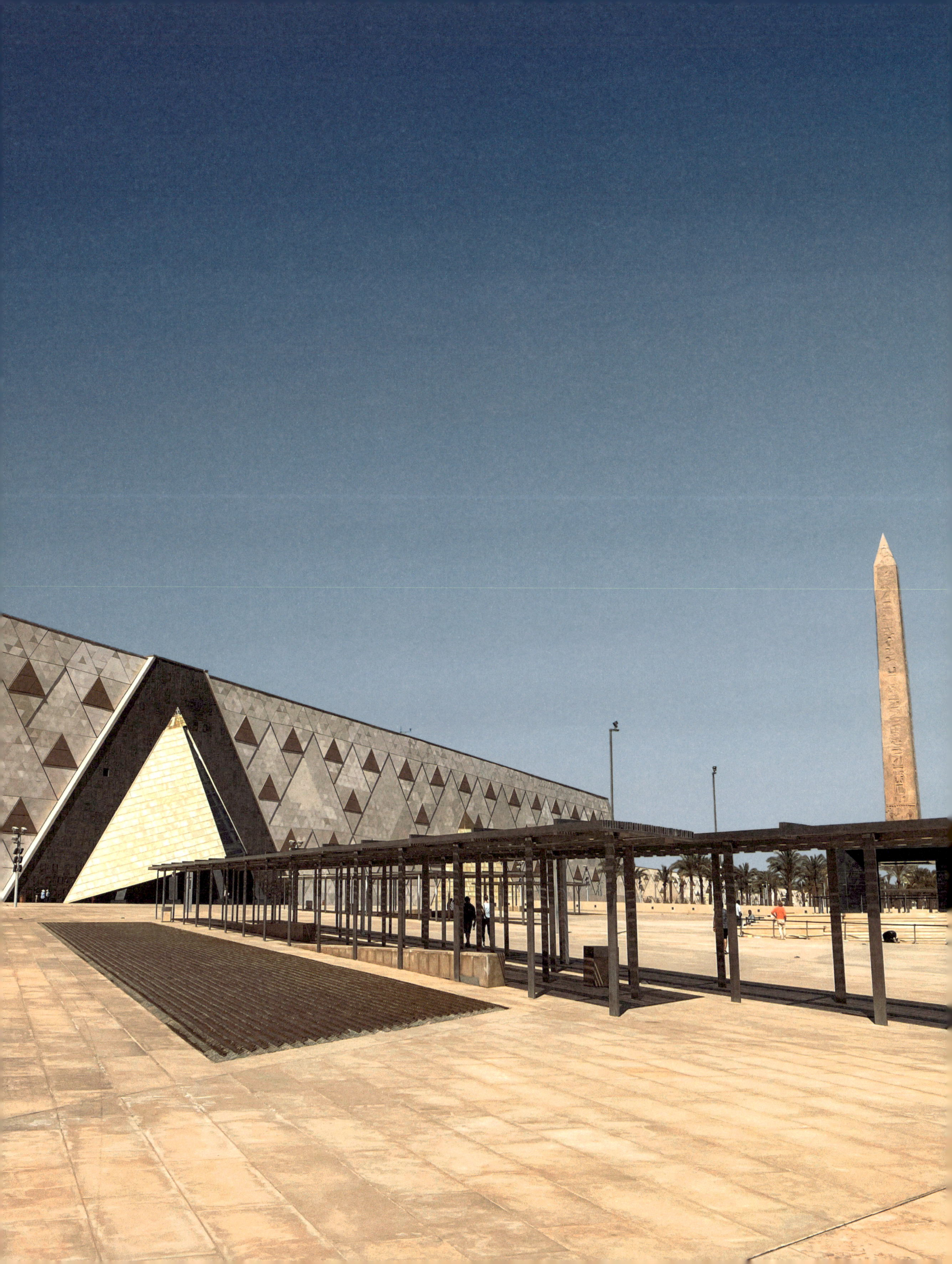

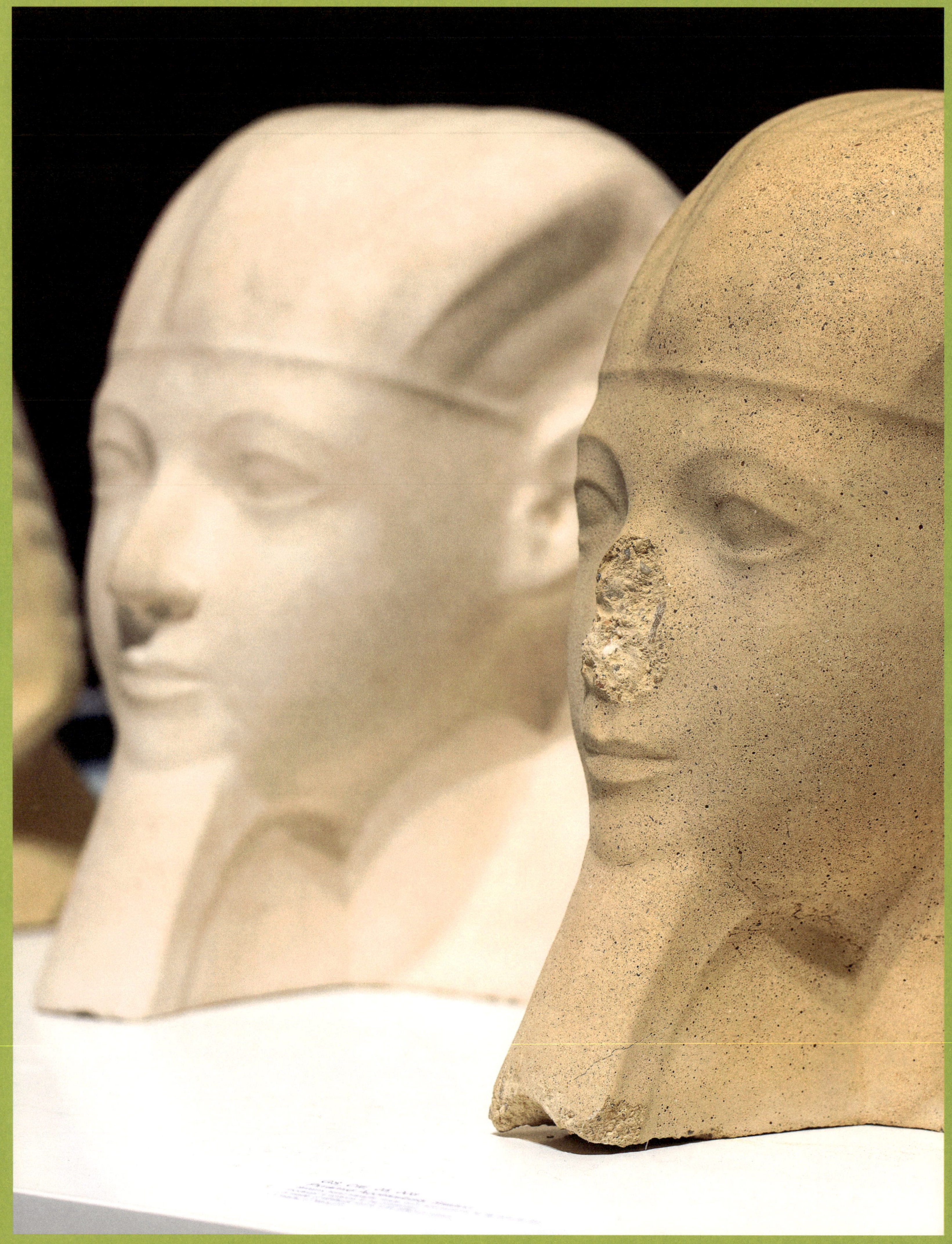

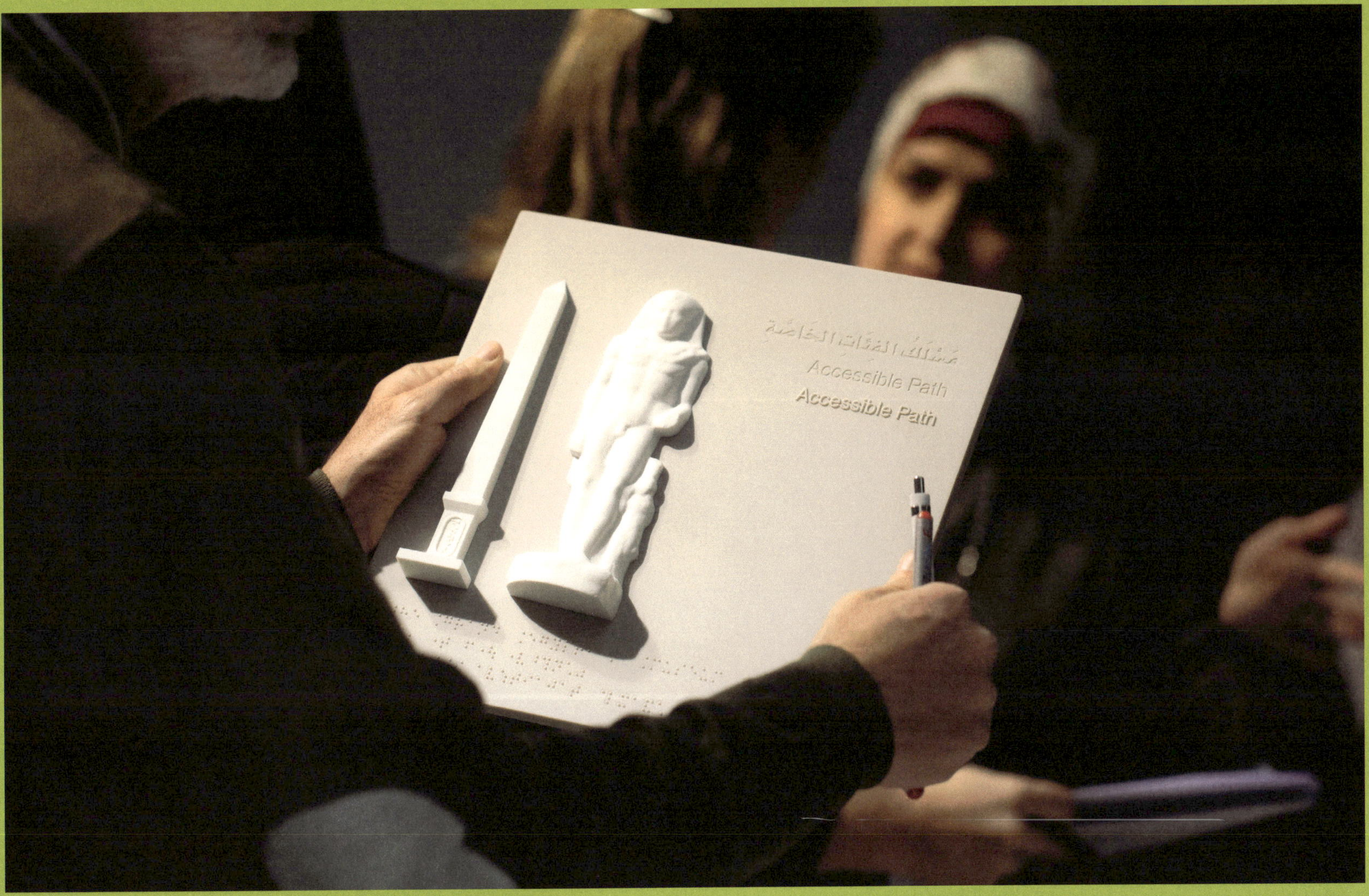

Accessible Path
Accessible Path

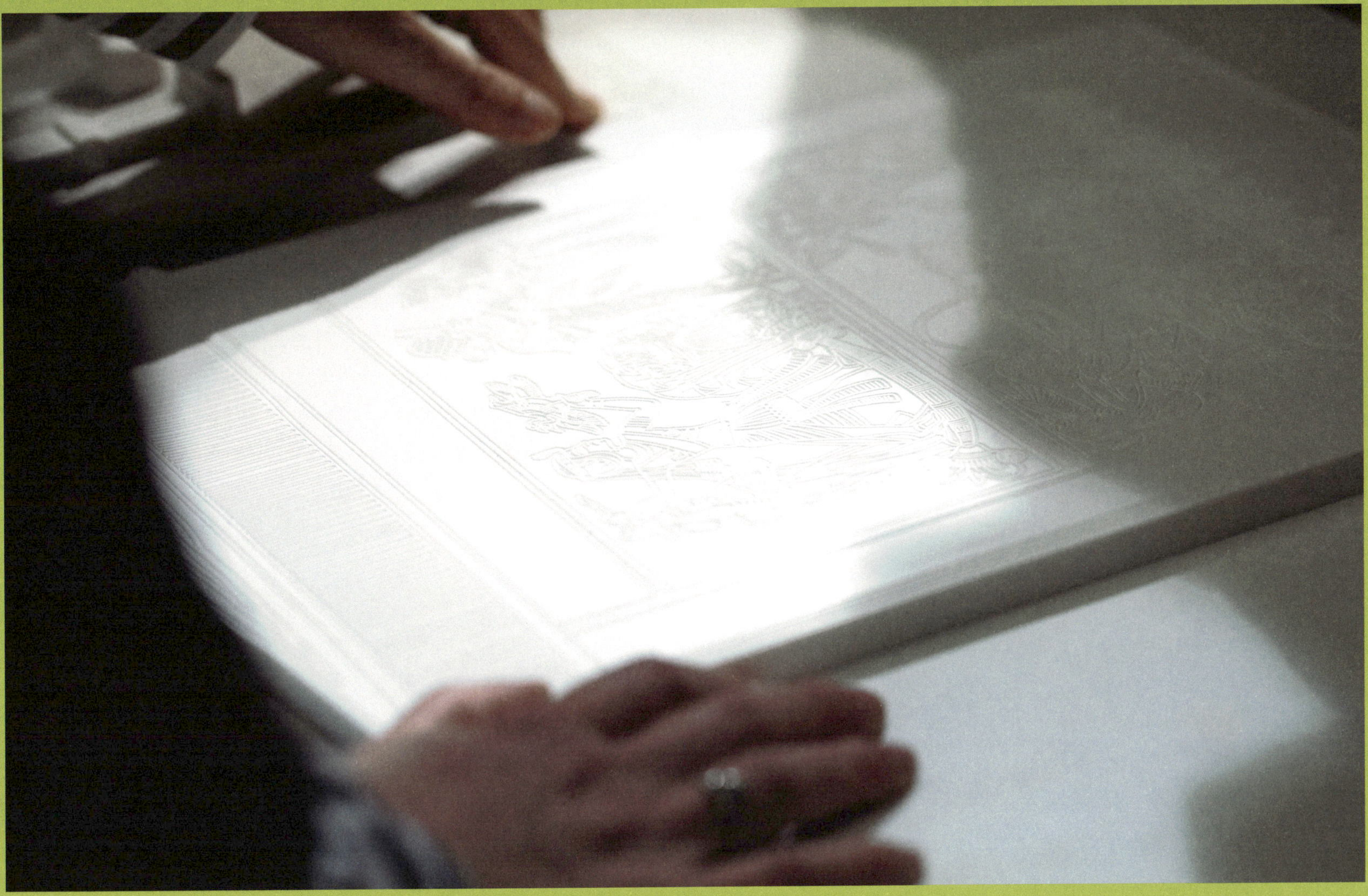

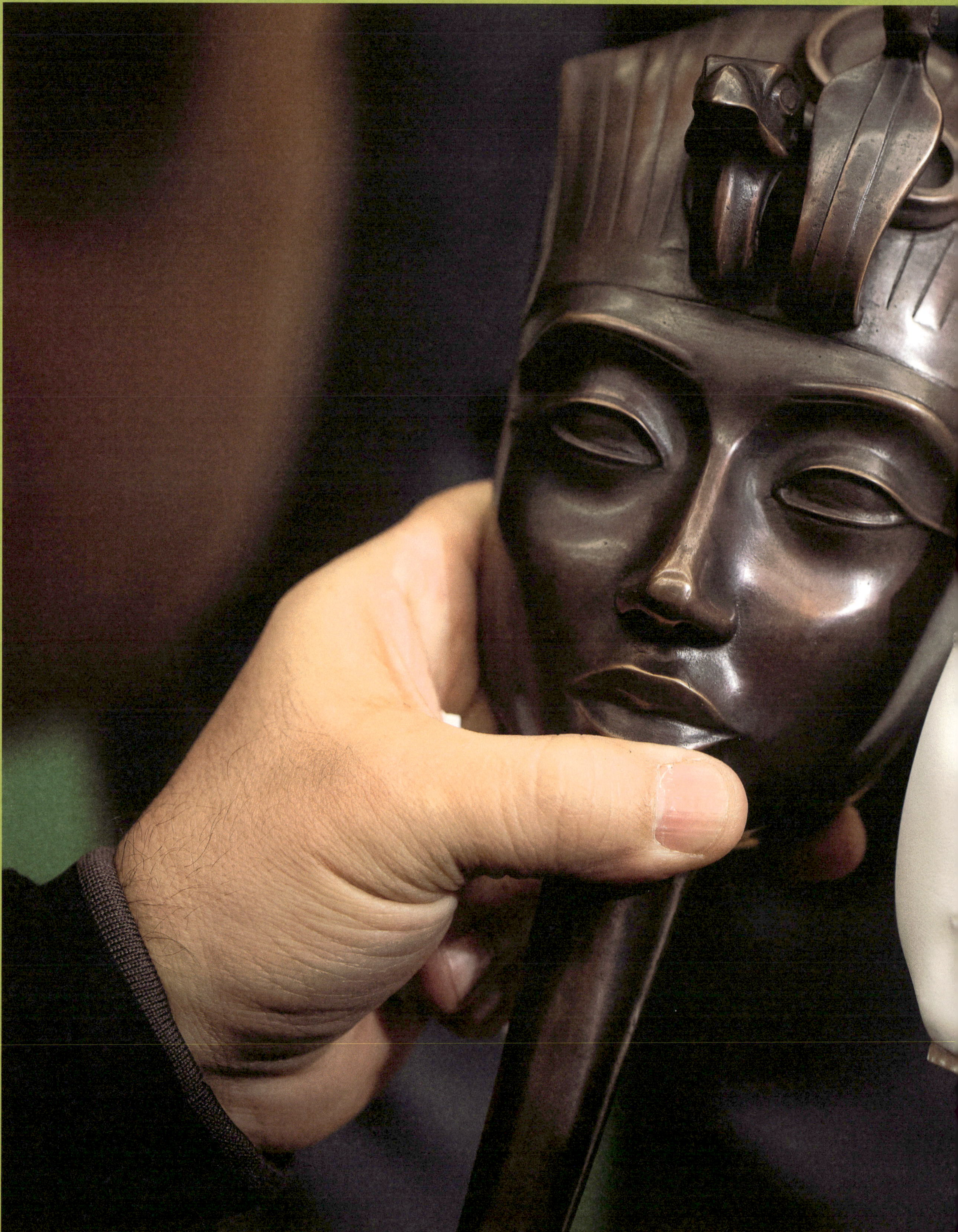

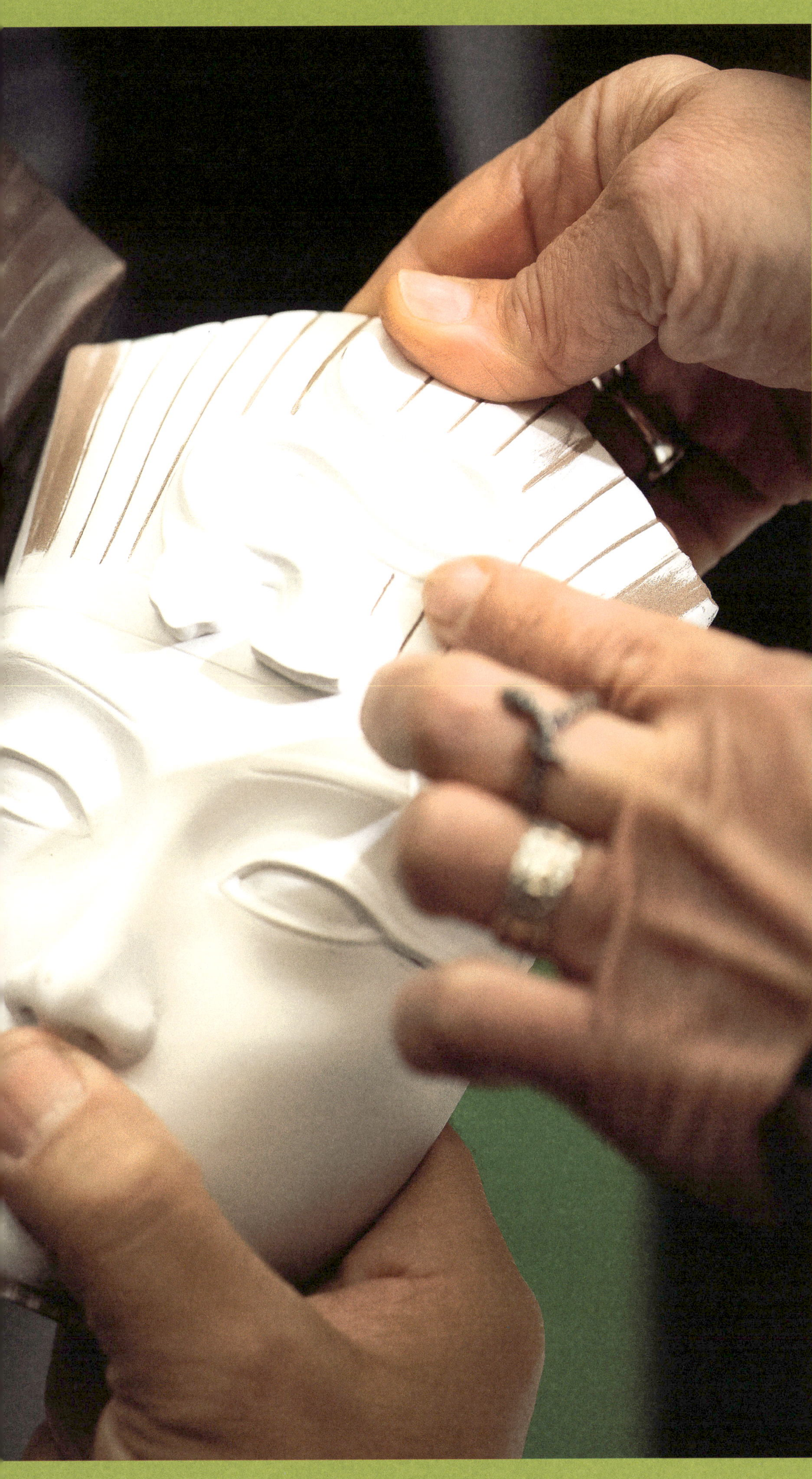

MUSEUMS WITH SIMILAR MEASURES

Waikato Museum

HAMILTON, NEW ZEALAND

Dedicated to the preservation of Maori culture and heritage, through traveling exhibitions and its own collections.

Museo Miraflores

GUATEMALA CITY, GUATEMALA

Protection and dissemination of the cultural and ancestral heritage of the Maya culture in the Kaminaljuyu metropolis, the most successful and prosperous in the Guatemala Valley.

Whitney Museum of American Art

NEW YORK, USA

Program for the inclusion of indigenous communities, perspectives, and artists.

Museum of Islamic Art

DOHA, QATAR

The Museum of Islamic Art (MIA) stands out as a beacon of cultural exchange and serves as a tribute to the lasting impact of Islamic art and civilization.

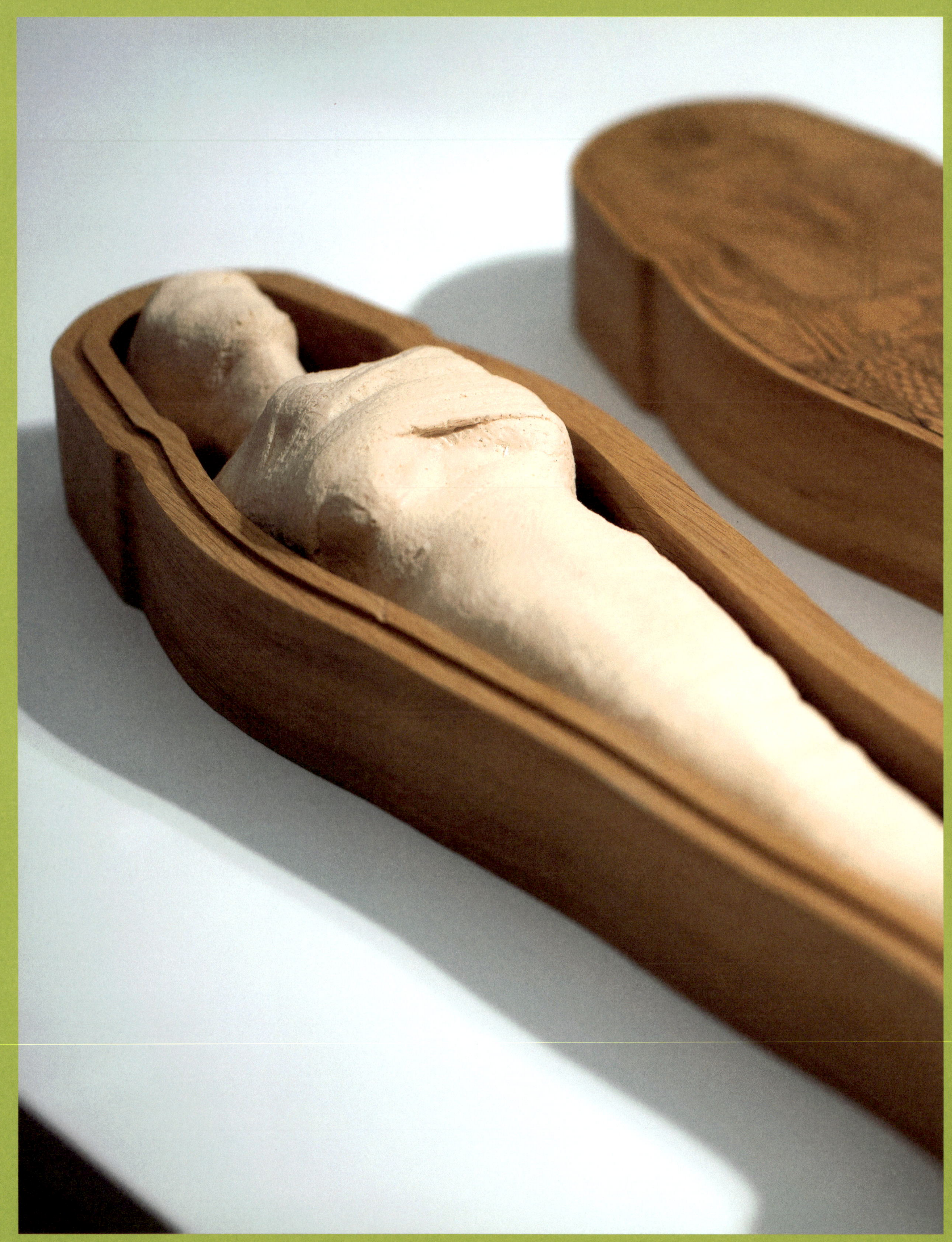

“Innovation at the Grand Egyptian Museum comes from linking ancient Pharaonic culture with modern museography without losing its identity.”

Barış Çözer

Director of Museums and Exhibitions in the Middle East at ACCIONA

33 COLLABORATION NETWORKS AND ALLIANCES

ALLIANCES SDG 13 / 17

Collaborate to go further. Collaborate to lead the transition to a new model. Creating collaborative sustainability networks that will enable the culture industry to pursue the implementation of a joint strategy on sustainable development is fundamental for creating an atmosphere conducive to innovation and the ongoing improvement of processes.

MuseoCycle

Network connecting museums to extend the life of surplus exhibition furniture.

NEMO – Network of European Museum Organizations

This network represents over 30,000 museums in 40 countries across Europe. One of its key initiatives is sustainable transition, supported by a working group on sustainability and climate action. This group promotes research, advocacy, and the exchange of knowledge and experiences.

Gallery Climate Collection

International community of arts organizations working to reduce environmental impacts in museums.

ICOM – International Council of Museums

Creation of a model guide to help museums face the challenge of sustainability in its different dimensions.

Coalition of Museums for Climate Justice

Museum partnerships to lead in strengthening public awareness on climate change.

CIMAM – International Committee for Museums and Collections of Modern Art

Establishment of a working committee to develop measures and provide applicable resources for the sustainable development of museums.

Guggenheim Museum Bilbao

BILBAO, SPAIN

Agreement with Ecoalf company to produce ecological employee clothing.

Museo Nacional Thyssen-Bornemisza

MADRID, SPAIN

Exhibition tour, in collaboration with ACCIONA, linking art and sustainable development in terms of ecology, economy and society.

National Children's Museum

WASHINGTON, D.C., USA

Children's exhibit *Heroes of Climate Action*, sponsored by Nickelodeon.

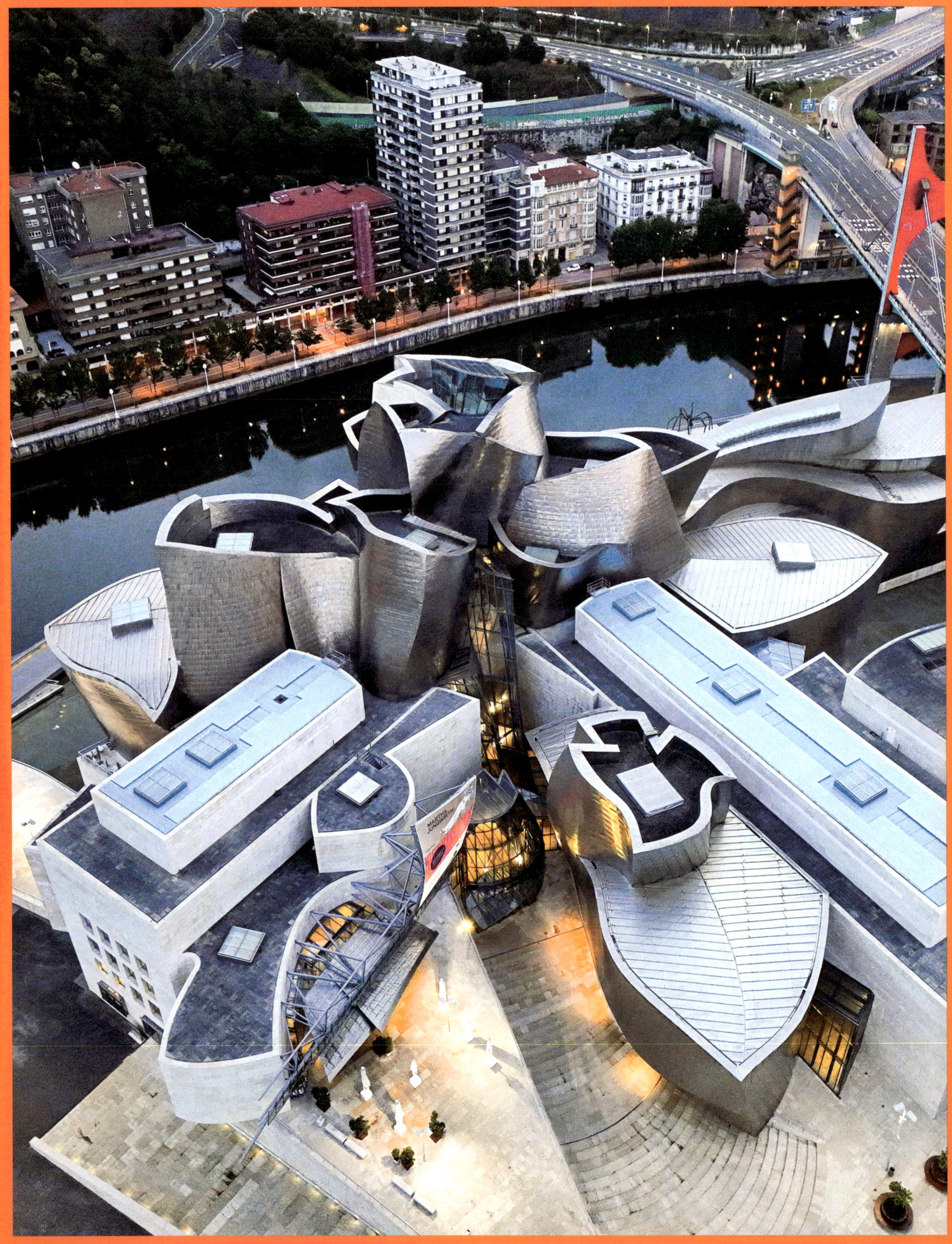
MARTHA
JUNGWIRTH

“Working together as a community and sector, rather than individually, increases the likelihood of achieving our goals.”

Heath Lowndes

Gallery Climate Coalition

Designed by Woulfe

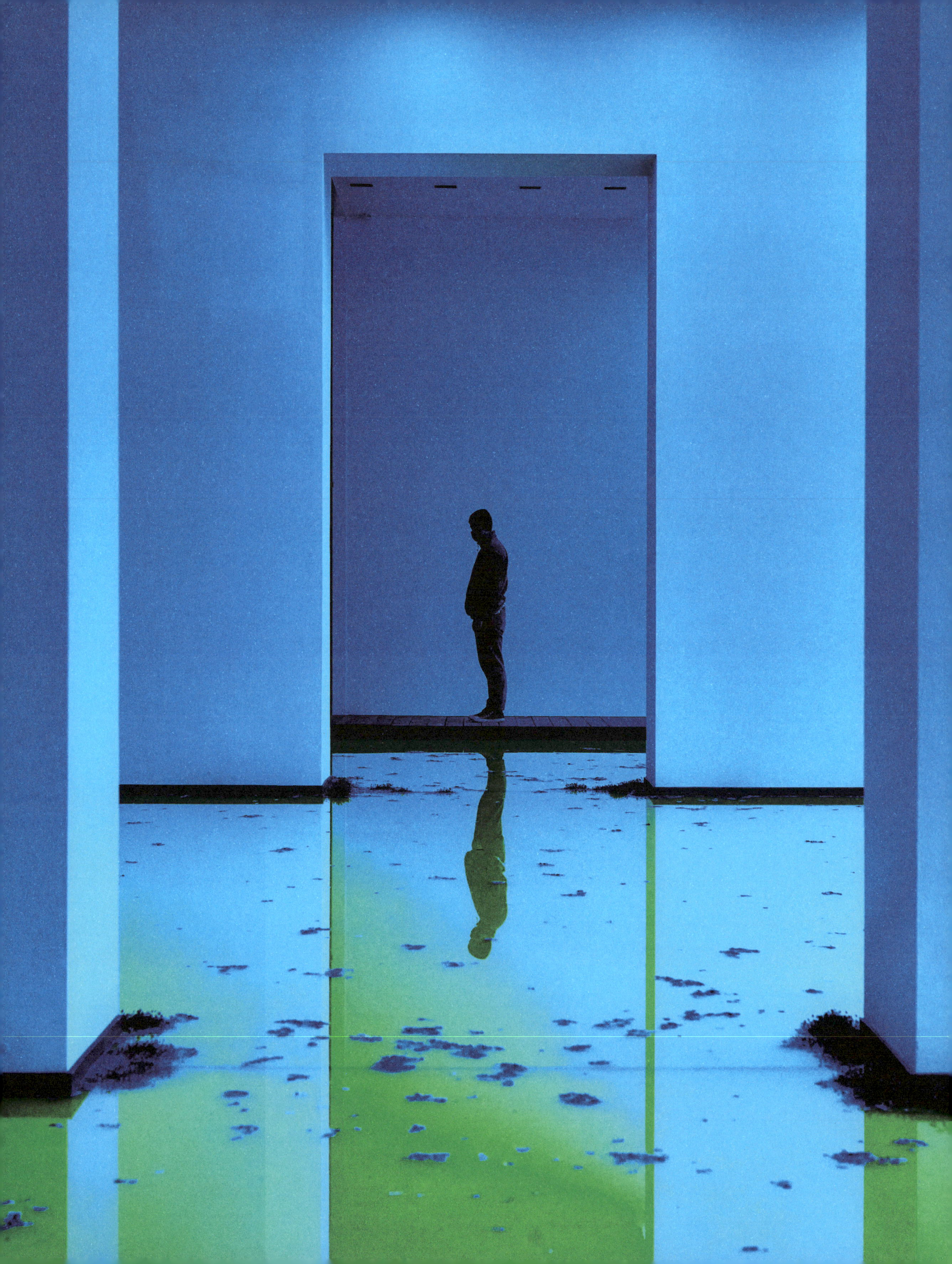

A FUTURE FOR OUR SECTOR'S CLIMATE RESPONSIBILITY

Sarah Sutton
CEO and Co-founder, Environment and Culture Partners

In his foreword, Alfons Martinell highlighted the compelling need to consider future needs in our present pursuits and pointed out that to do so is a moral responsibility. I agree. The cultural sector, as educators, researchers, and communicators, has a responsibility and opportunity to demonstrate its full potential as a valued community resource. I believe that many in our professions do and will accept this responsibility, enough of us to achieve a transformation that is widespread and wonderful, even if it is slow, uneven, and sometimes tedious.

So, when I'm asked if I'm hopeful about the human response to climate change, my response is "yes." This is because there are so many smart and motivated people working on the climate crisis, and so many committed people in our field. They are doing excellent work to find a different and better path. I know because we see them, work with them, and read about many of them in these pages. So yes, I'm hopeful.

But for that hope to last, it must be shared broadly and replenished every day.

Early on in the sustainability movement, fifty years or more ago, the clearest symbol of thoughtful environmental action was a brown paper bag: so simple and plain that it shouted "low impact" (at least to those avoiding plastic). Many people, however, were put off by the complete absence of design and color, and, by extension, the lack of pleasure and appeal in the brown-bag approach to the world and our future. It sent a message of austerity that obscured the potential for creativity, joy, and impact that is such a part of thoughtful environmental action and design.

The continuous creativity and reinvention we see in the climate actors of the cultural sector is the antithesis to that plain approach. We see their masterful integration of cultural buildings with natural landscapes, the creative use and reuse of materials in exhibitions and construction, and exciting innovations in building systems and surfaces and in designs that make them adaptive to less predictable, more extreme conditions and needs.

Creativity, curiosity, and courage are embedded in our professional nature. These traits facilitate innovation and encourage cooperation that leads to change at scale. When we plan to activate these characteristics, if we can be curious ourselves and encourage others to be curious with us, if we can be creative in our approach and our solutions and help others to be creative with us, and if we have the determination to jump toward a future, not stand back and guard ourselves, then we will create the change we need.

Whether our focus is arts, science, culture, heritage, living collections, or another area, we have a remit to build on past and present knowledge, and the experience to guide our future. This work deserves to expand beyond trend-like responses and fashionable preoccupations, to become fully integrated as the best of regular practice.

We have lost so much ground if the return to or realization of nature-based approaches passes for exciting. If the changes in our world and its climate are so profound that we find ourselves celebrating the tiny islands of biodiversity that we create at a single museum site, then our situation is indeed dire, and our solutions are not yet enough. It is incumbent upon the creative, curious, and courageous to bring about their return. The shift is important: these practices should have been obvious, but at least now we can make them ubiquitous.

What more should our sector do to move us to a safer, healthier, more just, and joyful future? We can start by aligning with (and then enhancing and expanding) the United Nations Paris Agreement's near-term 2030 goal to reduce GHG emissions by at least 50%. Advancing approaches in pursuit of ambitious goals is critical.

- Reduce emissions by 65% from 2020 baselines of transportation of art, artifacts, exhibits, materials, and professionals as well as the public.
- Reduce emissions by 65% from 2020 baselines of onsite energy consumption.
- Make climate action and resilience plans a core requirement for art/artifact loans and museum accreditations.
- Make Bizot Group guidelines or better common practice in buildings with environmental management.
- Expect all museums to identify climate action as part of their social role and responsibility.

Each of us can contribute to progress:

- Start or move forward in your climate journey, now. Faster. All the time. Learn what you need to learn. Share what you know. Scale for the future, not the fantastic.
- Design for high-efficiency, low-energy projects using only clean and renewable sources.
- Eliminate the use of gas or oil; require new equipment to be electric. Prioritize clean energy generation and always install battery backups with solar.
- Allow only low-impact materials, whether that means fewer, less volatile, reused and refashioned, or even better.
- Be a part of creating a field-wide expectation that exhibit and building fabrication must be sustainable for the Earth's future, not just the budget or traffic, or for now.
- And, just in case, design for disaster.

Our colleagues and supporters must repeatedly hear our strong, clear voices—drawn from practice and commitment and buttressed with our values and convictions. They must see that the entire culture sector has a responsibility and is exercising its distinct ability to prioritize climate action as a key pillar of its charitable, educational, community-driven mission.

From the examples here, I am most passionate about the last topic in this text: Alliances.

"Alliances: Collaborate to go further." This means "to lead the transition to a new model," to "pursue the implementation of a joint strategy on sustainable development," which is "fundamental for creating an atmosphere conducive to innovation and the ongoing improvement of processes" (key no. 33 of this book).

This is where my hopefulness is refreshed every day. Climate work and the blending of action across two distinct domains (culture and environment) require an interconnection of ideas and contexts, and systems thinking, that cannot be advanced in isolation. And the work requires skills contributed by all aspects of our field and those who can help us. Let us be generous partners to each other, positive examples for those who are watching, and relentless as we move ahead.

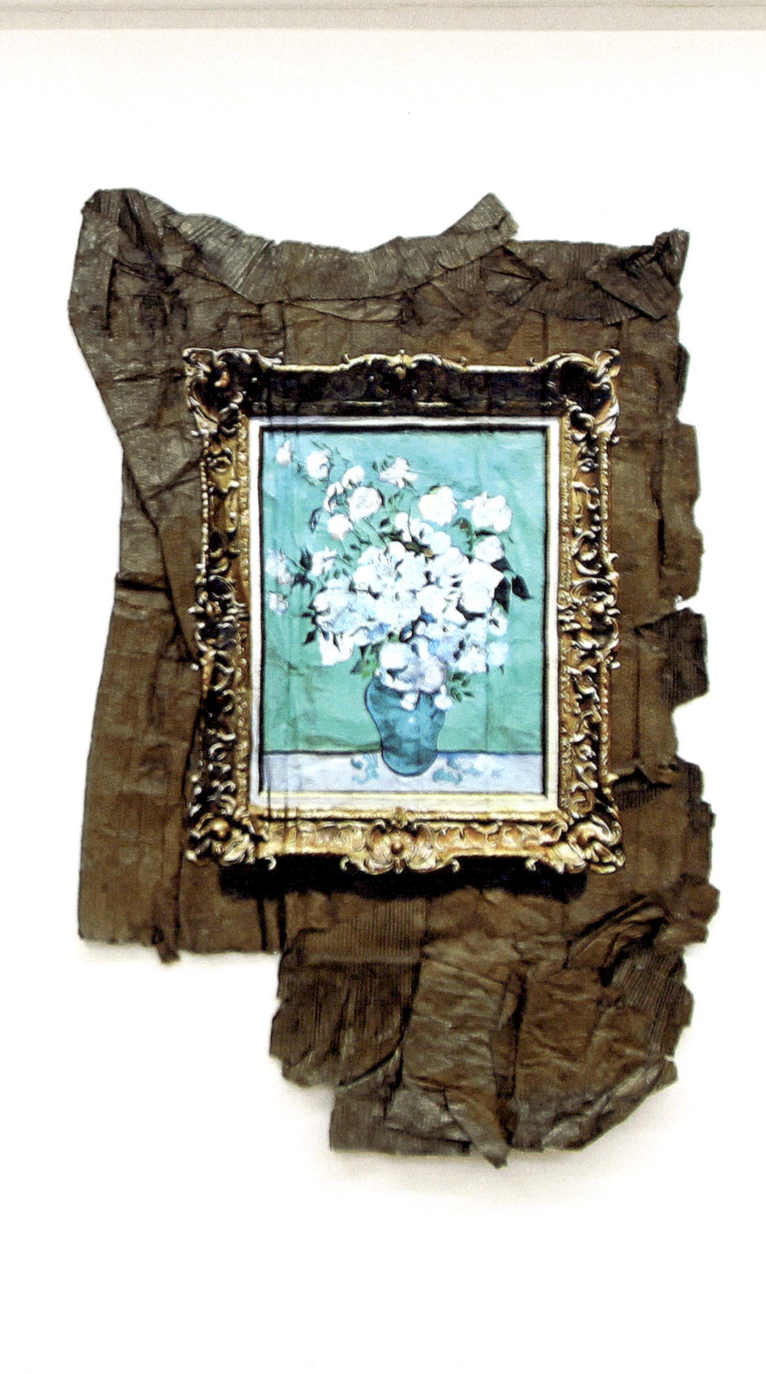

ANNEXES

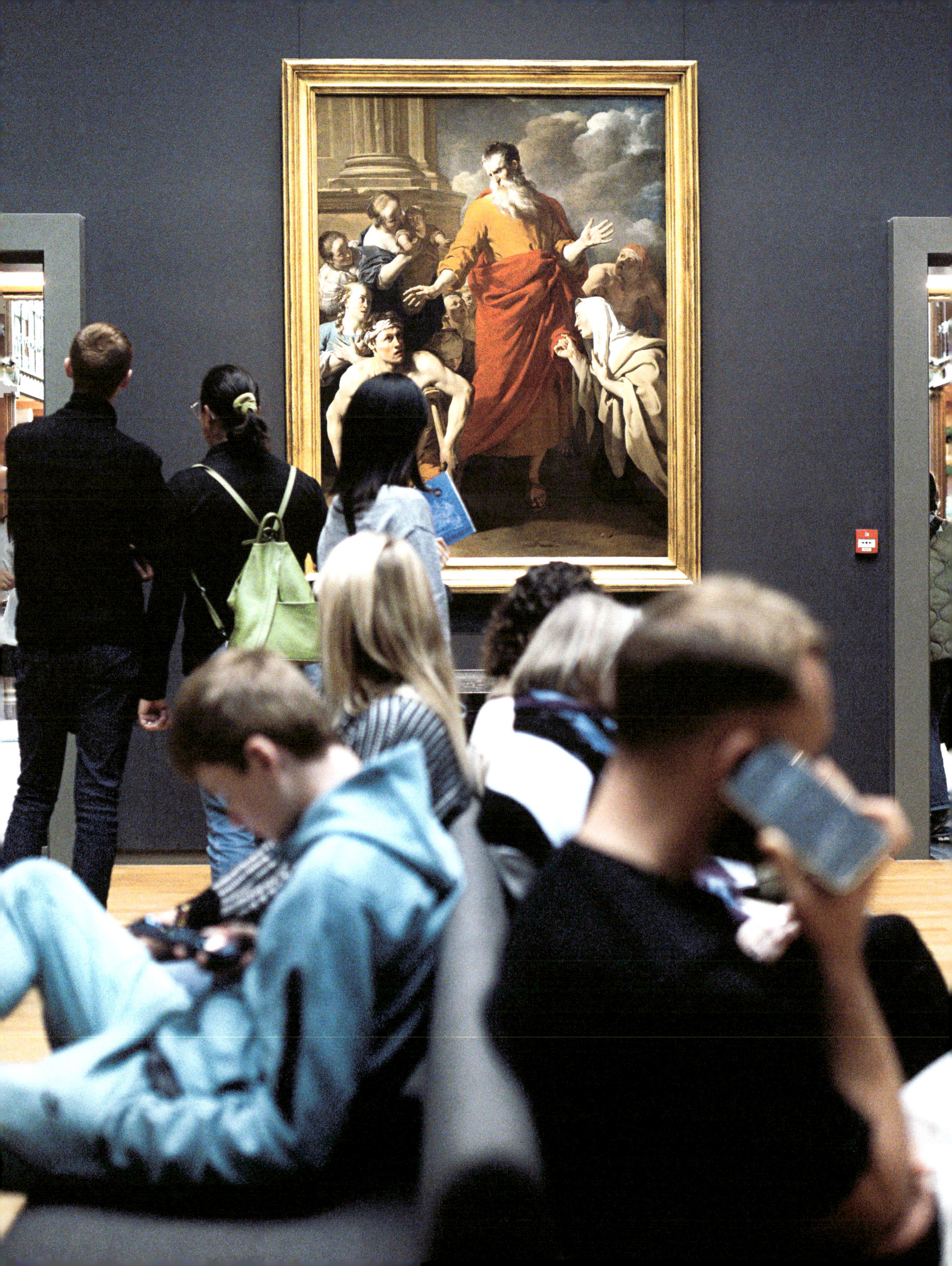

INTERNATIONAL CERTIFICATIONS

Sustainability certifications consist of evaluation and verification by an independent body specialized in construction and/or management, focusing on sustainability and environmental performance. There are two main types:

- Sustainable construction certification
- Environmental management and/or energy management certifications

While the initial cost and effort to obtain these certifications are high, the long-term benefits include cost reductions through optimized processes, consumption savings, and reduced maintenance costs.

It's crucial to see the certification process not as an end but as a means of enhancing the museum's sustainable performance.

The main types of certifications are described below.

SUSTAINABLE CONSTRUCTION CERTIFICATIONS

LEED

Created by the U.S. Green Building Council, this is an internationally recognized system that was introduced in 1993. Over 100,000 LEED-certified buildings exist across more than 150 countries.

There are five different categories for certification:

- Building design and construction
- Interior design and construction
- Operation and maintenance of buildings
- Cities and communities
- Design and construction of residential housing

To achieve certification, projects must meet requirements across various areas: location and transportation, sustainable site development, water efficiency, energy and atmosphere, materials and resources, indoor environmental quality, innovation, and regional priority. The total points determine the certification level: certified, silver, gold, or platinum.

LEED Certification is valid for a period of one to five years, after which a recertification process must be passed.

Examples of LEED-certified museums

National Museum of African American History & Culture

WASHINGTON, D.C., USA
LEED BD+C.
New Construction
(2009 version). Gold
Scorecard 66/110

Dallas Museum of Art

DALLAS, TEXAS, USA
LEED O+M.
Existing Buildings
(2008 version). Silver
Scorecard 44/91

Museum of Northern Arizona

FLAGSTAFF, ARIZONA, USA
LEED BD+C.
New Construction
(2.1version). Platinum
Scorecard 57/69

BREEAM

BREEAM (Building Research Establishment Environmental Assessment Methodology Certification) is an established building environmental impact assessment methodology implemented in ninety countries, with over 590,000 buildings certified since 1990. It offers a version for non-residential buildings adapted to local languages, regulations, and construction practices, plus an international version for those without specific adaptations.

The certification process involves earning points based on compliance across ten categories: management, health and wellness, energy, transportation, water, materials, waste, land use and ecology, pollution, and innovation. BREEAM certification has five levels: correct, good, very good, excellent, and exceptional.

Examples of BREEAM-certified museums

Van Gogh Museum

AMSTERDAM, THE NETHERLANDS
BREEAM Certificate:
Very Good (2023)

Rijksmuseum

AMSTERDAM, THE NETHERLANDS
BREEAM Certificate:
Excellent (2021)

Manchester Museum

MANCHESTER, UNITED KINGDOM
BREEAM Certificate:
Very Good (2021)

ENVIRONMENTAL AND ENERGY MANAGEMENT CERTIFICATIONS

ISO 14001

This is an international standard developed by ISO (International Organization for Standardization) that aims to implement an environmental management system, based on the PDCA (Plan-Do-Check-Act) cycle for continuous improvement. The system includes environmental objectives and targets, policies, and procedures for achieving them, defined responsibilities, personnel training activities, documentation, and a system for monitoring changes and progress. Additionally, the standard mandates the evaluation of compliance with applicable environmental legal requirements.

Examples of museums with ISO 14001 certification

Guggenheim Museum Bilbao
BILBAO, SPAIN

Natural History Musem
LONDON, UNITED KINGDOM

Vasa Museum
STOCKHOLM, SWEDEN

ISO 50001

This is an international standard developed by ISO (International Organization for Standardization) to enhance and sustain an energy management system, grounded in the PDCA (Plan-Do-Check-Act) continuous improvement cycle. This standard aims to perpetually improve the efficiency and energy performance of organizations by analyzing energy consumption, identifying improvement opportunities, and reducing greenhouse gas emissions.

Examples of museums with ISO 50001 certification

Musée du Louvre
PARIS, FRANCE

CaixaForum Barcelona
BARCELONA, SPAIN

Salar Jung Museum
HYDERABAD, INDIA

EMAS

This is a voluntary certification regulation introduced by the European Union in 2009, entailing a legal commitment. It mandates full compliance with relevant environmental legislation for organizations and requires the publication of an externally verified environmental statement. This standard is considered more rigorous than ISO 14001, holds legal significance for public administrations, and applies within the European Union.

Examples of museums with EMAS certification

Museo de la Ciencia Cosmocaixa
BARCELONA, SPAIN

Museu Serralves
PORTO, PORTUGAL

Fundació Joan Miró
BARCELONA, SPAIN

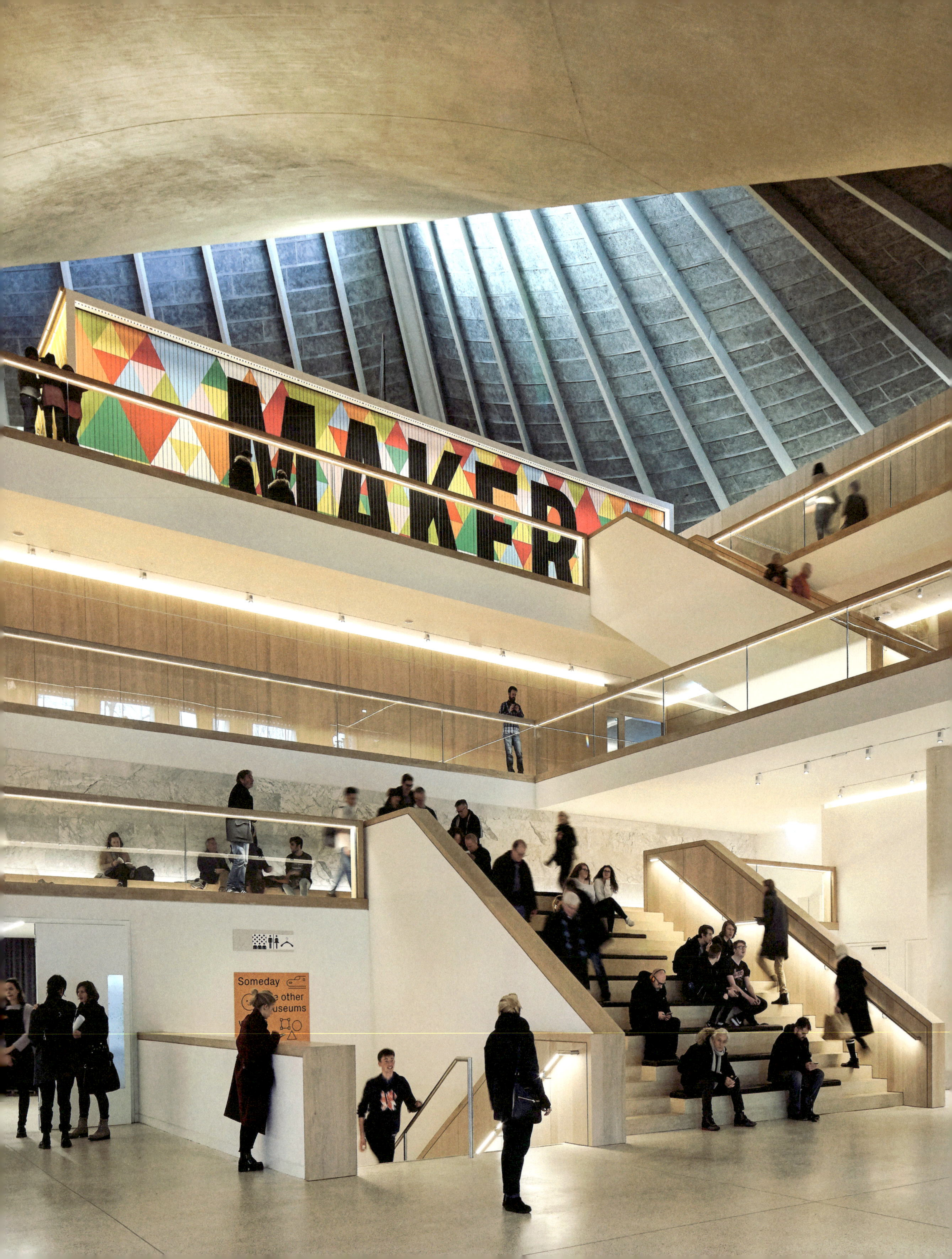
MAKER
Someday
other

USEFUL TOOLS FOR SUSTAINABILITY MANAGEMENT IN MUSEUMS

The following links provide information and access to various practical tools and resources for museum organizations and institutions concerned with or engaged in the sustainability of their activity.

Unlike a traditional bibliography, this collection primarily includes practical materials such as toolkits, manuals, guides, reports, management plans, and carbon footprint calculators, rather than theoretical books or articles.

GENERAL

Best Practice Guidelines

Handbook of best practices for the art world.

GALLERY CLIMATE COALITION (GCC), UNITED KINGDOM

Climate Resources Bank

Sustainability initiatives resource bank.

MUSEUMS ASSOCIATION, LONDON, UNITED KINGDOM

Climate Action. Advice and tips

Advice and tips for implementing a sustainability strategy in the museum.

MUSEUMS GALLERIES SCOTLAND, UNITED KINGDOM

Creative Climate Tools

Resource hub for practical tools and support on how to take climate action now.

JULIE'S BICYCLE, UNITED KINGDOM

Toward a Sustainable Culture

Hacia una cultura sostenible: a practical guide for integrating the 2030 Agenda in the culture industry, prepared by the Spanish Sustainable Development Network (REDS).

RED ESPAÑOLA PARA EL DESARROLLO SOSTENIBLE (REDS), SPAIN

Museums in the Climate Crisis

A report containing information and recommendations for the sustainable transition in Europe.

NETWORK OF EUROPEAN MUSEUM ORGANIZATIONS (NEMO), BERLIN, GERMANY

Sustainability and Museums: A Workbook for Improving Operations, Engaging Communities, and Creating Partnerships

A handbook to make museums more sustainable and get communities involved in the process.

NATIONAL INFORMAL STEM EDUCATION (NISE) NETWORK, USA

Culture and Local Development: Maximising the Impact. Guide for Local Governments, Communities and Museums

This guide offers local governments, communities and museums a road map for defining a common agenda of local development.

ICOM AND OCDE

Common Conceptual Framework for the Sustainability of Ibero-American Museum Institutions and Processes

Marco Conceptual Común de Sostenibilidad de las Instituciones y Procesos Museísticos Iberoamericanos: a compilation of essential reflections and concepts related to sustainability in the museums of Ibero-America.

IBERMUSEOS. THE SPACE OF IBERO-AMERICAN MUSEUMS, SPAIN / PORTUGAL

Museums and the Sustainable Development Goals

Los museos y los Objetivos de Desarrollo Sostenible: a practical guide for museums, galleries, the culture industry, and their partners.

IBERMUSEOS. THE SPACE OF IBERO-AMERICAN MUSEUMS, SPAIN / PORTUGAL

CARBON FOOTPRINT

Guide to calculating the carbon footprint and developing an improvement plan for an organization

MINISTRY FOR ECOLOGICAL TRANSITION AND THE DEMOGRAPHIC CHALLENGE, SPAIN

Carbon Literacy for Museums. Toolkit overview

A guide to help museums become aware of how they can reduce carbon emissions at the individual, community, and organizational levels.

CARBON LITERACY PROJECT, UNITED KINGDOM

ENERGY EFFICIENCY

A Practical Guide for Sustainable Climate Control and Lighting in Museums and Galleries

MUSEUMS AND GALLERIES QUEENSLAND, AUSTRALIA

SUSTAINABLE BUILDINGS

Arts Green Book. Sustainable Buildings

This green book provides a series of guidelines for promoting sustainability in built structures.

ARTS COUNCIL ENGLAND, UNITED KINGDOM

Fit for the Future: Investing in Environmentally Sustainable Building

A guide that explains the social, economic, and cultural benefits of investing in sustainable buildings.

ARTS COUNCIL ENGLAND AND JULIE'S BICYCLE, UNITED KINGDOM

SUSTAINABLE EXHIBITIONS

Museum Freecycle UK

Museum materials exchange and reuse website.

MUSEUM FREECYCLE UK, UNITED KINGDOM

Exhibition Design for Our Time

A guide to reducing the environmental impact of exhibitions.

DESIGN MUSEUM, LONDON

Sustainable Development Guide: Resources for Exhibitions

Guía de desarrollo sostenible: Recursos para exposiciones: a guide on how to efficiently manage material resources in the conceptual stage of exhibition design.

EVE MUSEUMS + INNOVATION, SPAIN

Exhibit Materials Use Management Guide

Guía de gestión de uso de materiales para exposiciones: a practical guide to sustainability, climate control, and lighting in museums and galleries.

EVE MUSEUMS + INNOVATION, SPAIN

Waste & Materials Collections Care: Packing, Storage & Transport

A complete guide for the arts sector that provides key advice on how to reduce waste.

KI CULTURE, AMSTERDAM, THE NETHERLANDS

ACCESSIBILITY AND INCLUSION

A Guide for Museums. Accesibility Toolkit

ACCESS SMITHSONIAN is a resource guide with accessibility measures that can be implemented in museums.

SMITHSONIAN INSTITUTION, WASHINGTON DC, USA

Accessibility Manual for Museums

Manual de accesibilidad para museos: this handbook explains the basic concepts of accessibility and includes a best practices guide and applicable legislation.

IBERMUSEOS. THE SPACE OF IBERO-AMERICAN MUSEUMS, SPAIN / PORTUGAL

Facing Change

Insights from the American Alliance of Museums Diversity, Equity, Accessibility, and Inclusion Working Group.

AMERICAN ALLIANCE OF MUSEUMS, USA

Toward an Inclusive Culture: Museums for Everyone

Kultura inclusiboaren bidean Guztientzako museoak: a guide to help cultural agents devise more accessible and inclusive cultural practices.

(BASQUE/SPANISH). K6 GESTIÓN CULTURAL-ELKARTU, SPAIN

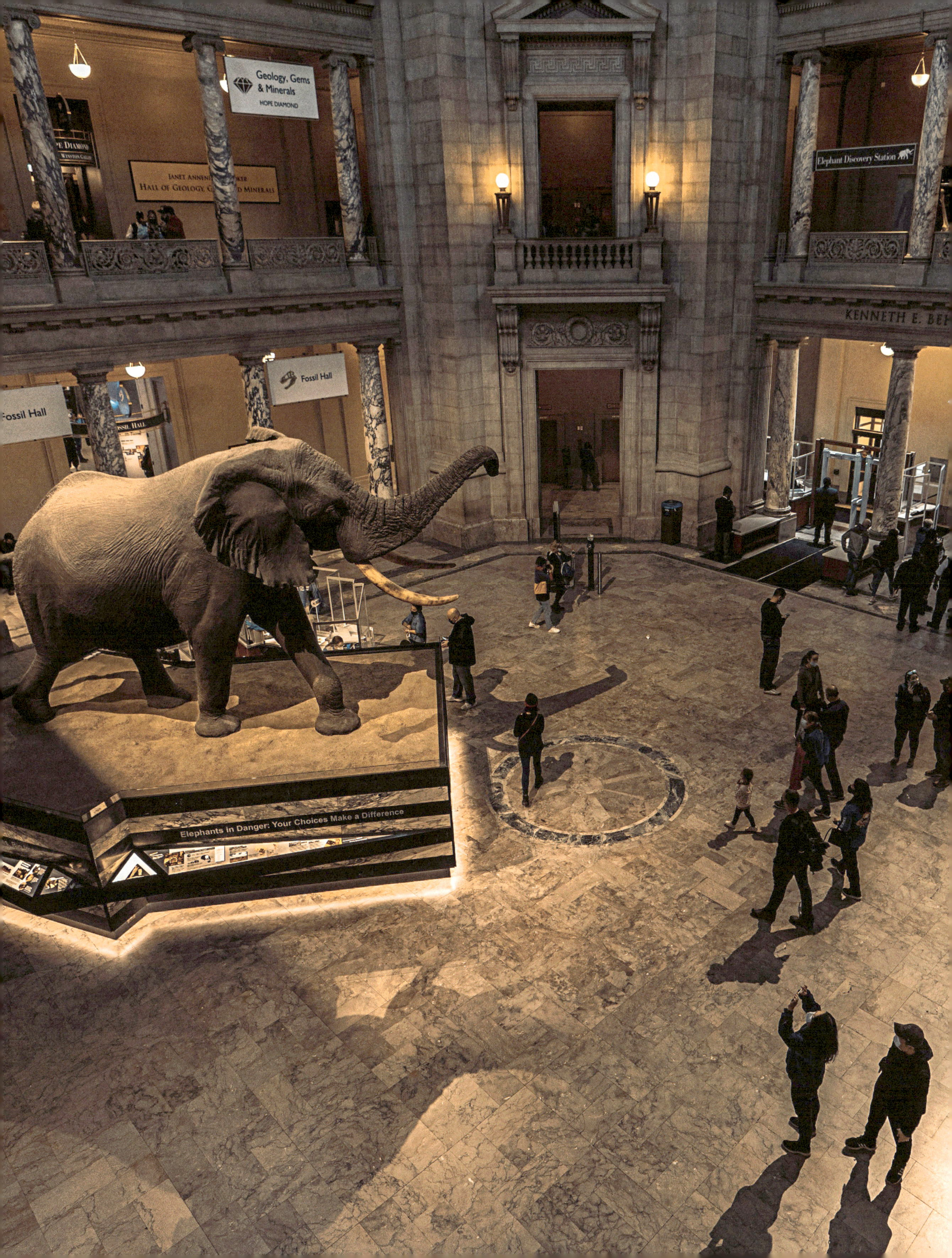
Geology, Gems & Minerals
HOPE DIAMOND
Elephant Discovery Station
Fossil Hall
Fossil Hall
Elephants in Danger: Your Choices Make a Difference

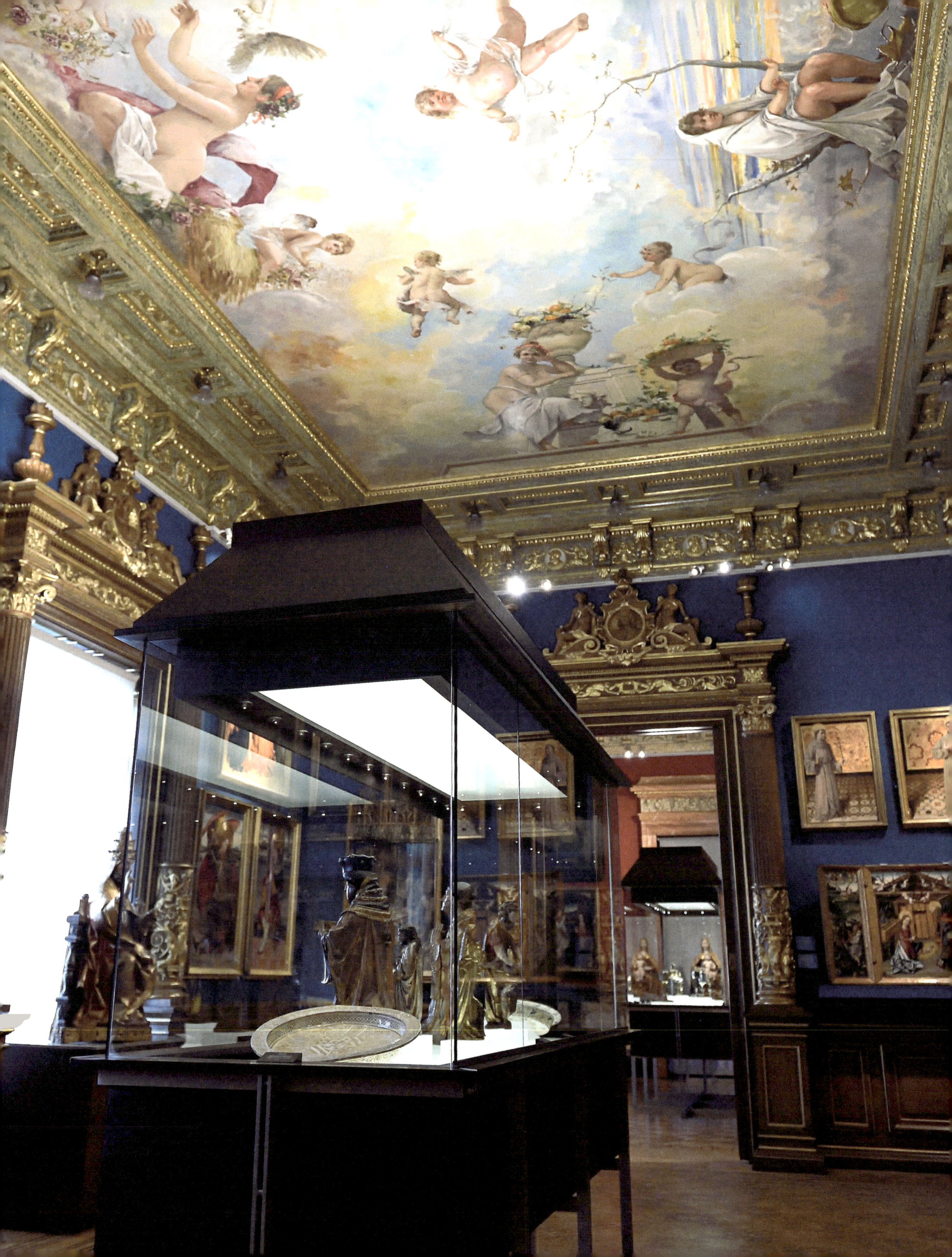

10 SIMPLE MEASURES FOR MUSEUMS STARTING ON THE ROAD TO SUSTAINABILITY

Aligning museum institutions with social and environmental responsibility begins with initial steps that facilitate subsequent actions.

The ten measures outlined below were chosen for their ease of implementation and are based on a prior commitment to making each museum an agent of the positive change necessary for the planet's sustainability.

For successful implementation, it is crucial to set specific, quantifiable goals and periodically assess the effectiveness of the actions we are taking to achieve them.

Each measure listed below includes a brief description, followed by information on museums that have already implemented them:

1 INTERNAL RECOGNITION OF THE CLIMATE EMERGENCY

Acknowledge this through internal documents shared with employees or an external policy. This acknowledgment serves as a foundation for integrating sustainable values into the museum's strategy and can include forming specific work teams. A starting point for sustainable action.

Museums & Heritage: Creative Climate Actions Starts Here. Julie's Bicycle

Guide with tips and recommendations for getting started in climate action.

Museums for Climate action

Brings together ideas and resources for museums to meet the challenges posed by the climate emergency.

Museo Nacional Thyssen-Bornemisza

MADRID, SPAIN

The museum's core purpose document, in the values section, incorporates concepts such as sustainability, climate emergency and adoption of the SDGs.

2 RESPONSIBLE WATER CONSUMPTION

This involves implementing simple measures such as installing flow reducers and presence sensors on faucets, dual-flush cisterns in toilets, and regulating water pressure in the building.

Museo Lázaro Galdiano

MADRID, SPAIN

Selective installation of flow restrictors in restroom faucets.

3 USE OF RENEWABLE ENERGY AND GOOD ENERGY EFFICIENCY PRACTICES

The goal is to guarantee that the energy used in the museum comes from sustainable sources and to use it efficiently.

Museu Nacional d'Art de Catalunya

BARCELONA, SPAIN

All energy consumed is guaranteed to be of renewable origin. In addition, presence detectors have been installed for lighting control in the exhibition rooms. These same detectors regulate the lighting for security, cleaning, and maintenance when the rooms are closed to the public.

Museo Cueva Pintada

GRAN CANARIA, SPAIN

Installation of photovoltaic panels to power the museum facility.

Musée du Louvre

PARIS, FRANCE

The pyramid of the Louvre in Paris has replaced its 4,500 xenon lamps with 3,200 LED technology light points.

Museo del Prado

MADRID, SPAIN

Integral lighting project with LED technology.

Museo Lázaro Galdiano

MADRID, SPAIN

In 2024, the museum reduced its energy consumption by more than 40% compared to the previous two years, thanks to a lighting project using LED technology that ensures optimal conservation of the artworks and user comfort.

4 CIRCULAR DESIGN AND USE OF SUSTAINABLE MATERIALS IN EXHIBITIONS

Use of configurable modular systems that allow or encourage their reuse across different museum activities. Optimization of the logistics and transportation of materials and simplification of the installation process.

Exhibition *Materia gris. Nuevos materiales para la era post-fósil*

(Gray Matter: New Materials for the Post-fossil Era).

CENTROCENTRO, MADRID, SPAIN

5 ACCESSIBILITY, INCLUSION, AND PROMOTION OF DIVERSITY

Implementation of various measures to ensure that the physical spaces of museums and the exhibited content are accessible to people with mobility, comprehension, and/or communication difficulties.

Accessibility in Museums

Manual of best practices for professionals and institutions of the Association of Museographers and Museologists of Andalusia, Spain.

ASOCIACIÓN DE MUSEÓGRAFOS Y MUSEÓLOGOS DE ANDALUCÍA, SPAIN

Excellence in DEAI

This manual proposes measures for achieving excellence in diversity, equity, accessibility, and inclusion.

AMERICAN ALLIANCE OF MUSEUMS, USA

6 MINIMIZATION AND SEGREGATION OF WASTE

Reduction of the consumption of paper, plastics, and packaging in all aspects of museum operations, such as stores, cafeterias, and exhibitions. Community involvement to achieve proper segregation of waste for later reuse or recycling.

Museo de Historia Natural de Valparaíso

VALPARAÍSO, CHILE

Recycling actions with the community.

High Museum of Art

ATLANTA, USA

Minimization of single-use containers in catering areas.

7 PROMOTION OF SUSTAINABLE MOBILITY FOR EMPLOYEES AND VISITORS

Installation of bicycle and personal mobility vehicle parking facilities, development of sustainable mobility programs for visitors and employees, and installation of charging stations for electric vehicles.

Museo Cerralbo

MADRID, SPAIN

The museum, through the #museoprobici project, promotes the use of bicycles to access the museum, with a place to park bikes and lockers for panniers, helmets, etc.

8 CALCULATION, VERIFICATION, AND REDUCTION OF THE CARBON FOOTPRINT

Measurement of the carbon footprint using reliable systems and implementation of a program of measures to reduce greenhouse gas emissions for both the museum operations and its visitors.

Museo Moderno

BUENOS AIRES, ARGENTINA

The museum has measured its carbon footprint and launched a plan for improvement opportunities.

9 EMPLOYEE TRAINING AND RAISING AWARENESS ABOUT SUSTAINABILITY AMONG VISITORS AND THE COMMUNITY

Launch of public information campaigns or designated awareness-raising spaces.

Museu Nacional d'Art de Catalunya

BARCELONA, SPAIN

Dissemination among employees of simple, easy-to-apply tips on good environmental practices.

Museo Lázaro Galdiano

MADRID, SPAIN

Creation of a working group focused on promoting responsible consumption among employees and visitors. Preparation of an employee newsletter with ideas and environmental tips, as well as practical initiatives implemented by the museum.

10 INFORMATION TO THE SUPPLY CHAIN

Alignment of products and service suppliers with the sustainability commitments and requirements adopted by the museum.

Natural History Museum

LONDON, UNITED KINGDOM

Detailed document on the museum's purchasing strategy in which sustainability plays a very relevant role.

Museu d'Art Contemporani de Barcelona

BARCELONA, SPAIN

Purchasing, responsible consumption, and recycling policy document.

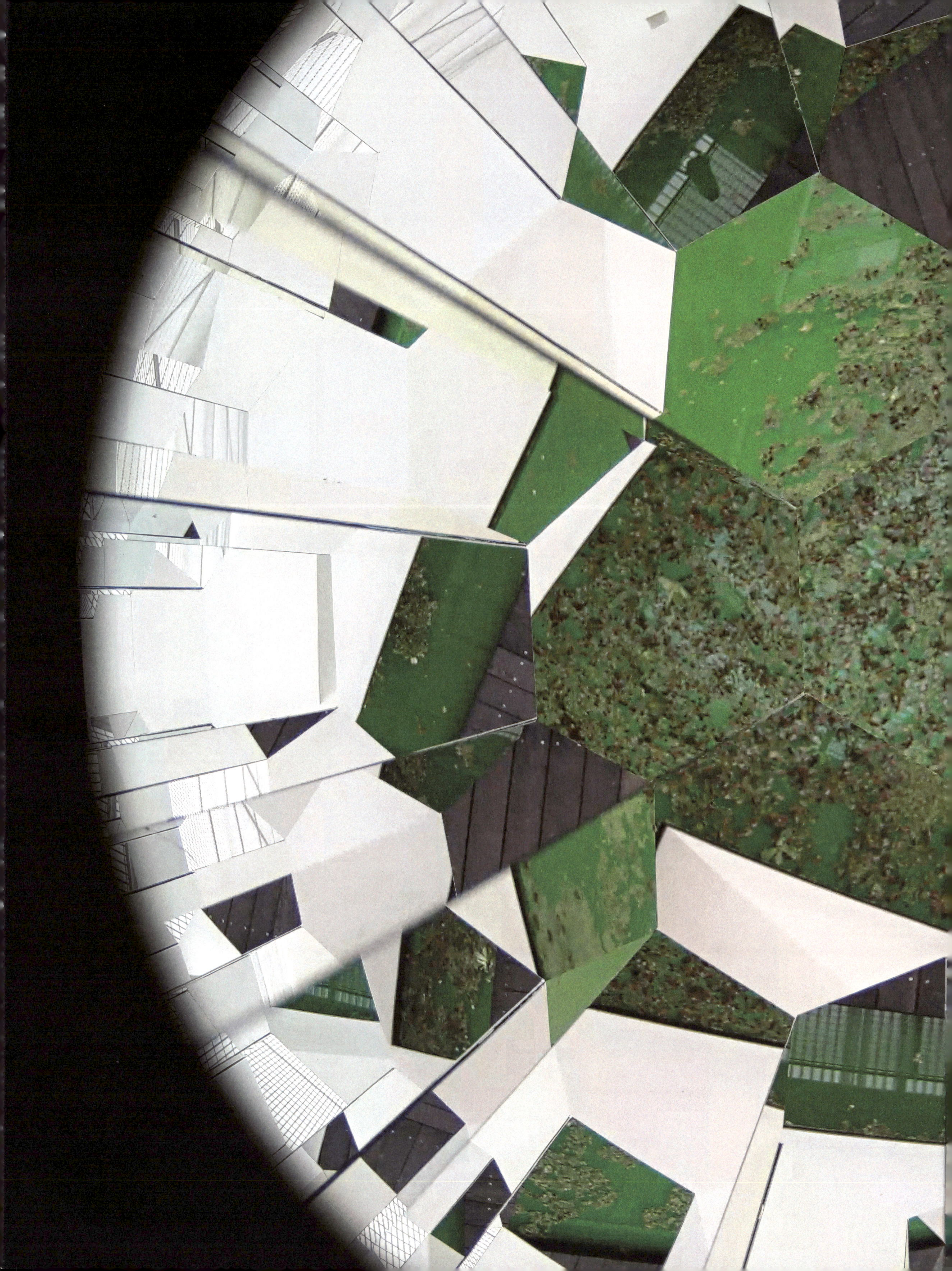

CANADA

- Biôdome
- Royal Ontario Museum

UNITED STATES

- Arizona-Sonora Desert Museum
- Art Institute of Chicago
- Aspen Art Museum
- Brooklyn's Children Museum
- California Academy of Sciences
- Children's Museum of Pittsburgh
- Cincinnati Museum Center
- Dallas Museum of Art. *Speechless: Different by Design* exhibition
- Discovery Museum
- Exploratorium
- Field Museum
- Haggerty Museum of Art
- High Museum of Art
- Museum of Northern Arizona
- Museum of the Moving Image
- National Children's Museum. *Climate Action Heroes* exhibition
- National Museum of African American History and Culture
- Natural History Museum of Utah
- Pérez Art Museum Miami
- Perot Museum of Nature and Science
- Phipps Conservatory and Botanical Gardens
- San Francisco Museum of Modern Art
- Smithsonian American Art Museum
- The Climate Museum
- The Dalí Museum
- The Huntington
- The Metropolitan Museum of Art
- The Museum of Contemporary Art
- Whitney Museum of American Art
- Young At Art Museum

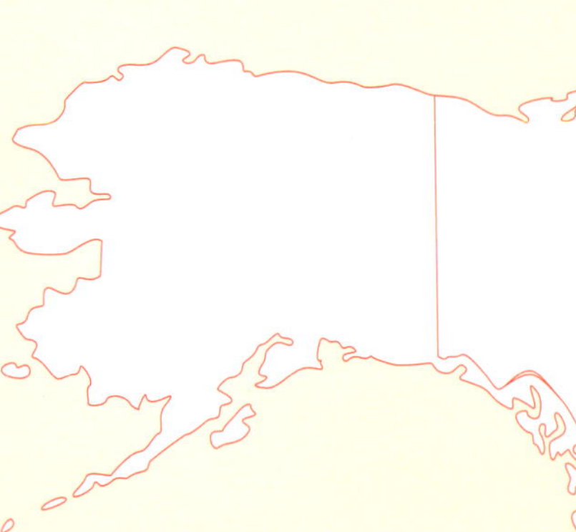

CLASSIFICATION OF MUSEUMS BY CATEGORY

- INTEGRATION OF NATURE
- CONSTRUCTION MATERIALS
- WATER USE
- BUILDING ENERGY EFFICIENCY
- PROTECTION AND PROMOTION OF BIODIVERSITY
- CIRCULAR EXHIBITION DESIGN
- ENVIRONMENTAL IMPACT ASSESSMENT OF EXHIBITIONS
- EXHIBITION MATERIALS
- POSITIVE IMPACT OF EXHIBITION PROJECTS
- ACCESSIBILITY, INCLUSION, AND DIVERSITY
- TRAINING OF EMPLOYEES AND WORK TEAMS
- ENVIRONMENTAL EMERGENCIES
- SUSTAINABLE MOBILITY
- CARBON FOOTPRINT
- VISITOR EDUCATION AND AWARENESS
- INTEGRATION OF MUSEUMS IN THE COMMUNITY
- PRESERVATION OF MEMORY AND HERITAGE
- ALLIANCES

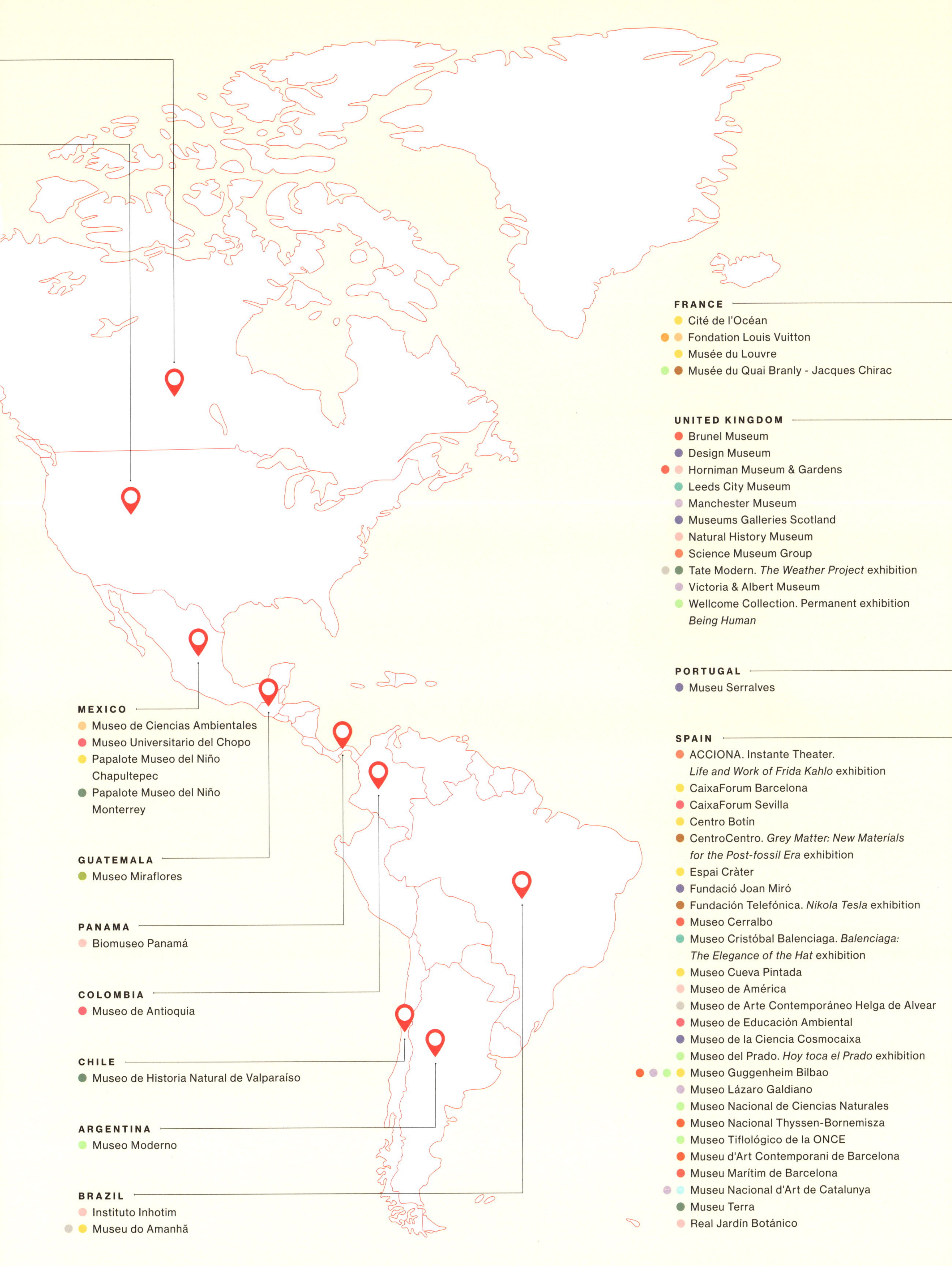
FRANCE
Cité de l'Océan
Fondation Louis Vuitton
Musée du Louvre
Musée du Quai Branly - Jacques Chirac
UNITED KINGDOM
Brunel Museum
Design Museum
Horniman Museum & Gardens
Leeds City Museum
Manchester Museum
Museums Galleries Scotland
Natural History Museum
Science Museum Group
Tate Modern. *The Weather Project* exhibition
Victoria & Albert Museum
Wellcome Collection. Permanent exhibition *Being Human*
PORTUGAL
Museu Serralves
SPAIN
ACCIONA. Instante Theater. *Life and Work of Frida Kahlo* exhibition
CaixaForum Barcelona
CaixaForum Sevilla
Centro Botín
CentroCentro. *Grey Matter: New Materials for the Post-fossil Era* exhibition
Espai Cràter
Fundació Joan Miró
Fundación Telefónica. *Nikola Tesla* exhibition
Museo Cerralbo
Museo Cristóbal Balenciaga. *Balenciaga: The Elegance of the Hat* exhibition
Museo Cueva Pintada
Museo de América
Museo de Arte Contemporáneo Helga de Alvear
Museo de Educación Ambiental
Museo de la Ciencia Cosmocaixa
Museo del Prado. *Hoy toca el Prado* exhibition
Museo Guggenheim Bilbao
Museo Lázaro Galdiano
Museo Nacional de Ciencias Naturales
Museo Nacional Thyssen-Bornemisza
Museo Tiflológico de la ONCE
Museu d'Art Contemporani de Barcelona
Museu Marítim de Barcelona
Museu Nacional d'Art de Catalunya
Museu Terra
Real Jardín Botánico
MEXICO
Museo de Ciencias Ambientales
Museo Universitario del Chopo
Papalote Museo del Niño Chapultepec
Papalote Museo del Niño Monterrey
GUATEMALA
Museo Miraflores
PANAMA
Biomuseo Panamá
COLOMBIA
Museo de Antioquia
CHILE
Museo de Historia Natural de Valparaíso
ARGENTINA
Museo Moderno
BRAZIL
Instituto Inhotim
Museu do Amanhã

Iluminar no es solo proyectar
luz, sino también sombra.

Museo Lázaro Galdiano

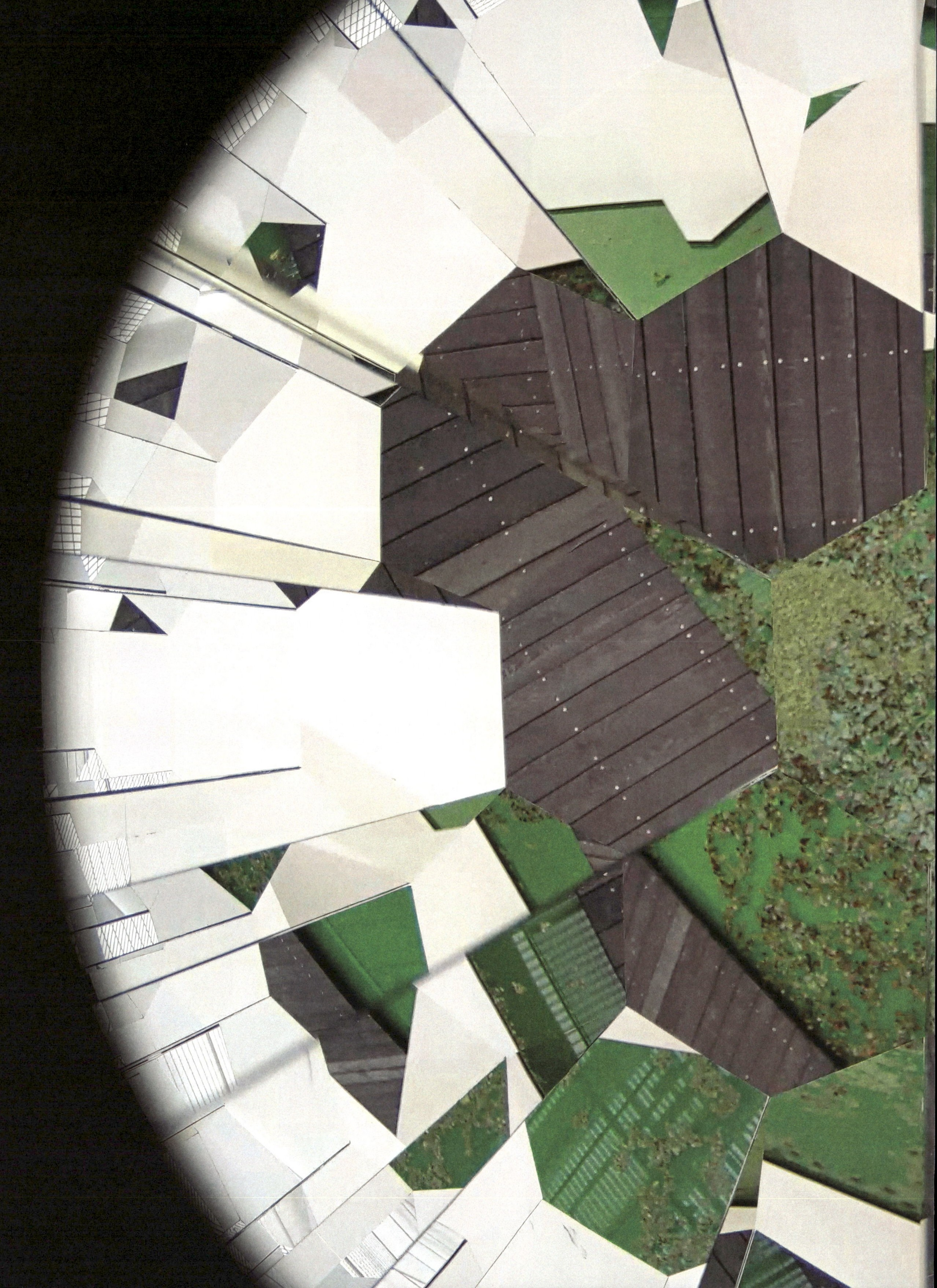

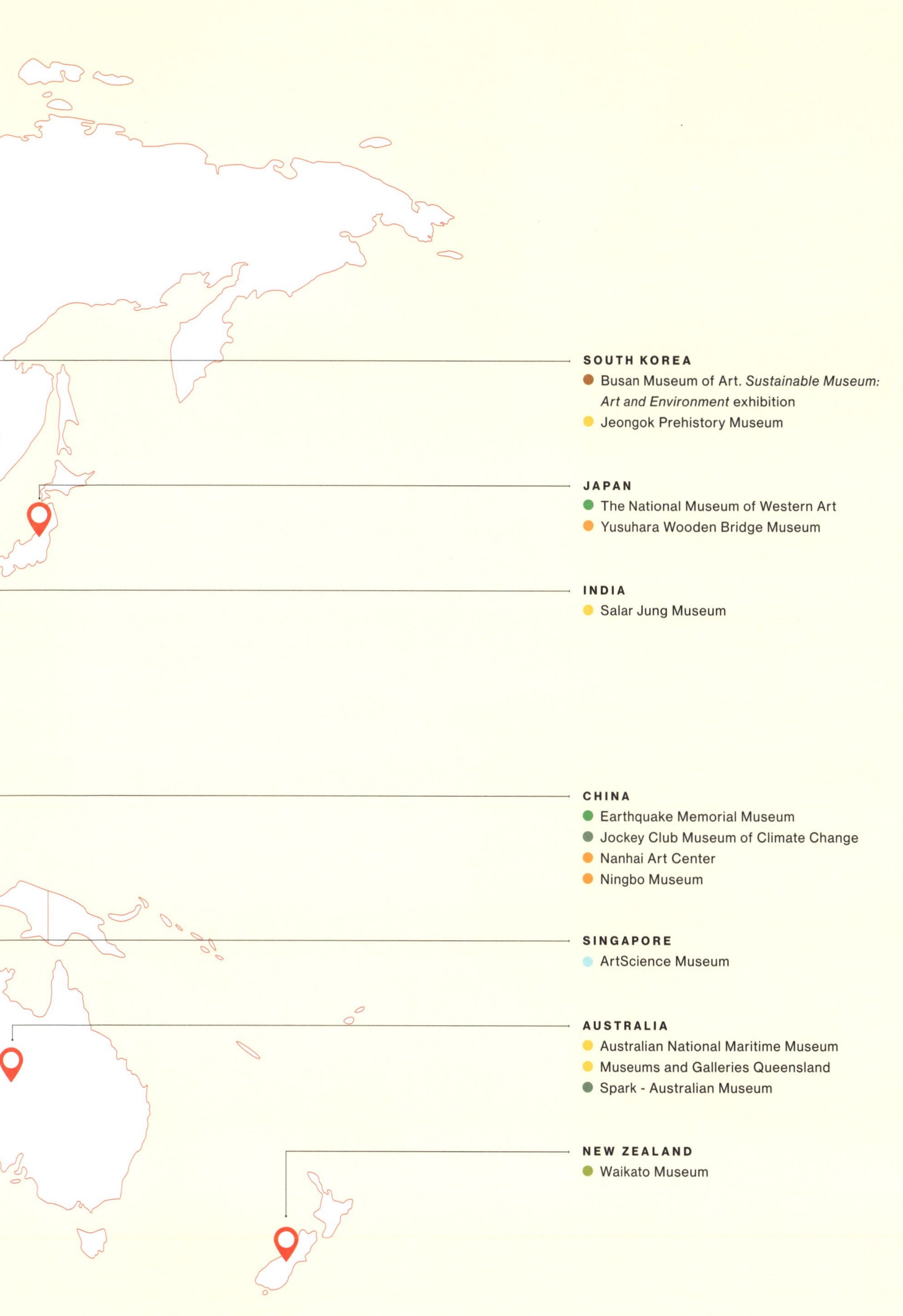

SOUTH KOREA
- Busan Museum of Art. *Sustainable Museum: Art and Environment* exhibition
- Jeongok Prehistory Museum

JAPAN
- The National Museum of Western Art
- Yusuhara Wooden Bridge Museum

INDIA
- Salar Jung Museum

CHINA
- Earthquake Memorial Museum
- Jockey Club Museum of Climate Change
- Nanhai Art Center
- Ningbo Museum

SINGAPORE
- ArtScience Museum

AUSTRALIA
- Australian National Maritime Museum
- Museums and Galleries Queensland
- Spark - Australian Museum

NEW ZEALAND
- Waikato Museum

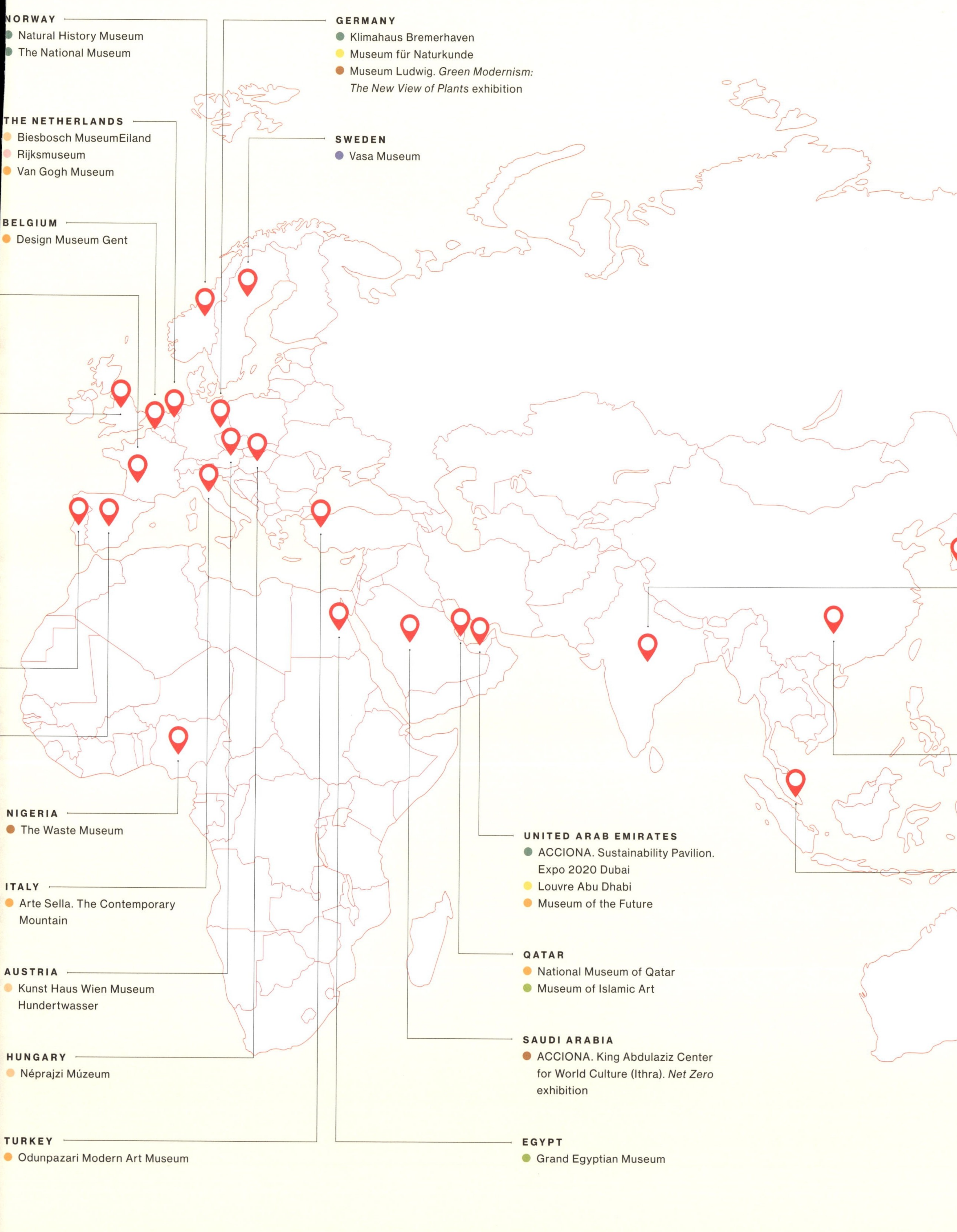

NORWAY
Natural History Museum
The National Museum
GERMANY
Klimahaus Bremerhaven
Museum für Naturkunde
Museum Ludwig. *Green Modernism: The New View of Plants* exhibition
THE NETHERLANDS
Biesbosch MuseumEiland
Rijksmuseum
Van Gogh Museum
SWEDEN
Vasa Museum
BELGIUM
Design Museum Gent
NIGERIA
The Waste Museum
UNITED ARAB EMIRATES
ACCIONA. Sustainability Pavilion. Expo 2020 Dubai
Louvre Abu Dhabi
Museum of the Future
ITALY
Arte Sella. The Contemporary Mountain
QATAR
National Museum of Qatar
Museum of Islamic Art
AUSTRIA
Kunst Haus Wien Museum Hundertwasser
SAUDI ARABIA
ACCIONA. King Abdulaziz Center for World Culture (Ithra). *Net Zero* exhibition
HUNGARY
Néprajzi Múzeum
TURKEY
Odunpazari Modern Art Museum
EGYPT
Grand Egyptian Museum

EDITION
ACCIONA Cultural Engineering, S.A.U.

CONTENT
Ramón Rodríguez Alonso
Ivonne Varas Ebert
Pedro A. García López
Robert Muro
Clotilde Entrecanales Carrión
Alfons Martinell
Sarah Sutton

COORDINATION
Clotilde Entrecanales Carrión
Ramón Rodríguez Alonso
Paula Novo García
Laura Artaza Armesto
Elena María Fernández López

DESIGN AND GRAPHIC EDITION
unberbau

TRANSLATION
David Cánovas Williams

PROOFREADING
Art in Translation

PRE-PRINT
Museoteca

PRINT
Artes Gráficas Palermo

PRODUCTION AND DISTRIBUTION
La Fábrica

ISBN
978-84-10024-45-8

DL
M-24378-2024

Printed in Spain

PHOTOGRAHIC CREDITS
Ahmed Fawzy Elaraby / Alamy Stock Photo: 249.
Basil Morin: 86-87
Biomuseo Panamá (photo: Fernando Alda): 117, 118-119, 120, 121, 122-123.
Boaz Rottem / Alamy Stock Photo: 236-237.
CaixaForum Sevilla (photo: Fundación "la Caixa"): 241, 242-243, 244-245, 246.
California Academy of Sciences: 27, 28, 29, 30-31.
Chris A Selby / Alamy Stock Photo: 196-197.
Creative Commons Attribution-Share Alike 4.0 International: 153, 216, 266, 279, 280.
Design Museum, London (photo: Gareth Gardner): 154-155, 156.
Design Museum, London (photo: Hufton + Crow): 149, 150, 151, 152, 272.
Dietmar Rabich: 88.
Eduardo Eckenfels: 1.
Espai Cràter (Ajuntament d'Olot): 111, 112-113, 114.
Espai Cràter, *El edificio que educa* (illustration: Clara Kozak): 115.
Museo Cristóbal Balenciaga; outside of the museum (photo: Museo Cristóbal Balenciaga / Idoia Unzurrunzaga): 165.
Fundación Marcelino Botín-Sanz de Sautuola y López; view of the Centro Botín (photo: Stéphane Aboudaram): 91.
Fundación Marcelino Botín-Sanz de Sautuola y López; view of the Pachinko (photo: Enrico Cano): 92-93
Fundación Marcelino Botín-Sanz de Sautuola y López; view of the exhibition *Roni Horn: I am paralyzed with hope, Centro Botín*, Santander, 2023 (photo: Vicente Paredes): 94.
Gent Waste Brick for DINF (photo: Design Museum Gent): 43.
Grand Egyptian Museum (photos: Niccolo Guasti): 250, 251, 252-253, 254.
Guilherme Vieira: 213.
Horniman Museum & Gardens: 207.
Iluminando (illustration: Museo Lázaro Galdiano): 293.
Jansos / Alamy Stock Photo: 208-209.
Jeongok Prehistory Museum (sketches: Anouk Legendre, XTU Architects): 103.
José Luis López de Zubiria: 6.
Julio Anaya Cabanding and AISHONANZUKA, Hong Kong: 11, 264.
Klimahaus Bremerhaven: 227, 228-229, 230-231.
Life and Work of Frida Kahlo, exhibition (photos: Juan Rayos and Ana Amado): 167, 168-169, 171.
MAD Architects and Nanhai Art Center: 45, 46, 47, 48-49, 50.
Manchester Museum: 187, 188, 189, 190-191, 192.
Museo de América; peregrine preservation action at the museum: 131.
Museo Guggenheim Bilbao (photos: FMGB Guggenheim Bilbao Museoa): 105, 106-107, 108, 258.
Musée du Quai Branly – Jacques Chirac, photo Vincent Mercier: 133, 134-135.
Museo Nacional del Prado: 181, 182-183, 184.
Museu del Disseny – DHub: 159, 160, 161, 162-163.
Museum of the Moving Image: 239.
Mutisia clematis, detail (Real Jardín Botánico-CSIC): 125.
Mwintirew: 85.
National Museum of Qatar – Qatar Museums: 53, 54-55, 56-57.
National Museum of Qatar – Qatar Museums (illustration and photo: Ahed AlKhatib, courtesy of artist): 58.
Natural History Museum, Oslo. Ítima foto: Jarli&Jorda: 219, 220, 221, 222-223.
Néprajzi Múzeum (sketch: Marcel Ferencz): 33.
NGV Triennial 2023, NGV International, Melbourne. Photo: Sean Fennessy: 16.
Net Zero Exhibition (photos: Phil Handforth): 139, 140-141, 142, 143, 144-145.
Ningbo Museum (photos: Nigbo Museum): 35, 36-37, 38, 39, 40-41.
Odunpazari Modern Museum, Eskişehir (photo: Studio Naaro): 61, 62-63, 64-65, 66.
Olafur Eliasson; neugerriemschneider, Berlin; Tanya Bonakdar Gallery, New York / Los Angeles (photo: Mark Niedermann): 8, 260.
Olafur Eliasson; neugerriemschneider, Berlin; Tanya Bonakdar Gallery, New York / Los Angeles (photo: Patricia Grabowicz): 294-295.
Olafur Eliasson; neugerriemschneider, Berlin; Tanya Bonakdar Gallery, New York / Los Angeles (photo: Anders Sune Berg): 15.
PACE Gallery: 12.
Papalote Museo del Niño; *Toco, juego y aprendo*: 233
Paul Quayle / Alamy Stock Photo: 195.
Snøhetta 2024 and Museo de Ciencias Ambientales, Guadalajara: 21, 22-23, 24.
Stephen Chung / Alamy Stock Photo: 127, 128-129.
studiomarcovermeulen and Biesbosch Museum: 77, 78, 79, 80-81, 82.
Symphony, traveling exhibition (photo: Fundación "la Caixa"): 137.
The Dalí Museum, St. Petersburg, Florida: 201, 202-203, 204.
The Huntington Library, Art Museum, and Botanical Gardens: 69, 70, 71, 72-73, 74.
The Museum of Contemporary Art (MOCA): 198.
Tomaz Silva / Agência Brasil: 216
Under the Forest (Axionometry: ACCIONA): 225.
VinnyWiki: 214-215.
Waste (creativity: Candida Pestana): 147
Wellcome Collection: 173, 174-175, 176-177.
wendy connett / Alamy Stock Photo: 235.
XTU architects (photo: Iwan Baan): 97, 98, 99, 100-101, 102.

ACCIONA Cultural Engineering S.A.U.
Avda. de la Gran Vía de Hortaleza, 3
28033 Madrid
cultura.acciona.com/es